MW01285875

Responsible, Sustainable, and Globally Aware Management in the Fourth Industrial Revolution

Ziska Fields
University of KwaZulu-Natal, South Africa

Stefan Huesig
Chemnitz University of Technology, Germany

A volume in the Advances in
Business Strategy and Competitive
Advantage (ABSCA) Book Series

Published in the United States of America by
  IGI Global
  Business Science Reference (an imprint of IGI Global)
  701 E. Chocolate Avenue
  Hershey PA, USA 17033
  Tel: 717-533-8845
  Fax: 717-533-8661
  E-mail: cust@igi-global.com
  Web site: http://www.igi-global.com

Copyright © 2019 by IGI Global. All rights reserved. No part of this publication may be reproduced, stored or distributed in any form or by any means, electronic or mechanical, including photocopying, without written permission from the publisher.
Product or company names used in this set are for identification purposes only. Inclusion of the names of the products or companies does not indicate a claim of ownership by IGI Global of the trademark or registered trademark.

Library of Congress Cataloging-in-Publication Data

Names: Fields, Ziska, 1970- editor. | Huesig, Stefan, 1972- editor.
Title: Responsible, sustainable, and globally aware management in the fourth
  industrial revolution / Ziska Fields and Stefan Huesig, editors.
Description: Hershey : Business Science Reference, [2019]
Identifiers: LCCN 2018032001| ISBN 9781522576389 (hardcover) | ISBN
  9781522576396 (ebook)
Subjects: LCSH: Sustainable development--Technological innovations. | Social
  responsibility of business. | Industrial management--Environmental aspects.
Classification: LCC HC79.E5 R474 2019 | DDC 658.4/08--dc23 LC record available at https://lccn.
loc.gov/2018032001

This book is published in the IGI Global book series Advances in Business Strategy and Competitive Advantage (ABSCA) (ISSN: 2327-3429; eISSN: 2327-3437)

British Cataloguing in Publication Data
A Cataloguing in Publication record for this book is available from the British Library.

All work contributed to this book is new, previously-unpublished material.
The views expressed in this book are those of the authors, but not necessarily of the publisher.

For electronic access to this publication, please contact: eresources@igi-global.com.

Advances in Business Strategy and Competitive Advantage (ABSCA) Book Series

ISSN:2327-3429
EISSN:2327-3437

Editor-in-Chief: Patricia Ordóñez de Pablos Universidad de Oviedo, Spain

MISSION

Business entities are constantly seeking new ways through which to gain advantage over their competitors and strengthen their position within the business environment. With competition at an all-time high due to technological advancements allowing for competition on a global scale, firms continue to seek new ways through which to improve and strengthen their business processes, procedures, and profitability.

The **Advances in Business Strategy and Competitive Advantage (ABSCA) Book Series** is a timely series responding to the high demand for state-of-the-art research on how business strategies are created, implemented and re-designed to meet the demands of globalized competitive markets. With a focus on local and global challenges, business opportunities and the needs of society, the **ABSCA** encourages scientific discourse on doing business and managing information technologies for the creation of sustainable competitive advantage.

COVERAGE

- Differentiation Strategy
- Customer-Orientation Strategy
- Ethics and Business Strategy
- Co-operative Strategies
- Cost Leadership Strategy
- Economies of Scale
- International Business Strategy
- Foreign Investment Decision Process
- Joint Ventures
- Value Creation

IGI Global is currently accepting manuscripts for publication within this series. To submit a proposal for a volume in this series, please contact our Acquisition Editors at Acquisitions@igi-global.com or visit: http://www.igi-global.com/publish/.

The Advances in Business Strategy and Competitive Advantage (ABSCA) Book Series (ISSN 2327-3429) is published by IGI Global, 701 E. Chocolate Avenue, Hershey, PA 17033-1240, USA, www.igi-global.com. This series is composed of titles available for purchase individually; each title is edited to be contextually exclusive from any other title within the series. For pricing and ordering information please visit http://www.igi-global.com/book-series/advances-business-strategy-competitive-advantage/73672. Postmaster: Send all address changes to above address. © © 2019 IGI Global. All rights, including translation in other languages reserved by the publisher. No part of this series may be reproduced or used in any form or by any means – graphics, electronic, or mechanical, including photocopying, recording, taping, or information and retrieval systems – without written permission from the publisher, except for non commercial, educational use, including classroom teaching purposes. The views expressed in this series are those of the authors, but not necessarily of IGI Global.

Titles in this Series

For a list of additional titles in this series, please visit:
https://www.igi-global.com/book-series/advances-business-strategy-competitive-advantage/73672

Global Considerations in Entrepreneurship Education and Training
Luísa Cagica Carvalho (Instituto Politécnico de Setúbal, Portugal & CEFAGE - Universidade de Évora, Portugal) and Ana Dias Daniel (Universidade de Aveiro, Portugal)
Business Science Reference • © 2019 • 322pp • H/C (ISBN: 9781522576754) • US $215.00

Innovation and Social Capital in Organizational Ecosystems
Brychan Celfyn Thomas (University of South Wales, UK) and Lyndon John Murphy (Cardiff Metropolitan University, UK)
Business Science Reference • © 2019 • 341pp • H/C (ISBN: 9781522577218) • US $225.00

Cases on Corporate Social Responsibility and Contemporary Issues in Organizations
Alexandros Antonaras (University of Nicosia, Cyprus) and Paraskevi Dekoulou (University of Nicosia, Cyprus)
Business Science Reference • © 2019 • 402pp • H/C (ISBN: 9781522577157) • US $225.00

Women Entrepreneurs and Strategic Decision Making in the Global Economy
Florica Tomos (University of South Wales, UK) Naresh Kumar (Universiti Malaysia Kelantan, Malaysia) Nick Clifton (Cardiff Metropolitan University, UK) and Denis Hyams-Ssekasi (University of Bolton, UK)
Business Science Reference • © 2019 • 411pp • H/C (ISBN: 9781522574798) • US $215.00

Linking Cultural Dimensions and CSR Communication Emerging Research and Opportunities
Maria Palazzo (University of Salerno, Italy)
Business Science Reference • © 2019 • 169pp • H/C (ISBN: 9781522579465) • US $165.00

Evidence-Based Initiatives for Organizational Change and Development
Robert G. Hamlin (University of Wolverhampton, UK) Andrea D. Ellinger (The University of Texas at Tyler, USA) and Jenni Jones (University of Wolverhampton, UK)
Business Science Reference • © 2019 • 749pp • H/C (ISBN: 9781522561552) • US $495.00

For an entire list of titles in this series, please visit:
https://www.igi-global.com/book-series/advances-business-strategy-competitive-advantage/73672

701 East Chocolate Avenue, Hershey, PA 17033, USA
Tel: 717-533-8845 x100 • Fax: 717-533-8661
E-Mail: cust@igi-global.com • www.igi-global.com

Editorial Advisory Board

Sulaiman O. Atiku, *Pentecost University College, Ghana*
Christo Bisschoff, *North West University, South Africa*
Ezekiel J. Fayomi, *Ekiti State University, Nigeria*
Cecile Nieuwenhuizen, *University of Johannesburg, South Africa*
Cobus Oosthuizen, *Milpark Business School, South Africa*
Chris Schachtebeck, *University of Johannesburg, South Africa*

Table of Contents

Section 1
Impact and Challenges of the Fourth Industrial Revolution on Responsible, Sustainable, and Globally Aware Management

Section 2
Imagination and New Concepts to Solve Global Business, Innovation, and Sustainability Challenges

Section 3
Global Responsible and Sustainable Management Competencies to Drive Responsible and Sustainable Business Practices

Section 4
Global Responsible Governance and Regulation of Digitalization and Potentially Disruptive Technologies

Section 5
Applications and Reflections of Innovative Technologies and Global Responsible and Sustainable Management

Detailed Table of Contents

Section 1
Impact and Challenges of the Fourth Industrial Revolution on Responsible, Sustainable, and Globally Aware Management

Digitization and sustainability are two mega-trends. There are a lot of opportunities and threats discussed. However, a compiled and industry-wide analysis of SWOTs is missing. After a review of the literature on digitization and sustainability and compiling a SWOT table, a concept map is developed for visualizing key topics in light of digitization and sustainability. In addition, for illustrating unconscious knowledge, two exemplifying systemic structural constellations are presented in this context as well. The results show immense tensions between sustainability and digitization, but also offer progressive patterns. In light of a development towards sustainability, digitization is both boon and bane and often needs a clear analysis of all relevant issues and a careful handling in order to be progressive. Digital transformation requires a precise and honest value basis and sustainability added value. Therefore, societal progress and strict law regulation will be needed.

Industry 4.0, and in general, digital technologies, represent a fundamental model shift towards decentralization and individualized production. With this, the development of new services and business models based on the internet is encouraged. Somehow, this forces traditional supply chains to evolve into highly adaptative networks. Companies have to consider their internal resources and the benefits of getting closer to partners in the supply chain. In this sense, the implementation of these technologies is accompanied by a series of sustainable implication at economic, environmental, and social levels.

Section 2
Imagination and New Concepts to Solve Global Business, Innovation, and Sustainability Challenges

Imagination is an often-overlooked integral element of human progress, in general, and innovations, in particular. In this chapter, it is argued that the examination of the diffusion and evolution of imaginations and their manifestation as innovations can help to understand the imaginative roots of innovations and to create a responsibly chosen path into a sustainable future. Science fiction as a specific area of manifested imagination is used to show how manifested imaginations influence the social imagination in general and certain individuals like scientists and innovators in particular. It is even used to sell ideas (or make them stick) and give them heritage, again influencing the social imagination. And the accelerated fusion, development, and progress of technologies in the wake of the digitalization is enabling fast and vast diffusion and distribution of imaginations, creating a need to explore, understand, and responsibly utilize imaginations.

A closer look at innovation for and from emerging markets reveals that a variety of different terms and concepts related to this type of innovation exist. The objective of this conceptual work is to develop a theoretical classification framework based on a comprehensive literature overview that provides a starting point for structuring these different terms and concepts. After a first investigation and comprehensive search for the keywords "reverse," "frugal," "jugaad," and "bottom of pyramid" in the Google Scholar database, 19 different texts were identified and classified for further analysis. As a result, 33 identified terms concerning innovation for and from emerging markets, various spellings and synonyms are presented. Finally, a theoretical-based classification framework is derived and the criteria "market orientation," "determinants," "nature," "sophistication," "sustainability," "novelty," and "innovator type" was proposed. This classification framework could be used for further research and teaching in innovation, responsible, and sustainable management disciplines.

Section 3
Global Responsible and Sustainable Management Competencies to Drive Responsible and Sustainable Business Practices

Chapter 5
Sangeeta Trott, ITM-SIA Business School, India

The main purpose of the chapter is to understand the role of marketing in creating awareness and action for sustainability in the fourth industrial revolution. The chapter is sequenced as follows: It begins with a brief introduction, followed by exploring the relationship between marketing and sustainability. The chapter then explains how marketing can play an important role in developing awareness and action at various phases of sustainability with suitable examples. The chapter then discusses the various issues which one faces in sustainability and ends with a conclusion. The chapter has great theoretical and managerial implications.

Chapter 6
Martin Albert, Chemnitz University of Technology, Germany
Friedrich Mickel, Chemnitz University of Technology, Germany

Sustainability is a concept that has increased in popularity constantly over recent years. During this time, the discipline of project management begun to focus on sustainability, but literature shows that the topic of sustainable project management is still incipiently explored. Therefore, the goal of the chapter is to identify connections between sustainability and project management, which is achieved through the literary review of 46 different texts. These sources were analyzed using a bibliometric analysis and a qualitative content analysis. As deductive and inductive derived categories "definition project management," "definition sustainability," "definition sustainable project management," "affected areas," "principles of sustainable project management," and "project manager" were defined. In order to develop the profession of sustainable project management, focusing upon the verification of theoretical findings with empirical research is suggested.

Section 4
Global Responsible Governance and Regulation of Digitalization and Potentially Disruptive Technologies

Chapter 7

Henry Frank Wissink, University of KwaZulu-Natal, South Africa

This chapter is an effort to promote and guide thinking about the global and local challenges in how governments respond to innovative and disruptive projects and technologies. The chapter is based on the considerations of and concerns regarding the challenges and changes that we face on a global scale and how it impacts on the notion and need for innovation. Not all inventions or innovations are disruptive or serve the interest of the public at large, and some even may have serious harmful consequences or impacts. These may be unforeseen or sometimes deliberately obscured and perhaps just serve the narrow interests of profiteers. Governments are required to consider their roles and plan to be responsible and proactive to ensure that the best interests of both the business and public sector are pursued for the purposes of long-term sustainability.

Chapter 8

Dagmar Gesmann-Nuissl, Chemnitz University of Technology, Germany

No other technology has been mentioned as frequently as blockchain technology. No less than a technical revolution should go along with it. In addition to a brief introduction to the functionality of the blockchain technology, this chapter will also highlight various fields of application and the related legal challenges in international trade. The transport industry may be mentioned as an example. Especially in the transportation of goods, a large number of documentation obligations must be adhered to and permits must be obtained. Packing lists, export licenses, and product certificates are examples of this. All mentioned documents are based on the same data set, namely the details of the type, origin, and quantity of the goods. Large parts of these documents must be carried along with the goods and presented on instructions, which causes considerable bureaucracy and makes transportation more difficult and expensive. These documents could be displayed on the blockchain in the future.

Section 5
Applications and Reflections of Innovative Technologies and Global Responsible and Sustainable Management

Chapter 9

Katja Schneider, Chemnitz University of Technology, Germany
Marlen Gabriele Arnold, Chemnitz University of Technology, Germany

The global textile industry offers huge potentials regarding the transformation towards sustainability. These improvements require a facilitation of business model innovations embedding shifting consumer demands. How can the textile industry drive responsible and sustainable business practices in terms of social sustainability? Tackling this question, a qualitative content-based analysis of current literature conducted highlights main themes and concepts on business model innovations, textile industry, and social sustainability. In addition, an exploratory multiple case study design was used. Results show social sustainability patterns are seldom and often linked to external pressures. This chapter proposes a reorientation towards stronger holistic and inclusive approaches for sustainability and reflects on socio-cultural aspects linked to sustainable textile business models. Progressing sustainability in the textile industry needs both a single consideration of environmental and social issues as well as an integrative and systemic perspective in academia as well as in practice.

Chapter 10

Indira Padayachee, University of KwaZulu-Natal, South Africa
John Mukomana, University of KwaZulu-Natal, South Africa

Port terminals play an integral role in the transportation logistics chain by providing cargo handling, storage, and warehousing services to a range of shipping lines, freight forwarders, and cargo owners. This chapter reports on a case study aimed at determining the challenges and limitations experienced with the current information and communication technology used in port terminals in Durban and examines how technological, organizational, and environmental factors influence port automation. A quantitative approach was adopted, and a questionnaire was designed to collect data. The findings revealed that adequate technology needs to be acquired, and the compatibility and complexity of the technology have the biggest influence on the automation of terminal ports in Durban. Communication with stakeholders and

IT skills retention were found to be the most important organizational factors and customer readiness emerged as an important environmental factor influencing the automation of port terminals in Durban.

In the midst of the Fourth Industrial Revolution, the proliferation of the technology revolution is changing the mindset of people relating to waste management. The mobility of people to the different places of African continent, a hike in industrial advancements, and the increase in the rise of goods consumption among others are fueling the generation of waste across Africa. Although the waste management industry plays a crucial role, reports have shown in the last decade that environmental degradation, pollution, and non-compliances by the activities of waste management companies prevail and impinge on environmental performance. Waste has now become one of the most significant environmental issues that requires attention. This chapter emphasizes on the landscape of the sector of waste management and the challenges facing the waste industry in Africa. The chapter ends with propositions to address those issues in a view to promote environmental performance and ensure responsible management of emerging African markets in the era of the Fourth Industrial Revolution.

The Fourth Industrial Revolution and increased environmental awareness is forcing business leaders to adapt to the changing environment in functional areas such as the supply chain. This chapter focuses on the role of green supply chain management in achieving a sustainable competitive advantage, exploring the factors that affect green supply chain management initiatives at a leading pharmaceutical manufacturer in Durban. The study used a descriptive and exploratory case study approach in which in-depth interviews were conducted with 10 participants. Content analysis was used to analyze the collected data. The findings of the study reveal that the main factors affecting green supply chain management initiatives include high costs, lack of government support, and pressure to reduce selling prices. Since a limited number of studies have been conducted on this topic, the findings and recommendations of this work contribute to the existing body of research knowledge.

Foreword

Responsible, Sustainable, and Globally Aware Management in the Fourth Industrial Revolution addresses three interconnected aspects of the contemporary and future-oriented management education for the leaders and academics of tomorrow. First, it provides an overview of advanced technologies and their interplay with business and society. This combination is important given because management is increasingly affected by and empowered through technologies such as blockchain or artificial intelligence. Second, it introduces the concept of the Fourth Industrial Revolution, which requires sustainable and responsible management practices and values beyond the single focus on short-term profit gains. And finally, these aspects must be embedded in a broader understanding of global challenges and opportunities to account for the complexities of the growing, interconnected, and transnational business environment.

This book could not be timelier. By focusing on responsible and sustainable management practices, leaders and academics require the necessary skills to make use of innovative technologies and to understand the impact of these technologies. To ensure responsible and sustainable management practices, they also need to be aware of the global impact of their decisions. Managers should therefore understand the impact of their business processes on the environment and use responsible, sustainable and globally applicable management practices to leverage the opportunities of the Fourth Industrial Revolution.

The book addresses various topics related to this context and critically reflects on the importance and impact of new technologies. These technological overviews can also help academics that are familiar in the field to better navigate through theoretical concepts, recent technologies and their implications for application and society. In particular, the sustainable implications of Industry 4.0 and the omnipresent impact of digitization are discussed. Moreover, it introduces the role blockchain technology can play in the context of international trade of goods from a legal perspective, as well as how governments and public policy makers could deal with such potentially disruptive and innovative technologies. In addition, the authors describe specific applications on (1) how port terminal automation will be affected by technologies of the Fourth Industrial Revolution, (2) how responsible and sustainable business model innovation in the textile industry should look like, and (3) how blockchain technology can be applied to the global south by analyzing the waste management industry of Africa as well as the green supply chain management initiatives in a south African pharmaceutical supply chain. These practical case studies provide managers and academics helpful examples of real solutions to global challenges, and will help in increasing awareness for responsible and sustainable management practices. Finally, the academic community will also benefit from the interdisciplinary insights and composition of this book. By providing novel insights for the somewhat neglected roots of innovations such as imagination, which is exemplified in science fiction and a novel classification framework for concepts of innovation for and from emerging markets, the book enables much needed guidance for students and scholars of innovation. I wish all the credits, attention and success this book deserves for the authors.

Claudia Doblinger
Technical University of Munich, Germany

Preface

There are different approaches to the practice, research and education for responsible and sustainable development (Arevalo & Mitchell, 2017). Typically, sustainable topics also have a specific property; sustainable objectives are rarely consistent (Albert et al., 2017). For managers, students and academics to become more aware of these contradictions, especially in the age of digitalization and in the Fourth Industrial Revolution requires new ways of education. With a focus on responsible and sustainable management practices, they need to be able to use innovative technologies and understand the impact of these technologies, as well as becoming more globally aware of their decisions to ensure responsible and sustainable management. Management should therefore truly understand the impact of their business processes on the environment and use responsible, sustainable and globally aware management to survive and thrive in the Fourth Industrial Revolution with their various stakeholders.

Even more so, in times of a growing and interconnected, global business environment and novel, sometimes potentially disruptive technologies, frequently described in the concept of the Fourth Industrial Revolution. The Fourth Industrial Revolution or 4IR, is proposed as the fourth major industrial era since the initial Industrial Revolution of the 18th century (Kagermann, 2015; plattform-i40.de, 2019). Industry 4.0 has become a buzzword for the current and future trends of automation and data exchange in manufacturing technologies especially put forward from government, scholars and practitioners from Germany (plattform-i40.de, 2019). It includes cyber-physical systems, the Internet of things, cloud computing and cognitive computing. More recently, digitalization and technologies such as artificial intelligence, big data and analytics, autonomous vehicles and drones, 5G, 3D printing and even blockchain technologies are also subsumed under this umbrella term. Therefore, firms in the digital age operate in an environment that is characterized by the emergence of potentially disruptive, digital technologies (Yoo et al., 2012) and blurring industry boundaries (Porter & Heppelmann, 2014). Startups with novel business models such as from the so called sharing economy (Herrmann-Fankhänel, 2019) or platforms such Facebook and high-tech firms such as Google threaten existing industry structures (Teece, 2010; Yoo, Henfridsson & Lyytinen, 2010) and established companies face their traditional business models challenged and at risk (Bharadwaj et al., 2013). While traditional corporate innovation practice mainly focused on products and services, the digitalization forces the traditional industry to initiate and actively shape the next wave of innovation to address the challenges and opportunities of the Fourth Industrial Revolution (Kagermann, 2015).

So far, we have not experienced an industrial revolution before where technology and humans are so closely integrated, and this has a profound effect on how these changes will impact on managers and why it is critical for managers to be more responsible, more focused on sustainability and why it is critical to be globally aware. This publication aims to address complex and unknown issues around management, focusing on responsible, sustainable and globally aware practices and principles. It starts by exploring the individual and the changes needed in individual thinking and other cognitive processes. The assumption is that managers will not be able to manage organizations if they have not become more creative, using their imagination to view the future more and to manage businesses more effectively and efficiently.

This book is addressing these challenges by outlining various fields in this context are addressed, new technologies are critical reflected, and overviews are provided that help also academics familiar in the field to better navigate through the related theoretical concepts, recent technologies and their implications for application and society on different levels.

This comprehensive and timely publication aims to be an essential reference source, building on the available literature and joint expertise in the field of management, while providing for further research opportunities in this dynamic field. It is hoped that this text will provide the resources necessary for governments, nonprofit and for-profit organizations, and managers specifically to address sustainability needs in businesses and countries around the world.

The primary intended audience is scholar-practitioners and researchers who have the need for reference material regarding the subject matter of the proposed publication as outlined above. The secondary intended audience is undergraduate and postgraduate business students who require the same reference material. At the same time, while having academic rigor, the book is written in a way such that it can be understood by non-academics and non-specialists; it will be appealing to the general public.

This book was initiated on the basis of a multi-level, permanent and academic cooperation in responsible, sustainable and globally aware management education and practice. This cooperation was predominantly built on a bi-continental approach called "Joint Expertise". The "Joint Expertise" project supported by the German Academic Exchange Service, tried to establish such a responsible, sustainable and globally aware management education approach for master and doctoral students between the University of Technology Chemnitz, Faculty of Economics and Business Administration and the University of Kwazulu-Natal (UKZN), School of Management, IT and Governance (Herrmann-Fankhänel, et al. 2017). As we were looking for further knowledge generation and development we called out for more contributions on this topic all over the world to gather a maximum of expertise. As a result, we received many contributions that dealt closely with these and related issues from a variety of perspectives. After a rigorous editorial and blind review process the most interesting and advanced chapters were subsequently accepted for this publication. A good number of very valuable contributions were also received that, for a number of reasons, did not reach the acceptability threshold set for this book. For those who are interested in the numbers for this book, we received 29 proposal submissions, 4 were rejected and 24 accepted for submission of a full chapter. Finally, 17 full chapters were submitted and 12 finally accepted for publication. Here in the preface, we want to outline and reflect on the resulting contributions of our endeavor to collect and advance the body of knowledge on the responsible, sustainable and globally aware management education and practice in the Fourth Industrial Revolution:

Section 1 deals with "Impact and Challenges of the Fourth Industrial Revolution on Responsible, Sustainable, and Globally Aware Management" and the big picture of the presumed changes of Industry 4.0, and in general, digital technologies for sustainability in the context of responsible and globally aware management is outlined. In particular, Marlen Gabriele Arnold and Anne Fischer from the Chemnitz University of Technology in Germany address this section focus comprehensively in their chapter "Digitization and Sustainability: Threats, Opportunities, and Trade-Offs". They investigate the connection between digitization and sustainability by applying a SWOT analysis, review the literature on digitization and sustainability and develop a concept map for visualizing key topics in light of digitization and sustainability. In addition, for illustrating unconscious knowledge two exemplifying systemic structural constellations are presented. Their results suggest immense tensions between sustainability and digitization, but also offer progressive patterns. In light of a development towards sustainability, they critically evaluate digitization and except no panacea for sustainability but propose the need for societal progress and strict law regulation based on digital transformation that requires a precise and honest value basis and sustainability added value. In the chapter "Sustainable Implications of Industry 4.0", Jorge Tarifa-Fernandez from the University of Almeria in Spain takes a slightly different approach and more optimistic view towards Industry 4.0, and in general, digital technologies. For him both concepts represent a fundamental model shift towards decentralization and individualized production so that traditional supply chains have to evolve into highly adaptive networks. Therefore, one can expect a series of also positive sustainable implications at economic, environmental and social level. Both chapters reflect to some degree also the ongoing discussion between techno optimistic (see e.g. Brynjolfsson and McAfee, 2014) and pessimistic stances (Gordon, 2015; Cowen, 2011; Bloom et al., 2017; Nordhaus, 2015).

Section 2, "Imagination and New Concepts to Solve Global Business, Innovation, and Sustainability Challenges," provides a more theoretical lens towards global responsible innovation and its possible sustainability and business implications. Frequently, innovation and creative solutions towards sustainability need vision and foresight. Imagination is an often-overlooked integral element of human progress in general and innovations in particular, claims Julien Bucher from the Chemnitz University of Technology in Germany in his contribution "The Overlooked Roots of Innovations: Exploring the Relevance of Imagination on Innovation Using Science Fiction". In this chapter, he argues, that the examination of the diffusion and evolution of imaginations and their manifestation as innovations can help to understand the imaginative roots of innovations and to create a responsibly chosen path into a sustainable future. Moreover, Science Fiction as a specific area of manifested imagination might be also used to manifest imaginations' influence in the social imagination in general and certain individuals such as scientists and innovators in particular. Beyond this, its purposeful use as a marketing tool to sell or discredit ideas in the wake of the digitalization is also addressed. These ideas might be of specific interest of scholars of innovation and practitioners who are interested in the so called "fuzzy front end" of radical innovation processes and discuss that in the context of responsible and globally aware management (Stüer et al., 2010; Hüsig & Kohn, 2003; Hüsig, 2014). The responsible and globally aware management of innovation requires also a clear understanding and communication of innovation terms and concepts related to innovation for and from emerging markets – which is the point that Martin Albert and Stefan Hüsig again from the Chemnitz University of Technology in Germany want to make. The objective of their conceptual chapter "Towards a Classification Framework for Concepts of Innovation for and From Emerging Markets" is to develop a theoretical classification framework based on a comprehensive literature overview that provides a starting point for structuring these different terms and concepts. As a result, they are able to identify 33 terms concerning innovation for and from emerging markets, various spellings and synonyms. Finally, a theoretical-based classification framework is derived and the criteria 'market orientation', 'determinants', 'nature', 'sophistication', 'sustainability', 'novelty', and 'innovator type' is proposed. This classification framework could be used for further research and teaching in innovation, responsible and sustainable management disciplines.

In Section 3, "Global Responsible and Sustainable Management Competencies to Drive Responsible and Sustainable Business Practices", a more practical and managerial approach is at the center of the chapters. Consequently, Sangeeta Trott, from ITM-SIA Business School from India takes a closer look at "Marketing to Develop Environmental Sustainability, Awareness, and Action". The main purpose of this chapter is to understand the role of marketing in creating awareness and action for sustainability in the fourth industrial revolution. In her chapter she explains how marketing can play an important role in developing awareness and action at various phases of sustainability with suitable examples. However, "Sustainable Project Management" seems to be relevant not only for marketing purposes when it comes to the facilitation of Industry 4.0 technologies. Martin Albert and Friedrich Mickel from the Chemnitz University of Technology in Germany elaborate on recent developments in the discipline of project management that has begun to focus on sustainability, but literature shows that the topic of sustainable project management is still incipiently explored. Therefore, their chapter aims to identify connections between sustainability and project management. They performed a literature review of 46 different texts and analyzed them using a bibliometric analysis and a qualitative content analysis. In order to develop the profession of sustainable project management, focusing upon the verification of theoretical findings with empirical research is suggested.

Section 4 focuses on "Global Responsible Governance and Regulation of Digitalization and Potentially Disruptive Technologies". Here Henry Frank Wissink from the University of KwaZulu-Natal from South Africa has contributed a chapter called "Governance and Public Policy Challenges in Managing Disruptive and Innovative Technologies" that is an effort to promote and guide thinking about the global and local challenges in how governments respond to innovative and disruptive projects and technologies. His chapter is based on the considerations of, and concerns regarding the challenges and changes that humanity faces on a global scale and how it impacts on the notion and need for innovation. Since not all inventions or innovations are disruptive or serve the interest of the public at large, and some even may have serious harmful consequences or impacts it is or should be the role of governments to be responsible and proactive to ensure that the best interests of both the business and public sector are pursued for the purposes of long-term sustainability. This chapter clearly provides a novel facet to the ongoing discussion of the regulation and management aspects of disruptive innovation that should be of utmost relevance to practitioners and academics alike (Hüsig et al., 2014). In this regard, few technologies have been framed more disruptive than blockchain technology. This is what Dagmar Gesmann-Nuissl from the Chemnitz University of Technology in Germany is interested in from a legal perspective in her chapter "Blockchain Technology in International Trade in Goods". In her contribution she highlights various fields of application and the related legal challenges in international trade. Especially in the transportation of goods, a large number of documentation obligations must be adhered to and permits must be obtained. These documents could be displayed on the blockchain in the future and showcase the opportunities of the digitalization for potentially increased efficacy.

Finally, in Section 5, "Applications and Reflections of Innovative Technologies and Global Responsible and Sustainable Management", the focus is on concrete applications of 4IR technologies and approaches to increase sustainability of specific operations in various industries such as transportation, textile, waste management and pharmaceutical with a particular interest in the African context. However, technology is not the sole answer that offers huge potentials regarding the transformation towards sustainability. Katja Schneider and Marlen Gabriele Arnold, both from the Chemnitz University of Technology in Germany, show that these improvements might also require a facilitation of business model innovations embedding shifting consumer demands. Therefore, they take a closer look on how can the textile industry drive responsible and sustainable business practices in terms of social sustainability in their chapter called "Responsible and Sustainable Business Model Innovation in the Textile Industry: Exploring Approaches to Social Sustainability". Tackling this question, they conducted a qualitative content-based analysis of current literature which highlights main themes and concepts on business model innovations, textile industry and social sustainability. In addition, results of their exploratory multiple case studies show social sustainability patterns are seldom and often linked to external pressures. This chapter proposes a reorientation towards stronger holistic and inclusive approaches for sustainability and reflects on socio-cultural aspects linked to sustainable textile business models. Progressing sustainability in the textile industry needs both, a single consideration of environmental and social issues as well as an integrative and systemic perspective in academia as well as in practice. Indira Padayachee and John Mukomana from University of KwaZulu-Natal in South Africa focus on the digitalization in the transportation sector with their contribution "Factors Influencing Port Terminal Automation in the Fourth Industrial Revolution: A Case Study of Durban". Their chapter reports on a case study aimed at determining the challenges and limitations experienced with the current information and communication technology used in port terminals in Durban and examines how technological, organizational and environmental factors influence port automation. Their quantitative approach revealed that adequate technology needs to be acquired and the compatibility and complexity of the technology have the biggest influence on the automation of terminal ports in Durban. However, also communication with stakeholders and IT skills retention were found to be important organizational factors and customer readiness emerged as an important environmental factor influencing the automation of port terminals in Durban. In another contribution from the African continent Bibi Zaheenah Chummun, also from University of KwaZulu-Natal in South Africa looks at the "Environmental Performance in the Waste Management Industry of Africa: A Measure of Responsible Management". This chapter emphasizes on the landscape of the sector of waste management and the challenges facing the waste industry in Africa. In the midst of the Fourth Industrial Revolution, the proliferation of the technology revolution is changing the mindset of people relating to waste management. The mobility of people to the different places of African continent, a hike in industrial advancements and the increase in the rise of goods consumption among others are fueling the generation of waste across Africa that leads to environmental degradation, pollution and non-compliances by the activities of waste management companies prevail and impinge on environmental performance. Therefore, propositions to address those issues and ensure responsible management of emerging African markets in the era of the Fourth Industrial Revolution are provided. Finally, Aveshin Reddy and Micheline Juliana Naude, both from University of KwaZulu-Natal in South Africa take a look at "Factors Inhibiting Green Supply Chain Management Initiatives in a South African Pharmaceutical Supply Chain" in their chapter. There they focus on the role of green supply chain management in achieving a sustainable competitive advantage, exploring the factors that affect green supply chain management initiatives at a leading pharmaceutical manufacturer in Durban. In their study a descriptive and exploratory case study approach is used and their findings reveal that the main factors affecting green supply chain management initiatives include high costs, lack of government support, and pressure to reduce selling prices. Since a limited number of studies have been conducted on this topic, their findings and recommendations contribute to the knowledge on the Fourth Industrial Revolution and increased environmental awareness which is forcing business leaders to adapt to the changing environment in functional areas such as the supply chain.

As a conclusion, the editors are very satisfied with the result. We were able to gather a multidisciplinary cross-section of approaches from various subfields and countries to the practice, research and education for responsible and sustainable development in the age of digitalization and in the Fourth Industrial Revolution. As outlined above, many chapters contributed novel ideas, concept and approaches to the theme of the book and will enrich the ongoing discussion on the implications of the digitalization and the Fourth Industrial Revolution for responsible and sustainable development on a global scale. By doing so, we will help future managers, students and academics to become more globally aware of these issues and equip them with inspirations how a responsible, sustainable and global aware management education and practice in the Fourth Industrial Revolution—a "Management 4.0"—should be designed.

Ziska Fields
University of KwaZulu-Natal, South Africa

Stefan Huesig
Chemnitz University of Technology, Germany

REFERENCES

Albert, M., Breßler, J., & Hüsig, S. (2017). Expansive Learning through contradictions of sustainability. In J. A. Arevalo (Ed.), *Handbook of Sustainability in Management Education - In Search of a Multidisciplinary, Innovative and Integrated Approach.* Edward Elgar Publishing. doi:10.4337/9781785361241.00021

Arevalo, J. A., & Mitchell, S. F. (2017). Handbook of Sustainability in Management Education. In *Search of a Multidisciplinary, Innovative and Integrated Approach.* Edward Elgar Publishing. doi:10.4337/9781785361241

Bharadwaj, A., Sawy, O., Pavlou, P., & Venkatraman, N. (2013). Digital Business Strategy: Towards a Next Generation of Insights. *Management Information Systems Quarterly, 37*(2), 471–482. doi:10.25300/MISQ/2013/37:2.3

Brynjolfsson, E., & McAfee, A. (2014). *The second machine age: Work, progress, and prosperity in a time of brilliant technologies.* WW Norton & Company.

Cowen, T. (2011). *The Great Stagnation: How America Ate All the Low-Hanging Fruit of Modern History, Got Sick, and Will (Eventually) Feel Better.* New York: Dutton.

Die Geschichte der Plattform Industrie 4.0. (n.d.). Retrieved from https://www.plattform-i40.de/I40/Navigation/DE/Plattform/Plattform-Industrie-40/plattform-industrie-40.html

Gordon, R. J. (2015). *The Rise and Fall of American Growth: The U.S. Standard of Living since the Civil War.* Princeton, NJ: Princeton University Press.

Herrmann-Fankhänel, A. (2019). How to take Advantage of Online Platforms like the Sharing Economy does. In Co-Creation: Reshaping Business and Society in the Era of Bottom-up Economics. Springer. doi:10.1007/978-3-319-97788-1_7

Herrmann-Fankhänel, A., Dreßler, A., & Hüsig, S. (2017). JointExpertise – ein internationales Projekt mit Schwerpunkt auf Nachhaltigkeit sowie verantwortungsbewussten und global orientiertem Handeln. *CWG-Dialog, 2*(22), 5–6.

Hüsig, S. (2014). A Typology for Radical Innovation Projects based on an Innovativeness Framework. *International Journal of Innovation and Technology Management, 11*(4).

Hüsig, S., & Kohn, S. (2003). Factors Influencing the Front End of the Innovation Process: A Comprehensive Review of Selected Empirical NPD and Explorative FFE Studies. *10th International Product Development Management Conference*, Brussels, Belgium.

Hüsig, S., Timar, K., & Doblinger, C. (2014). The influence of regulation and disruptive potential on incumbents' sub-market entry decision and success in the context of a network industry. *Journal of Product Innovation Management, 31*(5), 1039–1056. doi:10.1111/jpim.12143

Kagermann, H. (2015). *Change Through Digitization—Value Creation in the Age of Industry 4.0.* In H. Albach, H. Meffert, A. Pinkwart, & R. Reichwald (Eds.), *Management of permanent change* (pp. 23–45). New York: Springer Gabler.

Nordhaus, W. D. (2015). *Are We Approaching an Economic Singularity? Information Technology and the Future of Economic Growth (No. w21547)*. National Bureau of Economic Research. doi:10.3386/w21547

Porter, M., & Heppelmann, J. (2014). How Smart Connected Products are Transforming Competition. *Harvard Business Review, 92*(11), 64–88.

Stüer, C., Hüsig, S., & Biala, S. (2010). How to Create and Sustain an Open and Radical Innovation Capability in the Fuzzy Front End? The Case of Vodafone R&D Germany and Selected Ongoing Radical Innovation Projects. *International Journal of Product Development, 11*(3/4), 196–219. doi:10.1504/IJPD.2010.033958

Teece, D. J. (2010). Business Models, Business Strategy and Innovation. *Long Range Planning, 43*(2), 172–194. doi:10.1016/j.lrp.2009.07.003

Yoo, Y., Boland, R. J. Jr, Lyytinen, K., & Majchrzak, A. (2012). Organizing for Innovation in the Digitized World. *Organization Science, 23*(5), 1398–1408. doi:10.1287/orsc.1120.0771

Acknowledgment

I would like to recognize Prof. Stefan Huesig and the Technische Universität Chemnitz team (Chemnitz University of Technology [CUT], Germany), as well as Prof. Henry Wissink and the team from the University of KwaZulu-Natal (UKZN, South Africa) for their hard work, dedication and commitment to share their expertise and knowledge to encourage academic collaboration between Germany and South Africa.

Prof. Ziska Fields

The editors would like to thanks to all reviewers who helped to ensure the high quality of the book's contributions, namely:

Ankit Katrodia

Ayansola Ayandibu

Brett van Niekerk

Christo Bisschoff

Cliford Madondo

David Cropley

Debbie Ellis

Ethel Abe

Harold Patrick

Henry Wissink

Idris Ganiyu

Indira Padayachee

Isaac Abe

Julien Bucher

Katja Schneider

Lindiwe Kunene

Mariki Eloff

Marlen Arnold

Martin Albert

Micheline Naude

Nicholas Biekpe

Nigel Chiweshe

Pfano Mashau

Sebastian Liebold

Sulaiman Atiku

Thokozani Mbhele

Special thanks go to the JointExpertise Team for all kinds of support:

Anja Herrmann-Fankhänel

Anne Dreßler

Henry Wissink

Both the editors would like to thank the IGI Global team for all their support during the publication process. We value your professionalism.

Ziska Fields
University of KwaZulu-Natal, South Africa

Stefan Huesig
Chemnitz University of Technology, Germany

Section 1
Impact and Challenges of the Fourth Industrial Revolution on Responsible, Sustainable, and Globally Aware Management

Chapter 1
Digitization and Sustainability:
Threats, Opportunities, and Trade-Offs

Marlen Gabriele Arnold
Chemnitz University of Technology, Germany

Anne Fischer
Chemnitz University of Technology, Germany

ABSTRACT

Digitization and sustainability are two mega-trends. There are a lot of opportunities and threats discussed. However, a compiled and industry-wide analysis of SWOTs is missing. After a review of the literature on digitization and sustainability and compiling a SWOT table, a concept map is developed for visualizing key topics in light of digitization and sustainability. In addition, for illustrating unconscious knowledge, two exemplifying systemic structural constellations are presented in this context as well. The results show immense tensions between sustainability and digitization, but also offer progressive patterns. In light of a development towards sustainability, digitization is both boon and bane and often needs a clear analysis of all relevant issues and a careful handling in order to be progressive. Digital transformation requires a precise and honest value basis and sustainability added value. Therefore, societal progress and strict law regulation will be needed.

DOI: 10.4018/978-1-5225-7638-9.ch001

Copyright © 2019, IGI Global. Copying or distributing in print or electronic forms without written permission of IGI Global is prohibited.

INTRODUCTION

According to Krys (2017), in particular seven megatrends will play a major role over the next 15 years: (1) demographic change, (2) globalisation and the markets of the future, (3) scarcity of resources, (4) climate change, (5) technology dynamics and innovation, (6) global science, and (7) sustainability and global responsibility. These profound changes can be grasped by specific aspects. Demographic change is particularly marked by a further increase in the world's population (United Nations, Department of Economic and Social Affairs, Population Division, 2017), a rising average age (Contis, Bennett, Mathers, Li, Foreman, & Ezzati, 2017) as well as migratory movements and migration to cities. Trend 2 captures the shift in global economic equilibria towards specific countries that have tended to play a subordinate role until now. The increasing scarcity of resources and the associated rise in prices and possible supply bottlenecks will continue to impact the company's activities in the future. Climate change and the associated threat to ecosystems (due to droughts, extreme storms, floods, etc.) will also continue to progress in the next 20 years. Trend 5 is especially characterised by a globally faster spread of technologies, which means that innovative companies in particular can benefit. Less developed countries will follow suit, especially in terms of innovation capacity. Digitisation and life sciences are crucial key technologies. In connection with the Global Knowledge Society, three changes need to be emphasized in particular: Increased dissemination of knowledge, slight improvement in gender equality and increased competition for qualified employees. On the one hand, trend 7 indicates an increased significance of sustainability due to limited resources, and on the other hand, the relevance of cooperation by governments at a global level. A growing influence on increasing sustainability is attributed to both the individual and the impact of NGOs (Krys, 2017).

Digitisation, digitalisation or digital transformation as well as sustainability belong to the main global megatrends today. However, there are lots of positive developments, but also negative consequences in terms of sustainability. In order to create holistic sustainable concepts, attention to fundamental developments is essential. In addition to a wide range of positive developments, potential risks and challenges have already been, but still must be identified, analysed and implemented in order to prevent exponential technology adaptations from leading to a complete lack of transparency of the overall system. So, how is a responsible and sustainable management possible taking all relevant values and opportunities and threats into account? The main questions of positive and negative impacts of digitisation concerning sustainability impacts will be discussed based on given conceptual and theoretical reflections as well as gained by results used systemic structural constellations. Systemic structural constellations are able to spatially map patterns, connections, structures and relationships within a system and can thus be used in a variety of ways, like depicting complex challenges spatially and visually in order to point out new possibilities as well as revealing and closing the gaps between knowledge and lack of action or to open up paths to more sustainable action (Arnold, 2018, 2016). Systemic structural constellations address the unconsciousness and are based on unconscious thinking and processes; they provide an excellent supplement to conventional research designs. After a review of the literature on digitisation and sustainability and compiling a SWOT table, a concept map is developed for visualising key topics in light of digitisation and sustainability. In addition, two exemplifying systemic structural constellations are presented for illustrating unconscious knowledge in this context, too.

BACKGROUND

The digital ecosystem describes an open information landscape (Dini, 2007) with particular emphasis on the adaptability, dynamics and self-organizing mechanisms of inter-organizational information systems and encompasses a holistic perspective on the inter-organizational system of action (Müller-Mielitz & Lux, 2016). Actors and innovations can develop competitively, independently and co-evolutionarily. If it is possible to generate and maintain a critical mass of users, success can be achieved in terms of economic and social sustainability (Müller-Mielitz & Lux, 2016). Platforms, exposed to network effects can lead to dysfunctional social distribution and participation processes, will become central (BKA, 2015). Furthermore, network effects, information asymmetries, opportune behaviour and negative assessments can have an impact on citizens' decisions and voting behaviour as well as on effectiveness and sustainability. Moreover, increasing digitisation may reduce the range of information and equal opportunities between technology-affine and technology-averse citizens. Technology-affine refers to the assumption that these users have a high degree of technological affinity and, for example, are more familiar with installation processes, because they have a strong connection to technology (Geisler, Zelazny, Christmann, & Hagenhoff, 2011). In contrast, technology-averse users show a high degree of technological repugnance and have a less experienced handling with technologies.

Prisecaru (2016) provides an overview of the main characteristics (energy resource, main technical achievement, main developed industries, transport means) of the fourth industrial revolution: Green Energies; Internet, Genetic Engineering, 3D Printer; High Tech Industries and Electric Car, Fast Train. All these points have a major impact on both industrial production and social relations as well as on people's relationship to production and its results. It is questionable, for example, whether strong productivity growth and technological progress lead to an improvement in

3

wealth or increase social inequalities and unemployment (Prisecaru, 2016), thus strengthening the integration of socially sustainable criteria. There is also considerable potential in the area of environmental sustainability. For example, technological progress enables a reduction in industrial waste and more efficient processes for the use of resources (Prisecaru, 2016), but can lead to increased resource consumption as a result (rebound).

In addition, the ongoing digitisation process is raising expectations for achieving the Sustainable Development Goals. For example, changes are emerging in a wide variety of sectors that can make a contribution to sustainability (Osburg & Lohrmann, 2017): In the healthcare sector for instance, people are benefiting from new technologies that make medical solutions more affordable, accessible and of higher quality. In the automotive sector, networked applications can save several hundred thousand lives and reduce traffic accidents considerably. In this context, digitisation supports a healthy life in accordance with SDG 3 (GeSI Report, 2015). The demand for a fair, integrative and qualitative high-quality education can be achieved by solutions in the sense of an open education such as MOOCs. (SDG 4). Likewise, specific adaptations can help to reduce greenhouse gas emissions and promote a market transformation towards renewable energies, thus complying with the SDG 13. Significant opportunities and challenges can be identified in the markets and their players. SDG 9 aims to build a resilient infrastructure, promote innovation and sustainable, inclusive industrialisation. The market perspective is also included in SDG 12 and aims at sustainable production and consumption patterns. However, this is only an excerpt of aspects that need to be included in the context of digitisation with a focus on sustainable design (Osburg & Lohrmann, 2017).

Such effects and possible rebound effects have not been sufficiently researched in the context of sustainability. Rebound effects can occur at both the micro and macro level. According to Greening, Greene, & Difiglio (2000), a four-part typology can be used to identify these effects. The direct rebound effect (1) can be assigned to the micro level and is characterized in particular by increased demand due to price reductions. These in turn are the result of technological improvements in the area of fuel consumption, which can reduce the necessary use of raw materials. Secondary effects (2) can also be observed (Greening et al., 2000), which are characterised by an increase in demand for alternative services and goods. An aggregation of behaviour at the micro level, which may still be moderate, could be significant at the macro level due to economy-wide effects (3), especially for fuel supply markets (Greening et al., 2000.). Finally, transformational effects (4), such as changes in social institutions or consumer preferences due to technological change may also occur (Greening et al., 2000). In order to grasp the variety of digitisation and digital transformation a comprehensive literature review follows resulting in a SWOT analysis.

LITERATURE REVIEW

Leonard & Graf von Kospoth (2017) emphasize this rapid development with linear humanity and point out that society needs ways to ensure the preservation of what makes us human. Hyper-innovations should therefore be made humanely sustainable. A complete lack of transparency must be exerted by pressure from governments, organisations and officials on the companies behind this trend. Furthermore, it is relevant to anchor the addictive potential (e. g. specific platform designs) of technological innovations in a collective understanding and to develop rules in order to establish a human balance. Drivers that endanger addiction must be identified and transparency ensured. While there are fears that the technological innovations could be turned against the whole world, there are also weakened opinions. According to Kissinger, the instructions by humans could be misinterpreted due to a lack of context (Sturgeon, 2018). It can have catastrophic consequences if the artificial intelligence does not meet human expectations. The first applications in which people were not able to keep up with the computer also became apparent and it is questionable whether the human brain is able to adapt identical abilities (Sturgeon, 2018).

Digital human rights and ethics must be anchored in the form of central rules for conducting business within the digital market (Leonard & Graf von Kospoth 2017). The German Ethics Council also concludes in a recent statement focusing on specific health-related areas of application that the traditional data protection law is no longer sufficient to meet the challenges of Big Data in the sectors examined by means of existing protection mechanisms and forms of action. It calls for a design and regulatory concept with the aim of protecting and respecting values such as sovereignty, justice, privacy, freedom, responsibility and solidity. The concept should be oriented towards data sovereignty in the sense of an extension of informational self-determination according to an interactive personality development while preserving privacy in a networked world (Deutscher Ethikrat, 2017, p. 27). The social sustainability aspect should be emphasised.

Osburg & Lohrmann (2017) provide an overview of different perspectives on aspects of sustainability within the digital world. The focus here is on leadership, mobility, working life and corporate responsibility, mainly addressing change and new models of digitisation. While the high relevance of digitisation is being discussed in all areas of life, the extent to which this is happening is slowly coming to light. Every change and new innovation can have far-reaching consequences for other areas and thus disrupt beneficial balances between society, the environment and the economy (Osburg & Lohrmann, 2017). In a workshop on the subject of "sustainable digitisation", the Ministry of the Environment was able to uncover both significant opportunities and risks as well as potential opportunities that digitisation could achieve. The focus was on resource efficiency through digitisation, intelligent energy systems, sustainable digitisation in society and digital education for sustainable development (MUKEBW, 2018). Both a promotion and a counteraction of resource efficiency can be caused by the digital change in the area of production (MUKEBW, 2018). While digitisation and digitalisation will be able to achieve considerable efficiency gains on one hand, it can also lead to immense negative effects on the other one. Santaris (2017) points out that digitisation and digital transformation seem to shift the demand for energy and resources on a global scale. Increased consumption would lead to a destruction of efficiency gains due to rebound effects (Erdmann & Hilty, 2010). Sustainability-focused concepts must always be integrated into the development of innovations by beginning - well aware that rebound effects will always be effective in the use phase.

Due to the implementation of the shared economy concept, the shift from product to service orientation can be observed in many sectors, which leads to the questioning of existing business models. Building on service-dominant logic and interorganisational governance models, Aksin-Sivrikaya & Bhattacharya (2017) establish a conceptual framework for a digital ecosystem integrating multi-stakeholder and value-co-creation. They also identify potential emerging sustainable governance models within a proposed ecosystem. Future challenges are transferred into three categories: (1) the design of business models in a digital environment, (2) interruptions of existing businesses, and (3) environmental and social problems due to digitisation. If we learn how to deal with these challenges correctly, sustainable governance models can lead to a reduction of costs and frictions associated with management, manufacturing, processing, energy use, logistics, production and information collection (Aksin-Sivrikaya & Bhattacharya, 2017). Strictly centred views will be eliminated and integrated business ecosystems and value creation activities within multi-stakeholder networks will increase. Fixed boundaries will therefore fade (Aksin-Sivrikaya & Bhattacharya, 2017). The following table summarises current literature-based SWOTs.

In total, on the one hand, digitisation implies the risk of the non-transparency of the overall system, on the other hand it can serve to make specific areas more transparent - for example, by creating trust and transparency through digital dialogue and symbolizing complexity. In the financial sector, the use of digital media can thus lead to an intensified customer relationship and the integration of topics such as environmental awareness, social responsibility and economic activity; in the social media sector can thus contribute to increased sustainability in the sense of increasing efficiency and holistic consulting (Behringer, 2017). Zinnöcker (2017) also uses digital measures to create transparency. Accordingly, digital measurements support and activate the visualisation and billing of individual energy consumption as well as the actors and their energy savings.

Table 1. SWOTs in the context of digitisation and sustainability

Strengths	Weaknesses
• digital ecosystems describe an open information landscape • digital ecosystems encompass a holistic perspective on the inter-organizational system of action	• lack of transparency • digitisation seems to shift the demand for energy and resources on a global scale • addictive potential (e. g. specific platform designs) of specific technological innovations • the traditional data protection law is no longer sufficient to meet the challenges of Big Data in the sectors examined by means of existing protection mechanisms and forms of action • environmental and social problems due to digitisation
Strengths and Weaknesses	
• complexity	
Opportunities	Threats
• **healthcare sector:** people are benefiting from new technologies that make medical solutions more affordable, accessible and of higher quality • **automotive sector:** networked applications can save several hundred thousand lives and reduce traffic accidents considerably • **education sector:** fair, integrative and qualitative high-quality education can be achieved by solutions in the sense of an open education such as MOOCs • **financial sector:** use of digital media can lead to an intensified customer relationship and the integration of topics such as environmental awareness, social responsibility and economic activity • **social media sector:** can contribute to increased sustainability in the sense of increasing efficiency and holistic consulting • **production sector:** • Material Flow Cost Accounting as a simulation and optimization tool for small and medium-sized enterprises in the manufacturing sector and control instrument in companies (e.g. by integration into existing Enterprise Resource Planning (ERP) environments • Learning networks for companies & integration of employees and their training and further education to increase resource efficiency • Environmental services 4.0: Digitisation opens up completely new possibilities and improved information for recycling companies. • Efficient production: Optimisation of internal material/energy efficiency, e.g. "One-piece-flow": no set-up times and production is started without any losses as well as a digital image of production can reveal optimization potentials • value chain 4.0: increasing modularization of companies → more interfaces between companies; transport of information along the value chain; the recyclability of production should already be taken into account at the design stage; definition of interfaces for resource efficiency and industry 4.0 • **decreased resource consumption in production due to** • Production is closer to the customer, is more demand-oriented → resulting in lower inventory levels and less overproduction • Product to Performance: product becomes less important, the benefit of the product becomes more important • Digitisation enables transparency of the by-product streams and better information across the value chain → optimizes the value chain • Losses in value added can be better evaluated through digitization and inefficient production can be avoided • digital measurements support and activate the visualisation and billing of individual energy consumption as well as the actors and their energy savings • specific adaptations can help to reduce greenhouse gas emissions and promote a market transformation towards renewable energies (SDG 13) • resilient infrastructure • promote innovation and sustainable, inclusive industrialisation • establish a human balance • sustainable governance models can lead to a reduction of costs and frictions associated with management, manufacturing, processing, energy use, logistics, production and information collection • by creating trust and transparency through digital dialogue and symbolizing complexity specific areas can become more transparent	• network effects can lead to dysfunctional social distribution and participation processes • information asymmetries, opportune behaviour and negative assessments can have an impact on citizens' decisions and voting behaviour as well as on effectiveness and sustainability • reduced range of information (lack transparency) and equal opportunities between technology-affine and technology-averse citizens • immense energy consumption • further rebound effects • every change and new innovation can have far-reaching consequences for other areas and thus disrupt beneficial balances between society, the environment and the economy • interruptions of existing businesses • Increased resource consumption in production due to: • Increasing complexity in the world of production, consumption and communication • Increasing technical and social innovation • Acceleration of processes in the areas of planning, production and logistics • a shortening of product lifetimes (not because of reduced shelf life, but because of faster product innovations • Extension of possibilities (product features, services...) & product offers • Increasing the specificity of customer requirements • Increase or shift in demand for products and services • a constantly growing individualisation of consumer wishes and products

continued on following page

Table 1. Continued

Opportunities and Threats
• opportunity to reduce the use of resources concerning an increasing scarcity of resources • far-reaching changes in processes, products, processes and business models • considerable efficiency gains on one hand, that can also lead to a negative effect (rebound) on the other one • digital human rights and ethics must be anchored in the form of central rules for conducting business within the digital market • the design of business models in a digital environment • rapid development of technologies • sector-specific requirements • new designs and regulatory concepts • shift from product to service orientation • integrated business ecosystems and value creation activities within multi-stakeholder networks

Sources: Aksin-Sivrikaya & Bhattacharya, 2017; Behringer, 2017; BKA, 2015; Deutscher Ethikrat, 2017; Dini, 2007; Erdmann & Hilty, 2010; GeSI Report, 2015; Greening at al., 2000; Müller-Mielitz & Lux, 2016; MUKEBW, 2018; Leonard & Graf von Kospoth, 2017; Osburg & Lohrmann, 2017; Santaris, 2017; Sturgeon, 2018; Zinnöcker, 2017

(Source: Own representation)

METHODS

Beside analysing relevant literature in the topic sustainability and digitisation (both, English and German papers and literature) addressing challenges, opportunities and risks, and compiling a SWOT analysis, a concept map generated by content analysis of English papers was generated in order to analyse current linkages between sustainability and digitisation and digitalisation. Final, results of systemic structural constellations were integrated to combine conscious-based and unconscious-based knowledge.

A total number of 112 texts (scientific articles and summaries; e.g. Bondarouka & Brewster (2016); of acknowledged scientific journals; e.g. The International Journal of Human Resource Management, Human Geographies – Journal of Studies and Research in Human Geography, Journal of Security and Sustainability Issues, Journal of Urban Regeneration and Renewal) relating to the period 2015-2018 and accessible in the Ebsco and Scopus databases were included in the analysis. Within the Ebsco and Scopus databases, the keywords "digitisations" and "sustainability" were used as filters.

Content analysis can help to explore specific concepts from text-based information and uncover their structures and interdependencies. From a given amount of data, it filters out the most frequently occurring topics (Zawacki-Richter & Latchem, 2018). The computer-aided content analysis which is used under the purpose of this study may serve to map a specific area of research (Zawacki-Richter & Latchem, 2018). Smith & Humphreys (2006) highlight the advantages of such automated processes. Human analysis requires considerable financial and time resources to avoid the subjectivity associated with the method. For example, coders must be trained in advance, dictionaries and codebooks validated and intercoder reliability tested (Smith & Humphreys, 2006, p. 262). In addition to cost savings, automation can shorten the analysis process. At the same time, it is a simplification when very large amounts of data are to be examined (Smith & Humphreys, 2006). In the context of this investigation the content analysis software Leximancer^{LM} (2017) was used for this research. This includes a two-stage process of simultaneous information extraction. For each of these levels (semantic and relational) a different algorithm is used (Smith & Humphreys, 2006). In the context of our analysis it produced a concept map which represents key concepts and the semantic structure of topics for the articles examined. Leximancer^{LM} has already been used for several content analyses of academic journals (Zawacki-Richter & Latchem, 2018). Analyses up to now relate amongst others to the Journal of Communication (Lin & Lee, 2012), Journal of International Business Studies (Liesch, Håkanson, McGaughey, Middleton, & Cretchley, 2011), Distance Education (Zawacki-Richter & Naidu, 2016) and the Journal of Cross-Cultural Psychology (Cretchley, Rooney, & Gallois, 2010).

The software generates a visual map whereby similar concepts are bundled (Zawacki-Richeer & Latchem, 2018). According to Smith and Humphreys (2006, p. 264) "The map is an indicative visualization that presents concept frequency (brightness), total concept connectedness (hierarchical order of appearance), direct interconcept relative co-occurrence frequency (ray intensity), and total (direct and indirect) interconcept co-occurrence (proximity)". Harwood, Gapp, & Stewart (2015) were able to demonstrate stable results using Leximancer^{LM} and a manual grounded theory approach. Nevertheless, it is of great importance always to pay attention to expert judgment and analytical sensitivity with regard to interpretation (Zawacki-Richeer & Latchem, 2018). In addition, the interpretation requires both knowledge and a thorough understanding of the context and theme of the study (Zawacki-Richeer & Latchem, 2018).

Moreover, facing this variety and complexity in the context of digital change, new approaches, methods and models are increasingly relevant for generating holistic sustainable concepts identifying strengths and challenges in organisations, institutions and companies. Meeting the requirements of current and future reality, e.g. complex strategic decision-taking, environmental behaviours and the maintenance or preserving of resilience of systems, scientific tools and practices often lack in complete mapping (Walker et al., 2002). According to Wade (2004, p. 194), constellations are a method meeting the mentioned challenges, because they "provide powerful and creative ways to clarify and resolving complex, possibly intractable issues associated with organisations." In addition, they offer the opportunity to experiment with specific solutions in a secure environment and thus support decision making (Wade, 2004). Intuition and unconscious knowledge play a major role in the area of relevant decision-making processes (Rosselet, 2013), therefore, unconsciousness should be integrated beside conscious-based methods.

In particular, top managers are often confronted with a variety of tasks, information and decisions that have to be taken in a very short time. Agor (1986) was able to show that the majority of the executives he examined trusted their intuition in particularly important decisions. A significant advantage of the systemic structural constellations over many other methods is that they allow the integration of both unconscious and hidden knowledge in the area of decision-making processes (Arnold 2018, Arnold 2016). Accordingly, a wider range of knowledge on a topic can be skimmed off. Systemic structural constellations can be used to train a careful handling of digitised systems and as an instrument for mapping relationship structures within a system for the analysis and creation of possible changes to these structures (Kopp, 2013). Depending on the system under consideration, specific constellations can be used. The common feature of the constellations is that they aim to show the correlation between the individual system elements (Kopp, 2013). According to Arnold (2016, p. 22), the three central components of this method are a group of people who participate on a voluntary basis as representatives (1), an issue-holder (2) and a facilitator or process manager (3). An important component is also the so-called representative perception. This means that the representatives serve as resonators for the hidden and implicit knowledge (Arnold 2016, Rosselet, 2013). According to Schlötter (2005) representative perception is a basic ability of all humans. High-quality constellations are rule-guided and follow main structures.

Table 2. Methodical design of the Application of Systemic Structural Constellation

Topic	Digitisation and Sustainability: Threats, Opportunities and Non-Conformity
Question/Goal	Which possibilities and threats dominate in the context of digital change and its sustainable development? Are there any overlaps in the results of the methods used? • Content-based: new hypotheses and theory development concerning Digitisation and Sustainability
Participants	Issue-holders: professors, researchers, students Representatives: experienced researchers and students from Chemnitz University of Technology
Year	Autumn 2017 and Spring 2018
Duration	Up two hours including reflexion
Research design	Exploratory case study
Data collection	Observation, interviewing, testing as well as heuristics
Data preparation	Video, protocol, joint reflexion
Data interpretation	Interpretative-hermeneutic methods, reference analysis

(own source)

There are five key phases in systemic structural constellation work (Arnold, 2018): (1) Starting with clarifying the context the constellator and the issue-holder clear up the concern and issues by figuring out the goal and key involved elements. In scientific contexts, beside practitioners researchers or professors (educated as a constellator) can take the part of the issue-holder. (2) The selection of representatives for representing the core elements (agreed on in step 1) of the specific system is taken by the issue-holder by intuition or based on unconscious decision. (3) Initial constellation and first pattern are formed by the issue-holder as he or she positions all representatives/elements in the room. That special positioning and grouping is called structural constellation. It enables the recognition of spatial perspectives, arrangements, distances, and directions. So, underlying dynamics of the represented and focused situation can become more visible and conscious (Arnold, 2018). The selected representatives can also position in the room themselves – following their impressions where to position best in the given systemic constellation. (3) Process work enables diverse interventions facilitating solutions, testing simulations or gaining new hypotheses, etc. Finding a solution, forming a final constellation setting or the issue-holder is satisfied with the current patterns, the constellation process will be finished. (4) In the Closure the representatives are released from their work and will be thanked for their service and assistance (Arnold, 2018). (5) A final reflexion on new insights and strategic options follows. Systemic structural constellation processes take 20 minutes up to two hours.

Within the scope of the chapter tangible examples of applications with students, carried out at the Chemnitz University of Technology, will be presented. Table 2 gives an overview of the methodical design. One of the constellations figures out tensions between technology-avers and -affine people in the context of sustainability and digitisation. The other focussed on health care and consisted the following elements *Sustainability*, *Digitisation*, *Company*, *Organisational Members*, *Health Care Effects* and *Competition*.

Limitations

It should be noted that the study has covered a period from 2015 to 2018. Digitisation is subject to constant change, which makes it virtually impossible to fix it in time. It only seems feasible to show a trend that reflects prevailing topics. The articles were accessed through the two databases: Ebsco and Scopus, but not limited to specific journals. It should be noted, however, that only accessible articles could be included. Only English articles and books were used. However, it may also be of interest to include literature in other languages and other types of sources. As already mentioned, Leximancer^{LM} can be used to create concept maps. Algorithms serve to find the most frequently occurring terms (Zawacki-Richter & Latchem,

2018). However, the co-word analysis should be viewed critically. According to Leydesdorff (1997, p. 418) "words change both in terms of frequencies of relations with other words, and in terms of positional meaning from one text to another." It should be noted that "the fluidity of networks in which nodes and links may change positions is expected to destabilize representations of developments of the sciences on the basis of co-occurrences and co-absences of word" (Leydesdorff, 1997, p. 418). Some authors point out that the words within a co-word analysis are only to be seen as indicators for the links between individual concepts (Courtial, 1998). Others see particular possibilities to carry out a narrative investigation concerning a specific subject in the co-occurrence of words (Liesch et al., 2011; Sowa, 2000). With regard to the maps created with Leximancer^{LM}, a careful interpretation and knowledge of the overall topic is indispensable (Zawacki-Richter & Latchem, 2018).

This is comparable to the systemic structural constellations. They have a high objectivity and reliability (Schlötter, 2005), but also face the reliability-validity dilemma (Lamnek, 1988). Meeting external validity a joint discussion and reflexion for balancing different perspectives and points of view is essential in scientific contexts (Arnold, 2018). As the main focus, here, is set on unconscious knowledge, the main quality criteria should assess how useful a constellation is to address new questions, formulate promising hypotheses and widening the context and understandings. However, in order to produce high quality in constellation settings, the frame-set of the constellator, how open-minded and respectful and how experienced she or he is, have strong impact on the outcome. In addition, the representatives can also manipulate the results when not being open-minded, but having strict frames or expectations. Therefore, hidden work, e.g. using tags, t-shirts, etc. for differentiation, is most successful – as it focuses on representation fundamentally. In addition, when repeating constellations, there might never be identical positioning, but always comparable patterns. So, the results of the constellation work was not interpreted as absolute truth, but as helpful patterns and indicators for challenges in complex settings addressing sustainability and digitisation. However, this method sensitises students to the topic and on the other hand, completely new impulses for reflexions, progress and changed frames can be generated, which can be used by the companies themselves.

SOLUTIONS AND RECOMMENDATIONS

In this section, our results of the concept maps and systemic structural constellations will be discussed on the background and literature review.

Concepts Maps

The following fifteen topics are associated with the literature studied: *Data*, *Design*, *Digital*, *Market*, *OECD*, *Online*, *People*, *Performance*, *Projects*, *Public*, *Results*, *Species*, *Sustainable*, *Use*, and *Value*. Figure 1 shows the concept map of the analysed texts.

The topics with the most common strokes are *digital* (13610), *sustainable* (11191), *use* (10396), *data* (9701), *design* (6166), the latter is already green. Warmer colours (of the other themes) show that these are the most frequently occurring themes within the texts studied. In particular, the interpretation will focus on the first three topics. Leximancer^{LM} makes it possible to visualize the concepts related to the topics. "Digital"

Figure 1. Concept map for the analysed literature

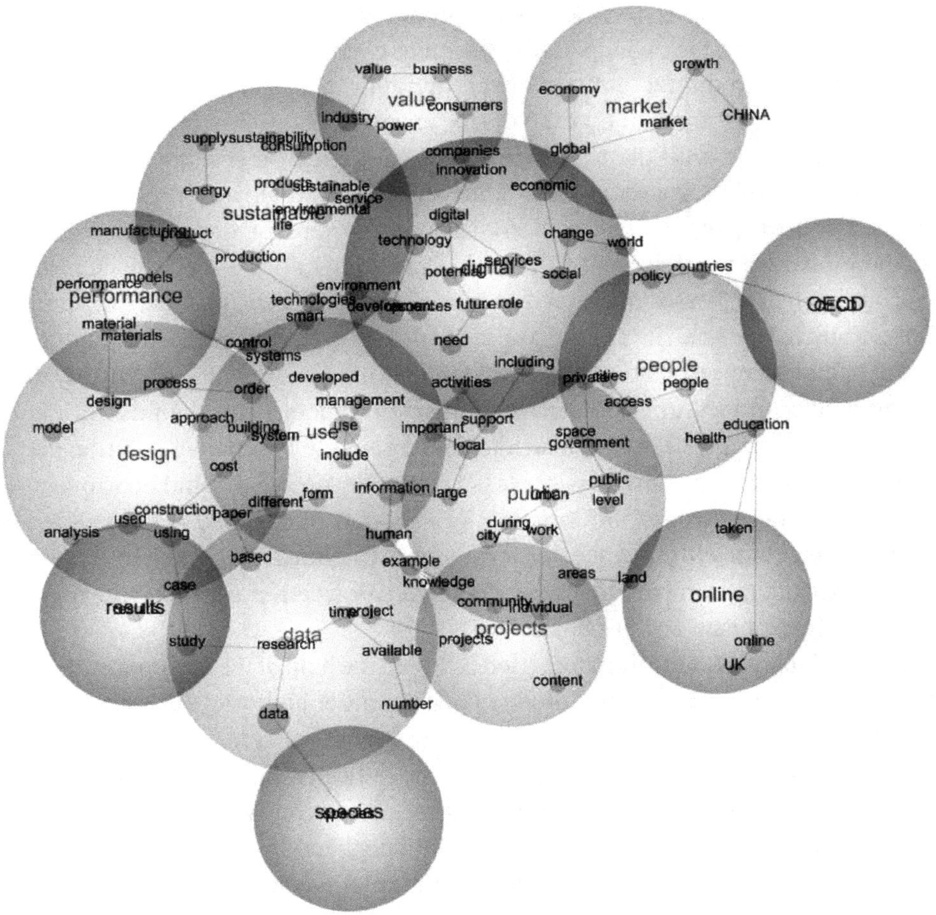

is associated with the following concepts for the texts used: *digital, development, services, social, economic, technology, future, need, potential, including, world, change, innovation*. The concepts *sustainable, sustainability, production, products, energy, technologies, environmental, product, smart, manufacturing, life, supply* and *consumption* are associated with "sustainability". *Use, information, system, different, systems, management, order, important* represent the concepts in connection with the theme bubble "use".

Linking the topics *digital* and *sustainable,* it has to be emphasised that the analysis merely shows one direct link path between the two thematic bubbles (*sustainable* and *digital*). The directly related concepts are: *sustainable, environmental, life, production, technologies, (smart), environment, development (resources), technology, digital.* These topics reflect the analysed SWOTs (see table 1), as well. So, there is a high congruency. With regard to a sustainable design of digital change, the main focus seems to be on production. Extracts of the used literature with keywords such as manufacturing processes, production and production phase reflect this. An indirect connection between the two topics also becomes clear. The concept of technologies, which is linked to digital and sustainable through further concept points, is also included in the *use* area. In this sector, for example, the following problems may arise in connection with the use of digital technologies: According to Bondarouk & Brewster (2016), concrete case studies show that employees prefer to receive information from people rather than from a digital system. Incongruent frameworks can therefore result in divergent views and conflicting information. This in turn can be accompanied by losses in the area of processes, resistance and false expectations (Bondarouk & Brewster, 2016). According to this, it seems to be quite relevant on the part of social components to leave people in the function of superiors. In any case, it should be examined in advance what concrete problems a digital transformation can entail in such a case in order both to find a socially acceptable solution and to protect the company against possible losses. Another problem could be irreversible damage to data security if information systems are outsourced (Bergere, 2016). Even in connection with advanced metering infrastructure and the electronic storage of customer data, problems may arise in the area of data protection (Sooknanan, Bahadoorsingh, Joshi, & Sharma, 2016).

The first analysis of the literature used (without the help of the Leximancer[LM] tool) shows *digitisation* presents a multitude of opportunities and risks that must be taken into account in order to achieve sustainable change in the overall system. But which areas are in focus and where could a sustainable design be particularly relevant? The following is a list of the main results in connection with the Leximancer[LM] programme used. The structuring of the following sections is intended on setting the thematic focus of the analysis. Selected interrelationships have been integrated. In addition, the subheadings are used to illustrate the areas of topics that overlap and are bordering on the first analysis (SWOT). Since the use phase, especially in connection with potential rebound effects, is a major focus in connection with technological progress, opportunities and risks of this concept bubble are explained in a separate section.

Results concerning the specific topics and its concepts after analysis by the programme, which specify above listed points, complete or acknowledge them:

Global Development

Not only specific sectors (see table 1), but also global industries and specific groups of countries face new challenges. According to Alexander (2017), constant innovations in corporate technologies and an increase in the virtualisation of social spaces are key drivers of a transformation of the global retail industry. This could cause some difficulties, especially for emerging countries. According to Conschafter (2017), cities can also be made usable as respite from the digitised world. Thus, future urban planning should reflect not only the advantageous and unobtrusive integration of technologies for people, but also the most appreciated places of the past. It should be emphasized that this integration must take place for all economic and social backgrounds and therefore a complete participation of all people should be striven for (Conschafter, 2017). He sees the risk of excluding certain groups, for example, in the decline in car traffic and car ownership. In addition to the exclusion of certain groups, according to Matser (2017), there is also the risk of an increased distance between customers and employees (business sector). Furthermore, there may be increased staff shortfalls if this problem is not counteracted in advance by means of increased attention (Matser, 2017). In specific sectors, such as services, fewer people are expected to be needed and unemployment is expected to rise. This can lead to output and quality increases (Matser, 2017), and suitable political measures are necessary to compensate an increased unemployment.

Demand for Sustainability and the Inclusion of Specific Groups

According to Lyons, Mokhtarian, Dijst, & Böcker (2018), it is necessary to understand how the basic social needs for the various approaches (to goods, people, services, opportunities) can be met sustainably. Uncertainties about future access depending on affordability and social preferences should also be taken into account. Scenario planning can play a decisive role here, for example by mapping divergent future perspectives and promoting group thinking (Lyons, Mokhtarian, Dijst, & Böcker, 2018.). Beside avoiding or reducing uncertainties as ways of including the various groups, Conschafter (2017) calls for the design of the built environment_and addressing it through appropriate policies to counteract the exclusion of specific groups. He identifies great potential for artificial intelligence, increasing automation and the associated efficiency gains, and the use of renewable technologies to create environmentally friendly cities of the future. However, in order to achieve this and to create a resilience of the cities, it is relevant that the cities themselves push this forward, for example with the creation of green spaces (Conschafter, 2017). Lifelong learning can be seen as an essential way of promoting social inclusion. Both younger and adult groups of the labour market or the unemployed should be included (Dias, Alemdra, & Silva, 2017). For specific groups, such as the elderly, it is often a considerable challenge to face completely new challenges. A change is also increasingly expected on the consumer side to solve global environmental concerns. They must also assume responsibility in social, economic, ethical and ecological areas (Fuentes & Sörum, 2018). In order to meet this complex challenge, one should never start at just one point.

Company

In the future, it may be particularly relevant for companies to combine different types of innovation (organisational innovation, marketing, process, service and product innovation) in order to set themselves apart from other competitors (Luciana & Stan 2017). On the one hand, there are also clear effects on social factors in the field of digital, whose changes are also accompanied by market-economy transformations. On the other hand, the graphic shows no connection line between the theme bubbles *people* and the *market*. Thus, there should be greater importance regarding the inclusion of this concept (*people*) in the areas of *market* and *digital*.

In the automotive sector, green services can play a particularly important monitoring and control function for sustainable measures, such as in the area of raw material recycling (Opazo-Basáez, Vendrell-Herrero, & Bustinza, 2018). It is relevant to integrate these projects with digital skills in the case of implementation effectively, taking into account the respective performance and sustainability objectives of the company (Opazo-Basáez, Vendrell-Herrero, & Bustinza, 2018). In addition, intelligent materials can provide significant opportunities to contribute to the sustainability of digital measures. These can be activated, for example, by specific environmental impacts and thus transformed (Teoh, Chua, Liu, & An, 2017). This could lead to other energy sources being saved. An increased service life can be particularly useful for products whose production phase has a considerable negative impact on the environment. The associated increase in efficiency leads to a reduction in the energy required for recycling materials (Dominish et al., 2018). This has both positive environmental effects and cost savings on the company side. However, potential rebound effects should always be considered in the context of efficiency improvements (Greening, Greene, & Difiglio, 2000). It is useless to extend the service life of products by means of new technologies if this results in higher consumption, which in turn increases the resource usage. Informing consumers about potential risks should be done by both the state and the companies themselves.

A study of 100 Canadian companies in 2015 shows that both management commitment and stakeholder pressure will lead to environmentally friendly supply practices and waste-free production. In this way, more innovative products, new skills, environmental improvements and financial gains can be increased (Rajala, Hakanen, Mattila, Seppälä & Westerlund, 2018). Under the focus of a sustainable design of the manufacturing processes, economically effective processes and products should predominate. According to Da Silva et al. (2017), these contribute to optimising energy procurement and consumption, the environmental impact, the safety of employees and society and the use of natural resources. Industry 4.0 can make a significant contribution to minimise the environmental damage. Intelligent systems, in the area of production, can achieve a reduction of the following main areas: overproduction, production waste, goods movements and energy consumption (Kamble, Gunasekaran, & Gawankar, 2018). According to Kamble et al. (2018) products can be made clearly identifiable by means of intelligent systems. This can help to facilitate the challenge of increasing complexity in the area of manufacturing processes (Kamble et al., 2018). It is crucial to analyse the effects of such systems (products, factories) (Kamble et al., 2018). These smart technologies seem to play a decisive role, especially with regard to sustainable development.

Specific Challenges and Opportunities in Connection With the Theme Bubble Use

According to Gebhardt (2017), ecosystems are directly related to a high degree of complexity and constant change. Managers must be able to cope with these tasks and take irrational behavior and complex system logic into account (Gebhardt, 2017). A control of social systems should include both belief systems and emerging characteristics (Gebhardt, 2017). Here, systemic structural constellations could support respective development. In connection with a stable design of storage management, long-term strategies and intelligent filter systems represent a major challenge (Scholz, 2016). This problem relates in particular to the problem of digital preservation of information. While printed paper makes it possible for a very long time to preserve information, such as cultural heritage, less than 20% of the information transmitted globally (in relation to 2007) could be stored in the context of technical ageing (Scholz, 2016).

There is considerable potential for optimization in the automotive sector. For example, real-time access to the entire system can improve flowing and stationary traffic and its safety (Rammler, 2017) (see table 1). A combination of infotainment systems and standard communication technologies can contribute to an increase in well-being, especially in conurbations, where, for example, waiting times can be bridged. Here entertainment, communication, information and work can play a major role (Rammler, 2017). The adaptation of e-government systems can contribute an increased benefit for municipalities in electronic transactions with stakeholders along the whole value chain (Khilji, Duan, Lewis, Bukoye, & Luton, 2017). According to Toonen & Bush (2018), fish attraction devices can help to get a more accurate picture of the shape of oceanic space using information and sensor technologies. It is relevant to make information and communication technology more environmentally friendly and energy efficient through appropriate measures, as they are used generously in the area of digital information over its entire life cycle (Chowdhury, 2016). In sum, according to the literature, central rebound effects can be: energy overconsumption, underestimation of human needs and ability to adapt, unlearn of diverse cap-/abilities, etc. (further see table 1). These rebounds might even get worse when differentiating technology-avers and technology-affine people.

Systemic Structural Constellations

Figuring out main challenges, a constellation was conducted containing the following (hidden) elements: Digitisation, Sustainability, Opportunities and Bounds, Technology-affine and Technology-avers (figure 2).

Issue-holder were a sustainability professor and a group of scientists and students in the field of sustainability management. The whole constellation work was conducted in a hidden way, meaning only the constellator knew what the respective representatives were representing. The single elements or respective representatives were asked to find a good place in the room related to the given system and searched their position themselves. The representatives were asked for their feelings, wishes to move and differences they can explain. After a first round of expressing their inner pictures and ideas, the representatives were allowed to move and interact further. This procedure was repeated until a final constellation was found as all representatives explicated a stable context. The figures convey pivotal expressions of the respective elements. The interpretation is based on the statements, the positions and systemic principles (Arnold, 2016).

In the beginning, it became quickly obvious technology-affine and technology-avers are in clear tensions and two different poles – as they positioned vis-à-vis (figure 2). During the constellation these two poles oriented towards digitisation and sustainability, but becoming more open for other positions and got more balanced. The element *Technology-affine* wanted to push digitisation without any constraint. In the beginning *Sustainability* mainly focussed on *Bounds* and *Technology-avers*, but changed to a more open-minded and balanced position stating *Opportunities*

Figure 2. Initial constellation representing technology-avers versus -affine people
(own source, figures © Antonia Wetzel)

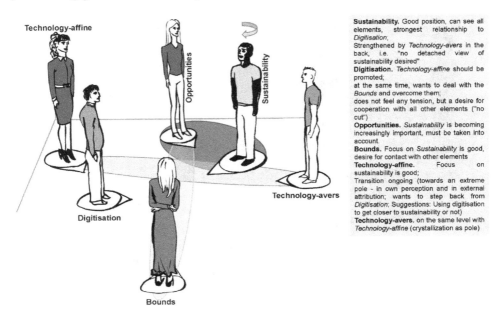

Sustainability. Good position, can see all elements, strongest relationship to *Digitisation*;
Strengthened by *Technology-avers* in the back, i.e. "no detached view of sustainability desired"
Digitisation. *Technology-affine* should be promoted;
at the same time, wants to deal with the *Bounds* and overcome them;
does not feel any tension, but a desire for cooperation with all other elements ("no cut")
Opportunities. *Sustainability* is becoming increasingly important, must be taken into account.
Bounds. Focus on *Sustainability* is good, desire for contact with other elements
Technology-affine. Focus on sustainability is good;
Transition ongoing (towards an extreme pole - in own perception and in external attribution; wants to step back from *Digitisation*; Suggestions: Using digitisation to get closer to sustainability or not)
Technology-avers. on the same level with *Technology-affine* (crystallization as pole)

can operate as a mediating element; and a case-based analysis should be conducted in order to figure out all opportunities and bounds or SWOTs for taking sustainable decisions (figure 3). This is in line with Santarius' (2017) argument digitisation and digital transformation should be analysed case-based as well as support and strengthen sufficiency and overall sustainability. Yet, he already observed severe rebounds, as overconsumption, immense energy consumption, etc. So, in terms of sustainability, digital transformation needs a clear value basis and sustainability added value. In terms of responsible management, digitisation and digital transformation has to be reflected before implementing assumed digital progress. A company should assess digital changes against a sustainability framework, including social, environmental and economic indicators, case-wise. Part of a responsible management is also lab-orientation, meaning first simulating complex transformational processes in selected corporate parts before implementing digital change and devices company-wide. Therefore, societal progress and strict law regulation will be needed, too.

Moreover, stressing health as a particular focus in the constellation work, the following figure presents the initial constellation of the second conduced constellation. Particularly for the element *Organisation*, a clear area of conflict between the elements *Competition* and *Organisational Members* emerged within the constellation (see figure 4). Companies must be able to withstand competition in the face of

19

Figure 3. Finial constellation representing technology-avers versus -affine people
(own source, figures © Antonia Wetzel)

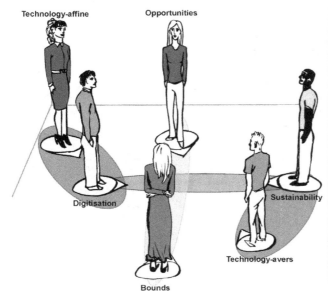

Sustainability. strongest connection to *Digitization*; does not see *Opportunities* as a connecting element; Opportunities and risks are only seen in terms of digitisation, not in terms of sustainability - "there are connections, but not in every case or not at all levels" Proposal: "there should be separate opportunities and risks for sustainability";
In the process - after a change of position of Technology-avers: loss of reinforcements; distances itself from *Digitisation*, sees *Digitisation* as a danger, more disadvantages than advantages; at the same time more opportunities for *Digitisation* than for *Sustainability* are perceived
Digitization. Coherent positioning; desire for proximity to *Opportunities* - these should predominate as legitimation for own element
Opportunities. Bounds as connecting element; nevertheless desire to turn to both elements *Sustainability* and *Digitisation* (no two delimited topics)
Bounds. No special reference to elements; desire for distance to all elements; wish that all elements - except *Opportunities* - turn with the back ("show cold shoulder")
Technology-avers. with all connected, would like to have contact with all, at the same time proximity to the element *Sustainability* desired; *Technology-avers* does not necessarily mean sustainability-avers; Desire for constant connection to *Technology-affine*, so that a whole is created
Technology-affine. wants to be close to *Digitisation*, because progress is pivotal; would like to go even further away from *Bounds*, but *Digitisation* does not go along with; *Bounds* should not come closer; sees *Opportunities* as a link between *Sustainability* and *Digitisation*

Figure 4. Initial constellation representing sustainability and digitisation in health contexts
(own source, figures © Antonia Wetzel)

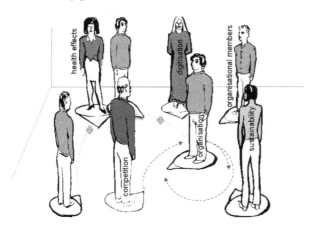

Health effects. Feels the urge to sit down and feels exhausted

Organisation. would like to focus on employees, but does not want to ignore competition; wants to be progressive for competition; wants to do everything right for organisational members

Sustainability. regards employees as central, the following 3 areas are relevant: organisation, digitisation, organisational members, neutral tendency towards others

Digitisation. is focused on company, health does not matter

Organisational members. feel equally weakened and attracted by sustainability, because it stands for the success of the company; the element also wants to keep an eye on the competition; expresses its interest in other organisations; feels the impulse to focus on health; wants to take care of it, even if others may have to put back; neutral attitude to other elements.

Competition. wants to keep an eye on everyone; feels a strong urge to move; wants to be able to react quickly when health becomes worse digital change, but they must not ignore their employees. The *Company* felt that it was consistently driven by *Competition*. For the *Employees*, direct health effects were of particular relevance, and *Sustainability* was of secondary importance for this element in the course of the installation process. However, strong tensions and various trade-offs occurred and were not easy to solve. The versatile connections, topics and linkages can also be seen in figure 1. The concept map shows various influences and connections concerning digitisation and sustainability, like people, public, market, value, performance, design and use, etc. So, companies have to consider diverse topics and challenges for managing digitisation, digitalisation and digital transformation successfully. The constellation makes obvious that organisations cannot focus on all aspects at the same time and often prioritise topics. Likewise, sustainability is not always on the top agenda.

The constellation also showed that the inputs for a sustainable development of corporate structures should be provided directly by the company itself (see figure 5).

So, as stated above, people are benefiting from new technologies that make corporate solutions more affordable, accessible and of higher quality and can support health at all. However, there are also strict limitations by human that have to be considered for digital transformation. These results are absolutely in line with Leonard & Graf von Kospoth's (2017) arguments that rapid digital transitions have

Figure 5. Final constellation representing sustainability and digitisation in health contexts
(own source, figures © Antonia Wetzel)

Organisation. feels disrupted by competition; moves into a position that balances sustainability and digitisation (similar distance), even if competition gets in the way of the company; end position: feels uncomfortable, as competition is only partly in focus

Sustainability. Seeks contact to organisational members

Organisational members. orient towards the company and health effects; in the final position: sustainability has been pushed into the background ever since health effects came closer

Competition. feels the urge to turn; wants to keep an eye on everything and feels quite comfortable in the middle; sees itself in a central role; runs around digitisation and sustainability, in the end it positions itself towards the company and digitization;
moves closer to health effects during the formation process, so that the members of the organisation are more satisfied; it is also important for the element to take other factors into account;
It takes a while for the competition to take a firm position

to be aligned and balanced with humanity, and digital innovations should be made humanely sustainable. Sustainability can be a concept for reorientation towards humanity and human limits beside environmental boundaries.

CONCLUSION AND FUTURE RESEARCH DIRECTIONS

There are a lot of opportunities and risks concerning sustainability in the context of digitisation and a digital transformation. Increased affordability, accessibility, quality, speed, transparency, etc. could be opportunities in a digital transformation. Main rebound effects to be considered are: network effects, security lags, increasing information asymmetries, immense energy consumption, mass consumption, loss of sufficiency, lack of humanity, etc. This is in line with the results of the constellation work. Immense tensions between sustainability and digitisation occurred within the constellations, but there were also linked and progressive items. So, in light of a development towards sustainability, digitisation is both, boon and bane, and often needs a clear analysis of all relevant issues and a careful handling in order to be progressive. Digital transformation requires a precise and honest value basis and sustainability added value. In the context of sustainability and digital transformation, responsible and sustainable management requires a holistic technology and environmental assessment, a clear emphasis of human values and a proactive orientation towards balanced concepts of planet, people and profit. Responsible management should assess digital changes against a sustainability framework, including social, environmental and economic indicators, case-wise. In addition, applying a lab-orientation, meaning first simulating complex transformational processes in selected corporate parts before implementing digital change and devices company-wide, is helpful to identify corporate and value-chain driven rebound effects or unstainable properties. So, a company can govern before deep (irreversible) transformational processes have happened. Therefore, societal progress, innovative incentives and strict law regulation will be needed.

Further research is need on real-effect rebounds for estimating environmental harm, social stress and economic losses on micro-, meso- and macro-levels. Protected or regional separated real labs could indicate possible changes and rebounds and indicate sustainable solutions, incentives and restrictions before implementing digital systems on a large scale. Moreover, generalisable trade-offs and rebounds should be figured out more intensively. Therefore, a cross-industry study should be conducted, both cross section and longitudinal section. Final, patterns should be investigated how digitisation, digitalisation and digital transformation can serve developments towards sustainability and not thwart sustainability goals in a big way. Here, pivotal digitised limitations have to be discussed, too.

REFERENCES

Agor, W. H. (1986). The logic of intuition: How top executives make important decisions. *Organizational Dynamics, 14*(3), 5–18. doi:10.1016/0090-2616(86)90028-8

Aksin-Sivrikaya, S., & Bhattacharya, C. B. (2017). Where Digitalization Meets Sustainability: Opportunities and Challenges. In T. Osburg & C. Lohrmann (Eds.), *Sustainability in a Digital World. CSR, Sustainability, Ethics & Governance*. Cham: Springer. doi:10.1007/978-3-319-54603-2_3

Alexander, B. (2017). Disruption of the Retail Ecosystem: The South African e-Retail Imperative. *Proceedings Of The European Conference On Management, Leadership & Governance*, 32-39.

Arnold, M. (2016). *Systemic Structural Constellations and Sustainability in Academia: A New Method for Sustainable Higher Education*. Taylor & Francis. doi:10.4324/9781315403465

Arnold, M. G. (2018). Combining conscious and unconscious knowledge within human-machine-interfaces to foster sustainability with decision-making concerning production processes. *Journal of Cleaner Production, 179*, 581–592. doi:10.1016/j.jclepro.2018.01.070

Behringer, C. (2017). Digitalisierung und CSR in der Finanzberatung. In A. Hildebrandt & W. Landhäußer (Eds.), *CSR und Digitalisierung. Management-Reihe Corporate Social Responsibility*. Berlin: Springer Gabler. doi:10.1007/978-3-662-53202-7_54

Bergere, F. (2016). Ten years of PPP: An initial assessment. *OECD Journal on Budgeting, 15*(1), 31–123. doi:10.1787/budget-15-5jm3rx2qbxbq

Bondarouk, T., & Brewster, C. (2016). Conceptualising the future of HRM and technology research. *International Journal of Human Resource Management, 27*(21), 2652–2671. doi:10.1080/09585192.2016.1232296

Bundeskartellamt (BKA). (2015). *Digitale Ökonomie – Internetplattformen zwischen Wettbewerbsrecht, Privatsphäre und Verbraucherschutz*. Tagung des Arbeitskreises Kartell-recht. Retrieved July 13, 2018, from https://www.bundeskartellamt.de/SharedDocs/Publikation/DE/Diskussions_Hintergrundpapier/AK_Kartellrecht_2015_Digitale_Oekonomie.pdf?__blob=publicationFile&v=2

Chowdhury, G. G. (2016). How to improve the sustainability of digital libraries and information Services? *Journal of the Association for Information Science and Technology, 67*(10), 2379–2391. doi:10.1002/asi.23599

Conschafter, S. J. (2017). Charting a path for cities in the Second Machine Age with or without the car: A focus on the human experience. *Journal of Urban Regeneration and Renewal, 10*(2), 116–127.

Courtial, J. P. (1998). Comments on Leydesdorff's article. *Journal of the American Society for Information Science, 49*(1), 98–98. doi:10.1002/(SICI)1097-4571(199801)49:1<98::AID-ASI14>3.0.CO;2-1

Cretchley, J., Rooney, D., & Gallois, C. (2010). Mapping a 40-year history with Leximancer: Themes and concepts in the Journal of Cross-Cultural Psychology. *Journal of Cross-Cultural Psychology, 41*(3), 318–328. doi:10.1177/0022022110366105

Da Silva, F. M., Bártolo, H. M., Bártolo, P., Almendra, R., Roseta, F., Almeida, H. A., & Lemos, A. C. (2017). Challenges for Technology Innovation: An Agenda for the Future. In *Proceedings of the International Conference on Sustainable Smart Manufacturing*. Lisbon, Portugal: CRC Press.

Dias, A. C., Almendra, R., & Silva, F. (2017). Design education facing Europe 2020—a reflection on demands: FAULisbon as the case study. In Challenges for Technology Innovation (Vol. 287, No. 292, pp. 287-292). Routledge in association with GSE Research.

Dini, P. (2007). A Scientific Foundation for Digital Ecosystems. In F. Nachira, A. Nicloai, & ... (Eds.), *Digital Business Ecosystems, Information Society and Media* (pp. 24–47). Luxembourg: Office for Official Publications of the European Communities.

Dominish, E., Retamal, M., Sharpe, S., Lane, R., Rhamdhani, M., Corder, G., ... Florin, N. (2018). "Slowing" and "Narrowing" the Flow of Metals for Consumer Goods: Evaluating Opportunities and Barriers. *Sustainability, 10*(4), 1096. doi:10.3390u10041096

Erdmann, L., & Hilty, L. M. (2010). Scenario analysis. *Journal of Industrial Ecology, 14*(5), 826–843. doi:10.1111/j.1530-9290.2010.00277.x

Ethikrat, D. (2017). Big Data und Gesundheit–Datensouveränität als informationelle Freiheitsgestaltung. *Vorabfassung vom, 30.*

Fuentes, C., & Sörum, N. (2018). Agencing ethical consumers: Smartphone apps and the socio-material reconfiguration of everyday life. *Consumption Markets & Culture,* 1–26.

Gebhardt, C. (2017). Humans in the Loop: The Clash of Concepts in Digital Sustainability in Smart Cities. In T. Osburg & C. Lohrmann (Eds.), *Sustainability in a Digital World. CSR, Sustainability, Ethics & Governance* (pp. 85–93). Cham: Springer. doi:10.1007/978-3-319-54603-2_7

Geisler, S., Zelazny, M., Christmann, S., & Hagenhoff, S. (2011, June). Empirical analysis of usage and acceptance of software distribution methods on mobile devices. In *Mobile Business (ICMB), 2011 Tenth International Conference on* (pp. 210-218). IEEE.

GeSI Report. (2015). *System Transformation: how digital solutions will drive progress towards the sustainable development goals.* Accenture Strategy. Retrieved March 14, 2018, from www.systemtransformation-sdg.gesi.org

Greening, L. A., Greene, D. L., & Difiglio, C. (2000). Energy efficiency and consumption—the rebound effect—a survey. *Energy Policy, 28*(6-7), 389–401. doi:10.1016/S0301-4215(00)00021-5

Harwood, I., Gapp, R. P., & Stewart, H. J. (2015). Cross-check for completeness: Exploring a novel use of Leximancer in a grounded theory study. *Qualitative Report, 20*(7), 1029–1045.

Kamble, S. S., Gunasekaran, A., & Gawankar, S. A. (2018). Sustainable Industry 4.0 framework: A systematic literature review identifying the current trends and future perspectives. *Process Safety and Environmental Protection, 117*, 408–425. doi:10.1016/j.psep.2018.05.009

Khilji, N., Duan, Y., Lewis, R., Bukoye, T., & Luton, U. K. (2017, July). Incorporating Knowledge Management Tools in the UK Local Government towards Improved Planning Support Services. In *ICICKM 2017 14th International Conference on Intellectual Capital Knowledge Management & Organisational Learning: ICICKM 2017* (p. 122). Academic Conferences and Publishing Limited.

Kontis, V., Bennett, J. E., Mathers, C. D., Li, G., Foreman, K., & Ezzati, M. (2017). Future life expectancy in 35 industrialised countries: Projections with a Bayesian model ensemble. *Lancet, 389*(10076), 1323–1335. doi:10.1016/S0140-6736(16)32381-9 PMID:28236464

Kopp, U. (2013). Systemische Nachhaltigkeitskompetenzen für Führungskräfte–Erfahrungen mit Aufstellungsarbeit in der Managementaus- und weiterbildung. *Die Unternehmung, 67*(2), 126–151. doi:10.5771/0042-059X-2013-2-126

Krys, C. (2017). Megatrends–Rahmenbedingungen für unternehmerische Nachhaltigkeit. In CSR und Strategisches Management (pp. 45-65). Springer Gabler. doi:10.1007/978-3-662-49457-8_2

Lamnek, S. (1988). Qualitative Social Science. In Methodology. Beltz PVU.

Leonhard, G., & von Kospoth, C. A. G. (2017). Exponential technology versus linear humanity: Designing a sustainable future. In T. Osburg & C. Lohrmann (Eds.), *Sustainability in a Digital World. CSR, Sustainability, Ethics & Governance* (pp. 77–83). Cham: Springer. doi:10.1007/978-3-319-54603-2_6

Leydesdorff, L. (1997). Why words and co-words cannot map the development of the sciences. *Journal of the American Society for Information Science, 48*(5), 418–427. doi:10.1002/(SICI)1097-4571(199705)48:5<418::AID-ASI4>3.0.CO;2-Y

Liesch, P. W., Håkanson, L., McGaughey, S. L., Middleton, S., & Cretchley, J. (2011). The evolution of the international business field: A scientometric investigation of articles published in its premier journal. *Scientometrics, 88*(1), 17–42. doi:10.100711192-011-0372-3

Lin, J., & Lee, S. T. (2012, November). Mapping 12 years of communication scholarship: themes and concepts in the Journal of Communication. In *International Conference on Asian Digital Libraries* (pp. 359-360). Springer. 10.1007/978-3-642-34752-8_53

Lyons, G., Mokhtarian, P., Dijst, M., & Böcker, L. (2018). The dynamics of urban metabolism in the face of digitalization and changing lifestyles: Understanding and influencing our cities. *Resources, Conservation and Recycling, 132*, 246–257. doi:10.1016/j.resconrec.2017.07.032

Matser, I. (2017). Leading Change in Ongoing Technological Developments: An Essay. In Sustainability in a Digital World. Springer International.

Ministerium für Umwelt, Klima und Energiewirtschaft Baden-Württemberg (MUKEBW). (2018). *Digitalisierung als Motor für mehr Nachhaltigkeit. Runder Tisch "Nachhaltige Digitalisierung" des Umweltministeriums.* Retrieved from https://www.nachhaltigkeitsstrategie.de/erleben/rueckblick/nachhaltige-digitalisierung.html

Müller-Mielitz, S., & Lux, T. (Eds.). (2016). *E-Health-Ökonomie.* Springer-Verlag.

Opazo-Basáez, M., Vendrell-Herrero, F., & Bustinza, O. F. (2018). Uncovering Productivity Gains of Digital and Green Servitization: Implications from the Automotive Industry. *Sustainability, 10*(5).

Osburg, T., & Lohrmann, C. (Eds.). (2017). *Sustainability in a Digital World. CSR, Sustainability, Ethics & Governance*. Cham: Springer. doi:10.1007/978-3-319-54603-2

Prisecaru, P. (2016). Challenges of the fourth industrial revolution. *Knowledge Horizons. Economics, 8*(1), 57.

Rajala, R., Hakanen, E., Mattila, J., Seppälä, T., & Westerlund, M. (2018). How Do Intelligent Goods Shape Closed-Loop Systems? *California Management Review, 60*(3), 20–44. doi:10.1177/0008125618759685

Rammler, S. (2017). Digital Fuel for the Mobility Revolution: The Opportunities and Risks of Applying Digital Technologies to the Mobility Sector. In T. Osburg & C. Lohrmann (Eds.), *Sustainability in a Digital World. CSR, Sustainability, Ethics & Governance* (pp. 159–171). Cham: Springer. doi:10.1007/978-3-319-54603-2_13

Rosselet, C. (2013). *Andersherum zur Lösung; Die Organisationsaufstellung als Verfahren der intuitiven Entscheidungsfindung*. Zürich: Versus. doi:10.24096/9783039097371

Santarius, T. (2017). Die dunkle Seite des „smart everything" – Gesellschaft revolutionieren statt Wachstum generieren. Agora, 42(2), 70-74.

Schlötter, P. (2005). Familiar language and its discovery. System constellations are not random - the empirical evidence [Vertraute Sprache und ihre Entdeckung. Systemaufstellungen sind kein Zufallsprodukt - der empirische Nachweis, in German]. Carl-Auer-Verlag.

Scholz, R. W. (2016). Sustainable digital environments: What major challenges is humankind facing? *Sustainability, 8*(8), 726. doi:10.3390u8080726

Smith, A. E., & Humphreys, M. S. (2006). Evaluation of unsupervised semantic mapping of natural language with Leximancer concept mapping. *Behavior Research Methods, 38*(2), 262–279. doi:10.3758/BF03192778 PMID:16956103

Sooknanan, D., Bahadoorsingh, S., Joshi, A., & Sharma, D. P. (2016). Smart Grid Analysis for the Caribbean Region. *West Indian Journal of Engineering, 38*(2).

Sowa, J. F. (2000). *Knowledge representation: logical, philosophical, and computational foundations* (Vol. 13). Pacific Grove, CA: Brooks/Cole.

Stan, L. (2017). The management of innovation in the context of structural funds. *Manager*, 25.

Sturgeon, N. (2018, July 10). Henry Kissinger pens ominous warning on dangers of artificial intelligence. *RT Question More*. Retrieved July 13, 2018, from https://www.rt.com/news/432425-henry-kissinger-artificial-intelligence/

Teoh, J. E. M., Chua, C. K., Liu, Y., & An, J. (2017). 4D printing of customised smart sunshade. In Challenges for Technology Innovation (Vol. 105, No. 108, pp. 105-108). Routledge in association with GSE Research.

Toonen, H. M., & Bush, S. R. (2018). The digital frontiers of fisheries governance: Fish attraction devices, drones and satellites. *Journal of Environmental Policy and Planning*, 1–13. doi:10.1080/1523908X.2018.1461084

United Nations, Department of Economic and Social Affairs, Population Division. (2017). *World Population Prospects: The 2017 Revision, Key Findings and Advance Tables*. Working Paper No. ESA/P/WP/248.

Walker, B., Carpenter, S., Anderies, J., Abel, N., Cumming, G., Janssen, M., ... Pritchard, R. (2002). Resilience management in social-ecological systems: A working hypothesis for a participatory approach. *Conservation Ecology*, 6(1), 14. doi:10.5751/ES-00356-060114

Zawacki-Richter, O., & Latchem, C. (2018). Exploring four decades of research in Computers & Education. *Computers & Education*, *122*, 136–152. doi:10.1016/j.compedu.2018.04.001

Zawacki-Richter, O., & Naidu, S. (2016). Mapping research trends from 35 years of publications in Distance Education. *Distance Education*, *37*(3), 245–269. doi:10.1080/01587919.2016.1185079

Zinnöcker, T. (2017). Nachhaltigkeit, Energiewende und Digitalisierung. In A. Hildebrandt & W. Landhäußer (Eds.), *CSR und Digitalisierung. Management-Reihe Corporate Social Responsibility*. Berlin: Springer Gabler. doi:10.1007/978-3-662-53202-7_15

Chapter 2
Sustainable Implications of Industry 4.0

Jorge Tarifa-Fernández
https://orcid.org/0000-0002-6031-8526
University of Almeria, Spain

ABSTRACT

Industry 4.0, and in general, digital technologies, represent a fundamental model shift towards decentralization and individualized production. With this, the development of new services and business models based on the internet is encouraged. Somehow, this forces traditional supply chains to evolve into highly adaptative networks. Companies have to consider their internal resources and the benefits of getting closer to partners in the supply chain. In this sense, the implementation of these technologies is accompanied by a series of sustainable implication at economic, environmental, and social levels.

1. INTRODUCTION

Recent changes in technological and international issues have heightened the need for companies to keep abreast of their competition and, in general, of what disturbs their stability (Ngai et al., 2011; Sanders, 2007). This situation has accelerated the pace of innovation concerning its discovery, implementation, introduction, and diffusion into the market. This issue has grown in importance in light of the recent emergence of digital technologies associated with the concept of Industry 4.0. In general, it represents a fundamental model shift towards decentralization and individualized production (Lasi et al., 2014; Linkov et al., 2018). This shift mainly encourages the development of new services and business models based on the Internet, which

DOI: 10.4018/978-1-5225-7638-9.ch002

Copyright © 2019, IGI Global. Copying or distributing in print or electronic forms without written permission of IGI Global is prohibited.

somehow forces traditional supply chains to evolve into highly adaptative networks (Duarte and Cruz-Machado, 2018). Many companies have already taken the first steps towards a connected industry. However, the road to a positive development goes through a process of evolution rather than a revolution. Alongside this evolution, companies have to consider sustainability to remain competitive and also follow the current trend.

The concept of sustainability refers to the maintenance of the well-being over a long period, which inherently implies people, planet and profit (Elkington, 1994; Kuhlman and Farrington, 2010). Companies have to manage the resources needed for production, knowing that those essential today may be substituted by others tomorrow (Kuhlman and Farrington, 2010). The main objectives of sustainability should include the reduction of inequalities, decent work, and responsible consumption and production (Linkov et al., 2018). In this sense, sustainability should be considered as the central focus to guarantee both the resources needed and the impact on future generations.

The relationship between humankind and nature comprises two opposing views, one that stresses adaptation and harmony, and another that sees nature as something to be conquered (Kuhlman and Farrington, 2010). Thus, companies have to deal with fundamental decisions. On the one hand, companies have to develop their strategy and find the position they feel most comfortable with under one of these perspectives. On the other hand, it is unknown whether digital technologies will be able to offer solutions in the future. Hence, companies must take advantage of their current benefits to manage the resources that are more appealing to them in the best possible conditions. In sum, if companies make the proper choice and follow the right guidelines, they will obtain benefits from the implementation and development of digital technologies.

The arrival of Industry 4.0 and, therefore, digital technologies, pose a new scenario in which most companies are naïve. This situation increases the uncertainty of companies regarding their perception of the pros and cons of implementing digital technologies. On the one hand, there is a wide range of technologies under the umbrella of Industry 4.0, which makes it problematic to assess which one would fit each company better. On the other hand, as it is difficult to foresee the future behavior of these technologies, most companies prefer to wait for others to act and observe their evolution. For the sake of generalization, different digital technologies are not presented. That pertains to each company, depending on the industry it develops its activity.

Sustainability has been a topic of great interest in the past and is still gathering companies' attention. This issue has demonstrated to be relevant to create competitive advantages and allow companies to remain profitable for a more extended period.

This importance makes it attractive to combine with other hot topics, such as digital technologies.

Hence, this chapter aims to outline the main possibilities that digital technologies have to offer to companies to influence their sustainability at three levels (economic, environmental and social). It also aims to raise awareness of the importance of considering sustainability in any area of the company, even when there is skepticism on its effectiveness. This chapter is organized as follows: Section 2 illustrates the Fourth Industrial Revolution and how it is manifested at a global (intelligent supply chain) and company level (Industry 4.0). Section 3 presents the main arguments likening digital technologies and sustainability. Finally, Section 4 offers a discussion and the main conclusions.

2. THE FOURTH INDUSTRIAL REVOLUTION

2.1. Introduction

The essence of the Fourth Industrial Revolution is the digitalization of all physical assets and the integration into digital ecosystems with partners in the supply chain (Sanders et al., 2016, Zhong et al., 2017). The concept of Industry 4.0 mainly represents this revolution, which, in a general sense, describes the introduction of Internet technologies into the industry (Gabriel and Pessl, 2016). That is, it comprises the set of strategies and actions leading to the application of advanced information and communication systems and future-oriented technologies (Sanders et al., 2016) with the aim of bringing the virtual and physical worlds closer (Prause, 2016). Despite this, Lasi et al. (2014) understand Industry 4.0 as a wide range of current concepts (e.g., smart factory or cyber-physical systems) whose clear classification is not possible in individual cases. Geissbauer et al. (2016) also state that Industry 4.0 consists of three essential elements: (a) digitalization and integration with members of the supply chain; (b) digitalization of the products and services offered, and (c) digital business models and customer access.

The relationship between digital technologies and companies makes necessary to review the knowledge bases applied to operations management in order to allow a progressive implementation. This analysis can be carried out through two distinct, although mutually interrelated, levels. The first level is strategic in nature and responds to the planning needs of all actions that would integrate individual companies into an intricate network of relationships. The companies involved must be cohesive enough to share both a common thought and vision. These circumstances lead to the concept of the intelligent supply chain (Yan et al., 2014). The second level is of an operational nature and oversees the control of all actions and activities that organizations have to carry out. In this way, if the production process works correctly, the proposed objectives will be achieved. In order to meet current trends, these efforts must be made by maintaining a permanent connection both within the company itself and with the rest of the partners in the supply chain (Leuschner et al., 2013). The concept of Industry 4.0 would encompass this perspective. Although each level is responsible for solving problems within its own field of action, strategic or operational, both must be related in order to understand that they are complementary and that the decisions made in each one will have an undeniable impact on the development of the other.

The adaptation process to this new revolution happens, unquestionably, by digitalizing the business. A high dose of commitment and collaboration are undoubtedly needed on the part of different elements such as people, things and the business itself (Ferreti and Schiavone, 2017). In this sense, the machinery must be organized autonomously, while the supply chains are interlinked automatically. Thus, orders can be transformed directly into data for manufacturing, and the equipment can negotiate virtually the necessary actions to carry out the subsequent steps. This connection is possible through the creation and strengthening of a close link between the physical and virtual parts (Del Giudice, 2016, Haddud et al., 2017).

The implementation of digital technologies causes the boundaries of organizations to become fuzzy in comparison to traditional companies (Flyverbom et al., 2017). These new business models, which are due to different forms of value creation, are becoming dominant. For instance, as digital technologies become the norm for most companies, the phenomenon of "platform business" is gaining attention (Prause, 2016). Under this phenomenon, value creation consists mostly in offering products, services, or technologies that provide the foundation upon which external firms can develop their complementary products, technologies, or services (Gawer and Cusumano, 2014). Changes like these can also push customers and consumers to adapt to the new situation, creating considerable uncertainties still to uncover.

2.2. Intelligent Supply Chain

Factors such as globalization and the increase in competition have been critical in driving companies to develop strategic and collaborative relationships within the supply chain (Lambert and Cooper, 2000; Wisner and Keah, 2000). In this situation, uncertainty has a dominant presence, which forces organizations to realize the importance of their supply chain partners. Companies have to see in them the opportunity to develop, under a strategic perspective, a competitive advantage that allows all members to remain competitive in the markets (Qi et al., 2011; Narasimhan and Kim, 2002). In this way, companies have developed their relationships with suppliers and customers by trying to integrate them into their decision-making systems.

Thereby, companies would link the maintenance of these relationships over time to their general interests (Cao and Zhang, 2011). Before this change, the conception of rivalry was between companies. However, these relationships change the focus, while competitiveness begins to focus on the level of supply chains.

The level of development of the relationships within the supply chain goes through a continuum range, running from mere transactional relationships to specific interconnected systems (Ellram, 1991; Webster, 1992). When relations between partners within the supply chain surpass personal boundaries without losing their own identity, the concept of an intelligent supply chain emerges.

Under these circumstances, the intelligent supply chain is a general supra-organizational phenomenon in which organizations within the same supply chain are involved in a collective action through motivation, learning and continuous work, and the development of competencies with the aim of unraveling the complexity of problems at the supply chain level and creating an efficient and sustainable ecosystem (Gonzalez-Chiñas, 2010). For an ideal development and functioning of collaborative relationships, the organizations involved must have common elements that respond to similar organizational profiles. Thus, features such as the predisposition towards innovation and the dissemination of permanent information, the search for new ways of doing things, respect for the environment, proactivity or reflection on social problems will shape the common base upon which to develop a joint thought (Bowersox et al., 2003; Golicic et al., 2003). Therefore, companies must seek the supply chain partners that fulfill the requirements each company consider appropriate.

In a general sense, the purpose of the intelligent supply chain comprises obtaining an economic, social and environmental change (being the latter understood as permanent). The achievement of said changes means that organizations have to work simultaneously at two levels: individual and collective. The former implies that companies focus on their internal management, trying to adapt to the demands agreed upon by the supply chain. The latter, in the collective sphere, implies that organizations have to work on maintaining the connection with the rest of the members (Geissbauer et al., 2016). While the first answers to an individual action with global restrictions, the second responds to a joint strategic alignment. Although both approaches might perform at different points in time, they have to emerge simultaneously. An effortless exchange of information needs to happen in both directions so that a certain cohesion between both of them exists and, thus, an optimal objective can be achieved. Otherwise, inconsistencies such as redundant work or setting conflicting goals could be detrimental to a good development (Ngai et al., 2011, Sanders et al. 2016).

Once the organizations have decided to get involved in these processes, they have to show a certain level of long-term commitment towards all the members of the supply chain (Roehrich et al., 2014). This process will help them strengthen their participation and stability within the group while reducing uncertainty, distrust, and opportunism (Zhou et al., 2015). Internally, the responsibility for the change rests with the top managers, resulting essential in the early stages of the relationship (Costa et al., 2017, Hoejmose et al. 2012). They are also in charge of searching the necessary actions to converge towards the intelligence of the supply chain. The aim is to create an ecosystem in which suppliers, partners, and customers are immersed in the co-creation and capture of added value (Geissbauer et al., 2016).

Each company should act on internal aspects to get closer with their partners within the supply chain. Therefore, the enrichment of each company starts in-house to allow for a proper out-house development. In doing so, for instance, elements as necessary as information may flow flawlessly. According to Gonzalez-Chiñas (2010), there are five main points on which companies should focus to improve their supply chain relationships:

1. Human Resources. This is one of the most important points, as dealing with human resources represents the base of every company. At this point, the focus is on seeking the commitment and motivation of workers by extending their skills. Companies have to offer them the freedom to make decisions autonomously within their scope and be aware of their worries and concerns. These actions intend to reach a mutual understanding between workers and the company. In short, it is about generating an alignment between the personal objectives of workers and those of the company.

2. Learning. It is directly related to the first one because it aims to provide workers with the know-how to work as a team and to benefit from everyone's knowledge, which allows them to speed up the resolution of problems. It is, therefore, a process of socialization and adaptability that would enable workers to break down individual barriers and include them within collective or global thinking. Among others, practices such as workgroups or quality circles help to encourage this type of stimuli.

3. Cultural change. Companies have to support the cultural change within them to remain proactive and continuously alert to disruptive situations. They must change the pre-established standards and favor the transition, easing the path for employees. With this, companies promote the creativity and innovation capacity of their workers, which allows them to see things continuously in a unique way, moving away from routine and uninspiring thoughts. At the same time, companies generate a new knowledge base in line with their sustainability objectives which, in turn, will allow them to improve their adaptability.

4. Future vision. Companies must create an image of their future trajectory by establishing a shared aspiration. To do this, they must create and firmly

establish a business identity. This determination would be like defining the personality of each company, that is to say, what firms usually do or how they behave when facing certain stimuli. It means that not only workers should feel identified with the company, but there must also be a company identity towards which all workers think of as their point of reference. The interaction of the company with both the environment in general and the rest of companies within the supply chain are responsible for forging this identity. In this way, each company will act and behave according to the behavior of the others. At this point, the coordination between all of them within the supply chain is of vital importance, so that each action is in line with the rest. This alignment allows the identification of each business identity within the supply chain.

5. Internal procedures. They focus on understanding the individual performance within the supply chain. The objective is to achieve a systematic thinking that guides and structures the execution of each company's knowledge and ideas.

2.3. Industry 4.0: The Interconnectedness

The expansion of the Internet, along with the digitalization of information, has led to a greater automation of processes (Caputo et al., 2016). This development has been critical in allowing the advance of new technological developments and, therefore, an autonomous and interconnected work (Brettel et al., 2014, Haddud et al., 2017, Yu et al., 2016). Consequently, networks have been created so that the integration between the physical and information systems has favored the form of the basis of a new industrial revolution (Lasi et al., 2014, Sanders et al., 2016). The essence of this revolution has been determined by the adaptation of technologies, first into the productive processes and then into all the companies, to cover the gap between the physical and the virtual. This has been possible thanks to the concept of Industry 4.0, understood as the digitalization of supply chains that allows the implementation of emerging technologies with the ultimate goal of obtaining a more efficient and flexible production, while increasing their quality and decreasing their costs (Brettel et al. 2014, Prause, 2016, Sanders et al., 2016). Therefore, Industry 4.0 pursues the achievement of efficient products adapted to the needs of increasingly demanding consumers, who consider both the optimization of resources and the awareness of their responsible use.

Industry 4.0 becomes a facilitator of a fluid exchange of information, allowing, in turn, the enrichment of communication between people, things, machines, and systems (Gabriel & Pessl, 2016). In short, it allows operations to be aggregated and data to be analyzed for autonomous decision-making (Ford & Despeisse, 2016, Haddud et al., 2017). For instance, if something unpredictable happens in an internal process, the response time may decrease. This benefit comes from the interconnection developed in real time (including workers) that allows having the information needed to solve problems permanently available. Therefore, this new conception of the industry has the potential to solve the most common barriers related to the scarcity of resources, such as obtaining adequate communication, monitoring or supervision of processes or the integration of their own internal operations as well as with the rest of the partners in the supply chain (Sanders et al., 2016).

The implementation of the technologies associated with Industry 4.0 results in a set of advantages for organizations (Müller et al., 2018). Among them, it can be highlighted: (a) allowing the development of the identity and communication for each partner within the supply chain; (b) inducing mass customization of information and communication technologies in manufacturing; (c) encouraging and ensuring an improvement in cooperation among employees; (d) allowing to plan production in real time and the dynamic self-optimization of the machinery; (e) favoring the degree of automation, so that intelligent and self-optimizing machines in the production line can synchronize themselves with the value chain as a whole. Despite these advantages, once companies enter the dynamic of Industry 4.0, they will need to reinvent their capabilities at faster rates if they intend to be on the front line.

3. TOWARDS SUSTAINABLE MANAGEMENT

3.1. Introduction

The traditional vision of industrial management has not considered its environment as an important agent when it comes to its development. The environment represents the place where companies obtain resources and place products with no value in the market, that is, the physical media where companies develop their activity. Considering a broader perspective, management should contemplate the deterioration that companies' activities have on the environment in which they operate. This consideration implies recognizing social and environmental approaches (Seuring and Müller, 2008). Under this situation, the industry has adopted a different attitude, trying to adapt to the new demands. In this sense, digital technologies have increasingly influenced the way members of society perceive, think about, and engage with nature (Kahn, 2011). Therefore, the technologies comprising Industry 4.0 might become responsible for addressing this change.

The main idea is that Industry 4.0 makes use of emerging information technologies so that business and engineering processes are integrated, allowing production to operate in a flexible, efficient and green way and maintaining quality and low cost (Wang et al., 2016). In this manner, all efforts are focused on achieving a significant improvement in the well-being of the society as a whole, bearing in mind its natural environment. For instance, the generation of large amounts of data and the creation of centralized data repositories, to exploit them at a later date, can determine relationships, predict behaviors and establish dependencies between companies, workers and the environment (Linkov et al., 2018). Also, big data facilitates calculations and the processing of relationships between consumer needs and their functions for large amounts of data (Sanders et al., 2016). For instance, to face the diversification of consumer needs, Toyota popularized the concept of the SMED system (Single-Minute Exchange of Die) with which the reduction in change times was evident. Modern manufacturing systems tend towards mass customization, so they cannot afford to increase the time between changes in product variants. In this sense, systems equipped with self-optimization and machines with behavior towards learning allow companies to adapt the machinery according to the products and produce small batches (Ford and Despeisse, 2016, Gogate and Pande, 2008). All this results in faster changes in the parameters of the machines according to the instructions given. The adaptation time of organizations is substantially reduced due to the ability of their decision-making machinery and its fluid communication with other elements (Sanders et al., 2016). Therefore, one of the critical points of Industry 4.0 is to determine whether the technologies applied can provide the correct information for the appropriate purpose at the right time to generate added value, or if, on the contrary, they can identify themselves as intruders.

The development of an intelligent industry is based, therefore, on a holistic perspective that allows a broad and complete knowledge of both the company itself and its relationships through the supply chain (Preuveneers and Ilie-Zudor, 2017). Said perspective entails an integral connection of the company both internally and with all the external agents participating in the supply chain process. Although this, initially, seems an easy task to accomplish, firms have to rely on the current development of their operational capabilities. In doing so, firms increase the base upon which to build their new capabilities to face digital transformation. This is of great importance as the implementation of digital technologies, disruptive in nature, generates an upsetting situation resulting in a brand-new organization.

For instance, computer science enables the creation of intelligent machines that work and react like humans (Moudud-Ul-Huq, 2014). According to Linkov et al. (2018), machines will be able to learn from their experience and make their own decisions without further input from humans beyond the initial design of the machine. Hence, digital technologies change the essential parts of a firm, such as its corporate structures, processes, culture, and abilities and skills related to human resources. This poses the challenge of developing new operational capabilities inherent to digital technologies, commonly known as digital operational capabilities. These enhanced capabilities arise as an adaptation to new circumstances based on previous ones.

Accordingly, new routines and processes become the sources of these capabilities, being also sensitive to employee networks and inter-organizational relationships.

Under this development, Industry 4.0 offers the first advantage: it allows a new way of doing things sustainably. Thus, due to the interconnection created, companies can implement new management models based on the sustainable allocation of products, materials, energy, and water (Stock and Seliger, 2016). In order to achieve this, they rely on certain practices such as intelligent logistics, intelligent supply networks, and self-sufficient supply (Stock et al., 2015). These changes provide a more efficient form of management based on the creation of value by connecting with the intelligence elements. In this way, the sustainability and efficiency of the resources become the focus of the design of industrial manufacturing processes, assuming at this level the fundamental framework conditions to guarantee the success of the products (Lasi et al., 2014).

Current studies have partially demonstrated that Industry 4.0 and all the technologies associated influence the way companies conceive the business and their relationships with other members of the supply chain, highlighting the crucial role of customers (Ittmann, 2015; Lasi et al., 2014; Yu et al., 2016). Although the application of Industry 4.0 comes in several and diverse forms, the following sections try to provide an overall view of how (and most of the time, why) digital technologies represent a challenge when dealing with relevant issues such as sustainability.

3.2. Environmental Sustainability

In broader terms, the production process carried out in companies favors the deterioration of the environment due to two main reasons: (a) scarce natural resources are consumed at a higher rate than the regeneration rate of the environment itself; and (b) emissions and waste are generated at a rate that exceeds the assimilation rate of the environment (Goodland, 1995). Many of the alterations suffered by the natural environment, such as global warming or environmental pollution, have been due, mainly, to industrial production (e.g., greenhouse gas emissions, spills into the sea or tire landfills) in which companies have disregarded the environmental cost (Fischer, 2017).

For its part, the technologies associated with Industry 4.0 generate enormous amounts of data, which provide valuable information available to companies. These data come primarily from both within the company, obtained from interdepartmental relationships, and outside, derived from its relations with other companies (mainly suppliers and customers) within the sector (Botta et al., 2016; Ittmann, 2015). In this sense, companies have to optimize the use of this information to create new sustainable business models. These new models make the most of the information available and are developed from the competition in the long-term, which becomes crucial in order to maintain a comparative advantage (Prause, 2015). Hence, this perspective, alongside with a more profound knowledge of their activities, can provide companies' products with other characteristics, such as functionality or accessibility, that surpass the merely physical ones (Stock & Seliger, 2016).

Data availability allows companies to schedule tasks and processes intelligently. The balance achieved from this helps to reduce energy consumption (Ding et al., 2017; Fysikopoulos et al., 2014). Also, this leads to the prediction of its consumption and, therefore, it favors a more responsible use (Shrouf & Miragliotta, 2015). Managing the product lifecycle and its activities, such as recycling or invert logistic, can be achieved thanks to the interconnection of data and information. Eventually, said management allows the reduction of greenhouse gas emissions (Peukert et al., 2015) and it also favors waste reduction and resource consumption (Herrmann et al., 2014; Stock & Seliger, 2016). Counting with data transparency throughout the supply chain stimulates the optimization of several processes that directly affect delivery accuracy, unnecessary waiting times or product quality (Qi et al., 2015).

In most manufacturing companies, the equipment is usually long-lasting and essential. Thus, reconditioning it with sensors and devices allows to equalize every piece of equipment, while promoting cyber-physical systems through the creation of value. In short, companies go from having a problem of depreciation of their equipment to an alternative to buying new production equipment (Stock and Seliger, 2016) and, therefore, contributing to the economic sustainability of the company (through a more efficient use of resources and avoiding the economic implication of buying new equipment) and being more environmentally friendly (reusing the old equipment and avoiding the environmental costs of disposing of it). Another example of environmentally friendly production technology is additive manufacturing as it requires fewer resources than traditional manufacturing and hardly generates waste, while reducing transport logistic by decentralization (Gabriel & Pessl, 2016).

For companies, being part of an interconnected ecosystem requires a continuous improvement perspective to be more and more efficient. It also implies the identification of the processes to be integrated and a deeper understanding of the best business models under a sustainable point of view (Ford & Despeisse, 2016). Therefore, it is easier to assess the alternatives or scenarios by making available the tools to capture, analyze and report information concerning the sustainability of the company.

A clear example of this is Omron UK, a provider of industrial automation, healthcare and electronic components that faced the decision of implementing Industry 4.0 in the packaging line. The most significant improvement in this line was having all the elements integrated so that the data could be exchanged between them. It was controversial in older equipment because most of the time there was not any indication about the working capacity, which made it difficult to assess their productivity. Electronically capturing the data could require changing the working process to make sure the information is logged correctly and not illegible in paper form. This could require some small technical upgrades of the equipment to add additional sensors to capture operating data, convert existing analog information into a digital format or add a data communication module to provide remote data capture and control. Starting the data analysis to check the efficiency of the line requires the primary data capture process to be completed. It will also be possible to monitor the device condition, permitting preventive maintenance type functionality (Rossek, 2018). Therefore, having a good understanding of how well the packaging line is running allows to redirect investment on less efficient parts. At the same time, it allows companies to develop a strategy to migrate the lines in order to enable smart and flexible production. Although the direct benefit of reusing this equipment with digital technology is efficiency, there is also an environmental benefit behind this. By adding sensors to the old equipment, its useful life is extended. This enlargement means that through digital technologies the concept of "reuse" is reinvented as the full potential of certain assets is shown.

Under this perspective, the main benefit is manifested mainly for the company, that is, digital technologies do not allow any damage to the natural environment. They allow companies to reuse the equipment that would be otherwise discharged into the natural environment without ensuring a proper recuperation process. However, companies do not focus their efforts on producing more sustainable products (or services) by using digital technologies. Few people are concerned about the characteristics given by Industry 4.0 that make products more environmentally friendly. In this sense, generating environmental value for customers remains a challenge (Man & Strandhagen, 2017).

3.3. Economic Sustainability

The immediate benefits of Industry 4.0 are the optimization of the processes because of the transparency and interconnection (Oesterreich & Teuteberg, 2016), which eventually increase efficiency, quality, customization, and flexibility (Hossain & Muhammad, 2016; Peuker et al., 2015). This improvement requires the production of "smart products" that increase competitiveness (Porter & Heppelmann, 2015). Besides, the transparency gained both intra- and inter-organizational allows to lower logistics costs (Hofmann & Rüsch, 2017; Zhong et al., 2015).

An interconnected industry provides companies with the ability to manage the life cycle of their product to make it more sustainable. The process involves practices such as recycling, reusing or recovering the value of the product at the end of its useful life. Also, during this process, products can be redesigned with the aim of improving the degree of compliance with the needs of consumers and, therefore, their welfare. For this, companies can make use of information systems to capture the essential parts involved in re-manufacturing or to apply new services to consumers.

In a well-designed production system and under an "in time" philosophy, the materials should be available only at the time of manufacture and should not be waiting for prolonged periods or stored as inventory (Satoglu et al., 2018). Each process has to add value and result in a continuous flow of operations. In many cases, flow failures are due to errors in the calculation of inventory, capacity shortage, and centralized control systems, leading to delays in the decision processes. Thus, devices such as RFID can help eliminate the errors associated with the inventory through accurate tracking in real time. Then, an error-free inventory status helps maintain a low inventory level and a timely order of goods (Sanders et al., 2016).

As a rule, companies carry out preventive and periodic maintenance of machinery and facilities. However, failures are, in most cases, difficult to predict and control. In an intelligent industry, the machinery is interconnected through the information and communication systems in a way that it sends error notifications to the shop-floor and maintenance personnel (Sanders et al., 2016). At the same time, information systems can reprogram work to mitigate the impact of the fault. In addition, with more advanced analytical methods and in a big data environment, machines are equipped to be self-aware and perform self-maintenance. This machinery can assess its state of operation, and use the data obtained from another mechanism to avoid potential problems due to maintenance (Sanders et al., 2016). Thus, machine-worker communication, self-maintenance systems, and predictive maintenance control can improve productive and preventive maintenance in any industry.

Product quality is of vital importance in an industrial manufacturing process. The processes must always be under control, and this results in the development of different techniques to evaluate processes. Factors such as the reduction of the useful life of the products, development times and the increase of the complexity of the products mean that control processes are at a constant risk. Within a 4.0 environment, the sequence of operations to be performed on a given product is already inserted in support of that product. This information is transferred to the machinery so that the automatic operation is carried out, which in turn is shown with a better visualization interface for manual operations. Also, man-machine interfaces use a much more attractive and intuitive display, which helps avoid problems in the production process. In this sense, the internet of things helps with the integration of different methods that add value by combining information and data from different machines. The advanced analysis combines business intelligence with the management of process workflows. These technologies facilitate traceability, visibility, and localization throughout the production process in such a way that they eventually ensure the production of defect-free products to be sold to consumers (Sanders et al., 2016). Data availability in real time allows companies to manufacture customized products and offer customization solutions. This type of products usually generates higher margins than mass-produced ones.

The business model generated through Industry 4.0 allows increasing the capacity in order to adapt to the demand, a greater personalization of the customer service and, therefore, an improvement in the after-sales service. Also, it favors the reduction in design, production and sales times, which ultimately leads to a shortening of the production chains and thus making them more profitable.

KUKA, a company leader in robotics, has developed a cloud-based software application, used by friction welding machines, to integrate itself into "smart production" alongside other cloud solutions already implemented. All machine, production, and process data can be retrieved via a secure internet connection and automatically analyzed (via PC, laptop, tablet or smartphone). Friction welding machines communicate with the cloud via the Industry 4.0 standards and the Kuka Reome Service Client (a local edge gateway that handles the control functions and data communication with the cloud). The detection and elimination of problems in a reasonable timeframe require visualization of essential status data from anywhere in the production system and monitoring the welding process in real time. With the condition-based maintenance feature, the actual condition of machine components is factored into the calculation of maintenance intervals for the first time using sensor data. In that way, maintenance expenditure can be reduced up to 75%. It is also possible to link and analyze essential process variables and send messages (e.g., to the maintenance technician's smartphone), ultimately leading to an increased uptime and even higher productivity of the friction welding machines (Kuka, 2017).

As it can be seen, the principal advantage of digital technologies for this company is cost reduction. Its core responsibility is the interconnectedness derived, in this case, from the use of cloud-based software. Using this software has made information flows faster and, therefore, workers are able to make decisions with no delay. The company could reduce response times, that is to say, any problem can be solved in real time, saving the costs associated if the implication of more staff were necessary. Thus, one person with accurate information can act and be sure they are making the right decision. Besides, as the real state of the machinery is known to the company, maintenance costs can be dramatically reduced because the exact moment in which to carry out maintenance tasks is known.

3.4. Social Sustainability

In general, the transition to a connected industry entails, in most cases, a substantial investment in information technologies (Vázquez-Casielles et al., 2017). Most of them simplify, and even substitute, the work done by the workers. This fact provokes some hesitation on the part of human resources, which can face complex situations, such as dismissals, mitigation of their responsibilities or substantial changes in their working conditions.

On the contrary, an increase in their satisfaction is the most remarkable benefit for employees. It comes from, among others, the application of intelligent assistance systems and the human-machine interfaces (Herrmann et al., 2014; Peukert et al., 2015). Currently, it is not possible to foresee whether digital technologies could reduce the number of employees because of process automatization, or if, on the contrary, it compensates with the of new jobs (Bonekamp and Sure, 2015; Kubicek and Korunka, 2017). What seems to be clear regarding human resources is the necessity of changing the mindset in order to handle the challenges of implementing digital technologies rather than acting automatically (Leonhardt and Wiedemann, 2015; Müller et al., 2018.

The role of human resources is vital for companies that want to introduce new developments in their production processes as crucial as intelligent factories. Thus, according to Stock and Seliger (2016), there are three key points of action to address social change: (a) increase training in different information and communication technologies; (b) increase self-motivation and creativity through original approaches to organization and work design based on cyber-physical systems (e.g., gamification); and (c) increase general motivation through incentive systems considering smart data so that personalized attention can be provided.

Many of these actions can also undermine the concept of sustainability, which means that the commitment of both parties is necessary to carry out the most efficient transition possible.

Human resources are responsible for working and creating products and services, so they should give appropriate importance and flexibility to the recognition of their ideas and suggestions. However, in most cases, workers find it difficult to convey their opinions and feedback on their jobs. This situation changes in a connected industry environment since workers can provide information on production conditions instantaneously and in real time through their own devices (e.g., smartphones and tablets). All workers have smart portable devices fully integrated into the company's network. In short, this represents a comfortable environment for workers since it allows them to share and store their worries and suggestions in the workplace. In this way, those responsible can check the availability of workers and relocate them to different operations through their devices. Also, worker support systems simplify the evaluation of workers regarding speed, reliability, performance factors, and motivation. All this contributes to a better development of empowerment and workers' involvement in the organization (Sanders et al., 2016).

For companies, it is essential to foster a robust digital culture and supervise the change in management through good leadership which, in turn, is controlled by top management. This support will be decisive when assessing the expected returns to carry out the investment in a particular technology. Therefore, it is essential to employ staff with the necessary skills (e.g., intelligence, creativity, empathy) to develop this technology. Organizations must attract, retain and train digital natives as well as other employees who will then feel comfortable in a work environment based on a dynamic ecosystem to achieve sustainability with human resources.

As physical tasks will be less relevant in the future, expertise in the field of new communication technologies regarding planning, execution and decision-making processes, control or programming or in the fault and error correction becomes increasingly important (Gabriel and Pessl, 2016). This will imply two different effects. On the one hand, older workers will be freed from physical strain, which will be then translated into an improvement in their health, and, on the other hand, new professions will arise, which means new opportunities for younger people. However, it is also possible that some workers, be it younger or not, will not conceive having to interact with machines when it comes to receiving orders from them. This is a risk that managers should contemplate when thinking about developing a digital transformation.

Welspun Group, the Indian conglomerate, decided to include their almost 15,000 workers in the digital transformation. For that, the company started an initiative to introduce at the same time 500 of their workers into the cashless economy using the Unified Payment Interface (UPI) application. The workers downloaded and installed the UPI application and were trained in its use for online transactions. In a short time, these workers were able to use the application to, among others, make purchases and transfer money. The company intended to train the rest of the workers in the digital form (Mukherjee, 2017).

In doing so, those families were empowered to lead a digital lifestyle in the future. This kind of initiatives can be considered as a way of acting directly on the workers' motivation while reducing the resistance to change. With this, the company encourages workers to become familiar with digitalization and, therefore, to see its positive aspects. In this way, when the company decides to implement specific digital technologies, workers will have a preconceived image based on their recent experience provided by the company itself. On the one hand, the use of these technologies motivates workers while strengthening their position within the company. On the other hand, the use of similar techniques in real and working life fosters their creativity and lays the foundation for the development of a steady digital culture. Somehow, the company intends to increase the collective well-being generated with workers.

4. DISCUSSION AND CONCLUSION

Sustainability is a relevant issue of increasing concern. This topic claims for a re-evaluation, as other elements confront and question its effectiveness. Despite having been widely studied, it is a broad term with so much meaning yet to be discovered and currently presents new challenges in diverse areas. Its association with digital technologies, far from being casual, responds to the necessity of reassuring effectiveness.

Industry 4.0 challenges the understanding of sustainability as it considers new ways to improve the benefit, the natural environment, and society. However, the reluctance of companies to implement digital technologies and the duration of their availability as a source of competitive advantage undermine the development of their potential. Consequently, proving their effects on sustainability will be subjected to top management predisposition. This fact opens unexplored avenues for both researchers and practitioners.

Industry 4.0 seems to have a positive effect on sustainability (be it environmental, economic or social). However, there is still no correspondence with a significant impact, as most of the effects are relevant at small-scale. For instance, regarding the natural dimension, digital technologies act directly on tasks related to reducing, reusing and recycling, which reflect a traditional caring for the natural environment. In the same line, the economic impact essentially bases its advantage on cost takeout, overlooking other approaches, such as revenue increase or value creation. It seems that the repercussions on these two dimensions derive from the side effects rather than from being proactive and innovative. On the contrary, the effect of digital technologies on social aspects is controversial as it directly threatens jobs continuity or stability. In this sense, automatization tries to replace most of the mechanical and repetitive jobs in a more radical way than in precedent situations.

Although this increases pressures and uncertainty (e.g., offering more sustainable products because of the use of data gathered through a more interconnected company is not currently guaranteed), Industry 4.0 requires workers with a wide range of new skills, which in turn will lead to the creation of new jobs. Besides, it seems that the environmental benefits are directly connected with economical ones. For instance, reusing machinery with new technological applications reduces not only waste generation but also the costs associated with buying new equipment. However, this connection seems to be indirect regarding employees. Thus, companies need to invest in the development of ability-enhancing practices if they intend to readapt their workers to the new situation.

Nowadays, fulfilling a set of requirements to obtain a comparative advantage is not sufficient. Society demands another type of actions beyond the traditional limits over which sustainability seems to be currently working. This means that the implementation of digital technologies is not entirely connected with the sustainability problems companies face. In this sense, Industry 4.0 poses the challenge of controlling all the information that flows from suppliers to customers. It will depend on how it is obtained and used. When everything is connected and produces data and information, sustainability is subjected to responsible use. This interconnectedness leads companies to consider a parallel strategy to the implementation of digital technologies with the objective of being sustainable. That is, it seems that Industry 4.0 still has a long way ahead to implement sustainable changes and make them last longer because of the novelty of the approach and its recent application.

REFERENCES

Bonekamp, L., & Sure, M. (2015). Consequences of Industry 4.0 on human labour and work organisation. *Journal of Business and Media Psychology*, 6(1), 33–40.

Botta, A., De Donato, W., Persico, V., & Pescapé, A. (2016). Integration of Cloud computing and Internet of Things: A survey. *Future Generation Computer Systems*, 56, 684–700. doi:10.1016/j.future.2015.09.021

Bowersox, D. J., Closs, D. J., & Stank, T. P. (2003). How to master cross-enterprise collaboration. *Supply Chain Management Review*, 7(4), 18–27.

Brettel, M., Friederichsen, N., Keller, M., & Rosenberg, M. (2014). How Virtualization Decentralization and Network Building Change the Manufacturing Landscape An Industry 4.0. *Perspective*, 8(1), 37–44.

Cao, M., & Zhang, Q. (2011). Supply chain collaboration impact on collaborative advantage and firm performance. *Journal of Operations Management*, 29(3), 163–180. doi:10.1016/j.jom.2010.12.008

Caputo, A., Marzi, G., & Pellegrini, M. M. (2016). The Internet of Things in manufacturing innovation processes: Development and application of a conceptual framework. *Business Process Management Journal*, 22(2), 383–402. doi:10.1108/BPMJ-05-2015-0072

Costa, G., Mavrommatis, A., Vila, M., & Valdes, S. (2017). Collaborative Relationships Between Manufacturers and Retailers: A Supply Chain Collaboration Framework. In F. Martínez-López, J. Gázquez-Abad, K. Ailawadi, & M. Yagüe-Guillén (Eds.), *Advances in National Brand and Private Label Marketing. Springer Proceedings in Business and Economics*. Cham: Springer. doi:10.1007/978-3-319-59701-0_21

De Man, J. C., & Strandhagen, J. O. (2017). An Industry 4.0 Research Agenda for Sustainable Business Models. *Procedia CIRP, 63*, 721–726. doi:10.1016/j.procir.2017.03.315

Ding, K., Jiang, P., & Zheng, M. (2017). Environmental and economic sustainability-aware resource service scheduling for industrial product service systems. *Journal of Intelligent Manufacturing, 28*(6), 1303–1316. doi:10.100710845-015-1051-7

Duarte, S., & Cruz-Machado, V. (2018). Exploring Linkages Between Lean and Green Supply Chain and the Industry 4.0. In *Proceedings of the Eleventh International Conference on Management Science and Engineering Management. ICMSEM 2017. Lecture Notes on Multidisciplinary Industrial Engineering.* Springer.

Elkington, J. (1994). Towards the sustainable corporation: Win-win-win business strategies for sustainable development. *California Management Review, 36*(2), 90–100. doi:10.2307/41165746

Ellram, L. M. (1991). Supply-chain management: The industrial organization perspective. *International Journal of Physical Distribution & Logistics Management, 21*(1), 13–22. doi:10.1108/09600039110137082

Ferretti, M., & Schiavone, F. (2016). Internet of Things and business processes redesign in seaports: The case of Hamburg. *Business Process Management Journal, 22*(2), 271–284. doi:10.1108/BPMJ-05-2015-0079

Fischer, C. (2017). Environmental protection for sale: Strategic green industrial policy and climate finance. *Environmental and Resource Economics, 66*(3), 553–575. doi:10.100710640-016-0092-5

Flyverbom, M., Deibert, R., & Matten, D. (2017). The Governance of Digital Technology, Big Data, and the Internet: New Roles and Responsibilities for Business. *Business & Society*, 1–17.

Ford, S., & Despeisse, M. (2016). Additive manufacturing and sustainability: An exploratory study of the advantages and challenges. *Journal of Cleaner Production, 137*, 1573–1587. doi:10.1016/j.jclepro.2016.04.150

Fysikopoulos, A., Pastras, G., Alexopoulos, T., & Chryssolouris, G. (2014). On a generalized approach to manufacturing energy efficiency. *International Journal of Advanced Manufacturing Technology, 73*(9-12), 1437–1452. doi:10.100700170-014-5818-3

Gabriel, M., & Pessl, E. (2016). Industry 4.0 and sustainability impacts: Critical discussion of sustainability aspects with a special focus on future of work and ecological consequences. *Annals of the Faculty of Engineering Hunedoara, 14*(2), 131.

Gawer, A., & Cusumano, M. A. (2014). Industry platforms and ecosystem innovation. *Journal of Product Innovation Management, 31*(3), 417–433. doi:10.1111/jpim.12105

Geissbauer, R., Vedso, J., & Schrauf, S. (2016). Industry 4.0: building the digital enterprise: 2016 global industry 4.0 survey. PwC.

Gogate, A. S., & Pande, S. S. (2008). Intelligent layout planning for rapid prototyping. *International Journal of Production Research, 46*(20), 5607–5631. doi:10.1080/00207540701277002

Golicic, S. L., Foggin, J. H., & Mentzer, J. T. (2003). Relationship magnitude and its role in interorganizational relationship structure. *Journal of Business Logistics, 24*(1), 57–75. doi:10.1002/j.2158-1592.2003.tb00032.x

Gonzalez-Chiñas, D. (2010). *La cadena de suministro inteligente*. Retrieved from https://cadenadesuministro.wordpress.com/2010/08/09/la-cadena-de-suministro-inteligente/

Goodland, R. (1995). The concept of environmental sustainability. *Annual Review of Ecology and Systematics, 26*(1), 1–24. doi:10.1146/annurev.es.26.110195.000245

Haddud, A., DeSouza, A., Khare, A., & Lee, H. (2017). Examining potential benefits and challenges associated with the Internet of Things integration in supply chains. *Journal of Manufacturing Technology Management, 28*(8), 1055–1085. doi:10.1108/JMTM-05-2017-0094

Herrmann, C., Schmidt, C., Kurle, D., Blume, S., & Thiede, S. (2014). Sustainability in manufacturing and factories of the future. *International Journal of Precision Engineering and Manufacturing-green Technology, 1*(4), 283–292. doi:10.100740684-014-0034-z

Hoejmose, S., Brammer, S., & Millington, A. (2012). "Green" supply chain management: The role of trust and top management in B2B and B2C markets. *Industrial Marketing Management, 41*(4), 609–620. doi:10.1016/j.indmarman.2012.04.008

Hofmann, E., & Rüsch, M. (2017). Industry 4.0 and the current status as well as future prospects on logistics. *Computers in Industry, 89*, 23–34. doi:10.1016/j.compind.2017.04.002

Hossain, M. S., & Muhammad, G. (2016). Cloud-assisted industrial internet of things –enabled framework for health monitoring. *Computer Networks*, *101*, 192–202. doi:10.1016/j.comnet.2016.01.009

Ittmann, H. W. (2015). The impact of big data and business analytics on supply chain management. *Journal of Transport and Supply Chain Management*, *9*(1), 1–9. doi:10.4102/jtscm.v9i1.165

Kahn, P. H. (2011). *Technological nature: Adaptation and the future of human life*. MIT Press.

Kubicek, B., & Korunka, C. (2017). The Present and Future of Work: Some Concluding Remarks and Reflections on Upcoming Trends. In *Job Demands in a Changing World of Work* (pp. 153–162). Cham: Springer. doi:10.1007/978-3-319-54678-0_9

Kuhlman, T., & Farrington, J. (2010). What is sustainability? *Sustainability*, *2*(11), 3436–3448. doi:10.3390u2113436

Kuka. (2017). *Into the cloud with KUKA SmartConnect.frictionwelding*. Retrieved from https://www.kuka.com/en-ch/press/news/2017/09/industrie-40-innovation-award

Lambert, D., & Cooper, M. (2000). Issues in supply chain management. *Industrial Marketing Management*, *29*(1), 65–83. doi:10.1016/S0019-8501(99)00113-3

Lasi, H., Fettke, P., Kemper, H. G., Feld, T., & Hoffmann, M. (2014). Industry 4.0. *Business & Information Systems Engineering*, *6*(4), 239–242. doi:10.100712599-014-0334-4

Leonhardt, F., & Wiedemann, A. (2015). *Realigning Risk Management in the Light of Industry 4.0*. Amsterdam: Academic Press. 10.2139srn.2678947

Leuschner, R., Rogers, D. S., & Charvet, F. F. (2013). A Meta-Analysis of Supply Chain Integration and Firm Performance. *The Journal of Supply Chain Management*, *49*(2), 34–57. doi:10.1111/jscm.12013

Linkov, I., Trump, B. D., Poinsatte-Jones, K., & Florin, M. V. (2018). Governance strategies for a sustainable digital world. *Sustainability*, *10*(2), 440. doi:10.3390u10020440

Moudud-Ul-Huq S. (2014). The Role of Artificial Intelligence in the Development of Accounting Systems: A Review. *IUP Journal of Accounting Research & Audit Practices*, *13*(2), 7-19.

Mukherjee, S. (2017). *Welspun initiates digitization drive towards cashless economy.* Retrieved from https://techseen.com/2017/01/11/welspun-digitization-cashless/

Müller, J. M., Kiel, D., & Voigt, K. I. (2018). What drives the implementation of Industry 4.0? The role of opportunities and challenges in the context of sustainability. *Sustainability, 10*(1), 247. doi:10.3390u10010247

Narasimhan, R., & Kim, S. (2002). Effect of supply chain integration on the relationship between diversification and performance: Evidence from Japanese and Korean firms. *Journal of Operations Management, 20*(3), 303–323. doi:10.1016/S0272-6963(02)00008-6

Ngai, E. W., Chau, D. C., & Chan, T. L. A. (2011). Information technology, operational, and management competencies for supply chain agility: Findings from case studies. *The Journal of Strategic Information Systems, 20*(3), 232–249. doi:10.1016/j.jsis.2010.11.002

Oesterreich, T. D., & Teuteberg, F. (2016). Understanding the implications of digitisation and automation in the context of Industry 4.0: A triangulation approach and elements of a research agenda for the construction industry. *Computers in Industry, 83*, 121–139. doi:10.1016/j.compind.2016.09.006

Peukert, B., Benecke, S., Clavell, J., Neugebauer, S., Nissen, N. F., Uhlmann, E., ... Finkbeiner, M. (2015). Addressing sustainability and flexibility in manufacturing via smart modular machine tool frames to support sustainable value creation. *Procedia CIRP, 29*, 514–519. doi:10.1016/j.procir.2015.02.181

Porter, M. E., & Heppelmann, J. E. (2015). How smart, connected products are transforming companies. *Harvard Business Review, 93*(10), 96–114.

Prause, G. (2015). Sustainable business models and structures for Industry 4.0. *Journal of Security and Sustainability Issues, 5*(2), 159–169. doi:10.9770/jssi.2015.5.2(3)

Prause, G. (2016). E-Residency: A business platform for Industry 4.0? *Entrepreneurship and Sustainability Issues, 3*(3), 216–227. doi:10.9770/jesi.2016.3.3(1)

Preuveneers, D., & Ilie-Zudor, E. (2017). The intelligent industry of the future: A survey on emerging trends, research challenges and opportunities in Industry 4.0. *Journal of Ambient Intelligence and Smart Environments, 9*(3), 287–298. doi:10.3233/AIS-170432

Qi, Y., Zhao, X., & Sheu, C. (2011). The impact of competitive strategy and supply chain strategy on business performance: The role of environmental uncertainty. *Decision Sciences*, *42*(2), 371–389. doi:10.1111/j.1540-5915.2011.00315.x

Qiu, X., Luo, H., Xu, G., Zhong, R., & Huang, G. Q. (2015). Physical assets and service sharing for IoT-enabled Supply Hub in Industrial Park (SHIP). *International Journal of Production Economics*, *159*, 4–15. doi:10.1016/j.ijpe.2014.09.001

Roehrich, J. K., Grosvold, J., & Hoejmose, S. U. (2014). Reputational risks and sustainable supply chain management: Decision making under bounded rationality. *International Journal of Operations & Production Management*, *34*(5), 695–719. doi:10.1108/IJOPM-10-2012-0449

Rossek, D. (2018). *Implementing Industry 4.0 in packaging*. Retrieved from http://www.connectivity4ir.co.uk/article/149744/Implementing-Industry-4-0-in-packaging.aspx

Sanders, A., Elangeswaran, C., & Wulfsberg, J. (2016). Industry 4.0 implies lean manufacturing: Research activities in industry 4.0 function as enablers for lean manufacturing. *Journal of Industrial Engineering and Management*, *9*(3), 811–833. doi:10.3926/jiem.1940

Sanders, N. R. (2007). An empirical study of the impact of e-business technologies on organizational collaboration and performance. *Journal of Operations Management*, *25*(6), 1332–1347. doi:10.1016/j.jom.2007.01.008

Satoglu, S., Ustundag, A., Cevikcan, E., & Durmusoglu, M. B. (2018). Lean Transformation Integrated with Industry 4.0 Implementation Methodology. In F. Calisir & H. Camgoz Akdag (Eds.), *Industrial Engineering in the Industry 4.0 Era. Lecture Notes in Management and Industrial Engineering*. Cham: Springer. doi:10.1007/978-3-319-71225-3_9

Seuring, S., & Müller, M. (2008). From a literature review to a conceptual framework for sustainable supply chain management. *Journal of Cleaner Production*, *16*(15), 1699–1710. doi:10.1016/j.jclepro.2008.04.020

Shrouf, F., & Miragliotta, G. (2015). Energy management based on Internet of Things: Practices and framework for adoption in production management. *Journal of Cleaner Production*, *100*, 235–246. doi:10.1016/j.jclepro.2015.03.055

Stock, T., Bietz, T., Alva, D., Swat, M., Seliger, G., and Bähre, D. (2015). Design and Control of Manufacturing Systems for Enabling Energy-Efficiency and-Flexibility. *The Journal of Innovation Impact*, 438-49.

Stock, T., & Seliger, G. (2016). Opportunities of sustainable manufacturing in industry 4.0. *Procedia CIRP, 40*, 536–541. doi:10.1016/j.procir.2016.01.129

Vázquez-Casielles, R., Iglesias, V., & Varela-Neira, C. (2017). Manufacturer–distributor relationships: Role of relationship-specific investment and dependence types. *Journal of Business and Industrial Marketing, 32*(8), 1245–1260. doi:10.1108/JBIM-10-2016-0244

Wang, S., Wan, J., Li, D., & Zhang, C. (2016). Implementing smart factory of industrie 4.0: An outlook. *International Journal of Distributed Sensor Networks, 12*(1), 1–10. doi:10.1155/2016/3159805

Webster, F. E. Jr. (1992). The changing role of marketing in the corporation. *Journal of Marketing, 56*(4), 1–17. doi:10.1177/002224299205600402

Wisner, J., & Keah, C. (2000). Supply chain management and its impact on purchasing. *The Journal of Supply Chain Management, 36*(4), 33–42. doi:10.1111/j.1745-493X.2000.tb00084.x

Yan, J., Xin, S., Liu, Q., Xu, W., Yang, L., Fan, L., ... Wang, Q. (2014). Chen, Bo., Wang, Q. (2014). Intelligent supply chain integration and management based on cloud of things. *International Journal of Distributed Sensor Networks, 10*(3), 624839. doi:10.1155/2014/624839

Yu, X., Nguyen, B., & Chen, Y. (2016). Internet of things capability and alliance: Entrepreneurial orientation, market orientation, and product and process innovation. *Internet Research, 26*(2), 402–434. doi:10.1108/IntR-10-2014-0265

Zhong, R. Y., Huang, G. Q., Lan, S., Dai, Q. Y., Chen, X., & Zhang, T. (2015). A big data approach for logistics trajectory discovery from RFID-enabled production data. *International Journal of Production Economics, 165*, 260–272. doi:10.1016/j.ijpe.2015.02.014

Zhong, R. Y., Xu, X., Klotz, E., & Newman, S. T. (2017). Intelligent Manufacturing in the Context of Industry 4.0: A Review. *Engineering, 3*(5), 616–630. doi:10.1016/J.ENG.2017.05.015

Zhou, Y., Zhang, X., Zhuang, G., & Zhou, N. (2015). Relational norms and collaborative activities: Roles in reducing opportunism in marketing channels. *Industrial Marketing Management, 46*, 147–159. doi:10.1016/j.indmarman.2015.01.014

KEY TERMS AND DEFINITIONS

Digital Technologies: All types of equipment or application that use the information in a coded form.

Environmentally Friendly: Any product, service, policy, or set of actions that promote reduced, minimal, or no harm on the environment.

Fourth Industrial Revolution: Transition to new systems based on the structures of the previous digital revolution and characterized by its velocity, scope, and impact.

Industry 4.0: It is a phase within the Fourth Industrial Revolution that focuses on diverse technologies such as automation, machine learning, and real-time data.

Intelligent Supply Chain: A higher level of interconnection between firms within a supply chain with common purposes.

Man-Machine Interface: It is a software that shows the status of the process and allows the execution of the order. It represents the means of interaction between the operator and the machines.

Smart Products: They are products and services that rely on digital technologies to perform specific functionalities.

Section 2
Imagination and New Concepts to Solve Global Business, Innovation, and Sustainability Challenges

Chapter 3
The Overlooked Roots of Innovations:
Exploring the Relevance of Imagination on Innovation Using Science Fiction

Julien Bucher
Chemnitz University of Technology, Germany

ABSTRACT

Imagination is an often-overlooked integral element of human progress, in general, and innovations, in particular. In this chapter, it is argued that the examination of the diffusion and evolution of imaginations and their manifestation as innovations can help to understand the imaginative roots of innovations and to create a responsibly chosen path into a sustainable future. Science fiction as a specific area of manifested imagination is used to show how manifested imaginations influence the social imagination in general and certain individuals like scientists and innovators in particular. It is even used to sell ideas (or make them stick) and give them heritage, again influencing the social imagination. And the accelerated fusion, development, and progress of technologies in the wake of the digitalization is enabling fast and vast diffusion and distribution of imaginations, creating a need to explore, understand, and responsibly utilize imaginations.

DOI: 10.4018/978-1-5225-7638-9.ch003

Copyright © 2019, IGI Global. Copying or distributing in print or electronic forms without written permission of IGI Global is prohibited.

INTRODUCTION

On the way back to earth in 1969, the crew of the Apollo 11 mission was voicing their personal impressions and experiences of the trip to the moon and the landing on it in U.S. prime time television. Neil Armstrong kicked off the transmission from their capsule with the following words:

"Good evening. This is the commander of Apollo 11. A hundred years ago, Jules Verne wrote a book about a voyage to the Moon. His spaceship, Columbia, took off from Florida and landed in the Pacific Ocean after completing a trip to the Moon. It seems appropriate to us to share with you some of the reflections of the crew as the modern-day Columbia completes its rendezvous with the planet Earth and the same Pacific Ocean tomorrow." (Armstrong 1969)

Neil Armstrong decided to connect this special moment in human history with an imaginative idea of space travel and landing on the moon emerged in the Science Fiction novel by Jules Verne. Verne introduced with his moon travel story the possibilities in the future without having the technology or any context actually to realize this vision of man in space. But he spread the imagination of it in his writings 100 years before the actual moon landing was realized.

On February 6th, 2018 the private spaceflight company SpaceX launched its innovative Falcon Heavy rocket from Launch Pad 39A at the Kennedy Space Center, the same site, that the team of the Apollo 11 mission took off from. On this test flight, the main technical spectacle was the successful launch of the "most powerful operational rocket in the world", ending with the simultaneous landing of the two side boosters of the rocket – and the crash of its center core. Musk, known for its various business ventures like Tesla, SpaceX, Neuralink and the Boring Company (not to forget his early ventures, Zip2 and X.com, which later merged with Confinity to become PayPal), also used the rocket to launch a Tesla Model 3 into the orbit. Besides that, being an impressive cross-promotional marketing decision, he also shed light on its imaginative influences: On the main screen of the car "DON'T PANIC!" was displayed, written in capital letters like an imperative or a shout and obviously contradicting itself – just like the book it is referencing, Douglas Adams "The Hitchhiker's Guide to the Galaxy" (Adams 1989). In this humorous Science Fiction series, the protagonist finds this eponymic guide and the first thing he reads, since it is written on its envelope, is the short imperative Musk borrowed: "DON'T PANIC".

These two words seem to remind anyone involved in the project and watching the spectacle, that they are experiencing a milestone, a potential breakthrough or failure in the history of space travel – but whether the case, DON'T PANIC! – in the end, this is just a small step, the ideas behind and desires that spawned and drive this project are quite old and have been discussed and explored for centuries, captured and preserved for later discourses in media artifacts that influence and are influenced by the social and individual imagination.

In this chapter it is argued, that imagination is an often overlooked integral element of the human progression in general and innovations in particular and that the examination of the diffusion and evolution of imaginations and their manifestation as innovations can help to understand the imaginative roots of innovations and help to create a responsibly chosen path into a sustainable future. Focusing on Science Fiction as a specific area of manifested imagination, it will be argued that Science Fiction is influencing the social imagination in general and certain individuals like scientists and innovators in particular, and that it is even used to sell certain ideas (or make them stick) and give them heritage, again influencing the social imagination – besides the discussion and conceptualization of technological and social fictions already mentioned before.

The article is structured in the following way: At first, the basics are covered with paragraphs on imagination, innovation, and the Information Age, Imagination Age, and the Fourth Industrial Revolution. Then the focus shifts to Science Fiction with a short explanation on the selection of this specific field and an exploration of research on Science Fiction. Historic and present case examples of Science Fiction in the context of innovation, research & development and value creation in general, are used in the course of the chapter to show how Science Fiction is and could be used to foster innovations and to explore and possibly prepare for their implications and consequences.

IMAGINATION

Schütz (1971) described humans as the constructors of their own daily lifeworld. In dependence on the individual selective and interpretative activity, the individual sets and develops structures of relevance in the social and cognitive construction of the lifeworld, that influence which and how themes and aspects are perceived and are integrated. Imaginations have an influence on these constructions and the lifeworld. These individual constructions and the knowledge related to them are intersubjectively effective because the context of meaning emerges in the mutual living and acting together. Castoriadis (1997: 322) argued, that imagination is socio-historical and that imagination and the social imaginary, or in his own words, the "social instituting imaginary", do "create – ex nihilo", produce something from nothing.

Castoriadis (1997, 1998) distinguishes two basic types of imaginations, primary and secondary imagination. Primary or radical imagination is the individual imagination and creates ex nihilo, from nothing. Such imagination is "*before* the distinction between 'real' and 'fictitious'" and creates "forms", that can be images but are not solely or prevalent, they are "in the main significations and institutions (each of those being impossible without the other)" (Castoriadis 1997: 322). But individuals are not the only ones creating these significations and institutions. The same applies to the instituting social imaginary, the imagination of the anonymous collective, the society, and, "more generally, the social-historical field", secondary imagination, in contrast, is "either reproductive or simply combinatory (and usually both)" (Castoriadis 1997: 322).

In a globalized and connected world with increasingly open processes of innovation and value creation, imaginations of the future are developed and influenced by organizations as well as individuals, using the tools of propaganda like marketing, persuasion and acts of (digital) public speech, exploiting the opportunity to reach big crowds using the digital infrastructure to frame imaginations or certain aspects of them and to set agendas. Infrastructure is here used as a term to signify resources, that within a certain system or organisation are free or affordable and accessible, including material resources (like books in libraries, public traffic, the energy, water, mobility or health infrastructure) and immaterial resources like information, knowledge, relief, help and entertainment (Frischmann 2005, Frischmann 2012, Bucher 2016). The digital infrastructure mentioned encompasses all the readily and affordable (or even free) available resources needed to participate in the digital world, like the www as a globally accessible technology, the availability of affordable access to it (via e.g. WiFi hotspots or mobile data), affordable technology to actually use it, like smartphones, tablets or laptops and actual applications like social media platforms, forums, blogs, messenger, online software and encyclopaediae (Bucher 2016). The www and the proliferation of information technology create an infrastructure that makes it easier than ever before in the history of the human kind to access information – and to spread and influence it. And this does not refer to a certain, potentially established group, like organized or already influential actors, but to everyone that has access and the capability to do so. This way imaginations are developed in an interaction that is based on interest and less bound by classic barriers, like distance and cultural norms and idiosyncrasies, which does not mean, that they don't matter anymore in such processes, but they lost their power as a barrier that prevents interaction from the get-go. Social imagination in the Imagination Age is an interactive and highly communicative process of collective creation of visions of the future that select, integrate and exclude, develop and reinterpret existing imaginations, paving the way for innovations to come. These paths of imaginative ideas give the open and uncertain future, full of risks and opportunities, a morphing, evolving and not necessarily consistent structure that provides orientation.

In the wake of the uprising and proliferation of digital network technologies and equipment to use it, the distribution of social imaginations across cultures and nations has become way easier and extensive (Weller/Bucher 2016). As Appadurai pointed out, „electronic media offer new resources and new disciplines for the construction of imagined selves and imagined worlds." (Appadurai 1997: 3) The digital network and information technologies increased the accessibility of manifested imaginations across borders, cultures, and languages substantially.

Regarding the relevance of media in the global circulation of imaginations Hans Georg Soeffner (2004) emphasizes the influence of media and especially the visuals in media. Through the repeatability and reproducibility of contents in new media multiple perspectives of signification and interpretation are possible and increase the possible discourses. In this way, more habits occur and imaginations are generated.

Social change, as well as technological innovation, depend on one another. While social change processes rely on technology to share and retrieve information, to communicate and organize (think about the ways of organizing and influencing people, about printers to produce flyers, letters, and networks to communicate), the development and diffusion of technologies is in part based on manifested social imaginations (or sediments of the social imaginary), especially regarding the exploitation of their functionalities (offering new possibilities, easier access and/or usage.

INNOVATION

Innovations are new products, services, business models, technologies, forms of organization, social patterns, institutions and behavior among other new material or immaterial things that may be coined (or advertised) as innovations. Schumpeter (1912, 1942), framed innovations as one key economic activity to generate economic growth and human progress. According to him, innovation is an act of creative destruction, where a product or a service or complete product lines are replaced by a new one. This kind of innovations is nowadays considered radical innovations, entirely new, unseen products, services, business models or technologies. But such high-impact is not necessarily the case, a lot of innovations are just minor improvements regarding the functionality, accessibility or other aspects of an existing product or service, called incremental innovations (Abernathy/Utterback 1978). The minimum improvement may be considered the design innovations. Redesigns, improved and in the best case more attractive and better usable versions of existing products or services. Incremental innovations keep product lines and services as well as markets alive by constantly improving what already exists. Disruptive are innovations (services, products, business models, technologies) that start in a niche or at the bottom end of a market, underperforming in certain aspects (at the beginning), disrupt and replace whole major markets (Christensen 1997) – the prime example here is the digital, sensor-based photography that disrupted the analog, chemistry-based photography (e.g. Ho/Chen 2018). Innovation research also focused on the context of innovations, e.g. on innovation systems (Lundvall 1985) and innovation ecosystems (Oh et al. 2016), and on the social behavior regarding innovations, their adoption, and diffusion (Rogers 2003). And they have looked at Innovations, not only to distinguish them from each other but also to understand and improve them. Innovation has been conceptualized as a process in several ways, as linear processes with certain sequential, overlapping or parallel phases (e.g. Thom 1992, Ulrich/Eppinger 1995, Hughes et al. 1996, Witt 1996, Brockhoff 1999), with certain stages and gates (Cooper 1983, Cooper/Kleinschmidt 1990, Cooper 1996) and as processes that include iteration and repetition of phases and elements.

In the last fifteen years, open processes of innovation (Chesbrough 2003) gained popularity. Open Innovation encourages to exploit the opportunities of global digital networks using crowdsourcing (outside-in open innovation). It also emphasizes the opportunities of the global market to monetize and/or generate value using potentially unused or not further pursued intellectual property and technology. It can be monetized through licensing, exchanged for other intellectual property or technologies or even made open source. Most concepts of innovation processes out there share two similarities: the same starting and ending point, with the final phase being the realization and diffusion of the innovation and the first phase being a problem to solve or an invention or inventive idea (see e.g. Verworn/Herstatt 2000). And this invention seems just to emerge from nothing, or from the magma of the social imaginary like Castoriadis described it. I believe most radical inventions (and innovations) have a history of manifested imaginary ideas that document how this ground-breaking idea has been a part of the social imaginary before its realization and that the inventor and the innovator probably were influenced by these ideas. The innovation process could be considered as dyadic – one half is the imagination part and the other one is the realization part. The realization is a creative process: realizing the innovation, getting the necessary organization and business running, getting to the market – the goals are already defined and the common problems and their solutions are worked on. The first part, the imaginative process, and its history has been widely neglected so far. Influenced by the social imaginary, cultural narratives, and ontologies, as well as certain individuals and groups, imaginations are spread using media and conserved this way, conserved to be consumed, forgotten and rediscovered, inspiring reinterpretations and reimaginations over time. This can be illustrated quite good coming back to Elon Musk, this time it is about his transport system Hyperloop. The idea to transport people in tubes like pneumatic post is almost as old as these document transportation systems and have been repeated and illustrated quite often, e.g. in the animated TV-Series Futurama and the Jetsons, which Musk even mentioned himself in an interview with business insider (Lynley 2012), before publishing his idea in a white paper (Musk 2013). There are two different ways, that these imaginations influence individuals, groups and societies: They cater to human desires and give them (an imaginative, individual as well as shared) expression, a shape, a graspable function, a meaning, and create evolving imaginations of the future. Professionals and scholars, as well as adolescents and so-called nerds and geeks, are naturally interested in fictions that tackle their field of interest and explore the imaginative future developments regarding the disciplines, technologies or aspects of human life, that they are personally and/or professionally interested in and their imagination about human and technological progression is in turn influenced by the description or explication of the imaginations, their inherent logic, their implications, and possible consequences. They may agree or disagree, but once they are interested and engaged in these imaginations and their narratives, these fictional imaginations will influence and shape their imagination of the future.

In the economic sciences it is still pretty common, to conceptualize the modern, individual human as an entity that is making decisions based on rational choices, not really considering inherent human factors that influence decision making, like experiences, desires, opinions and imaginations, that themselves relate to the socio-cultural environment and history and the social imaginary. Imaginations accumulate, evolve and interrelate in the course of history and influence the social imaginary, in a globalized and connected world even easily across societies and geographical distinctions. Thus I argue, that the way of human progression, the future, is not (primarily) shaped by rational decision, but by imaginations of the future, of technological advances and the opportunities they present, of new social systems, norms and institutions, new ways of interacting, living and so on. Since decisions that shape the future are always made in the present, it follows to conclude, that "it is the future that shapes the present – or, to be more specific: it is the images of the future that shape present decisions." (Beckert 2013) Imaginations of the future create paths to follow, paths that may not work out as imagined before, because of e.g. trends, stagnating technological or social progression and misconceptions or just scientific advance and the falsification of certain assumptions. But they still create an imagination (or image) of the future that comes with certain expectations (and thus, the formulation of goals), something to replace the openness and the uncertainty associated with the future.

The history of mankind shows that cultural and social innovations are seemingly based on technological innovations and that the majority of institutions, businesses, societies, and individuals take time to adapt to them, the culture lags behind (Ogburn 1966). But then there are also the desires of the people, that influence the development of technologies and the selection of technologies to further pursue and fund as well as not only political but also socio-cultural changes. Opposing the technology-push concept economists coined the demand of the people, the potential customers and the market, market-pull or demand-pull (Godin/Lane 2013). The author argues that innovations, technological as well as social and economic, don't just emerge as one-of-a-kind phenomena out of the blue and that they aren't just based on the basic modes of innovation - adoption, modification, and combination of existing, realized things and concepts. Innovations in their early state as inventions, as theoretical concepts or even working prototypes, as well as their consequences, prerequisites and use cases have been imaginatively explored, creating trends and sustaining imaginations that culminate in a desire or need (you may think of the concept of the pulling market) for certain products, services, developments or changes, creating paths for upcoming trends and opportunities for scientific investigations and the creation of value.

This doesn't mean, that imaginative concepts, by all means, have to manifest in reality as innovations at a certain point in history or even at all. Still, the digital networks of the Information Age and the global proliferation of technology and media to access these networks is making a big difference when it comes to the accessibility of intellectual resources (like the invention and proliferation of speech or letterpress printing did before): Knowledge, imaginations and ideas from the own and especially other cultures, languages and time periods influence more people than ever before in the history of mankind, thanks to the benefits of the Information Age. Of course, this development has several shortcomings that create problems, like the easy diffusion of false information, redundant information instead of proven information and often the sheer amount of information. But this just means, that certain technologies are needed to index, search, select, evaluate and organize information as well as human competencies to tackle these tasks individually and successfully navigate in the seas of data and information as well as supporting technology (soft- and hardware). One of the main prerequisites for the manifestation of imaginations as innovations is the accessibility and proliferation of these imaginative concepts, and besides their aforementioned flaws the digital networks of the Information Age provide exactly this: the opportunity to publish and proliferate as well as access immaterial resources like knowledge and imaginations in the form of texts, images, sounds and multimodal combinations of them (like videos and narrated slide presentations/screen captures).

SCIENCE FICTION

But looking at the application of innovative technology and the realization of new services and products there seems to be an overlooked influence – the specific imaginative context of an innovation, the imaginations of the individuals that are involved in the process that influence the direction and scope, as well as the decision making and design of inventions and innovations. Human creativity is seldom able to create something that is completely new, it is usually based on the adaption, modification, and combination of existing, realized artifacts and concepts (Plessner 1928/1975). At least that is a common belief. Looking at Elon Musk there seems to be a missing basis for creativity – imaginative ideas. Referencing matching Science Fiction, like ideas of space travel during a spaceship launch does not only reference a funny idea but an imaginative influence. These imaginations most often can't be directly adapted for real-world use right away (with the exception of this rule being already exploited based on Johnsons (2011a) idea of 'Science Fiction Prototyping') and influence humankind, especially the creative, imaginative, inventive individuals that are often associated with innovation and have a dual function when it comes to the realization of innovations: They foster the development of hypothetical technology and forms of social and political organization by creating desires that can outlast generations and become embedded in culture (f.e. the desire to fly – in the terrestrial sky like Icarus, to the moon, to mars, to other solar systems etc.) and manifested imaginations as Science Fiction often discuss possible consequences and subsequent developments and innovations. But not only that. When it comes to the so-called 'hard Science Fiction', there seems to be a common overlapping of the social sphere of Science and the one of Science Fiction. Scientists are often interested in Science Fiction and even reference it, and Science Fiction Writers are mostly academics themselves. Science Fiction often thematizes and conceptualize imaginative technological and scientific advancements, as well as forms of societies, social interaction, human biological progression and habitation. And it doesn't surprise, that engineers may be interested in the technological aspects of Science Fiction and that physicists may like stories about space travel. But besides the inherent topological commonalities, hard Science Fiction has also methodical vicinity to science. If a Science Fiction concept is scientific possible and testable, it is not much different from a thought experiment (Horowitz/Massey 1991, Frappier et al. 2012) in the natural sciences, and if it explores imaginary social and individual futures of the body and the mind, it borders on being a thought experiment in philosophy. Science Fiction is often exploring the circumstances and consequences of the concepts and how societies and individuals change, react or adapt, emphasizing single aspects of the human character and social behavior, with a clear notion towards dystopic concepts, exploring the negative aspects and opportunities of technological innovations and social change to be harmful exploited.

Science Fiction seems to be a perfect field to explore the importance of imagination on innovation and in the innovation process. It is often referenced as inspiration, is used as tool for marketing and branding, used to influence the social imagination or to individually create thought experiments that leave the confinements of the own profession and imagine what happens, if the idea, experiment or technological concept you're engaged in works out, come to fruition and changes the world. Or not.

In scholarly publications, Science Fiction is not often referenced and when it happens it is mostly presented as an antagonist or the opposite to 'real' science. But there are exemptions. There are researchers in several disciplines of the humanities and social sciences that do research on Science Fiction. Some scholars regard certain Science Fiction authors as philosophers, e.g. Stanislaw Lem is advocated by Gräfrath (1993) and Swirski (2013, 2014 & 2015), and promote their ideas, style (or methodology), creativity or oeuvre in general. In the business and management sciences, Science Fiction is a topic or reference rarely seen. But there are some articles, mostly about Science Fiction Prototyping and scenario building. There is at least one scientific journal in English that focuses on Science Fiction in a broad way, 'Science Fiction Studies', as well as Journals dedicated to the close field of Future Studies, like the 'Journal of Future Studies' and 'Futures'. Science Fiction has also been headlining a few articles per year in the journal 'Technological Foresight and Social Change' for over 25 years and running. In the journal 'Research Policy' a discussion between Lundvall (2017), Archibugi (2017a, 2017b) and Steinmueller (2017) about Science Fiction, imagination and economic development was initiated by an article by Archibugi (2017a) about the possibilities for an economic recovery lead by the use of biotechnology like envisioned in the movie Blade Runner, fittingly titled "Blade Runner Economics. Will innovations lead the economic recovery?" Steinmueller has already investigated the relation between Science Fiction and innovation before, the historic case of the geosynchronous satellite quite accurately imagined by Arthur C. Clarke (Bassett, Steinmueller & Voss 2013).

Regarding individual scholars that deal with Science Fiction, there are for example the philosophers Russell Blackford (2017), who also writes Science Fiction himself, investigates the relation between Science Fiction and moral imagination and Thomas Michaud (2017), who is working on a topic quite close to this approach, showing and arguing, that Science Fiction and Imagination are elemental and constitutional for the emergence of Innovations. The historians Graf and Herzog (2016) conceptualize the history of the future in the twentieth century and emphasize the variance and simultaneity of the present future(s), the diverse actors, contexts, and articulations and provide a heuristic to analyze the pluralization of the future in the twentieth century.

The before mentioned Science Fiction Prototyping was coined and conceptualized by the director of future casting, interactions and experience research at the Intel Corporation as a method to forecast and design, by identifying and using (implementing or producing) already realizable ideas exploited from Science Fiction to generate value, new products and services (Johnson 2009, 2011a, 2011b). He also pointed towards the value that Science Fiction (and especially his SF prototypes) propose for scientific work (Johnson 2010). Looking at organizations that actually deal with technologies that are common topics in Science Fiction, one stumbles upon approaches, that are quite similar and predate Johnsons publication – e.g. ESA, the

European Space Agency, was already working with Science Fiction right at the beginning of the century, reviewing Science Fiction writings, artwork and films trying to identify imaginations, concepts of imaginative technology, like old, overlooked ideas, that with modern technologies and materials may be utilizable and exploitable nowadays (ESA 2004). In 2002 they launched the 'Clarke-Bradbury International Science Fiction Competition', that challenged young people to write Science Fiction short stories thematising technology in some way, aiming "to promote innovative ideas for future space technologies: recognise and pursue viable space technologies found in Science Fiction; and share the ingenuity and creativity of young minds with the general public." (ESA 2004:3) This shows, that this competition is not only an example of quasi Proto-Science-Fiction-Prototyping, but also for a strategic approach of a public organization to influence the social imagination by setting up incentives and an event to purposeful make young humans engage in science and imagination (especially imaginative technology and Science Fiction) and also make them share their experiences.

To create value and foster innovation responsibly, manifested imaginations, like Science Fiction concepts and narratives, imaginative explorations of the future can and should be utilized to manage and prepare for the future in a responsible and sustainable way, considering and discussing Hans Jonas' idea of the universal imperative to ensure the survival of genuine human life (Jonas 1985, Jonas 1984).

In the 1970s the German philosopher Jonas formulated one of the prime arguments for modern concepts like responsibility, sustainability and the protection of nature in his book "The Imperative of Responsibility: In Search of Ethics for the Technological Age" (Jonas 1984). His ethic is based on the categorical imperative that Immanuel Kant (1785, 1788) brought forth, but because of its teleological perspective, it also shares elements with utilitarian concepts (e.g. Bentham 1781/2009, Mill 1861, Singer 1979/1993). This becomes evident considering that Jonas' so-called ecological imperative has a teleological premise of action: The permanence of genuine human life. Responsible action thus is always an action that considers knowledge regarding the consequences of the action. Regarding the exploration, interpretation, and understanding of these consequences, there are distinct approaches. According to Flechtheim Jonas is arguing the case for a speculative philosophy (Flechtheim/Joos 1991: 74) in contrast to mathematical extrapolations. Jonas himself said that a new science (or art) of futurology, allowing us to see long-distance effects, will be an asset to the world of tomorrow, an asset new in its form and function (Jonas 1985: 65). The uncertainty, whether futurology is a science or an art, is referring to an immanent creative component, not only regarding future innovation but also their influence, usage, adoption and the explication of assumed consequences of (human) action. The literalization of scientific findings and knowledge is the domain of the Science Fiction. It is not only an alternative to mathematical extrapolations of the future but also offers opportunities to add a qualitative perspective to quantitative investigations.

Such investigations have already taken place, scattered among the various social sciences. Among these documented cases of the influence of technological concepts from Science Fiction that manifested in reality, later on, is the geosynchronous communication satellite, that was imagined and described in stories by Arthur C. Clarke (1961) and George O. Smith (1976). This is just one example among several investigated by Bassett, Steinmueller and Voss (2007:03) in their extensive working paper on the 'Mutual Influence of Science fiction and Innovation' that uncovered "multi-directional and on-going pathways connecting SF and science". Individual imaginations may also challenge and change the borders of the general social imagination. Heuser (2015) describes a historic case that changed the borders and the rules of the individual and social imagination. She argues that the idea of space travel is based on a new ontology of space, a homogeneous space, and was first virtually explicated around 1600 and most significantly promoted in the works of Giordano Bruno (De Immenso, 1591) and Johannes Kepler (Somnium, 1593/2010). Approx. 300 years later the imagination of space travel was realized and it is documented that the pioneers of space travel were aware of the roots of the innovation that they were working on and recognized them. Imaginations seemingly create paths underlying the evo- and revolution of technology and culture. These imaginations are restricted by the social and individual ontology of the specific subject. Regarding space and space travel she argues, that the ontology of space has changed again, providing the foundation for possible actual space travel to other stars and habitable exoplanets.

Fictitious, but plausible imaginations that have been realized as well as the ones that haven't or have not yet manifested as innovations, should be recognized and investigated, even more so in a period of time, where the proliferation of imaginative ideas is quicker and farther than ever before as is their potential realization. Creating new possibilities in form of opportunities and threats, as each technology does (Ortmann 2013), putting the individual in a position where it usually feels the urge to take a stance, creating ambiguities, desires as well as opposition and denial of innovation, change, and progression.

FROM THE INFORMATION TO THE IMAGINATION AGE

While I argue, that one of the main arguments to engage in research on imagination and Science Fiction is the proliferation of information technology and thereby the diffusion and accessibility of information and imaginations across cultures and geographical distinctions, the implications of the Information Age, some others go one step further and call the present period the "Imagination Age" (King. 2007, Magee

1993). The Imagination Age is introduced as the follow up to the Information Age, associated with the emergence of a new global culture and an imagination economy that is heavily based on collaboration, creativity, and imaginative thinking. Cox illustrated and captured the difference between the Imagination and the Information Age quite fittingly:

The Information Age's icon was the programmer hunched over a keyboard, working alone. By contrast, imagination and creativity are collaborative exercises, choruses rather than solos, so people skills and emotional intelligence emerge as assets in the Imagination Age (Cox 2017: 9f).

Imagination and the entities, that try to influence and use it, depend heavily on the distribution of imaginative ideas and artifacts that carry these evolving ideas over time, surpassing single human lives, systems, and borders. We seem to have entered a period in time that is shaped by the globalization of not only goods and economies, but also culture, imaginations, and ideas, fostered by digitalization and its digital distribution systems with accompanying networks and platforms, that allow these ideas to be conserved, spread, discussed, evolved and realized faster than ever before in human history. This is furthermore fostered by the advance of the Fourth Industrial Revolution. Following the Digitalization, the Fourth Industrial Revolution (Schwab 2015, Schwab 2017, Schwab/Davis 2018) is heavily based on the diffusion of the former, being "characterized by a fusion of technologies that is blurring the lines between the physical, digital, and biological spheres" (Schwab 2015). And the social networks, media, and platforms used to distribute imaginations, ideas, and fictions depend heavily on the before mentioned fusion of technologies. It has never been easier to communicate almost anything with almost anyone thanks to modern, web-based communication incorporating multimodal media that can be accessed, altered or created, and distributed easily using mobile devices. And it doesn't surprise, that some of the most iconic personalities of the business world use these platforms, networks and the media to share their inspirations and influences – for example Bill Gates and Mark Zuckerberg, that both emphasize the importance of reading for their success and publicly share book recommendations (Gates 2018, Zuckerberg 2015), spreading ideas and imaginations, directly addressing and influencing their followers as well as broader audiences indirectly through media outlets that cover and reiterate these lists, e.g. Business Insider, that spread the book recommendations by Jeff Bezos, Elon Musk and Bill Gates (Abadi 2018).

SYNOPSIS AND PROPOSAL OF AN AGENDA

This article tries to argue, that the individual as well as socio-historical imagination influence each other and create paths for later realized innovations, including technological advances, products, business models and forms of living as well as social organization. Using the field of Science Fiction, it was argued, that these imaginations or fictions don't predict the future, but they are documents of plausible ideas and concepts that recognize scientific progress and embed these ideas and concepts in narratives, creating scenarios and use cases for these imaginations. Manifested imaginations influence the social imagination through media, creating paths of imaginations, that are made up of evolving and often interrelating manifested imaginations historically embedded in the culture – e.g. in literature, movies, audiobooks and radio plays, video games and architecture. And these manifested imaginations in turn influence and inspire scholars, professionals, innovators and open-minded thinkers like kids and adolescents. Like that the power of imagination is leaving traces to be discovered and considered for upcoming or theoretical future technology, social-cultural changes and the general direction of the human race and life on earth and possibly beyond.

Coming from this proposition, it is recommended to consider and recognize imaginations, especially the narratives and imaginations that are popular among a wide spectrum of the society and the ones that are respected and consumed among professional and academic groups, to understand the front-end of the innovation process and the supposed 'emergence' of innovation to manage future innovations in a responsible way and ensure the continuance of human life. And responsibility, sustainability and the creation of a future worth living, are topics that are often explored and discussed in Science Fiction publications, which present themselves as a favorable and quite obvious form of influential manifested imaginations to be considered. They not only seem to be quite interrelated with the sciences and address break-through technological as well as social concepts but they also often emphasize the ethical aspects of imaginative (but plausible) developments, systems, technologies, social and cultural shifts, human progression and their implications and effects. Science Fiction provides scenarios that may not be perfectly accurate or plausible (anymore), but pose a magnificent starting point to discuss future innovations and developments and their assumed mechanisms, implications and ramifications. Science Fiction can be framed as a laboratory for thought experiments that cover complex scenarios of the future showcasing possible technologies, social and individual behavior and how these may be intertwined. Understood this way they offer an opportunity to discuss these designed scenarios of the future and manage the actual future considering these powerful imaginations. This approach offers an alternative to foresight and forecasting methods that focus on the extrapolation of the status quo, may it be using statistics or expert interviews.

REFERENCES

Abadi, M. (2018, January). 15 books Bill Gates, Jezz Bezos, and Elon Musk think everyone should read. *Business Insider*. Retrieved from https://www.businessinsider. de/bill-gates-jeff-bezos-elon-musk-favorite-books-2017-11

Abernathy, W. J., & Utterback, J. M. (1978). Patterns of industrial innovation. *Technology Review*, *52*(5), 109–119.

Adams, D. (1979). *The Hitchhiker's Guide to the Galaxy*. London, UK: Pan Books.

Appadurai, A. (2010). *Modernity at Large. Cultural Dimensions of Globalization* (9th ed.). Minneapolis, MN: University of Minnesota Press. (Original work published 1996)

Archibugi, D. (2017a). Blade Runner economics: Will innovation lead the economic recovery? *Research Policy*, *46*(3), 535–543. doi:10.1016/j.respol.2016.01.021

Archibugi, D. (2017b). The social imagination needed for an innovation-led recovery. *Research Policy*, *46*(3), 554–556. doi:10.1016/j.respol.2016.09.018

Armstrong, N. (1969). *Recorded live broadcast transcript*. Retrieved from http:// apollo11.spacelog.org/07:09:32:24/#log-line-639144

Bassett, C., Steinmueller, E., & Voss, G. (2013). *Better made up. The mutual influence of science fiction and innovation*. Nesta Working Paper, No. 13/07. Retrieved from http://www.nesta.org.uk/wp13-07

Beckert, J. (2013). Imagined futures: Fictional expectations in the economy. *Theory and Society*, *42*(3), 219–240. doi:10.100711186-013-9191-2

Bentham, J. (2009). *An Introduction to the Principles of Morals and Legislation*. Dover, UK: Dover Publications. (Original work published 1781)

Blackford, R. (2017). *Science Fiction and the Moral Imagination*. Springer. doi:10.1007/978-3-319-61685-8

Brockhoff, K. (1999): Forschung und Entwicklung: Planung und Kontrolle (5th ed.). München, Germany: Oldenburg.

Bruno, G. (1999). *De Immenso et Innumerabilibus Liber I-VI. Das Unermeßliche und Unzählbare.* 6 Bücher. Peißenberg: Skorpion-Verlag. (Original work published 1591)

Bucher, J. (2016). *Die Proliferation der Möglichkeiten und Anforderungen. Über Infrastrukturinnovationen und ihre wirtschaftliche und soziale Adaption.* Paper presented at the 1. interdisziplinäre Konferenz zur Zukunft der Wertschöpfung. Retrieved from http://www.openproduction.info/wp-content/uploads/2016/12/161205_Konferenzband_Zukunft-der-Wertschöpfung_2016_digital.pdf

Castoriadis, C. (1997). *The Castoriadis Reader* (D. A. Curtis, Trans. & Ed.). Cambridge, UK: Blackwell Publishers.

Castoriadis, C. (1998). *The Imaginary Institution of Society* (K. Blarney, Trans.). Cambridge, UK: MIT Press.

Christensen, C. M. (1997). *The innovator's dilemma: when new technologies cause great firms to fail.* Boston, MA: Harvard Business School Press.

Clarke, A. C. (1961). *A Fall of Moondust.* London, UK: Galloncz.

Cooper, R. G. (1983). A process model for industrial new product development. *IEEE Transactions on Engineering Management, 30*(1), 2–11. doi:10.1109/TEM.1983.6448637

Cooper, R. G. (1996). Overhauling the new product process. *Industrial Marketing Management, 25*(6), 465–482. doi:10.1016/S0019-8501(96)00062-4

Cooper, R. G., & Kleinschmidt, E. J. (1990). *New Products: The Key Factors in Success.* Chicago, IL: American Marketing Association.

Cox, M. W., & Alm, R. (2017). *The Imagination Age. America's fourth wave of economic progress.* Retrieved from https://www.smu.edu/-/media/Site/Cox/CentersAndInstitutes/ONeilCenter/Research/AnnualReports/2017AnnualReport.ashx?la=en

European Space Agency ESA. (2004): Tales of Innovation and Imagination: Selected Stories from the 2003 Clarke-Bradbury International Science Fiction Competition. D. Raitt & B. Warmbein (Eds.). Retrieved from www.esa.int/esapub/sp/sp546/sp546web.pdf

Flechtheim, O. K. & Joos, E. (1991). *Ausschau halten nach einer besseren Welt.* Berlin: Dietz.

Frappier, M., Meynell, L., & Brown, J. R. (2012). *Thought Experiments in Science, Philosophy, and the Arts*. London, UK: Routledge. doi:10.4324/9780203113271

Frischmann, B. M. (2005). An Economic Theory of Infrastructure and Commons Management. *Minnesota Law Review*, *89*, 917–1030.

Frischmann, B. M. (2012). *Infrastructure. The Social Value of Shared Resources*. New York: Oxford University Press. doi:10.1093/acprof:oso/9780199895656.001.0001

Gates, B. (2018). *5 books worth reading this summer*. Retrieved from https://www.gatesnotes.com/About-Bill-Gates/Summer-Books-2018

Godin, B., & Lane, J. P. (2013). *"Pushes and Pulls": The Hi(story) of the Demand Pull Model of Innovation, Project on the Intellectual History of Innovation* (Working Paper No. 13). Retrieved from http://www.csiic.ca/PDF/Demand-pull.pdf

Graf, R., & Herzog, B. (2016). Von der Geschichte der Zukunftsvorstellungen zur Geschichte ihrer Generierung. Probleme und Herausforderungen des Zukunftsbezugs im 20. Jahrhundert. *Geschichte und Gesellschaft (Vandenhoeck & Ruprecht)*, *42*(3), 497–515. doi:10.13109/gege.2016.42.3.497

Gräfrath, B. (1993). *Ketzer, Dilettanten und Genies. Grenzgänger der Philosophie*. Hamburg, Germany: Junius.

Heuser, M.-L. (2015). Raumontologie und Raumfahrt um 1600 und 1900. *Reflex*, *6*, 1–15.

Ho, J. C., & Chen, H. (2018). Managing the Disruptive and Sustaining the Disrupted: The Case of Kodak and Fujifilm in the Face of Digital Disruption. *The Review of Policy Research*, *35*(3), 352–371. doi:10.1111/ropr.12278

Horowitz, T., & Massey, G. (1991). *Thought experiments in science and philosophy*. Retrieved from http://philsci-archive.pitt.edu/3190/

Hughes, G. D., & Chafin, D. C. (1996). Turning New Product Development into a Continuous Learning Process. *Journal of Product Innovation Management*, *13*(2), 89–104. doi:10.1016/0737-6782(95)00112-3

Johnson, B. D. (2009). *Science Fiction Prototypes Or: How I Learned to Stop Worrying about the Future and Love Science Fiction*. Paper presented at the 5th International Conference on Intelligent Environments. Retrieved from https://www.researchgate.net/publication/220992681_Science_Fiction_Prototypes_Or_How_I_Learned_to_Stop_Worrying_about_the_Future_and_Love_Science_Fiction

Johnson, B. D. (2010). *Science Fiction for Scientists!! An Introduction to SF Prototypes and Brain Machines*. Paper presented at Creative-Science 2010. Retrieved from http://dces.essex.ac.uk/Research/iieg/papers/SF_Prototyping(Paper).pdf

Johnson, B. D. (2011a). *Science Fiction Prototyping: Designing the Future with Science Fiction*. San Rafael, CA: Morgan & Claypool.

Johnson, B. D. (2011b). *Love and God and Robots. The Science Behind the Science Fiction Prototype "Machinery of Love and Grace."* Paper presented at Creative-Science 2011. Retrieved from http://dces.essex.ac.uk/Research/iieg/abstracts_CS11/CS11_ Johnson(abstract).pdf

Jonas, H. (1984). The Imperative of Responsibility. In *Search of Ethics for the Technological Age* (H. Jonas & D. Herr, Trans.). Chicago, IL: University of Chicago Press. (Original work published 1979)

Jonas, H. (1985). *Technik, Medizin und Ethik: Zur Praxis des Prinzips Verantwortung*. Leipzig, Germany: Insel Verlag.

Kant, I. (1788). *Critic der practischen Vernunft*. Retrieved from http://www.deutschestextarchiv.de/book/show/kant_pvernunft_1788

Kant, I. (2004). Grundlegung der Metaphysik der Sitten. Immanuel Kant: Grundlegung zur Metaphysik der Sitten. Göttingen, Germany: Vandenhoeck & Ruprecht. (Original work published 1785)

Kepler, J. (2010). Der Traum, oder: Mond-Astronomie. Somnium sive astronomia lunaris. In Mit einem Leitfaden für Mondreisende von Beatrix Langner. Berlin: Matthes & Seitz. (Original work published 1593)

King, R. J. (2007). *The Emergence of a New Global Culture in the Imagination Age*. British Council Essays.

Lundvall, B.-Å. (1985). *Product innovation and user-producer interaction*. Aalborg, Denmark: Aalborg University Press.

Lundvall, B.-Å. (2017). Is there a technological fix for the current global stagnation?: A response to Daniele Archibugi, Blade Runner economics: Will innovation lead the economic recovery? *Research Policy, 46*(3), 544–549. doi:10.1016/j.respol.2016.06.011

Lynley, M. (2012). *Elon Musk Wants To Invent A Fifth Mode Of Transportation Called 'Hyperloop'*. Retrieved from https://www.businessinsider.com/elon-musk-is-kicking-around-an-idea-that-would-send-you-from-san-francisco-to-los-angeles-in-30-minutes-2012-7?IR=T

Magee, C. (1993). The Age of Imagination. Coming Soon to a Civilization Near You. *Second International Symposium: National Security & National Competitiveness: Open Source Solutions Proceedings, 1,* 95–98.

Michaud, T. (2017). *Innovation, Between Science and Science Fiction.* London, UK: ISTE Ltd. doi:10.1002/9781119427568

Mill, J. S. (1861). *Utilitarianism.* Retrieved from https://en.wikisource.org/wiki/Utilitarianism

Musk, E. (2013). *Hyperloop Alpha.* Retrieved from http://www.spacex.com/sites/spacex/files/hyperloop_alpha-20130812

Ogburn, W. F. (1966). *Social change: With respect to cultural and original nature.* Oxford, UK: Delta Books.

Oh, D.-S., Phillips, F., Park, S., & Lee, E. (2016). Innovation ecosystems: A critical examination. *Technovation, 54,* 1–6. doi:10.1016/j.technovation.2016.02.004

Ortmann, G. (2013). Brave New World und wie neu sie wirklich ist. *ZFO - Zeitschrift Führung + Organisation, 82*(5), 338-339.

Plessner, H. (1975). Die Stufen des Organischen und der Mensch. Einleitung in die philosophische Anthropologie (3rd ed.). Berlin: Walter de Gruyter. (Original work published 1928) doi:10.1515/9783110845341

Rogers, E. M. (2003). *Diffusion of innovations* (5th ed.). New York, NY: Free Press.

Schumpeter, J. A. (1912). Theorie der wirtschaftlichen Entwicklung. Berlin: Duncker & Humblot.

Schumpeter, J. A. (1942). *Capitalism, socialism and democracy.* New York, NY: Harper.

Schütz, A. (1971). Wissenschaftliche Interpretation und Alltagsverständnis menschlichen Handelns. In A. Schütz (Ed.), Gesammelte Aufsätze I. Das Problem der sozialen Wirklichkeit (pp. 3-54). Den Haag, The Netherlands: Martinus Njihoff. doi:10.1007/978-94-010-2858-5_1

Schwab, K. (2015, December). The Fourth Industrial Revolution. What It Means and How to Respond. *Foreign Affairs.* Retrieved from https://www.foreignaffairs.com/articles/2015-12-12/fourth-industrial-revolution

Schwab, K. (2017). *The Fourth Industrial Revolution.* London, UK: Portfolio Penguin.

Schwab, K., & Davis, N. (2018). *Shaping the Future of the Fourth Industrial Revolution: A guide to building a better world*. London, UK: Portfolio Penguin.

Singer, P. (2011). *Practical Ethics* (3rd ed.). Cambridge, UK: Cambridge University Press. (Original work published 1979) doi:10.1017/CBO9780511975950

Smith, G. O. (1976). *The Complete Venus Equilateral*. New York, NY: Ballantine.

Soeffner, H.-G. (2004). *Auslegung des Alltags – Der Alltag der Auslegung*. Konstanz, Germany: UVK.

Swirski, P. (2013). *From Literature to Biterature: Lem, Turing, Darwin, and Explorations in Computer Literature, Philosophy of Mind, and Cultural Evolution*. London, UK: McGill-Queen's University Press.

Swirski, P. (2015). *Stanislaw Lem: Philosopher of the Future*. Liverpool, UK: Liverpool University Press. doi:10.5949/liverpool/9781781381861.001.0001

Swirski, P., & Osadnik, W. M. (2014). *Lemography: Stanislaw Lem in the Eyes of the World*. Liverpool, UK: Liverpool University Press. doi:10.5949/liverpool/9781781381205.001.0001

Thom, N. (1992). Innovationsmanagement. Bern: Schweizerische Volksbank.

Ulrich, K. T., & Eppinger, S. D. (1995). *Product design and development*. New York, NY: McGraw-Hill.

Verworn, B., & Herstatt, C. (2000). *Modelle des Innovationsprozesses* (Working Paper No. 6). Retrieved from http://nbn-resolving.de/urn:nbn:de:gbv:830-opus-1607

Weller, A., & Bucher, J. (2016). Visualisierte Imaginationen der Lebenswelt und der Einfluss der Medien. In J. Raab & R. Keller (Eds.), Wissensforschung - Forschungswissen. Beiträge zum 1. Sektionskongress der Wissenssoziologie (pp. 595-607). Weinheim, Germany: Belz Juventa.

Witt, J. (1996). Grundlagen für die Entwicklung und die Vermarktung neuer Produkte. In J. Witt (Ed.), Produktinnovation. Entwicklung und Vermarktung neuer Produkte (pp. 169-183). München, Germany: Vahlen.

Zuckerberg, M. (2015). *A Year of Books*. Retrieved from https://www.facebook.com/ayearofbooks/

ADDITIONAL READING

Anderson, B. (1983/2016). *Imagined Communities. Reflections on the Origin and Spread of Nationalism*. London, UK: Verso.

Blackford, R. (2017). *Science Fiction and the Moral Imagination*. New York: Springer. doi:10.1007/978-3-319-61685-8

Fields, Z., Bucher, J., & Weller, A. (2019). *Imagination, Creativity and Responsible Management in the fourth industrial revolution*. Hershey, PA: IGI Global.

Hofstadter, D. R., & Dennett, D. C. (1985). *The Mind's I. Fantasies and Reflections on Self and Soul*. New York: Bantam Dell.

Chapter 4
Towards a Classification Framework for Concepts of Innovation for and From Emerging Markets

Martin Albert
Chemnitz University of Technology, Germany

Stefan Huesig
Chemnitz University of Technology, Germany

ABSTRACT

A closer look at innovation for and from emerging markets reveals that a variety of different terms and concepts related to this type of innovation exist. The objective of this conceptual work is to develop a theoretical classification framework based on a comprehensive literature overview that provides a starting point for structuring these different terms and concepts. After a first investigation and comprehensive search for the keywords "reverse," "frugal," "jugaad," and "bottom of pyramid" in the Google Scholar database, 19 different texts were identified and classified for further analysis. As a result, 33 identified terms concerning innovation for and from emerging markets, various spellings and synonyms are presented. Finally, a theoretical-based classification framework is derived and the criteria "market orientation," "determinants," "nature," "sophistication," "sustainability," "novelty," and "innovator type" was proposed. This classification framework could be used for further research and teaching in innovation, responsible, and sustainable management disciplines.

DOI: 10.4018/978-1-5225-7638-9.ch004

Copyright © 2019, IGI Global. Copying or distributing in print or electronic forms without written permission of IGI Global is prohibited.

INTRODUCTION

A closer look at innovation for and from emerging markets, respectively developing economies (e.g. Frugal Innovation or Reverse Innovation) reveals that a variety of different terms and concepts related to this type of innovation exist. This terminological complexity is difficult to keep track of and blurs the underlying concepts since many terms are used synonymously or the understanding is rather vague. Bhatti and Ventresca (2013) state in regards to *Frugal Innovation* that, "there is no theoretically embedded definition and there exist few if any conceptual models to base future research on" (p.1). Pansera (2014) concludes regarding *Innovation for Development*, "it is virtually impossible to classify the literature analysed into a set of clearly defined and fixed categories" (p.55). Regarding to *Jugaad*, Prabhu and Jain (2015) notice that "the jostling between terminology has contributed to much conceptual confusion that needs to be addressed" (p.856). The goal of our conceptual work is to analyze terms and concepts relating to innovation for and from emerging markets and to suggest theoretical based classification criteria in order to differentiate these terms and concepts. Based on the classification criteria, we propose a classification framework that could be used for further research and teaching in innovation, responsible and sustainable management disciplines. Accordingly, the underlying research questions of our conceptual chapter are:

- Which terms and concepts are used to describe innovation for and from emerging markets?
- Which classification criteria can be used to differentiate terms and concepts relating to innovation for and from emerging markets?

In order to resolve these questions, keywords relating to innovation for and from emerging markets are identified and used for searching the database of Google Scholar. Terms and concepts relating to innovation for and from emerging markets as well as classification criteria are analyzed, and a classification framework is presented. Implications for research and practice in innovation, responsible and sustainable management disciplines finalize this chapter.

METHOD AND DATA BASE

After a first investigation in regards to innovation for and from emerging markets (EM), respectively developing economies, the following keywords were identified: 'reverse', 'frugal', 'jugaad', and 'bottom of the pyramid / bottom of pyramid / bop'. These keywords were used for searching the database of Google Scholar. Google

Scholar was chosen since it is publicly accessible and one of the most comprehensive databases for research output in the relevant academic fields. The search revealed (on 30.03.2016) the following number of search results (bracketed) relating to various combinations of the keywords (and in combination with the Google search operators 'allintext:', 'OR', and '" "'):

- (201) allintext: reverse jugaad "bottom of the pyramid" OR "bottom of pyramid" OR bop
- (263) allintext: reverse frugal jugaad
- (279) allintext: frugal jugaad "bottom of the pyramid" OR "bottom of pyramid" OR bop
- (479) allintext: reverse frugal "bottom of the pyramid" OR "bottom of pyramid" OR bop

Thereafter, all texts were manually scanned for terms in relation to innovation for and from emerging markets. Thereby, we primarily focused on reviews, overviews, surveys, and summaries in order to cover the greatest possible term diversity. For further investigation, only texts that used eight different terms to describe innovation for and from emerging markets were considered. However, we did not control for or filter by indicator-based quality of the research material such as rankings or impact factors. In Table 1, shown below, we present the identified texts along with the type and the number of mentions of the various terms.

In the following section, we present the identified 19 different texts, and the corresponding terms and concepts related to innovation for and from emerging markets as well as potentially proposed classification criteria.

OVERVIEW OF IDENTIFIED LITERATURE

Bhatti and Ventresca (2012) look at 17 various terms related to the rhetoric surrounding of Frugal Innovation: Appropriate Technology, Below the Radar Innovation, BOP Innovation / Bottom of the Pyramid Innovation, Catalytic Innovation, Cost Innovation, Disruptive Innovation, Extreme Affordability, Frugal Engineering, Frugal Innovation, Inclusive Innovation, Innovation for Underserved / Market for Underserved / Underserved Population / Underserved Segments / Underserved Clients / Underserved Markets / Underserved Niches, Innovation under Constraints, Lean Engineering / Lean Product Development / Lean Manufacturing, more with less and for more people / MLM Innovation, Reverse Engineering, Reverse Innovation, Trickle up Innovation / Bottom up Innovation. Although no classification criteria are explicitly stated, terms and concepts could be distinguished in 1) the reason for

Table 1. Texts with (at least eight) various terms in relation to innovation for and from emerging markets

Text	Type of Text	Mentions of Various Terms
Bhatti & Ventresca, 2012	Working Paper	17
Bhatti, 2012	Working Paper	11
Brem & Wolfram, 2014	Journal Article	13
Bubel, Ostraszewska, Turek, & Tylec, 2015	Conference Paper	8
Chataway, Hanlin, & Kaplinsky, 2014	Journal Article	9
Hamacher, 2014	Master Thesis	16
Millard, 2014	Literature Review	8
Ostraszewska & Tylec, 2015	Journal Article	8
Pansera, 2013	Journal Article	20
Pansera, 2014	Doctoral Thesis	23
Pansera & Sarkar, 2016	Journal Article	16
Prabhu & Jain, 2015	Journal Article	18
Rawat, 2015	Conference Paper	10
Rosca, Arnold, & Bendul, 2016	Journal Article	18
Soni & Krishnan, 2014	Journal Article	18
Terrio, 2014	Master Thesis	13
Von Zedtwitz, Corsi, Søberg, & Frega, 2014	Journal Article	12
Zeschky, Winterhalter, & Gassmann, 2014a	Conference Paper	10
Zeschky, Winterhalter, & Gassmann, 2014b	Journal Article	8

Frugal Innovation ('why') and 2) how Frugal Innovation is achieved ('how'). As 'how' are classified: cost efficiency, minimally viable product, optimizing supply chains, rebuilding value chains, user centric design, local capacity building, creative improvisation, business model innovation. As 'why' are classified: profiting from new markets, investing with social impact, serving with an ethical mission.

Bhatti (2012) mentions 11 various terms in relation to innovation in emerging markets: Bricolage, Bottom of the Pyramid Innovation, Creative Improvisation, Design Thinking, Frugal Innovation, Innovation for Underserved / Underserved Market / Underserved Costumer / Underserved Communities, Jugaad, Lean Engineering, more with less and for more people / MLM Innovation, Reverse Engineering, Reverse Innovation / Reverse Diffusion. Although no classification criteria are stated, some indications of the theoretical model for Frugal Innovation may be of use. The model deals with the challenges of innovating for the underserved in emerging markets.

Derived indications include: social innovation deals with affordability constraints (Design Thinking), institutional innovation deals with institutional voids (Social Movements, Social Capital), business innovation deals with resource constraints (Bricolage, Improvisation, Jugaad, Reverse Engineering).

Brem and Wolfram (2014) analyze 13 various terms regarding innovative approaches from emerging markets and following their research question "What are applicable characteristics to delineate the terms from emerging markets?": Bottom-of-the-pyramid Innovation, Catalytic Innovation, Constraint-based Innovation, Extreme Affordability, Frugal Engineering, Frugal Innovation, Gandhian Innovation, Grassroots Innovation, Indigenous Innovation, Jugaad, more with less for more people / MLM Innovation, Reverse Engineering, Reverse Innovation. Sophistication, sustainability, and emerging market orientation are defined categories that differentiate and help evaluate different types of innovations.

Bubel et al. (2015) specify eight various concepts of innovativeness that originate from developing countries: BOP, Cost Innovation, Disruptive Innovation, Frugal Innovation, Gandhian Innovation, Good-enough Innovation, Jugaad Innovation, Reverse Innovation. They differentiate Cost, Good-Enough, Frugal, and Reverse Innovations in terms of technology (low, medium, high) and market novelty (low, medium, high), based on Zeschky et al. (2014b).

Chataway et al. (2014) mention nine various terms in relation to Inclusive Innovation: Appropriate Technology, Below the Radar Innovation, BOP Innovation, Frugal Innovation, Grassroots Innovation, Inclusive Innovation, Jugaad Innovation, Pro-Poor Innovation, Reverse Innovation. No overall classification criteria are stated.

Hamacher (2014) looks at 16 various terms behind emerging market innovation: BOP Innovation, Bricolage, Creative Improvisation, Disruptive Innovation, Frugal Engineering, Frugal Innovation, Gandhian Innovation, Good-enough Innovation, Inclusive Innovation, Innovation for Underserved / Underserved Markets, Jugaad Innovation, Low-cost Innovation, MLM / more with less for more (people), Resource-constrained Innovation, Reverse Innovation, Value Innovation. He does not state explicit classification criteria but refers among others to Bhatti (2012). Bhatti's indications of the theoretical model for Frugal Innovation for dealing with the challenges of innovating for the underserved in emerging markets includes: affordability constraints, institutional voids, and resource constraints.

Millard (2014) mentions eight various innovation theories in development contexts: Appropriate Technology, Bottom of the Pyramid / Base of the Pyramid / BoP, Frugal Innovation, Gandhian Approach, Inclusive Innovation, Jugaad Innovation, Reverse Innovation / Trickle-up Innovation. Although no classification criteria are explicitly stated, the summary indicates some commonalities among the terms including: openness, inclusiveness, participation (consumers, producers, business partners, innovators), focus on local resources, and independence from outside demands or inputs.

Ostraszewska and Tylec (2015) specify eight various concepts of innovativeness that originate from developing countries: BOP, Cost Innovation, Disruptive Innovation, Frugal Innovation, Gandhian Innovation, Good-enough Innovation, Jugaad Innovation, Reverse Innovation. To specify and differentiate the considered concepts of innovation, the following characteristics are stated, based on Christensen (1997), Zeschky et al. (2014b), Brem and Wolfram (2014), and Prahalad and Mashelkar (2010): orientation, aim, description, innovative strategy, and specificity. Furthermore, the various types of innovation are classified according to their ability to introduce changes (same for less, adapted for less, new for less) and the market where they are offered (emerging markets, developed markets), based on Zeschky et al. (2014b).

Pansera (2013) mentions directly or indirectly 20 various terms to provide an overview of theoretical approaches to describe innovation at the BOP respectively innovation in a resource-constrained environment: Appropriate Technology, Below-the-Radar Innovation, Blowback Innovation, BOP Innovation, Bricolage Innovation, Catalytic Innovation, Disruptive Innovation, Empathetic Innovation, Frugal Innovation, Frugal Reengineering, Gandhian Innovation, Grassroots Innovation, Inclusive Innovation, Indigenous Innovation, Innovation for Underserved / Underserved Markets, Jugaad, Low-cost Innovation, more with less and for more people / MLM Innovation, Reverse Innovation, Trickle-up Innovation. Although no overall classification criteria are stated, the author depicts main determinants that move heterodox innovators (Below-the-Radar Innovation as an umbrella term for BOP, Grassroots Innovation, Inclusive Innovation, and Jugaad): social needs, resource constraints, market affordability, institutional voids, and environmental concerns. Furthermore, he states that entrepreneurship and innovation at the BOP are classified into three types: poor framed as consumers (creation of new markets at the BOP), poor framed as co-producers (creation of alliances at the BOP), and poor framed as entrepreneurs/innovators (creation of institutional framework to include grassroots innovation in public policy).

Pansera (2014) looks at 23 various terms related to innovation for development: Appropriate Technology, Below-the-Radar Innovation, Blowback Innovation, BOP Innovation / Bottom of the Pyramid Innovation, Bricolage, Disruptive Innovation, Empathetic Innovation, Frugal Innovation, Gandhian Innovation, Good-enough Innovation, Grassroots Innovation, Inclusive Innovation / Inclusive Growth / Inclusive Development / Inclusive Innovation Systems / Inclusive Business Models, Indigenous Innovation, Indovation / Hindolence, Innovation for Underserved / Underserved Markets, Jugaad Innovation, Long Tail Innovation / Long Tailoring Innovation, Low-cost Innovation, more with less and for more people / MLM Innovation, Pro-

Poor Innovation / From-the-Poor, Resource-constrained Innovation / RCI, Reverse Innovation, Trickle-up Effect. He states no overall classification criteria, since he argues that "it is virtually impossible to classify the literature analyzed into a set of clearly defined and fixed categories" (p.55) and that "any taxonomy will degrade the complexity of each approach and would not take into account the fact that ideas, meanings and principles overlap and are dynamic in practically all the works considered" (p.55).

Pansera and Sarkar (2016) mention 16 various terms in relation to innovation at the BOP respectively innovation by the poor: Appropriate Technology, Below-the-Radar Innovation, Blowback Innovation, BOP Innovation, Bricolage Innovation, Disruptive Eco-Innovation, Empathetic Innovation, Frugal Innovation, Gandhian Innovation, Grassroots Innovation, Inclusive Innovation, Innovation by the Poor, Innovation for Underserved / Underserved Market / Underserved Costumer, Jugaad Innovation, Long Tail Innovation / Long Tailoring Innovation, Reverse Innovation. No overall classification criteria are stated.

Prabhu and Jain (2015) look at 18 various innovation constructs and theoretical domains related to Jugaad: Bricolage, Design Thinking, Disruptive Innovation, Effectuation, Frugal Engineering, Frugal Innovation, Gandhian Innovation, Grassroots Innovation, Improvisation, Inclusive Innovation, Indian Innovation, Indigenous Innovation, Innovation for Underserved / Underserved Communities, Jugaad Innovation, Lean Experimentation, Low-cost Innovation, more with less for more people / MLM Innovation, Reverse Innovation. The following elements are used to classify the various innovation constructs: frugality, flexibility, and inclusivity.

Rawat (2015) mentions 10 various terms inspired by Indian innovative traits: Bottom of the Pyramid Innovation, Frugal Innovation, Gandhian Innovation / Gandhian Engineering, Global Innovation, Grassroots Innovation, Inclusive Innovation, Indovation / Indian Innovation, Jugaad Innovation, MLM Innovation / More value for less cost for more people, Reverse Innovation. No overall classification criteria are stated.

Rosca et al. (2016) specify 18 various terms of innovation in the light of Frugal and Reverse Innovation: Blowback Innovation, Bottom of Pyramid Innovation, Catalytic Innovation, Cost Innovation, Disruptive Innovation, Frugal Engineering, Frugal Innovation, Gandhian Innovation, Global Innovation, Good-enough Innovation, Grassroots Innovation, Inclusive Innovation, Indigenous Innovation, Jugaad Innovation, Resource-constrained Innovation, Reverse Engineering, Reverse Innovation, Trickle-up Innovation. No explicit classification of the various terms is undertaken. Implicitly they state the following commonalities: impact, market opportunities, point of origin, target markets, sustainability impact. Furthermore, they distinguish the direction of innovation between (a) from developing countries to developing countries, (b) form industrialized countries to developing countries,

(c) from developing countries to industrialized countries (reverse), and (d) from industrialized countries to worldwide customers.

Soni and Krishnan (2014) look at 18 various key concepts that depict Frugal Innovation: Appropriate Technology, Bottom of pyramid Innovation, Bricolage, Disruptive Innovation, Effectuation, Frugal Engineering, Frugal Innovation, Gandhian Innovation, Grassroots-level Innovation, Improvisation, Inclusive Innovation, Indian Innovation, Innovation for Underserved / Underserved Markets / Underserved Customers, Jugaad, Lean Engineering, more with less for more / MLM Innovation, Reverse Engineering, Reverse Innovation. The various concepts are related to the nature of Frugal Innovation with three differentiations: mindset (Jugaad, Bricolage, Effectuation, Improvisation, Gandhian Innovation, Inclusive Innovation), process (Frugal Engineering, Lean Engineering), and outcome (Appropriate Technology, Disruptive Innovation, Bottom of Pyramid Innovation, Reverse Innovation). Furthermore, frugal innovators are classified into three types: grassroots-level, domestic-enterprise level, and MNC-subsidiary level.

Terrio (2014) looks at 13 various innovation concepts in developing countries: Blowback Innovation, Bottom of the Pyramid / BOP, Cost Innovation, Disruptive Innovation, Frugal Innovation, Gandhian Innovation, Global Innovation, Good-enough Innovation, Inclusive Innovation, Jugaad Innovation, Resource-constraint Innovation, Reverse Innovation, Trickle-up Innovation. No overall classification criteria are stated.

Von Zedtwitz et al. (2014) define 12 various terms relating to frequently used concepts of innovation for and from developing economies: Blowback Innovation, Cost Innovation, Disruptive Innovation, Frugal Innovation, Global Innovation, Indigenous Innovation, Innovation at the Bottom of the Pyramid, Jugaad / Gandhian Innovation, Resource-constrained Innovation, Reverse Innovation, Shanzhai Innovation, Trickle-up Innovation. No overall classification criteria are stated, but they distinguish the direction of innovation in 16 different possible combinations of two different specifications (advanced countries and developing countries) and four different categories (concept, development, primary market, and secondary market).

Zeschky et al. (2014a) mention 10 various terms concerning Resource-constrained Innovation: Base of the Economic Pyramid / Bottom of the Pyramid, Cost Innovation, Frugal Innovation, Gandhian Innovation, Global Innovation, Good-enough Innovation, Jugaad, Resource-constrained Innovation, Reverse Innovation, Trickle-up Innovation. They state the following criteria for a typology of Resource-constrained Innovation (as an umbrella term for Cost Innovation, Good-enough Innovation, Frugal Innovation, and Reverse Innovation) along with typical innovation traits and examples: product description, target customer, innovation strategy, type of innovation, and novelty of innovation.

Zeschky et al. (2014b) mention eight various terms in relation to innovations aimed at resource-constrained customers in emerging markets: Cost Innovation, Frugal Innovation, Gandhian Innovation, Good-enough Innovation, Jugaad, Resource-constraint Innovation / Resource-constrained Innovation, Reverse Innovation, Trickle-up Innovation. The following classification criteria are stated to categorize Cost, Good-enough, Frugal, and Reverse Innovations: market novelty and technical novelty. Furthermore, they state the same classification criteria as in their previously mentioned paper (Zeschky et al. 2014a).

RESULTS FOR THE IDENTIFIED INNOVATION CONCEPTS

As an initial result, we present in Table 2, the 33 identified concepts concerning innovation for and from emerging markets, classified by total mentions in the 19 texts.

Moreover, we further specified the identified terms and their various spellings and synonyms (c.f. Table 3). Different versions with hyphen are not included in Table 3. Along the combination of the main expression (e.g. 'frugal') with the phrase 'innovation' (e.g. 'frugal innovation'), other phrases can be found in the literature, for example 'solution', 'technology', 'product', 'service' or 'alternative' (e.g. 'frugal alternative'), and are also not included in Table 3.

Furthermore, the terms and concepts in relation to innovation for and from emerging markets were sometimes categorized in superordinate concepts. Millard (2014) considered these types of innovations as theoretical approaches to Social Innovation and Bhatti (2012), Hamacher (2014), and Pansera (2013, 2014) see these innovations embedded in the concept of Social Innovation. Pansera (2013, 2014) also name these types of innovation 'Heterodox Innovation' respectively "different, heterodox formulations of innovation and technical change in the so-called 'developing world'" (Pansera, 2014, p.14).

In Table 4, we present stated references with at least two mentions in the identified texts of the various terms in relation to innovation concepts for and from emerging markets.

Table 2. Terms in relation to innovation for and from emerging markets

Concept	Total Mentions
Frugal Innovation	19
Reverse Innovation	19
Jugaad Innovation	18
BOP Innovation	17
Gandhian Innovation	16
Cost Innovation	12
Disruptive Innovation	12
Inclusive Innovation	12
Grassroots Innovation	9
MLM Innovation (respectively phrase in conjunction with 'More', 'Less', 'More')	9
Resource-constrained Innovation	9
Trickle-up Innovation	9
Good-enough Innovation	8
Frugal Engineering	8
Innovation for Underserved (respectively phrase in conjunction with 'Underserved')	8
Appropriate Technology	7
Bricolage Innovation	7
Blowback Innovation	6
Indigenous Innovation	6
Below the Radar Innovation	5
Global Innovation	5
Reverse Engineering	5
Catalytic Innovation	4
Improvisation	4
Indovation (respectively 'Indian Innovation' or 'Hindolence')	4
Lean Engineering	4
Design Thinking	3
Empathetic Innovation	3
Pro-Poor Innovation	3
Effectuation	2
Extreme Affordability	2
Long Tail Innovation	2
Value Innovation	1
Vernacular equivalents in other languages	x

Table 3. Various spellings and synonyms of different terms in relation to innovation concepts for and from emerging markets

Concept	Various Spellings / Synonyms
Appropriate Technology	Intermediate Technology
Below the Radar Innovation	as umbrella term for BOP, Grassroots Innovation, Inclusive Innovation, and Jugaad
Blowback Innovation	Innovation Blowback, South-North Innovation Transfer, Reverse Innovation, Trickle-up Innovation
BOP Innovation	in conjunction with 'Innovation': BoP, Bottom of Pyramid, Bottom of the Pyramid, Base of the Pyramid, Bottom of the economic Pyramid, Base of the economic Pyramid, Bottom of the Economic Development Pyramid, Inclusive Innovation
Bricolage Innovation	Bricolage, Social Bricolage, Grassroots Innovation
Catalytic Innovation	
Cost Innovation	Low-cost Innovation, Frugal Innovation
Design Thinking	
Disruptive Innovation	
Effectuation	
Empathetic Innovation	
Extreme Affordability	
Frugal Engineering	Frugal Reengineering, Constraint-based Innovation
Frugal Innovation	Gandhian Innovation, Jugaad Innovation; as umbrella term for Jugaad, Bricolage, Effectuation, Improvisation, Gandhian Innovation, Inclusive Innovation, Frugal Engineering, Lean Engineering, Appropriate Technology, Disruptive Innovation, Bottom of Pyramid Innovation, and Reverse Innovation
Gandhian Innovation	Gandhian Engineering, Jugaad Innovation, Frugal Innovation
Global Innovation	Reverse Innovation
Good-enough Innovation	Frugal Innovation
Grassroots Innovation	Grassroots-level Innovation, Social Bricolage
Improvisation	Creative Improvisation, Jugaad Innovation
Inclusive Innovation	Inclusive Growth, Inclusive Development, Inclusive Innovation System, Inclusive Business Model, BOP Innovation, Gandhian Engineering
Indigenous Innovation	
Indovation	Indian Innovation, Hindolence
Innovation for Underserved	Innovation serving the Underserved, Solutions for Underserved, Innovating for the Underserved, Underserved Costumer, Underserved Communities, Underserved Population, Underserved Segments, Underserved Clients, Underserved Markets, Underserved Niches, Frugal Innovation, BOP Innovation, Jugaad
Jugaad Innovation	Jugaad, Gandhian Innovation, Frugal Innovation

continued on following page

Table 3. Continued

Concept	Various Spellings / Synonyms
Lean Engineering	Lean Engineering, Lean Product Development, Lean Manufacturing, Lean Experimentation
Long Tail Innovation	Long Tailoring Innovation
MLM (More value for Less cost for More people) Innovation	more with less for more, more with less for more people, more with less and for more people, more value for less cost for more people, Frugal Innovation
Pro-Poor Innovation	From-the-Poor-Innovation, Innovation by the Poor, Innovation for the poor by the poor
Resource-constrained Innovation	RCI, Resource-constraint Innovation, Innovation under Constraints, Constraint-based Innovation, Frugal Engineering; as umbrella term for Cost Innovation, Good-enough Innovation, Frugal Innovation, and Reverse Innovation
Reverse Engineering	
Reverse Innovation	Reverse Diffusion, Trickle-up Innovation, Blowback Innovation
Trickle-up Innovation	Trickle-up Effect, Reverse Innovation, Blowback Innovation, Bottom up Innovation
Value Innovation	
Vernacular equivalents of Bricolage, Frugal Innovation, and Indigenous Innovation in other languages	Arrangiarsi (Italy), Chapuza (Spain), DIY (USA), Gambiarra / Jeitinho (Brazil), Jua Kali (Kenya), Jugaad (India), Kanju (parts of Africa), Solution D / Systeme D (France), Zizhu Chuangxin / Jiejian Chuangxin / Shanzai (China)

DEVELOPMENT OF A CLASSIFICATION FRAMEWORK

As a first step to differentiate and classify the different terms and concepts related to innovation for and from emerging markets, we derive the following classification criteria from the analyzed papers. These criteria are presented in the following sections:

- market orientation
- determinants (of innovation for and from emerging markets)
- nature (of innovation for and from emerging markets)
- sophistication
- sustainability
- novelty
- innovator type

Table 4. References in relation to innovation concepts for and from emerging markets

Concept	References (at Least 2 Mentions)
Appropriate Technology	Kaplinsky, 1990; Kaplinsky, 2011; Schumacher, 1973; Smith, 2005
Below the Radar Innovation	Kaplinsky, 2011
Blowback Innovation	Brown & Hagel, 2005
BOP Innovation	Kanter, 2008; London & Hart, 2004; London, 2009; Prahalad & Hart, 2002; Prahalad, 2004; Prahalad, 2006; Prahalad & Mashelkar, 2010; Prahalad, 2012
Bricolage Innovation	Baker et al., 2003; Baker & Nelson, 2005; Gundry et al., 2011; Lévi-Strauss, 1966
Catalytic Innovation	Christensen et al., 2006
Cost Innovation	Von Hippel, 2005; Williamson, 2010; Zeng & Williamson, 2007
Design Thinking	Brown & Wyatt, 2010
Disruptive Innovation	Christensen, 1997; Hart & Christensen, 2002
Effectuation	Sarasvathy, 2001
Empathetic Innovation	Gupta, 2010; Gupta, 2012
Extreme Affordability	(no reference)
Frugal Engineering	Kumar & Puranam, 2012; Radjou et al., 2012; Sehgal et al., 2010
Frugal Innovation	Bound & Thornton, 2012; Gupta & Wang, 2009; Sharma & Iyer, 2012; Woolridge, 2010; Zeschky et al., 2011; Zeschky et al., 2014b
Gandhian Innovation	Prahalad & Mashelkar, 2010
Global Innovation	Von Zedtwitz et al., 2014
Good-enough Innovation	Gadiesh et al., 2007; Hang et al., 2010; Zeschky et al., 2014b
Grassroots Innovation	Seyfang & Smith, 2007
Improvisation	(only one mention) Bound & Thornton, 2012; Feldman & Pentland, 2003; Miner et al., 2001
Inclusive Innovation	George et al., 2012; Hall et al., 2012
Indigenous Innovation	Lazonick, 2004; Lu, 2000
Indovation (respectively 'Indian Innovation' or 'Hindolence')	(only one mention) Birtchnell, 2013; Krishnan, 2010; Sarasvathy, 2001; Tiwari & Herstatt, 2012
Innovation for Underserved (respectively phrase in conjunction with 'Underserved')	Prahalad, 2004; Prahalad & Mashelkar, 2010
Jugaad Innovation	Cappelli et al., 2010; Krishnan, 2010; Petrick & Juntiwasarakij, 2011; Prahalad & Mashelkar, 2010; Radjou et al., 2012; Sharma & Iyer, 2012
Lean Engineering	(only one mention) Ries, 2011; Womack et al., 1991
Long Tail Innovation	Anderson & Markides, 2007

continued on following page

Table 4. Continued

Concept	References (at Least 2 Mentions)
MLM Innovation (respectively phrase in conjunction with 'More', 'Less', 'More')	Prahalad & Mashelkar, 2010; Prahalad, 2012
Pro-Poor Innovation	Gupta, 2012
Resource-constrained Innovation	Ray & Ray, 2010; Ray & Ray, 2011
Reverse Engineering	Samuelson & Scotchmer, 2002
Reverse Innovation	Agarwal & Brem, 2012; Govindarajan & Ramamurti, 2011; Govindarajan, 2012; Govindarajan & Trimble, 2012; Immelt et al., 2009; Trimble, 2012
Trickle-up Innovation	Hart, 2011
Value Innovation	(only one mention) Kim & Mauborgne, 2005
Vernacular equivalents in other languages	Pansera, 2014; Prabhu & Jain, 2015; Radjou et al., 2012

Market Orientation

According to Brem and Wolfram (2014), "the terms vary concerning emerging, developed, or international markets in matter of sales or supply market" (p.12). For emerging market-oriented terms and concepts, emerging markets are the target market. In regards to global (respectively international) market-oriented terms, emerging and developed markets are combined, "either the concept originated in emerging markets but is applied in both or the BoP is the general focus without a specific sales market direction" (Brem & Wolfram, 2014, p.15). Developed market-oriented terms and concepts focus on developed markets as target markets (c.f. Table 5).

Table 5. Classification Criteria 'Market Orientation'

Emerging Market-Oriented	Global Market-Oriented	Developed Market-Oriented
• Jugaad Innovation • Gandhian Innovation • Frugal Innovation • Indigenous Innovation • Catalytic Innovation • Cost Innovation • Good-enough Innovation	• Reverse Innovation • Gandhian Innovation • Frugal Innovation • Frugal Engineering / Constraint-based Innovation • Grassroots Innovation	• Reverse Innovation

Based on Brem and Wolfram (2014), Ostraszewska and Tylec (2015), and Zeschky et al. (2014a, b)

For a more comprehensive classification, we suggest the classification criteria stated in Table 6 that specifies emerging market-orientation (excludes the category 'from developed markets to developed markets'), inspired by Rosca et al. (2016). This classification distinguishes between origin market ('from') and target market ('to').

For an even more detailed classification for 'market orientation', we refer to von Zedtwitz et al. (2015). They divide the idea of the origin market in 'concept' (the type of market respectively country, where a product is conceived) and 'development' (the type of market respectively country, where a product is developed). The idea of the target market is divided into 'primary market' (market, where the product is initially commercialized) and 'secondary market' (market, where the product is commercialized after the first commercialization). In our opinion, the division in 'primary market' and 'secondary market' is merged in the concept of 'global market', without consideration of the chronological sequence (first and second). However, with two different specifications (advanced countries and developing countries) in four different categories (concept, development, primary market, and secondary market) there are 16 different possible combinations in von Zedtwitz et al. (2015, p.18) "Map of Global Innovation Flows".

Table 6. Adapted Classification Criteria 'Market Orientation'

From Emerging Markets to Emerging Markets	From Emerging Markets to Global Markets	From Emerging Markets to Developed Markets	From Developed Markets to Global Markets	From Developed Markets to Emerging Markets
• Jugaad Innovation • Gandhian Innovation • Frugal Innovation • Indigenous Innovation • Catalytic Innovation • Cost Innovation • Good-enough Innovation	• Reverse Innovation / Global Innovation • Gandhian Innovation • Frugal Innovation • Frugal Engineering / Constraint-based Innovation • Grassroots Innovation	• Reverse Innovation / Blowback Innovation / Trickle-up Innovation	• "Classic Innovation" • (Grassroots Innovation)	• Appropriate Technology

Based on Brem and Wolfram (2014), Ostraszewska and Tylec (2015), Rosca et al. (2016), and Zeschky et al. (2014a, b)

Determinants (of Innovation for and From Emerging Market)

Determinants of innovation for and from emerging markets describe, "challenges of innovating for the underserved in emerging markets" (Bhatti, 2012, p.22) respectively main determinants that move innovation and technical change in the so-called 'developing world' (Pansera, 2013, p.15). According to Pansera (2013, p.16), the determinant 'Social Needs' describes solving social problems such as tackling poverty and its consequences, 'Resource Constraints' refers to the coping with scarce or inappropriate resources, and 'Market Affordability' respectively 'Affordability Constraints' (Bhatti, 2012) implies that the offered products or processes must be affordable. Furthermore, 'Institutional Voids' characterizes the market environment of innovations in emerging markets that includes faulty institutions, corruption, unclear property rights, inappropriate infrastructures, and cultural barriers. Lastly, the determinant 'Environmental Concerns' refers to the awareness of the environmental degradation caused by a fast development (c.f. Table 7).

Table 7. Classification Criteria 'Determinants'

Social Needs	Resource Constraints	Affordability Constraints	Institutional Voids	Environmental Concerns
• BOP • Grassroots Innovation • Inclusive Innovation • Gandhian Innovation • Indigenous Innovation • Catalytic Innovation	• BOP • Bricolage • Frugal Innovation • Frugal Engineering • Grassroots Innovation • Gandhian Innovation • Improvisation • Jugaad Innovation • Reverse Engineering • Reverse Innovation • Resource-constrained Innovation • Cost Innovation • Good-enough Innovation	• BOP • Design Thinking • Frugal Innovation • Jugaad Innovation • Inclusive Innovation • Gandhian Innovation • Cost Innovation • Good-enough Innovation • Reverse Innovation	• Frugal Innovation • Inclusive Innovation • Jugaad Innovation	• Grassroots Innovation • Frugal Innovation

Based on Bhatti (2012), Brem and Wolfram (2014), Ostraszewska and Tylec (2015), Pansera (2013), Prabhu and Jain (2015), and Zeschky et al. (2014a, b)

Nature (of Innovation for and From Emerging Markets)

Soni and Krishnan (2014) "highlight that "frugality", as a concept, has existed in various disciplines for a long time" (p.33). In their opinion, frugal innovations involve some combination of frugal mindset, frugal process, and frugal outcome (c.f. Table 8). A "frugal mindset is encouraged by a resource-scarce environment, weaker institutional intermediaries, and a higher tolerance for uncertainty. Frugal processes are espoused by poor property rights regime and a critical size of lead market; and frugal outcomes are influenced by the network-position of innovators, and the presence of critical lead-markets" (Soni & Krishnan, 2014, p.29).

Sophistication

According to Brem and Wolfram (2014), sophistication of a term related to innovation for and from emerging markets "is evaluated by the complexity of inherent processes as well as the interaction of the categories involved (communication and coordination level)" (p.12) (c.f. Table 9).

Sustainability

A closer look on the determinant 'Environmental Concerns', reveals that it can be further distinguished (c.f. Table 10). Brem and Wolfram (2014) suggest a classification in low/ medium/ high sustainability and thus in social responsibility and ecological responsibility.

Novelty

Zeschky et al. (2014a) "employed the established dimensions of product and market novelty (Ansoff, 1965) as a conceptual framework to analyze if and how the product examples [related to cost, good-enough, frugal, and reverse innovation] were new

Table 8. Classification Criteria 'Nature'

Mindset	Process	Outcome
• Jugaad • Bricolage • Effectuation • Improvisation • Gandhian Innovation • Inclusive Innovation	• Frugal Engineering • Lean Engineering	• Appropriate Technology • Disruptive Innovation • Bottom of Pyramid Innovation • Reverse Innovation

Based on Soni and Krishnan (2014)

Table 9. Classification Criteria 'Sophistication'

Low Sophistication (Almost No Coordination or Systematic Communication)	Low-Medium Sophistication	Medium Sophistication (at Least a Minimum Level of Communication Between People of the Same Group to Coordinate Them)	Medium- High Sophistication	High Sophistication (Sophisticated Level of Coordination, Communication, and Process Complexity)
• Jugaad Innovation • Grassroots Innovation	• Gandhian Innovation • Frugal Innovation	• Catalytic Innovation • Frugal Engineering / Constraint-based Innovation • Indigenous Innovation		• Reverse Innovation

Based on Brem and Wolfram (2014)

Table 10. Classification Criteria 'Sustainability'

Low Sustainability (No Social and Ecological Responsibility Included)	Medium Sustainability (Social or Ecological Responsibility Focused)	High Sustainability (Social and Ecological Responsibility Focused)
• Jugaad Innovation • Frugal Engineering / Constraint-based Innovation • Reverse Innovation	• Gandhian Innovation • Frugal Innovation • Catalytic Innovation • Indigenous Innovation	• Grassroots Innovation

Based on Brem and Wolfram (2014)

compared to existing standards" (p.5) (c.f. Table 11 and Table 12). "In the Ansoff matrix, innovations are distinguished according to their technical and market novelty; the matrix thus classifies innovations by whether they are market extensions based on existing technologies, original product development activities for existing markets, or newly developed products for entirely new markets" (Zeschky, Winterhalter, & Gassmann, 2014b, p.3).

Innovator Type

Soni and Krishnan (2014) state that frugal innovators operate at three levels: grassroots, domestic-enterprises, and MNC-subsidiaries (c.f. Table 13). "Grassroots-level frugal innovators are individuals or a group of people who attempt to solve a given

Table 11. Classification Criteria 'Technical Novelty'

Low Technical Novelty	Low-Medium Technical Novelty	Medium Technical Novelty	Medium-High Technical Novelty	High Technical Novelty
• Cost Innovation	• Good-enough Innovation • Jugaad Innovation • Reverse Innovation	• Good-enough Innovation • Gandhian Innovation	• Good-enough Innovation • Frugal Innovation	• Frugal Innovation • Disruptive Innovation

Based on Ostraszewska and Tylec (2015), and Zeschky et al. (2014a, b)

Table 12. Classification Criteria 'Market Novelty'

Low Market Novelty	Low-Medium Market Novelty	Medium Market Novelty	Medium-High Market Novelty	High Market Novelty
• Reverse Innovation • Cost Innovation	• Reverse Innovation • Good-enough Innovation	• Reverse Innovation	• Reverse Innovation	• Reverse Innovation • Frugal Innovation • Disruptive Innovation

Based on Ostraszewska and Tylec (2015), and Zeschky et al. (2014a, b)

Table 13. Classification Criteria 'Innovator Type'

Grassroots Innovators (Single Entrepreneurs, Local Communities, Micro Firms, Clusters of Micro-Firms)	Domestic-Enterprise Innovators (Cooperatives, Small Firms, Network or Clusters of Firms)	MNC-Subsidiary Innovators (National or Public Firms, Multinational Corporations)
• Frugal Innovation • Grassroots Innovation • Inclusive Innovation • Jugaad Innovation	• Frugal Innovation • Jugaad Innovation	• Frugal Innovation • BOP Innovation

Based on Pansera (2013), and Soni and Krishnan (2014)

problem adopting locally available ingenuity and in doing so creates a novel solution. […] [T]here are several domestic firms which have reconfigured their processes and business models to address the fledging domestic market mostly located at the base of economic pyramid. We call them as domestic-corporate frugal innovators. […] The last category includes the MNC-subsidiary frugal innovators. The large domestic market, coupled with cheap and good quality talent available in India and China has attracted several MNCs" (Soni & Krishnan, 2014, p.35).

SUMMARY, IMPLICATIONS AND OUTLOOK

Due to the high variety of terms and concepts related to innovation for and from emerging markets (e.g. 17 various terms in Bhatti & Ventresca, 2012; 16 in Hamacher, 2014; 20 in Pansera, 2013; 23 in Pansera, 2014; 16 in Pansera & Sarkar, 2016; 18 in Prabhu & Jain, 2015; 18 in Rosca, Arnold, & Bendul, 2016; and 18 in Soni & Krishnan, 2014), we provided a comprehensive overview of 33 of these terms and concepts and confirmed the synonymously use. Furthermore, we proposed a framework built on seven classification criteria, suggested from different authors to differentiate the terms and concepts in our chapter.

As a suggestion to visualize the classification (excluding the criteria determinants and nature of innovation for and from emerging market), we present in Figure 1 a radar chart using the example of Frugal Innovation and Reverse Innovation. By analyzing the different innovation concepts in a systematic manner and visualizing the results in form of a radar chart, we reduce complexity and make comparisons easier.

The next step should include classifying further terms and concepts that have not yet been classified by our proposed framework. In the course of this classification, it may be possible that some categories need to be modified and that new categories may be identified or need to be created. It will be a challenge to classify all terms and concepts related to innovation for and from emerging markets "into a set of clearly defined and fixed categories" (Pansera, 2014, p.55), because the definitions of terms related to innovation for and from emerging markets are manifold and dynamic. In order to illustrate this issue, we take the definition of BOP Innovation

Figure 1. Radar chart for the classification of frugal innovation and reverse innovation

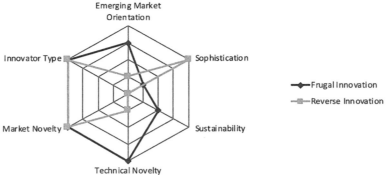

with regard to Prahalad (the poor as consumers) or to London and Hart (the poor as co-creators). Finally, the concepts are complex and full of overlapping ideas, meanings, characteristics, principles, and examples.

Based on these classification criteria, we propose that this classification framework could be used for further research and teaching in innovation, responsible and sustainable management disciplines. As an instruction tool, it could be used to raise awareness for blurry terminology in this area. This is especially relevant for the discourse and evaluation of cases, proposals and examples in sustainable innovation, responsible and sustainable management disciplines and practices. It could also act as a guide through the jungle of recent buzzwords that claim novelty and/or sustainability. Moreover, the classification framework could also be used for a critical discussion of the value added to many of these concepts or their use in specific contexts. This could aim for more responsibility in the research community of the innovation discipline as well as the practice for more disciplined and responsible use of concepts. Perhaps some frugality would add some value here, too.

However, based on the findings in our chapter we suggest that further research should focus on the theoretical and empirical consideration of the aspect of sustainability in concepts related to innovation for and from emerging markets. We see the potential in innovation for and from emerging markets to contribute to the idea of sustainability, e.g. frugal products as a concept for growth-neutral corporations (in the context of de-growth) or as a concept for a circular economy. Especially, more empirical research in this regard could enhance our understanding of related innovation concepts. Finally, further research could also illuminate the underlying schools of thought, networks and development trajectories over time that were created around these concepts. A historiographic approach could reveal the academic progress and might reveal the root concepts that other "me-too"-terminology adapted or even ignored. Using a quantitative approach based on word counts or other impact factors could distort real relevance by economies of attention and marking power by certain institutions. In retrospect, an intellectual history of this research stream and its usage in teaching or practice could be a promising endeavor.

REFERENCES

Agarwal, N., & Brem, A. (2012). Frugal and reverse innovation—literature overview and case study insights from a German MNC in India and China. *Proceedings of the 18th International Conference on Engineering, Technology and Innovation.*

Anderson, J., & Markides, C. (2007). Strategic Innovation at the base of the pyramid. *MIT Sloan Management Review, 49*(49116), 83–88.

Ansoff, H. I. (1965). *Corporate strategy*. New York: McGraw-Hill.

Baker, T., Miner, A., & Easley, D. (2003). Improvising firms: Bricolage, retrospective interpretation and improvisational competencies in the founding process. *Research Policy, 32*, 255–276. doi:10.1016/S0048-7333(02)00099-9

Baker, T., & Nelson, R. E. (2005). Creating something from nothing: Resource construction through entrepreneurial bricolage. *Administrative Science Quarterly, 50*(3), 329–366. doi:10.2189/asqu.2005.50.3.329

Bhatti, Y. (2012). *What is frugal, what is innovation? Towards a theory of frugal innovation* (SSRN Working Paper). Retrieved from Social Science Research Network website: https://papers.ssrn.com/sol3/papers.cfm?abstract_id=2005910

Bhatti, Y., & Ventresca, M. (2012). *The emerging market for frugal innovation - fad, fashion, or fit?* (SSRN Working Paper). Retrieved from Social Science Research Network website: https://papers.ssrn.com/sol3/papers.cfm?abstract_id=2005983

Bhatti, Y., & Ventresca, M. (2013). *How can 'frugal innovation' be conceptualized?* Said Business School Working Paper.

Birtchnell, T. (2013). *Indovation: Innovation and a Global Knowledge Economy in India*. Basingstoke, UK: Palgrave MacMillan. doi:10.1057/9781137027412

Bound, K., & Thornton, I. (2012). *Our frugal future: Lesson from India's innovation System*. London, UK: NESTA.

Brem, A., & Wolfram, P. (2014). Research and development from the bottom up - Introduction of terminologies for new product development in emerging markets. *Journal of Innovation and Entrepreneurship, 3*(9).

Brown, J. S., & Hagel, J. (2005). Innovation blowback: Disruptive management practices from Asia. *The McKinsey Quarterly, 1*(1), 35–45.

Brown, T., & Wyatt, J. (2010). Design thinking for social innovation. *Stanford Social Innovation Review, 8*(1), 30–35.

Bubel, D., Ostraszewska, Z., Turek, T., & Tylec, A. (Eds.). (2015). Innovation in developing countries - a new approach. In *Proceedings of the, 10th International Conference on European Integration - Realities and Perspectives (EIRP Vol.10)*. Galati, Romania: Danubius University Press.

Cappelli, P., Singh, H., Singh, J., & Useem, M. (2010). The India way: Lessons for the US. *The Academy of Management Perspectives, 24*(2), 6–24. doi:10.5465/amp.24.2.6

Chataway, J., Hanlin, R., & Kaplinsky, R. (2014). Inclusive innovation - an architecture for policy development. *Innovation and Development*, *4*(1), 33–54. doi:10.1080/2157930X.2013.876800

Christensen, C. M. (1997). *The innovator's dilemma: when new technologies cause great firms to fail*. Cambridge, MA: Harvard Business Review Press.

Christensen, C. M., Baumann, H., Ruggles, R., & Sadtler, T. M. (2006). Disruptive innovation for social change. *Harvard Business Review*, *84*(12), 94–101. PMID:17183796

Feldman, M. S., & Pentland, B. T. (2003). Reconceptualizing organizational routines as a source of flexibility and change. *Administrative Science Quarterly*, *48*(1), 94–118. doi:10.2307/3556620

Gadiesh, O., Leung, P., & Vestring, T. (2007). The battle for China's good-enough market. *Harvard Business Review*, *85*(9), 81–89.

George, G., Macgahan, A., & Prabhu, J. (2012). Innovation for inclusive growth: Towards a theoretical framework and a research agenda. *Journal of Management Studies*, *49*(4), 662–683. doi:10.1111/j.1467-6486.2012.01048.x

Govindarajan, V. (2012). A reverse innovation playbook. *Harvard Business Review*, *90*(4), 120–124.

Govindarajan, V., & Ramamurti, R. (2011). Reverse Innovation, Emerging Markets, and Global Strategy. *Global Strategy Journal*, *1*(3-4), 191–205. doi:10.1002/gsj.23

Govindarajan, V., & Trimble, C. (2012). *Reverse innovation: create far from home, win everywhere*. Boston, MA: Harvard Business School Press. doi:10.5437/08956308X5506003

Gundry, L. K., Kickul, J. R., Griffiths, M. D., & Bacq, S. C. (2007). Creating social change out of nothing: the role of entrepreneurial bricolage in social entrepreneurs' catalytic innovations. In G. T. Lumpkin & J. A. Katz (Eds.), *Social and sustainable entrepreneurship: Advances in entrepreneurship, firm emergence, and growth* (pp. 1–24). Bingley, UK: Emereld Group Publishing.

Gupta, A. (2010). Empathetic innovations: Connections across boundaries. In R. Mashelkar (Ed.), *Timeless Inspirator - Reliving Gandhi* (pp. 43–57). Pune, India: Sakal Papers.

Gupta, A. (2012). Innovations for the poor by the poor. *International Journal of Technological Learning, Innovation and Development*, *5*(1-2), 28–39.

Gupta, A., & Wang, H. (2009). *Getting China and India right: strategies for leveraging the world's fastest-growing economies for global advantage*. San Francisco, CA: Wiley.

Hall, J., Matos, S., Sheehan, L., & Silvestre, B. (2012). Entrepreneurship and innovation at the base of the pyramid: A recipe for inclusive growth or social exclusion? *Journal of Management Studies*, *49*(4), 785–812. doi:10.1111/j.1467-6486.2012.01044.x

Hamacher, S. (2014). *Exploring the frugal innovation process: an empirical study of a new emerging market phenomenon* (Master's thesis). Copenhagen Business School. Retrieved from http://studenttheses.cbs.dk/handle/10417/4943

Hang, C., Chen, J., & Subramian, A. M. (2010). Developing disruptive products for emerging economies: Lessons from Asian cases. *Research Technology Management*, *53*(4), 21–26. doi:10.1080/08956308.2010.11657637

Hart, S. (2011). Taking the green leap to the base of the pyramid. In T. London & S. L. Hart (Eds.), *Next Generation Business Strategies for the Base of the Pyramid. New Approaches for Building Mutual Value* (pp. 79–101). Upper Saddle River, NJ: Pearson Education.

Hart, S. L., & Christensen, C. M. (2002). The great leap: Driving innovation from the base of the pyramid. *MIT Sloan Management Review*, *44*(1), 51–56.

Immelt, J., Govindarajan, V., & Trimble, C. (2009). How GE is disrupting itself. *Harvard Business Review*, *87*(10), 56–65.

Kanter, R. M. (2008). Transforming giants. *Harvard Business Review*, *86*(1), 43–52, 136. PMID:18271317

Kaplinsky, R. (1990). *The Economies of Small: Appropriate Technology in a Changing World*. London, UK: Intermediate Technology Press. doi:10.3362/9781780440729

Kaplinsky, R. (2011). Schumacher meets Schumpeter: Appropriate technology below the radar. *Research Policy*, *40*(2), 193–203. doi:10.1016/j.respol.2010.10.003

Kim, W. C., & Mauborgne, R. (2005). *Blue ocean strategy: How to create uncontested market space and make competition irrelevant*. Boston, MA: Harvard Business School Press.

Krishnan, R. (2010). *From jugaad to systematic innovation: The challenge for India*. Bangalore, India: Utpreraka Foundation.

Kumar, N., & Puranam, P. (2012). *India inside: The emerging innovation challenge to the west*. Boston, MA: Harvard Business Press.

Lazonick, W. (2004). Indigenous innovation and economic development: Lessons from china's leap into the information age. *Industry and Innovation, 11*(4), 273–297. doi:10.1080/1366271042000289360

Lévi-Strauss, C. (1967). *The savage mind*. Chicago, IL: University of Chicago Press.

London, T. (2009). Making better investments at the base of the pyramid. *Harvard Business Review, 87*(5), 106–113.

London, T., & Hart, S. L. (2004). Reinventing strategies for emerging markets: Beyond the transnational model. *Journal of International Business Studies, 35*(5), 350–370. doi:10.1057/palgrave.jibs.8400099

Lu, Q. (2000). *China's leap into the information age: Innovation and organization in the computer industry*. New York, NY: Oxford University Press. doi:10.1093/ac prof:oso/9780198295372.001.0001

Millard, J. (2014). Development Theory. In J. Howaldt, A. Butzin, D. Domanski, & C. Kaletka (Eds.), Theoretical approaches to social innovation – a critical literature review (pp. 34-59). Collaborative project: Social Innovation - Driving Force of Social Change.

Miner, A., Bassof, P., & Moorman, C. (2001). Organizational improvisation and learning: A field study. *Administrative Science Quarterly, 46*(2), 304–337. doi:10.2307/2667089

Ostraszewska, Z., & Tylec, A. (2015). Reverse innovation – how it works. *International Journal of Business and Management, 3*(1), 57–74. doi:10.20472/BM.2015.3.1.004

Pansera, M. (2013). Frugality, grassroots and inclusiveness - new challenges for mainstream innovation theories. *African Journal of Science, Technology, Innovation and Development, 5*(6), 469–478.

Pansera, M. (2014). *Discourses of innovation and development - Insights from ethnographic case studies in Bangladesh and India* (Unpublished doctoral dissertation). University of Exeter, UK.

Pansera, M., & Sarkar, S. (2016). Crafting sustainable development solutions – Frugal innovations of grassroots entrepreneurs. *Sustainability, 8*(1), 1–25. doi:10.3390u8010051

Petrick, I. J., & Juntiwasarakij, S. (2011). The rise of the rest: Hotbeds of innovation in emerging markets. *Research Technology Management, 54*(4), 24–29. doi:10.5437/08956308X5404009

Prabhu, J., & Jain, S. (2015). Innovation and entrepreneurship in India - Understanding jugaad. *Asia Pacific Journal of Management, 32*(4), 843–868. doi:10.100710490-015-9445-9

Prahalad, C. K. (2004). *The fortune at the bottom of the pyramid: Eradicating poverty through profits*. Upper Saddle River, NJ: Pearson Education.

Prahalad, C. K. (2006). The innovation sandbox. *Strategy and Business, 44*, 1–10.

Prahalad, C. K. (2012). Bottom of the pyramid as a source of breakthrough innovations. *Journal of Product Innovation Management, 29*(1), 6–12. doi:10.1111/j.1540-5885.2011.00874.x

Prahalad, C. K., & Hart, S. L. (2002). The fortune at the bottom of the pyramid. *Strategy + Business, 22*, 2-14.

Prahalad, C. K., & Mashelkar, R. A. (2010). Innovation's Holy Grail. *Harvard Business Review, 88*(7), 1–11.

Radjou, N., Prabhu, J., & Ahuja, S. (2012). *Jugaad innovation: Think frugal, be flexible, generate breakthrough growth*. San Francisco, CA: Wiley.

Rawat, A. (2015). *SI, 2 - Trajectory of change - Remodelling India's national innovation system for sustainable development & inclusive growth*. Paper presented at the, 24th International Association for Management of Technology Conference (IAMOT '15), Cape Town, South Africa.

Ray, P. K., & Ray, S. (2010). Resource-constrained innovation for emerging economies: The case of the indian telecommunications industry. *IEEE Transactions on Engineering Management, 57*(1), 144–156. doi:10.1109/TEM.2009.2033044

Ray, S., & Ray, P. K. (2011). Product innovation for the people's car in an emerging economy. *Technovation, 31*(5–6), 216–227. doi:10.1016/j.technovation.2011.01.004

Ries, E. (2011). *The lean startup: How today's entrepreneurs use continuous innovation to create radically successful businesses*. New York, NY: Random House.

Rosca, E., Bendul, J. C., & Arnold, M. (2016). Business models for sustainable innovation - an empirical analysis of frugal products and services. *Journal of Cleaner Production, 20*, 133–145.

Samuelson, P., & Scotchmer, S. (2002). The law and economics of reverse engineering. *The Yale Law Journal, 111*(7), 1575–1663. doi:10.2307/797533

Sarasvathy, S. D. (2001). Causation and effectuation: Toward a theoretical shift from economic inevitability to entrepreneurial contingency. *Academy of Management Review, 26*(2), 243–263. doi:10.5465/amr.2001.4378020

Schumacher, E. F. (1973). *Small is beautiful.* New York: Harper & Row.

Sehgal, V., Dehoff, K., & Panneer, G. (2010). The importance of frugal engineering. *Strategy Business, 59,* 1–5.

Seyfang, G., & Smith, A. (2007). Grassroots innovations for sustainable development: Towards a new research and policy agenda. *Environmental Politics, 16*(4), 584–603. doi:10.1080/09644010701419121

Sharma, A., & Iyer, G. R. (2012). Resource-constrained product development: Implications for green marketing and green supply chains. *Industrial Marketing Management, 41*(4), 599–608. doi:10.1016/j.indmarman.2012.04.007

Smith, A. (2005). The alternative technology movement: An analysis of its framing and negotiation of technology development. *Human Ecology, 12*(2), 106–119.

Soni, P., & Krishnan, R. T. (2014). Frugal innovation - aligning theory, practice, and public policy. *Journal of Indian Business Research, 6*(1), 29–47. doi:10.1108/JIBR-03-2013-0025

Terrio, M. (2014). *Examining reverse innovation and collaboration: a case study in the context of Uganda* (Master's thesis). Aalto University. Retrieved from https://aaltodoc.aalto.fi/handle/123456789/15275

Tiwari, R., & Herstatt, C. (2012). Assessing India's lead market potential for cost-effective innovations. *Journal of Indian Business Research, 4*(2), 97–115. doi:10.1108/17554191211228029

Trimble, C. (2012). Reverse innovation and the emerging-market growth imperative. *Ivey Business Journal, 76*(2), 19–21.

Von Hippel, E. (2005). *Democratizing Innovation.* Cambridge, MA: MIT Press. doi:10.7551/mitpress/2333.001.0001

Von Zedtwitz, M., Corsi, S., Søberg, P. V., & Frega, R. (2015). A typology of reverse innovation. *Journal of Product Innovation Management, 32*(1), 12–28. doi:10.1111/jpim.12181

Williamson, P. (2010). Cost innovation: Preparing for a "value-for-money" revolution. *Long Range Planning*, *43*(2-3), 343–353. doi:10.1016/j.lrp.2009.07.008

Womack, J., Jones, D., & Roos, D. (1991). *The machine that changed the world*. New York, NY: Harper-Collins.

Woolridge, A. (2010). The world turned upside down. A special report on innovation in emerging markets. *The Economist*. Retrieved from http://www.economist.com/node/15879369

Zeng, M., & Williamson, P. J. (2007). *Dragons at your door: How Chinese cost innovation is disrupting the rules of global competition*. Boston, MA: Harvard Business School Press.

Zeschky, M. B., Widenmayer, B., & Gassmann, O. (2011). Frugal innovation in emerging markets. *Research Technology Management*, *54*(4), 38–45. doi:10.5437/08956308X5404007

Zeschky, M. B., Winterhalter, S., & Gassmann, O. (2014a). Resource-constrained innovation - Classification and implications for multinational firms. *Proceedings of the XXV Innovation for Sustainable Economy and Society Conference (ISPIM XXV '14)*.

Zeschky, M. B., Winterhalter, S., & Gassmann, O. (2014b). From cost to frugal and reverse innovation: Mapping the field and implications for global competitiveness. *Research Technology Management*, *57*(4), 20–27.

KEY TERMS AND DEFINITIONS

Bottom of the Pyramid: Approximately four billion people, living on less than US $2 a day, and coming from different cultures, ethnic groups, with diverse needs and abilities.

Classification: A process in which ideas and objects (inter alia terms and theories) are recognized, differentiated, and understood.

Emerging Markets: Countries that has some characteristics of a developed market and investing in more productive capacity but does not satisfy standards to be termed a developed market.

Frugal Innovation: A new solution, usually a product, which is generated through a new rethought process (compared to conventional innovation processes). Frugal innovation can be characterized by substantial cost reduction, concentration on core functionalities, and optimized performance level. Initiators can range from big multinational corporations to individuals and grassroots entrepreneurs. The market context is always an emerging one; sometimes the perspective expands to an industrialized market context.

Innovation: Innovation is an iterative, interactive, context-specific, multi-activity, uncertain, path-dependent process and the result of a new combination of ends and means from a certain perspective. From this perspective, someone must perceive a difference concerning the qualitative newness of an object compared to a prior status in a given context. This new combination must be realized, introduced and diffused into a specific context, which is the point of reference of the prior status.

Jugaad: An improvisational style of innovation with attention to the immediate needs of customers and consisting of overcoming limitations, like scarce resources.

Reverse Innovation: The development of new ideas and products in and for emerging markets, which will be introduced equally in developed markets. Focus on the flow of innovations from emerging markets to developed markets as compared to the predominant and historical flow from developed markets to from emerging markets.

Section 3
Global Responsible and Sustainable Management Competencies to Drive Responsible and Sustainable Business Practices

Chapter 5
Marketing to Develop Environmental Sustainability, Awareness, and Action

Sangeeta Trott
ITM-SIA Business School, India

ABSTRACT

The main purpose of the chapter is to understand the role of marketing in creating awareness and action for sustainability in the fourth industrial revolution. The chapter is sequenced as follows: It begins with a brief introduction, followed by exploring the relationship between marketing and sustainability. The chapter then explains how marketing can play an important role in developing awareness and action at various phases of sustainability with suitable examples. The chapter then discusses the various issues which one faces in sustainability and ends with a conclusion. The chapter has great theoretical and managerial implications.

INTRODUCTION

Sustainability has become a mega trend It is one of the most important concept of business thinking (Peattie, 2001). In 1987 World commission on environment and development called 'Brundtland commission" gave the term 'sustainable development'. The united Nations report on World Commission on Environment and development (1987) views sustainable development "as a kind of development that meets the needs of the present without compromising on the company ability to meet future generation". Sustainable development requires integration of various elements into sustainability viz; economic sustainability, social sustainability and

DOI: 10.4018/978-1-5225-7638-9.ch005

Copyright © 2019, IGI Global. Copying or distributing in print or electronic forms without written permission of IGI Global is prohibited.

environmental sustainability It has become the need of the hour. In order to make the planet highly sustainable. All countries are gearing for the noble cause. In view of increasing demand for sustainability companies have started incorporating sustainability due to the following reasons a) there is an increasing pressure upon companies to adopt sustainable practices on account of environmental and social legislations. b) companies themselves are concerned about the environment on account of increasing paucity of resources c) changes in the attitude of the people to adopt environmental practices. One of the most important aid in promoting sustainability is marketing. Marketing has been called, "ministers of propaganda of consumer culture". Marketing so far was based on assumption on infinite resources and environmental impact. In view of increasing concern for the environment there is an imperative need to redefine marketing in terms of product, price, place and promotion to meet the noble cause.(Kotler, 2011).Marketing comes to play an important role in decision making towards sustainability For example, reducing carbon dioxide, recycling waste etc. A study of the behaviour of the consumers towards sustainable products can help the organizations to better understand the role of marketing towards sustainability .Whenever a buyer is exposed with sustainable products; he will always try to understand the product from various aspects i.e, price, brand availability and in order to understand the concept of sustainability better it is always important to study the buyer's purchase decision. Hence, sustainable purchasing behaviour should be inculcated in the consumers in their daily food habits rather than purchase of big items The main objective of the chapter is to discuss how marketing can play an important role to develop environmental sustainability, awareness and action in the fourth industrial revolution.

BACKGROUND

The world has witnessed significant changes through various types of industrial revolution. The first industrial revolution (1820-1840) brought tremendous success for India's economic development; for instance, it used water and steam power to enhance production. The second revolution(1870-1914) laid emphasis on mass production; for instance, tele-communication changed the way India communicated using technology per se, and thus turned India into a global village. The third industrial revolution was characterised by Internet of Things (IoT), whereby it used electronics and information to automate production. The last and the current industrial revolution, the fourth in the list, lay emphasis on 'digital revolution'.

All the industrial revolutions witnessed significant growth on several important aspects of life, and the world strode forward boldly, making rapid progress on the socio-economic fronts; but, whatever came, was at the cost of the planet. Hence, sustainability and social innovation has thus become the need of the hour, adding another dimension to the fourth industrial revolution (i.e. Digital Revolution), commonly known as 'Industry 4' in Germany.

The fourth industrial revolution also known as 4.0 is rightly termed as the 'smart factory' (Dutton, 2014).A smart factory consists of a physical world with a decentralized form of decision-making. Industry 4.0 is concerned with various trends like digitization and connectivity (Horx 2015; Huer, 2015) It is also called 'sustainability revolution' as it can solve problems of the people and the planet. It involves disruptive technologies such as internet of things, robotics, virtual reality and artificial intelligence. It is the first of its kind with major emphasis on sustainability. Unlike Previous industrial revolutions were thrust down in the system in order to improve the socio- economics of the country, but unfortunately, this was at the cost of adhering to sustainability.

COMPONENTS OF FOURTH INDUSTRIAL REVOLUTION

The various components of fourth industrial revolution have been discussed below:

- **Interoperability**: Is concerned with the exchange of machines and equipment that perform the same functions. This helps in the creation of proper intelligent functions.
- **Decentralization**: One of the most important aspects of decentralization is to allow computers as well as companies to make decisions. This decentralization helps to grant more flexibility and also helps in gaining specialized knowledge.
- **Virtualization**: Is another important component of the industrial revolution in which a physical world is created. In case of failure a human being can be notified.
- **Real Time Capability**: Real time capability involves that the data collected is organized in real time. It includes plants that react to the failure of the machine and forward to another machine
- **Modularity**: Involves flexibility to the changing environment by replacing or expanding individuals which makes adding or removing production modules in an easy way.
- **Service Orientation**: Helps to be flexible and respond to market changes more quickly than they used in the enterprise.

Industry 4.0 and Sustainability

Industry 4.0 has a close connection with sustainability and each of the elements work towards sustainability. For example, interoperability helps to decrease industrial waste and also works faster in the adaptation of efficient processes. Decentralization helps in optimum allocation of the resources. Virtualization helps to decrease industrial waste and also helps in recycling of opportunities. Real time capabilities helps in better adaptation of demand curves, better use of the resources and faster adaptation of efficient resources. Modularity provides better usage of resources and longer machine life and service orientation helps in improved use of the products.

Marketing has come to play an important role in creating awareness and action in the era of fourth industrial revolution. Therefore, the main aim objective of the chapter is to explain the role of marketing in the fourth industrial revolution and how does it create awareness and action in the event of fourth industrial revolution. The chapter also spells out the theoretical and practical contributions of the study.

THEORETICAL FRAMEWORK

Relation Between Marketing and Sustainability

The two terms 'marketing' and 'sustainability' thereby may seem inter-related, but there is a huge difference between them.

Marketing and sustainability are effectively two diverse trends. In fact, marketing is considered as an 'antithesis of sustainability'; while the former (i.e. Marketing) is primarily a driver of consumption, the latter enables people around the world to satisfy their basic needs and desires. Therefore, there is a need to find out whether or not there's any link between marketing and sustainability.

Marketing is said to play a key role in sustainability; but, in effect, marketing plays a key role in decision-making in the effort towards sustainability by influencing the process of decision–making, which in turn influences the attitude and behaviour of consumers. Consumers, on the other hand, are predisposed to purchase sustainable products; therefore, their buying behaviour is influenced by various constructs like price, brand availability etc. However, research has shown that consumers find it hard to follow 'green practices'. The relationship between marketing and sustainability can thus possibly be termed as a 'chalk and cheese relationship'. However, to make marketing work towards sustainability, the following things are to be kept in mind, including: a) remove barriers like lack of choice, cost convenience, time and effort, b) a need to work closely with corporations c) changes in behaviour should be achieved by penalties when one talks of fourth industrial revolution marketing has come to play an important role. Marketing can rely on some of the very important features of fourth industrial revolution like internet of things, big data analytics to provide customized products to the customers and create awareness and action about sustainability.

However, marketing has an important role in the adoption of industrial revolution 4.0.Industry 4.0 is a technological revolution happening at the factory level. Changing the way products are made in the context of marketing seems to play a marginal role in respect of product. Marketing is at the base of decisions by the firms. They can help to increase flexibility and reduce production costs. Customization is an important asset in the fourth industrial revolution buying together B2B and B2C customers. Firms have started using customer centric business to understand the production and engage in the production process.

LITERATURE REVIEW

Few pieces of literature exists to explore the relationship between marketing and sustainability.

Peter Jones (2008) discussed the relevant issues regarding marketing and sustainability. Some believe that marketing does not play a role in achieving sustainability. While others believe that marketing can play an important role in achieving sustainability. Marketing has the potential to contribute to the establishment of more sustainable society. Marketers play an active role in seeking competitive advantage through environmental friendliness (Ajike et al., 2015).

Marketing plays an important role in shaping customer behaviour and influencing attitude and beliefs. As such marketing can play an important role in decision making. It plays an important role in carbon emission, recycling waste and adopting a healthier life (Elafy, Kortam 2014, Kumar et al 2012, Korlam and Gad, 2014) A study regarding investigating the needs of the customers will help to inculcate unsustainable behaviour. Research has found that empirical research has been established between environmental research and everyday behaviour.

MAIN FOCUS OF THE CHAPTER

This section of the paper will focus on the role of marketing in creating awareness and action in the fourth industrial revolution.

Role of Marketing Into the Dimensions of Sustainability

The three dimensions of sustainability can well be integrated with the marketing function in order to create awareness and action as a step towards sustainability. Marketing function is needed at each of the three pillars to create awareness and action about sustainable levels.

Marketing can be used as an important function to support sustainability at each of the areas as described below:

- **Economic Sustainability:** Alludes to the capacity of the economic system to promote growth of economic indicators, including distribution of personal income, mortgage and repayments etc. Industry 4.0 creates great opportunity for sustainable development through sustainable manufacturing

Industry 4.0 promotes the growth of sustainable manufacturing in the following ways:

- **New Business Models**: The concept of smart factory in industry 4.0 promotes new services. Marketing can play an important role in creating awareness about these services. In fact, the communication strategy should focus more on accessibility and functionality of the product.
- **Value Creation**: Smart factory concept promotes the use of closed loop product life cycle which encourages co-ordination between resources and cross factory. This facilitates recycle and reuse of the product. Marketing can play an important role in creating awareness and action regarding sustainability through its integrated marketing communications.
- **Equipment**: Industry 4.0 facilitates the efficiency of existing manufacturing equipment through the process of retrofitting This increases the efficiency of the machinery and results in lower costs of production. Marketing can play an important role in creating awareness about retrofitting through the concept of integrated marketing communications in B2B markets.
- **Social Sustainability**: Implies general well-being of mankind it is to expand people freedom and capabilities. Social sustainability includes access to resources, education, social stability and quality of the natural environment. Industry 4.0 promotes the use of social sustainability as it increases the efficiency of the workers through training in ICT which helps in decentralized decision making. Here, marketing plays an important role in creating awareness among employees and organization regarding training programs. Through continuous promotion campaigns it creates awareness among the

employees and youth regarding the importance of training in ICT. This act as an important driver to promote sustainability.

- **Environmental Sustainability**: Is one of the main pillars of sustainability; its indicators include air pollution, water pollution, areas of degraded land, rate of material flow, rate of energy etc. In here, marketing could possibly play an important role in creating awareness as to how to protect the environment and reduce the pollution for a sustainable living. Industry 4.0 holds great opportunity in reducing the impact of the environment. The main focus of industry 4.0 is to aim at environmental sustainability. Environmental sustainability can be achieved in the following ways:
  - ○ **Sustainable Business Models**: Industry 4.0 focusses on bringing sustainable business models that generate environmental and social benefits and reduce the negative impact of the environment. These new businesses helps to solve environmental problems and increase long term competitivess. The value creation in industry creates product cycle in the closed circuit which aims at efficient co-ordination of product, material and energy. The modernization of the plant helps to reduce the costs of the production thereby helping in sustainability. All these activities help to minimize waste water generation, efficient use of raw materials. All these play an important role in environmental sustainability. Marketing has an important role in help industry 4.0 towards sustainability. The effective sustainable designing of the product and increased promotion of green products in the market helps to reduce negative impact of the environment leading to increased sustainability.

The marketing function can also be integrated into the various levels of sustainability as shown in the Figure 1.

How Can Marketing Help in Sustainability?

The answer to this question lies with the marketers, who have to create a) competitive advantage b) build trust with customers c) develop marketing opportunities. Marketing in industry 4.0 can help in achieving these objectives towards sustainability.

Competitive advantage through brand innovation: marketers could use sustainability to create brand innovation, which would increase market growth. 'Sustainability' in itself could be used as the differentiator for good quality products; in fact, some businesses have tried to differentiate their products based on social and environmental impacts. Industry 4.0 creates new business models giving rise to new services, these services can help to reduce the negative impacts of the

Figure 1. Integration of marketing into the sustainability element

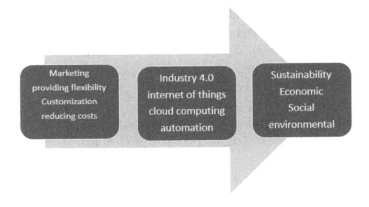

environment. Marketing can play an important role creating competitive advantage through continuous brand innovation.

Building trust with customers and society: some marketers feel that reputation and success may not be sufficient to preserve 'brands' in the long run. Marketers, thereby have an important role in building trust, whereby they should believe in more sustainable consumption. In industry 4.0 automation, product designing and recycling of products helps to build trust with the customers and the society.

Developing marketing opportunities: marketers today are increasingly interested in serving the poor; hence, they should identify opportunities for serving the poor by extending some products to the poor (to begin with), which for instance would include affordable packaging and maintaining brand values. Ultimately, serving the poor would serve as a great branding exercise for the marketers. Marketers play an important in industry 4.0 to develop environment and action about fourth industrial revolution. Through automation and aiming at effective product designing, products can be made available even to the bottom of the pyramid.

Marketing as a Tool to Create Awareness and Action Towards Sustainability

Marketing rests on four Ps of which one needs to be aware and take appropriate actions. Marketing can play a great role in creating awareness and action in the fourth industrial revolution by working on all the four p's of marketing when all the Ps of marketing are focused on improving the environment; marketing, which aims at sustainability of the environment is called green marketing.

Product

Product is the first 'P', an element of marketing mix. Marketing plays an important role in product development; right from the conceiving a product to its selling to the end consumer. Products aimed at the protection of the environment is called 'green product'. Right from the time of conception, 'green products' should be 'sustainable' and follow the rules of 'sustainable practices', effectively the 'environmental considerations'. For example, Toyota, Ford, Hyundai are some of the companies who are well known for 'green products'. ''Green' marketing needs to be incorporated at various levels of the Ps; some of the recent green product innovations are as follows:

- **Rechargeable Batteries:** Batteries are considered to be the most difficult items to be recycled, containing large number of environmentally hazardous materials. Hence, it is better to use rechargeable batteries, which give the option to charge the batteries when the charge is over.
- **Electric Cars:** One of the biggest contributions to green marketing in terms of checking pollution has been the introduction of electric cars. These cars run on electricity, and therefore reduce pollution.
- **LED Bulbs**: Another major breakthrough has been the introduction of LED energy conserving bulbs.
- **Product Design:** The design of a product also plays a very important role in product decisions. The product design should incorporate sustainability features, which in turn influences to a great extent the purchasing decisions of consumers today. Some of the best examples of sustainable designing includes LED bulbs, andthe concept of green hotels.
- **Imports EVX Ventures:** It is a sports car with sleek new aerodynamic vision that uses solar energy to drive; the car is powered by Solar Photo voltaic panelling along the exterior and a small 10KWH lithium battery within.
- **Green Hotels:** In the 'green hotel' right from the hotel's layout, to the use of material resources everything is environmentally friendly.
- **Green Cars:** Apart from being powered by Biofuels, electric vehicles/cars use efficient engines that reduce vehicle consumption of petroleum or any other forms of renewable energy throughout working life. Green cars thereby run on biofuels, solar energy and battery (as described earlier). In fact, even the tyres of the electric vehicles are made from bio-sourced organic materials.
- **The technology Used:** The technology used in manufacturing a product should be Eco friendly.
- **Packaging:** A green product should believe in green packaging too. Marketers promote the use of green packaging or eco packaging to prevent wastage. One of the best examples of green packaging is Macdonald. Very closely

associated with packaging, is the labelling; environment-friendly labelling of a product does help in deciding whether or not to buy a product per se. Research shows that most consumers have a positive green consciousness on eco labels (Cherian and Jacob,2012); they are considered to be the most appealing tools to judge the determination (Rashid, 2009).

Some examples of green packaging and labelling include the Cosmetible Cup: it is a special cup developed by KFC (a fast-food chain) containing a special biscuit wrapped in sugar-paper doubled with a layer of white chocolate.

Natural Clicquot 2 is another example of 100% biodegradable and isotherm packaging; made from potato starch and isotherm virtues, which in turn is 100% recyclable.

- **Nike in the Air**: Nike is packed with shoes in the air. The benefit of the product is that product that is transferred into packaging is made visible. The packaging provides the best possible presentation of the effectiveness of the shoes.It is also an innovative style of packaging.
- **Newton Eco Friendly Packaging**: The Newton Company designed a new way of packaging to pack their sports shoes made from 100% recyclable moulded carton; its ecological packaging allows it to minimize the weight and increase recyclability.
    - ○ **Eco Branding**: Brand is a name, a term symbol or a combination of both intended to distinguish a product from those of competitors. An Eco brand is a brand that is environment friendly.

Pricing

Pricing is the second 'P' of marketing. Green pricing or sustainable pricing refers to the marketable monetary value suggested for environmental activities, which reconciles the economic value of the environment. It is also defined as a reflection of the price that arises with production, environment and economic activities in a way that it creates profit for both companies and the consumers (Martin and Shouten, 2012). It also refers to the pricing done for environmental considerations; hence, pricing should take into account all the environmental factors. Sustainable pricing aims at fair payment of environment to add value to the operations carried outside the environment. Practicing ecological pricing on green products as demanded by the consumer is important for the protection of both environment as well as the consumer (Peattie and Charter, 2003)

Place

Place is the 3rd 'P' occupying an equally important place in marketing. It refers to a common point where buyers and sellers meet to satisfy each other's wants. In effect, 'place' refers to the distribution channel or the distribution network. Due to the growing consumption of the internet, most of the buying and selling are conducted online these days thereby reducing the cost. This is termed as 'green place'. A sustainable product achieves success by winning customers through suitable channels. The availability of a product has a great impact in attracting customers; therefore, marketing has to ensure wide availability of a product per se. Sometimes companies choose ecological partnership in order to develop environmental effects and they restructure logistics arrangement and make them more efficient (Dahlstorm, 2011).

Green Promotion

Last but not the least is the fourth and the most important aspect of marketing is known as 'promotion'. Promotion that focuses on environment is known as green promotion; this is done in the following ways: selecting a partner in such a way so that it promotes environmental protection. Environment friendly materials should be encouraged like for instance environment friendly bags. One of the biggest role the marketer has to play is in the field of designing the advertising messages. The advertising messages should be designed in such a way that it creates awareness among consumers regarding a product per se. The company tries to reduce communication materials, which has negative effects on the environment (Kotler, 2011). The strategic approach includes designing the communication process with regard to environmental benefits of the product. The entire process may include reducing the use of paper in the communication process, making it more environmental friendly and cost-effective (Banerjee, 2002).

The Integration of Four Ps of Marketing Into Sustainable Marketing Mix

Keeping in mind the role of marketing to drive more sustainability, many authors have integrated the four Ps of marketing into a sustainable marketing mix.

'Product' should be transformed into a 'customer product' wherein efforts should be made to minimize waste and pollution that occur during the process of production.

'Price' should be transformed into 'customer price'; i.e. the price set for a product should be formed by adding elements of ecological costs to the unit costs.

'Place' should be transformed into 'customer place', wherein efforts should be made to minimize waste and pollution that may be formed while transporting and selling the goods.

'Promotion' should be transformed into communication, wherein efforts should be made to effectively communicate among the stakeholders of developing responsibility for environment protection

Some Marketing Initiatives That Attempted to Create Environmental Awareness and Action

Tide Cold-Water Challenge

Tide began #turn cold-water campaign to switch from hot water to cold water in support of the Earth Day. The main reason for this initiative was to make an effort to save money and help to keep the clothes fresh for a longer period. The campaign #turn cold-water campaign encourages people to wash in cold water, helping to save electricity in turn. Cold-water washing saves energy in the following ways: a) it saves energy for 1 year; b) it saves power up to the power of the TV for four months.

This type of marketing campaign has created awareness on how saving energy can contribute towards the sustainability of the planet.

Diesel Global Warming

Diesel is one of the most luxurious ethnic garment manufacturers. They launched a marketing campaign to create awareness about sustainability titled 'Global warming ready'. The campaign involved launching a series of newspaper, magazine and billboards advertisements featuring various models posing in Diesel clothing in a world affected by raised water levels and temperature. This campaign served as a unique marketing campaign, as it provoked decisions regarding various societal issues. Some of the print ads for instance included are Tropical birds at St Marks Square, Sandy desert overtakes china wall, Tropical plant growing in Paris, New York City submerged etc. Diesel also partnered with a climate change watchdog known as www.shopglobalwar.org, to bring citizens to find solutions to global warming.

HSBC: No Small Change

It was one of the most successful award-winning campaigns introduced to create awareness among customers regarding sustainability. It won various awards like the communicator award, ECHO award, Green Office award, and was also featured in the Directory Magazine. The campaign involved encouraging customers to make commitments in making small changes that will benefit the environment, such as using recycled paper for brochures for instance. The campaign was based on the premise that it is by making small changes that society at large could bring about paradigm changes in the environment, where everyone played a role, albeit small. For instance, if HSBC's customers paid bills online, they qualified to receive a green living. Over a period of time, the campaign taught to reduce carbon footprints by using print ad posters, direct mail and creating online awareness. The ads contained some of the slogans like: 'Your money does not grow on trees, but it can help to plant a seed or two'; 'Free business checking is now available with good Karma'; 'Filling your car with recycled fry grease isn't the only way to go green'. The campaign did wonders in creating awareness and action.

Timberland Earth Keepers' Campaign

It is a unique campaign in which an earthkeeper has a goal of recruiting one million people to become a part of an online network designed for environmental change. The campaign includes online networking tools like changeagents.com, facebook page, youtube etc. All this is united in the earthkeeper channel widely known as www.earthkeeper.com. According to Timberland, an earthkeeper is a person who wants to protect the environment; without earthkeepers, the planet (i.e. earth) would suffer and face serious problems. Timberland thus set out to make a good idea into positive reality.

BMV Diesel Changes

This was one of the award winning campaigns in which the company tried to disclose information about environmental changes. Diesel cars in America are known to be noisy, causing lot of air pollution. BMV reached out to its customers through 2011 BMV 3 series Diesel commercial; the first half of the commercial, which picturized cars and trucks emitting smoke when BMV 335 enters the commercial in brilliant blue spreading the message of environmental protection.

GE Eco-Imagination Campaign

In May 2005 general electric, the world tenth largest population introduced $90 million eco-magnetic and advertising campaign, addressing some critical environmental challenges faced today; for instance, the need for cleaner and efficient sources of energy, reduced emission and abundance of clean water. The eco-imagination campaign was all about the future, focusing on unique energy, technology, manufacturing, and infrastructural capabilities, such as solar energy, hybrid locomotives, fuel cells and stronger materials. The campaign involved a print advertisement, featuring leaves sprouting from an electric power plant with a green aeroplane across the website in their online greeting. With tag lines like increasing business, green is green we are at the tipping point where energy efficiency and emission reduction is equally profitable, this campaign was a hit.

Volkswagen Fun Theory Campaign

Volkswagen launched its fun theory campaign in which reactions of people was noted to find out whether they would be interested in fun games by motivating people to take the staircase instead of the elevator for instance, wherein each staircase would have a different note to play.

SEVEN ISSUES IN MARKETING TO DEVELOP AWARENESS AND ACTION

"It is not easy to be green" (Noah & Bradley, 2012). Protect the environment and hurt the business. Even though green marketing plays a crucial role in the development of awareness and action associated with sustainability, there are some major issues associated with it.

1. **Compliance and Competitiveness:** One of the major challenges, which companies face today, is with regard to compliance and competitiveness. Environmental managers welcome an opportunity in which they strive for a win-win opportunity.
2. **It Is Never Easy to be Green**: Companies find it difficult to be green as the compliance costs are very high.
3. **Keeping up with the Jonesses:** As a rule, companies enhance shareholders' value by improving the efficiency and effectiveness of environmental spending, but the focus on these, obstructs the key competitive opportunity in those expenditures.

Green Product and Price

being energy efficient, multi-attribute and multi-phased analysis involves costs in research and development for instance; potentially higher costs for product take backs and/or transaction costs associated with third parties. The simple metric of 'green' puts the market towards energy efficiency in the user phase and can reduce other pollutants associated with electricity production for example. However, the major problem is attributing responsibilities for the mitigation of hosts, and the social impact generated by the demand of good. But, as roles and responsibilities shift, division of labour shifts in accordance, and the work, which was done by the government earlier, begins falling back on society, business and consumers. Environmental issues shift from end of the pipe affluent concerns and total material flows and relativity of risk, the use of criminal law is bought into question. As division of labour shifts, the need for spaces also shift. For example, there often seems to be tension between the environmental claims to be rigorous, comprehensive and comparable, vis a vis the need to create enough space for companies to communicate actions by talking to consumers and the supply chain. It is often said that the goodwill of the consumers and procurers is eroded by green claims.

ISSUES, PROBLEMS, AND CONTROVERSIES

One of the major issues in marketing is to develop awareness and action is Green-washing failure to meet the profit.

- **Green-Washing:** The growing demand for environment friendly products have persuaded manufacturers incorporate environment friendly practices. However, some companies in a haste to compete tend to mislead customers. This act of misleading consumers regarding environmentally friendly practices of the company is termed as green-washing. Green-washing is defined as the "act of misleading consumers regarding environmentally friendly practices of a company" (Pargual et al., 2011). India also seems to be affected by green-washing. Using the term 'green' beyond a certain point creates vagueness in consumer's mind (Zimmer et al., 1994) and they may do away with those products, which are actually environment friendly (Mayer et al., 1993). Green-washing seems to have a drastic effect in eroding consumer's confidence regarding environment friendly products and also the investor's confidence to invest in environmentally friendly firms (Delma & Burbano, 2011).

In late 1980 and 1990s, professional purchasers and individual consumers became interested in buying green products. These green products were accompanied by certain words like: earth friendly, 100% natural made with non-toxic ingredients etc. These terms were used without any effort to classify them, and therefore purchasers were often confused about these plans; this was commonly referred to as 'Advertising pollution'. However, the practice of green-washing did not completely disappear and was seen in some form or other. The term green-washing is shown by various sins which can be explained as follows:

- **Sin of the Hidden Trade-Off**: The word 'green' is based on a narrow set of environmental attributes; a product can be an energy efficient product, but it was possibly produced with the help of coal or contains neurotoxins such as mercury.

- **Sin of Proof:** Environmental claim cannot be substantiated by supporting information or third party certification.
- **Sin of Vagueness:** Claim is too broad or poorly defined.
- **Sin of Irrelevance:** Claim is truthful but unimportant or is not helpful.
- **Sin of the Lesser of Two Evils**: Claims are true within the product category as the product in whole is harmful.
- **Fibbing**: Manufacturers tend to mislead customers about environmental performance of a product, they claim that they meet environmental performance but actually they do not.
- **Unsubstantiated Claim:** Some manufacturers are unable to provide proof for their environmental claims, while others use words like green or eco. But, customers should be told the reason for it.

RECOMMENDATIONS

A recent report by the Forbes magazine in 2018 revealed that CMO's(chief marketing officer) in the organization should make the following changes .These should include the following:

1. **Rebalancing the Marketing Budget**: In order to integrate marketing with the fourth industrial revolution there is a strong need to rebalance the marketing budget. The organisations should compare which form of marketing is able to attract new customers and weigh the options like content marketing, email marketing, event and SEO .The resources should be deployed on the basis of whichever option are able to attract more customers.
2. **Modernising Marketing Tools**: For marketing to play an important role in the fourth industrial revolution it is important to modernize the marketing tools. Organizations should bank more on digital media tools in order to attract more customers rather than traditional methods like television, radio etc.
3. **Convert the Website Into Hard Working Tools**: One of the biggest assets to promote a product today is to create awareness through the website and maintain the website in such a way so that it attracts the attention of the consumer.
4. **Refresh Your Brand to Appeal to Your Customers**: For marketing to play a bigger role in the event of fourth industrial revolution it is important to refresh the brand appeals to the customers using Industry 4.0 tools like LOT
5. **Consolidate Marketing Resources That are Spread Across Organisations**: Another area where organisations have to work is to consolidate resources and spread it across the organisations.

IMPLICATIONS

- **Implications**: This paper makes an important contribution both academically and practically.
- **Theoretical Implication**: This chapter makes an important contribution in terms of theoretical implication as it is the first study to understand the role of marketing in creating awareness and action regarding the fourth industrial revolution.
- **Practical Implication**: The chapter is practically important as it will serve as a motivation to other marketing concerns to use marketing strategically to create awareness about the fourth industrial revolution.

FUTURE RESEARCH DIRECTION

This chapter adopts only an exploratory view of the topic. There is lot of scope of future research by extending the study to empirical research. Another interesting area of research is to find out the various issues and controversies related to the marketing role in creating awareness.

CONCLUSION

Marketing therefore has an important role to play in enhancing sustainability in the era of the fourth industrial revolution. The two terms, i.e. 'marketing' and sustainability seem inter-related, but in reality, there are huge differences between them. Marketing is said to play a key role in decision-making in an effort towards sustainability. It influences decision–making, which in turn influences the attitude and behaviour. Marketing can thereby be used as an important function to support sustainability at each of the following areas, i.e. economic sustainability, social sustainability and environmental sustainability. Marketing helps sustainability in the following ways: a) competitive advantage through innovation; b) building trust with customers and society; c) developing marketing opportunities. Not only that, even the four Ps are to be taken care of through marketing: for example, product: i.e. right from the time of inception of the product to the final procurement of the product, green aspects of the product should be taken care of. Even with regard to pricing, the price offered to consumers should be green pricing; a green place should be encouraged among the consumers, and green promotional strategies should be taken care However, in an effort to create sustainability, there is a need to transform marketing to create awareness about sustainability .

REFERENCES

Ajike & Neoma. (2015). Green marketing: A tool for achieving sustainable development of Nigeria. *International Journal of Advanced Research in Statistics, Management and Finance.*

Cavalho, Edson, & Mataers. (2018). Manufacturing in the fourth industrial revolution: A positive perspective in sustainable manufacturing. *Procedia Manufacturing, 21,* 671-678.

Duncu. (2013). The contribution of sustainable marketing for sustainable development. *Management and Marketing Challenges for the Knowledge Society, 8*(2), 385-400.

Jones, Clarke-Hill, Comfort, & Hillier. (2008). Marketing and sustainability. Marketing Intelligence and Planning, 26(2), 123-130.

Kortan, W., & Gad, G. (2014). Knowledge: for social innovation. *Journal of American Science, 10*(2), 143-147.

Peattie, K. (2001). Towards sustainability: The third age of green marketing. *The Marketing Review*, 2(2), 129–146. doi:10.1362/1469347012569869

Shahira, E.-A., & Korlam, W. (2014). Exploring environmental sustainability performance in the Cellular telecommunication industry in Egypt. In *Proceedings on 28th Environmental conference.* University of Oldenburg.

Upton, E. (2016). *The evolving relationship between sustainability and marketing.* Corporate Citizenship Briefing. News and Analysis on Resp.

Wang, W. Y. C., Pauleen, D. J., & Zhang, T. (2017). How social media applications affect B2B communications and improve business performance of SME. *Industrial Marketing Management, 54,* 4–14. doi:10.1016/j.indmarman.2015.12.004

Yeo, N. C. Y., Pepin, H., & Yang, S. S. (2017). Revolutionery technology adoption for manufacturing industry. *Proceedings of the 24th CIRP Conference on life Cycle Engineering,* 17-21.

Chapter 6
Sustainable Project Management

Martin Albert
Chemnitz University of Technology, Germany

Friedrich Mickel
Chemnitz University of Technology, Germany

ABSTRACT

Sustainability is a concept that has increased in popularity constantly over recent years. During this time, the discipline of project management begun to focus on sustainability, but literature shows that the topic of sustainable project management is still incipiently explored. Therefore, the goal of the chapter is to identify connections between sustainability and project management, which is achieved through the literary review of 46 different texts. These sources were analyzed using a bibliometric analysis and a qualitative content analysis. As deductive and inductive derived categories "definition project management," "definition sustainability," "definition sustainable project management," "affected areas," "principles of sustainable project management," and "project manager" were defined. In order to develop the profession of sustainable project management, focusing upon the verification of theoretical findings with empirical research is suggested.

DOI: 10.4018/978-1-5225-7638-9.ch006

Copyright © 2019, IGI Global. Copying or distributing in print or electronic forms without written permission of IGI Global is prohibited.

INTRODUCTION

Tom Taylor, the former chairperson of the Association for Project Management (APM), highlights that, "the planet earth is in a perilous position with a range of fundamental sustainability threats" and that, "Project and Programme Managers are significantly placed to make contributions to Sustainable Management practices" (APM, 2006, p. 1-7). Although the topic of sustainability is well known and much discussed, it is only recently related to the discipline of project management (Silvius & Schipper, 2014a, pp.41-43). This connection is an emerging, forward-looking area of research that continues gaining interest as it moves into the focus of both academics and practitioners (Silvius & Schipper, 2014a).

Otegi-Olaso et al. (2015) report over 560 publications (books, book chapters, journal articles, internet sites and conference papers) on this topic, of which almost 80% were published between 2004 and 2014, highlighting the many still open questions in terms of sustainability and project management (Marcelino-Sádaba, González-Jaen, & Pérez-Ezcurdia, 2015, p.14). Some authors conclude that the lack of integration between sustainability and project management is due to a present lack of research (Martens & Carvalho, 2015, p.30; Carvalho & Rabechini, 2017, p.1-2; Marcelino-Sádaba, González-Jaen, & Pérez-Ezcurdia, 2015, p.1). For example, Tufinio et al. (2013) point out a broad understanding of sustainability in literature and inside organisations, including the definition of the concept, standards and business practices. Marcelino-Sádaba et al. (2015) propose further research to identify effective and influentia project management areas for sustainable project management.

The purpose of this chapter is to investigate literature with a clear focus on publications, which discuss sustainability in the context of project management. The underlying research question for this work is:

- What are connections between sustainability and project management?

Following sub-question are:

- What are the definitions of sustainability, project management and sustainable project management?
- What are affected and influential areas of project management for sustainable project management?
- What are topics related to sustainable project management?

METHODS AND DATA BASE

To research the connection between sustainability and project management we followed the procedure of a literature review combined with bibliometric analysis and qualitative content analysis.

For the literature review, Cooper's method (Cooper, 1989) was chosen. In order to assure a clear research direction and a relevant database, the focus is set on the correct classification of the literature review and the problem formulation stage (Cooper, 1989). For the analysis of our identified data, we use Mayring's qualitative content analysis (Mayring, 2015). In this method, categories are created and subsequently analysed. To receive information from the material on quantitative aspects like the temporal evolution, the most productive author or recurrent institutions and countries, we refer to Ball and Tunger's bibliometric analysis (Ball & Tunger, 2005).

Literature Review

According to Machi and McEvoy (2012), "a literature review is a written document that presents a logically argued case founded on a comprehensive understanding of the current state of knowledge about a topic of study" (p.5). The stages of the literature review method of Cooper (1989) are problem formulation, data collection, data evaluation, analysis, interpretation, and public presentation. In our work, we focus on the first two stages of Cooper's method to cover the data collection. For the stage analysis, we conduct Mayring's (2015) qualitative content analysis.

As mentioned before our research focus is on the connection between sustainability and project management. Silvius and Tharp (2013) state that previous work is mostly interpretive by giving meaning to how the concepts of sustainability could be interpreted in the context of projects. They point out that, "a next step in research on the topic would preferably need to lead to more universal results" (Silvius & Tharp, 2013, p.xxiv). Therefore, our main objective is to find universal results on the connection between sustainability and project management. The second step in problem formulation stage is to determine explicitly which texts will be included in the review and which texts will be excluded. Therefore, a taxonomy of literature reviews is a solid starting point to set a framework (Cooper, Hedges, & Valentine, 2009).

In Table 1 the chosen classifications are highlighted. The first characteristic, focus, is used to identify methodological strengths and weaknesses in the research of sustainable project management. The first focus is on theories, the second is on finding practical implementations and applications. The goal of the review is to integrate and generalize findings across the literature, with the further ambition to critically analyse the research and identify central issues. The perspective of a

Table 1. Own presentation of the taxonomy for literature reviews

Characteristics	Categories			
Focus	Research Outcomes	Research methods	Theories	Applications
Goal	Integration	Criticism		Central issues
Perspective	Neutral representation		Espousal of position	
Coverage	Exhaustive	Exhaustive & Selective	Representative	Central or pivotal
Organization	Historical	Conceptual		Methodological
Audience	Specialized scholars	General scholars	Practitioners	General public

Source: (Cooper, Hedges, Valentine, 2009, p.4-5)

neutral representation gives the opportunity to present the review findings as facts, instead of individual interpretations. Doing so, facilitates the general exclusion of personal distortions in the analysis. The general purpose of the review is to locate and consider available literature on sustainable project management. To keep the number of articles of review manageable, the category exhaustive with selective citations is chosen, allowing the exclusion of non-academical literature. According to the various theories in the literature and the strong theoretical focus, this review is organised conceptually. The final characteristic is the audience. The primary audience for this chapter are scholars and practitioners with an interest in sustainable project management.

After the general framework is set, we carried out a first investigation on sustainability in project management. We identified the following keywords: 'project management', 'sustainability' and 'sustainable'. These terms were used for searching the database of Google Scholar (in combination with the Google search operator 'allintext:'). The search was carried out on 23.07.2017 with the following number of search results (bracketed):

- (291) allintext: "project management sustainability"
- (561) allintext: "sustainable project management"

We scanned all texts for terms relative to sustainable project management, focusing upon literature reviews, overviews, journal article and summaries in order to identify the wealth of available literature. Furthermore, the references on the available texts are observed. In order to form a more accurate list of result, the abstracts of each text were scrutinised under the following criteria: Does the paper analyse sustainability in the context of project management? We then excluded all texts, which consider sustainability exclusive from the project outcome, seen through the neglection of project management or the requirements of the project. In addition, only academic texts are considered. Altogether, we identified 46 texts for a further analysis. Table 2 presents these classified texts along with the corresponding type.

Bibliometric Analysis

Bibliometrics can be understood as collecting information of publications (Pritchard, 1969; Brookes, 1990; Potter, 1981). It is used for counting and analyzing the various aspects of scientific communication in written form (Ball & Tunger, 2005, p.15). Quotation analysis is a sub-area of bibliometrics, which mainly deals with quoted scientific publications (Ball & Tunger, 2005, p.15). The main object is the counting of quotations referring to a particular work or a particular scientist (Ball & Tunger, 2005, p.15). The greater the sum of the quotations, the greater the value of a work is estimated (Ball & Tunger, 2005, p.15). Bibliometric analyses provide information on the perception of publications by a research group or an institute in the field of specialist publications (Ball & Tunger, 2005, p.15). The analysis provides information on the impact of these publications and the related scientific results (Ball & Tunger, 2005, p.15). The goal of our bibliometric analysis is to find connections between sustainability and project management in the main characteristics of the texts. Thus, according to Andres (2012) our work applies a descriptive analysis that, "will offer a quick and even visual impression of certain aspects related to productivity in the given field of study" (p.13). Therefore, the identified texts from the literature review are used as a database. The focus of our bibliometric analysis belongs to the following aspects: temporal evolution, number of authors, institutions, countries and publisher. In addition, other indicators like the type of literature or the academic discipline of the authors are included in the bibliometric analysis (Andres, 2012, pp.13-21).

Qualitative Content Analysis

To analyse the content of the identified texts we use the qualitative content analysis according to Mayring (2015). The qualitative content analysis follows a certain systematic and is guided by a common procedure (Mayring, 2015, p.50). By forming categories and sub-categories, the material is segmented. Mayring (2015) provides a general model to carry out the qualitative content analysis and this model includes the following steps (p.62):

Table 2. Texts with various terms in relation to sustainable project management

	Text	Type of Text
1	Agarwal & Kalmár (2015)	Master Thesis
2	Aguilar-Fernandez, Otegi-Olaso, & Cruz-Villazón (2015)	Conference Paper
3	Albarosa & Masura (2016)	Master Thesis
4	Carvalho & Rabechini	Journal Article
5	Daneshpour (2015)	Journal Article
6	Deland (2009)	Conference Paper
7	Ebbesen & Hope (2015)	Journal Article
8	Gareis (2013)	Book chapter
9	Gareis, Heumann, & Martinuzzi (2010)	Conference Paper
10	Gareis, Heumann, & Martinuzzi (2011)	Journal Article
11	Goedknegt (2012)	Journal Article
12	Goedknegt & Silvius (2012)	Conference Paper
13	Hope & Moehler (2014)	Journal Article
14	Joseph & Marnewick (2016)	Journal Article
15	Keeys (2012)	Journal Article
16	Kirchhof & Brandtweiner (2011)	Conference Paper
17	Kivilä, Martinsuo, & Vuorinen (2017)	Journal Article
18	Labuschagne & Brent (2004)	Conference Paper
19	Marcelino-Sádaba, González-Jaen, & Pérez-Ezcurdia (2015)	Literature Review
20	Marnewick (2017)	Conference Paper
21	Martens & Carvalho (2015)	Journal Article
22	Martens & Carvalho (2013)	Journal Article
23	Michaelides, Bryde, & Ohaeri (2014)	Conference Paper
24	Nishida, Koshijima, & Umeda (2014)	Conference Paper
25	Oehlmann (2010)	Master Thesis
26	Okland (2015)	Literature Review
27	Otegi-Olaso, Aguilar-Fernández, & Cruz-Villazón (2015)	Conference Paper
28	Tufinio, Mooi, Ravestijn, Bakker, & Boorsma (2013)	Journal Article
29	Sánchez (2015)	Journal Article
30	Siew, Balatbat, & Carmichael (2016)	Journal Article
31	Silva (2015)	Journal Article
32	Silvius (2012a)	Conference Paper
33	Silvius (2012b)	Book Chapter
34	Silvius (2012c)	Working Paper

continued on following page

Table 2. Continued

	Text	Type of Text
35	Silvius (2016)	Journal Article
36	Silvius & Schipper (2010)	Conference Paper
37	Silvius & Schipper (2012)	Conference Paper
38	Silvius & Schipper (2014a)	Literature Review
39	Silvius & Schipper (2014b)	Journal Article
40	Silvius & Schipper (2015)	Journal Article
41	Silvius & Schipper (2016)	Journal Article
42	Silvius, Schipper, & Nedeski (2013)	Journal Article
43	Silvius, Schipper, Planko, van den Brink, & Köhler (2012)	Book
44	Silvius, van den Brink, & Köhler (2012)	Book Chapter
45	Talbot (2011)	Journal Article
46	Tam (2010)	Journal Article

1. Determination of the material
2. Analysis of the situation in which the text originated
3. Formal characteristics of the material
4. Direction of analysis
5. Theoretical differentiation of the research question
6. Determination of the analysis techniques (summary, explication, structuring), development of a category system
7. Definition of analysis units
8. Analysis steps using the category system and verification of the category system in theory and on the material,
9. Interpretation of the results in the direction of the main question and
10. Application of the content-analytical quality criteria

Relating to the determination of the analysis techniques, we used the types of deductive structuring and inductive summary. Following the type of structuring, we derived from the literature the categories 'definition project management', 'definition sustainability', 'definition sustainable project management', and 'affected areas'. Relating to the type of summary we additionally formed from the data material the following categories 'principles of sustainable project management', and 'project manager'. We evaluated all categories in the sense of the research question. Furthermore, each inductive build category is examined for the entire data material.

RESULTS

Bibliometric Analysis

Relating to the 46 identified texts Figure 1 shows a bar chart that illustrates the number of the selected articles in relation to the year of their publication. The number of articles increased in 2009 and grew continually until 2015. Peaks can be noticed in the years 2010, 2012 and 2015.

The temporal evolution of sustainable project management became increasingly popular in academic research within the last eight years. Several authors also recognize this development (Silva, 2015; Silvius & Schipper, 2015). Silva (2015) argues, "The topic of sustainability has experienced a growing interest in the general academic and professional community recently" (p.1). The author points out that the current academic literature is still exploring the link between sustainability and the field of project management (Silva, 2015). In line with that, Silvius & Schipper (2015) write, "The growing number of publications on the integration of sustainability into project management indicate that the topic is '… picking up momentum'" (p.335). Therefore, the topic of sustainable project management can be interpreted as a discipline which is still in its initial phase. The potentially low number of empirical research confirms this general image. Certainly, most of the current publications try to develop the topic conceptually rather than empirically.

Figure 1. Bar chart on the temporal evolution of articles of sustainable project management

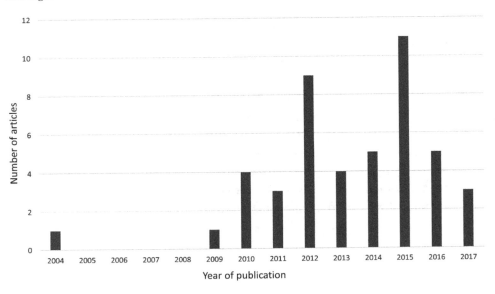

Table 3. Number of publications by institution of sustainable project management

Institution	Number of Publications	Country of Institution
University of Applied Sciences Utrecht	15	Netherlands
University of Sao Paulo	3	Brazil
Delf University of Technology	2	Netherlands
SKEMA Business School	2	France
University of the Basque Country	2	Spain
University of Johannesburg	2	South Africa
WU Vienna University of Economics and Business	2	Austria

Counted on the number of mentions (bracketed) of publications the most productive authors are Silvius, A.J.G. (14), Schipper, R. (8), Carvalho, M.M. (3), Gareis, R. (3), Goedknegt, D. (2), Heumann, M. (2), Hope, A.J. (2), Martens, M.L. (2), and Martinuzzi, A. (2). The author Silvius is recognized as the most productive author. It should be noted, that Silvius, Schipper and Goedknegt worked together on several publications. Authors with one publication are not mentioned.

Table 3 shows the number of publications relating to institutions. Noticeable is the University of Applied Science Utrecht with 15 publications. Institutions with a smaller publication number than two are excluded from the table.

We related all publications to their country of origin. The number of publications is bracketed: Netherlands (17), United Kingdom (4), Austria (4), Brazil (3), South Africa (3), Spain (3), Finland (2), France (2), Sweden (2), Australia (1), Argentina (1), Canada (1), Japan (1), North America (1), and Norway (1).

Overall, there are seven different types of text. The number frequency of occurrence is bracketed. The types of text are journal article (26), conference paper (12), book chapter (3), master thesis (3), literature review (3), working paper (1), and a book (1).

The publishers or the editors, which are responsible for the printing and distribution of the digital or printed publication, are listed below (the number of mentions is bracketed): Project Management World Journal (7), International Project Management Association (IPMA) (5), Project Management Institute (PMI) (3), International Journal of Project Management (3), Journal of Cleaner Production (3), Procedia Computer Science (2), Procedia Social and Behavioural Science (2), and other publishers with only one mention (21).

Looking at the academic discipline, we identify the following research fields (the number of mentions is bracketed): Project Management (33), Engineering (5), Information Systems (4), Project Management & Engineering (3), and Economics (1).

Regarding the research design 30 texts use a conceptional research design, three use work with an empirical approach, and 13 with a combination of both.

Qualitative Content Analysis

The following categories were derived from our identified texts: 'definition project management', 'definition sustainability', 'definition sustainable project management', 'affected areas', 'principles of sustainable project management', and 'project manager'.

Definition Project Management

In summary, six authors mention a complete definition of the term 'project management'. Marcelino-Sádaba et al. (2015) pretend, that the most widely accepted definition of project management was published by the Project Management Institute (PMI) in 2008, which refers to, "the application of knowledge, skills, tools and techniques to project activities to meet the project requirements" (p.2). A wide range of authors also uses this definition from the PMI (Okland, 2015, p.106; Joseph & Marnewick, 2016, p.536; Labuschagne & Brent, 2004, p.105). In contrast to the definition from the PMI, Nishida, Koshijima and Umada (2014) focus more on a time aspect. Therefore, Nishida et al. (2014) define project management as the, "management of a group of activities or initiatives with a defined deliverable and a definite starting point and end point" (p.2). Confronting the project management process, Kirchhof and Brandtweiner (2011) developed their own definition, "Project management is described as the management discipline of planning and controlling projects during their progress" (p.529).

We want to highlight, that only six out of 46 publications define the term project management. This potential low number of concrete definitions (13%) can be interpreted in terms of general clarity what project management is about. Most of the publications, that define the term, use the popular definition of the PMI (2013, p.416). Project management as a defined term appears since 1953 and has, therefore, a long tradition (Morris, Pinto, & Söderlund, 2012, p.17). It can be summarised that in both literature and in the selected publications, most related to the field of project management as we shown in our bibliometric analysis, there is a consensus about the understanding of the term 'project management'.

Definition Sustainability

67% of the publications state a definition of sustainability. The Brundtland (1987) report gives the most (97%) adopted definition of sustainability, which is, "to meet the needs of the present without compromising the ability of future generations to meet their own needs" (p.41). In this definition, an inter- and intra-generational aspect is concerned. Just Oehlmann (2010) presents two more definitions. The first is, "For business, sustainable development means adopting business strategies and activities that meet the needs of the enterprise and its stakeholders today, while protecting, sustaining and enhancing the human and natural resources that will be needed in the future" (Oehlmann, 2010, p.13). The second refers to the definition from the International Union for the Conservation of Nature (IUCN) (1991), "Improving the quality of human life while living within the carrying capacity of supporting ecosystems" (p.10).

Eleven publications report that sustainability is about inter-, and intra-generational equity (e.g. Ebbesen & Hope, 2015, p.4; Gareis, 2013, p.6; Goedknegt & Silvius, 2012, p.2). Eight texts mentioned a connection between the Brundtland report and an aspect on people, planet and profit or the three dimensions social, environmental, and economic (e.g. Marnewick, 2017, p.3; Okland, 2015, p.104; Talbot, 2011, p.39). In line with the three dimensions aspect, Silvius (2012a, p.3) argues that they should be 'harmonised'. Deland (2009, p.2) goes one step further and state that there must be a 'strong balance' between social, environmental and economic ideals, goals and results. According to this, various publications from Silvius and Schipper claim, "the report implies that sustainability requires also a social and an environmental perspective, next to the economical perspective, on development and performance" (Silvius, 2012c, p.2; Silvius & Schipper, 2012, p.2; Silvius & Schipper, 2015, p.338; Silvius & Schipper, 2016, p.10).

It is recognized that a conflict of goals between the dimensions can occur. To clear this up, a concept of strong and weak sustainability is suggested (Monto, Ganesh, & Varghese, 2005, p.32).

Furthermore, several authors emphasise that the Brundtland definition of sustainability may be interpreted by many organisations intuitively, but it remains difficult transferring the concept into business practice (Ebbesen & Hope, 2015, p.4; Goedknegt & Silvius, 2012, p.2; Hope & Moehler, 2014, p.359).

In addition to the Brundtland definition, 84% of the publications link sustainability to the concept of the 'Triple Bottom Line' or 'Triple-P'. This idea deals with economic (profit), social (people), and environmental (planet) aspects. Whereas 29% of the publications, which refer to the Triple Bottom Line approach, just named the concept, 71% propose an explanation. 27% of them mentioned that the Triple Bottom Line approach is about economic (profit), social (people), and environmental (planet) interests without a note on balancing these aspects (e.g. Tufinio, Mooi, Ravestijn, Bakker, & Boorsma, 2013, p.93; Carvalho & Rabechini, 2017, p.1). In contrast to that, 63% point out that the Triple Bottom Line is about the balance or harmony between the three areas (e.g. Ohelmann, 2010, p.31; Silvius, 2012a, p.3; Danishpour, 2015, p.321). In addition to that, Albarosa and Masura (2016) mentioned that the Triple Bottom Line approach is widely accepted, "but has also been the subject of critics for the difficulties related to its application" (p.1).

When it comes to the sub-categories 'economic dimension', 'social dimension' and 'environmental dimension', all publications designate these three dimensions. Therefore, just 40% of the literature mention their understanding of those. However, the publications differ in the interpretation of the dimensions. We want to demonstrate this with some examples.

Tam (2010) reports that the economic aspect is about, "increasing profitability through efficient use of resources (human, materials, financial), effective design and good management, planning and control" (p.18). Silvius et al. (2012) highlight that, "financial or economic performance indicators may include: sales, return-on-investment, taxes paid, monetary flows and profit" (p.10). Labuschagne and Brent (2004, p.104) propose that the economic aspects are clear. Some authors argue that the profit aspect implies all economic activities (e.g. Oehlmann, 2010, p.15; Marnewick, 2017, p.3). In addition, some authors agree on the interpretation of the economic dimension as maximising profit and reducing costs (e.g. Sánchez, 2015, p.325; Gareis, Heumann; & Martinuzzi, 2011, p.61).

This diversity in interpretation can also be noticed in the social dimension and environmental dimension. For Gareis et al. (2011) the social dimension is about, "security, equal opportunities, social justice, health and education" (p.61). Joseph and Marnewick (2016) emphasis that, "the social dimension refers to the communities in which organisations operate, as well as the employees of an organisation" (p.531). Labuschagne and Brent (2004) concedes that, "The social dimension concerns the technology's impact on the social systems in which it operates, as well as the organization's relationships with its various stakeholders during the development, operation and decommissioning of a technology" (p.6). In addition to that, Albarosa and Mesura (2016) deplore the tendency that the purpose of defining social sustainability, "have created a conceptional chaos, compromising the term's utility itself" (p.2).

Regarding the environmental dimension, various interpretations are given in the literature as well. This again can be illustrated with the following examples. Joseph and Marnewick (2016) argue that, "the environmental dimension is concerned with the physical environment that people inhabit" (p.531). Oehlmann (2010) states, "The Planet aspect involves reaching a balance between the environmental burden and the capacity of the Earth to carry environmental burdens" (p.15). According to Tam

(2010) the environmental aspect is about, "preventing harmful and irreversible effects on the environment by efficient use of natural resources, encouraging renewable resources, protecting the soil, water, air from contaminations and others" (p.18).

The topic of sustainability seems to be constructed around an agreed standard definition based on the Brundtland report and the Triple Bottom Line. All analysed publications, which use the Triple Bottom Line approach, refer to an economical, a social and an environmental dimension of sustainability. In contrast to that, there is a diversity by looking at the understanding of the three pillars of the Triple Bottom Line. As a result of our analysis, we noticed that the publications provide different interpretation on the social, economical and environmental pillar. Furthermore, there are stark differences when understanding the concept inside of organisations (Tufinio, Mooi, Ravestijn, Bakker, & Boorsma, 2013, p.98). Ebbesen and Hope (2013) underpinned this fact in their study, in which 17 project managers have been interviewed about their knowledge and their understanding of the concept of sustainability. They conclude that there was a particularly low level of understanding of the issue of sustainability (Ebbesen & Hope, 2013). Zuberbühler and Weiss (2017) imply that sustainability as a technical term is difficult to specify in usage (p.190). The concept can lead to misunderstandings because it is ambiguous and the core message used in the everyday speech does not satisfy the associations of the scholarship (Zuberbühler & Weiss, 2017). However, science has not yet agreed precisely on how to define sustainability (Howarth, 2010, p.445). If sustainability is determined in terms of a functioning ecosystem, then additional specifications are needed. It might be difficult to exactly determine how a functioning ecosystem with several sub-areas such as air, soil, water, fauna or flora interacts. Thus, sustainability requires above all a cross-linked and integrative perspective. This view underpins the fact that sustainability is a complex concept. In relation to the definitions from the selected publications, we see congruency in understanding the concept of sustainability as a holistic view based on the Brundtland report definition and the Triple Bottom Line approach. However, a definition of sustainability remains a difficult task due to the multidimensional perspectives, the complexity and the individual interpretations of the concept. Practical experience and empirical measurement are still necessary.

Definition Sustainable Project Management

This category refers to the question how sustainable project management is defined in the selected literature. Table 4 presents identified definitions of sustainable project management from the selected publications.

In overall, the selected definitions of sustainable project management differ in their scope of presentation. The differences become clear due to the involved actions according to what sustainability in project management is about. For example, the

Table 4. Definitions of sustainable project management

Author	Definition of Sustainable Project Management
Deland, 2009, p.11	"Sustainable Project Management is minimizing the resources that you and your team use to work a project from project initiation through close."
Ebbesen & Hope, 2013, p.5	"Sustainable project management seeks to ensure that projects incorporate sustainability principles throughout the project lifecycle and beyond."
Silvius et al., 2012, p.40	"Sustainability in projects and project management is the development, delivery and management of project-organized change in policies, processes, resources, assets or organizations, with consideration of the six principles* of sustainability, in the project, its results and its effects."
	* (1) balancing or harmonising social, environmental and economical interests; (2) both short-term and long-term orientation; (3) both local and global orientation; (4) values and ethics; (5) transparency and accountability; and (6) consuming income, not capital.
Silvius & Schipper, 2014a, p.79	"Sustainable Project Management is the planning, monitoring and controlling of project delivery and support processes, with consideration of the environmental, economical and social aspects of the life-cycle of the project's resources, processes, deliverables and effects, aimed at realising benefits for stakeholders, and performed in a transparent, fair and ethical way that includes proactive stakeholder participation."
Tam, 2010, p.18	"The promoting of positive and minimizing of negative sustainability impacts (economic; environmental; and social) within the process by which projects are defined, planned, monitored, controlled and delivered such that the agreed benefits are realized and contributing to a sustainable society."

definition from Deland (2009) and Ebbesen and Hope (2013) present two actions. In contrast to that, the definitions from Silvius et al. (2012) and Silvius and Schipper (2014a) present more than three actions.

Similarities can be noticed in the connection to the project management process. It is notable that the authors define sustainability in not only project management areas like processes, products or services but also as a holistic view for a business approach in order to describe a change in an organisation (Otegi-Olaso, Aguilar-Fernández, Cruz-Villazón, 2015, p.48). However, all definitions, except for one, emphasis a need to include sustainable aspects, like economic, social and environmental or sustainable principles.

It is remarkable that just five authors (teams) suggest a concrete definition of the term sustainable project management. This limited number of definitions can be explained by the fact that the research area, measured by the increase in publications, has only developed within the past eight years (see Figure 1).

Although it is possible to draw similarities between the definitions, there are also some significant differences in respect to the scope of the definitions. It is noticed that just Silvius and his team (e.g. Silvius & Schipper, 2014a) justify their definition based on extensive preliminary studies. This can be recognised by the fact that Silvius and his team revised their first definition of sustainable project management. They tried to classify principles of sustainability project management into a framework with six categories. According to Christensen (2006, pp.39-40), those categorisation schemes are indicators of a theory-building process. This ongoing struggle for a clearer defined terminology and categorisation on the definition of sustainable project management can help to understand the scope of sustainability in project management (Christensen, 2006, pp.40-41). This is necessary to build a descriptive theory via observation, categorisation, and association (Christensen, 2006). Thus, Silvius and his team can be considered as pioneers in the field of sustainable project management. However, the theory-building process must be regarded in differentiated terms. There is a lack of a common ground in the foundation of the framework. Especially when it comes to the concept of sustainability, it is difficult to create a shared understanding.

Writing in the journal 'Sustainable Development', Christen and Schmidt (2012, p.401) report reasons why definitions that include the concept of sustainability often fail. One reason could be that the definitions are insufficiently precise for clear instructions. It is often neglected that the society is a dynamic system (Christen & Schmidt, 2012). Adding specific goals to the definition might not consider this change process and therefore lose significance over time (Christen & Schmidt, 2012). If the definition is understood in terms of normative conditions, it may be guilty of paternalism (Christen & Schmidt, 2012). In addition, the term 'sustainability' is characterised by the individual perception of every single person and creates different interpretations due to its frequent and intensive use (Christen & Schmidt, 2012).

It can be summarised that defining the term 'sustainable project management' is a greater scientific challenge due to of the complexity of the term sustainability. One possible way to get closer to this problem might be to change the definitional strategy by developing a framework on a system-based approach, instead of generating a solid definition (Christen & Schmidt, 2012, p.402). This approach should start from a problem formulation analysis and could use meta-data of sustainability and project management to define the involved elements in sustainable project management (Christen & Schmidt, 2012). The approach should cover concrete actions, which affect the problems identified by the analysis (Christen & Schmidt, 2012).

Affected Areas

According to Martens and Carvalho (2015, p.30) the most reference guides in the project management area do not devote special attention to the issue of sustainability. Therefore, the authors highlight guides and important organizations: The Guide of the Project Management Body of Knowledge (PMBoK) (PMI, 2013), the PM Guide 2.0 (International Association of Project Managers, 2010), the Australian Institute of Project Management (AIPM) (2010), the APM, or the Projects in Controlled Environments PRINCE2 (Axelos, 2017).

We only consider the Guide of the PMBoK from the PMI (2013) and use their ten areas of knowledge as analysis criterions to identify affected areas of sustainability in project management (PMI, 2013). Affected areas are identified from the context and of the economic, the social and the environmental dimension of sustainability. It should be noted that some texts have an individual understanding of sustainability. However, for this analysis, the general understanding of the Triple Bottom Line and the Brundtland report is set as a framework for sustainability. Figure 2 presents the number of mentions of affected knowledge areas by sustainability. It can be declared that all knowledge areas are affected by sustainability.

In all, except for one text, it is described that the knowledge area of Project Integration Management is strongly affected by sustainability. Almost every text acknowledges that sustainable principles influence the project process, or areas of the project phases (e.g. Daneshpour, 2015; Deland, 2009; Gareis, 2013; Keeys, 2012). Kirchhof and Brandtweiner (2011) concede that the integration of sustainability in the project management process is already proofed by empirical findings (p.531). Due to the fact that the current environment is much more complex, the authors of the publications like Okland (2015), Otegi-Olaso et al. (2015), Silvius et al. (2012), or Silvius (2016) emphases that the boundary conditions for projects scope, time, cost and quality are stretched by considering sustainability. This will affect Project Scope Management, Project Time Management, Project Cost Management and Project

Figure 2. Bar chart on the number of mentions of affected knowledge areas by sustainability
Source: (own presentation, referring to (PMI, 2013))

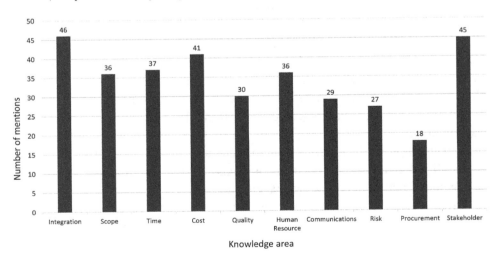

Quality Management. Therefore, it is recognized that companies can see sustainable thinking as a cost and not an investment issue (Aguilar-Fernandez, Otegi-Olaso, Cruz-Villazón, 2015, p.490). The project manager, representing Human Resource Management, is identified as a key person for sustainable project management (e.g. Albarosa & Masura, 2016; Carvalho & Rabechini, 2017; Hope & Moehler, 2014). In line with that, Goedknegt (2012) emphasis that, "a project manager is intrinsically motivated to work on a sustainable project and achieve sustainable result" (p.10). According to Communications Management, Kirchhof and Brandtweiner (2011) state that, "if a company decides to establish sustainability, it is essential to communicate the corresponding actions and make them transparent to the company's environment" (p.530). Silvius (2012d) proposes, that companies are integrating ideas of sustainability in their marketing and corporate communications (p.1). When it comes to the area of Project Risk Management, Oehlmann (2010, p.12) insists that sustainability involves some risk as well. Gareis (2013) argues, "differentiation in economic, ecologic, and social risks as well as in local, regional, and global risks allows for differentiated risk response measures" (p.14). Procurement Management is the knowledge area with the fewest mentions. Therefore, Goedknegt and Silvius (2012) deplore the tendency that, "public organizations are integrating criteria on sustainability in their procurement policies" (p.4). In contrast to that, almost every analysed text assume that Stakeholder Management is affected by sustainability. Labuschagne and Brent (2004) emphasis that, "Businesses are increasingly paying more attention to the social dimension of sustainable development, mainly due to an experienced shift in stakeholder pressures from environmental- to social-related concerns" (p.112). Silvius (2012c) agrees when he writes, "The pressure on companies to broaden its reporting and accountability from economic performance for shareholders, to sustainability performance for all stakeholders has increased" (p.2).

So all ten knowledge areas affected by sustainability. Still, not all areas are dealt with equally. Differences occur due to the research design, the knowledge about project management and sustainability, or the intention behind the publication. For example, the publication by Silvius et al. (2013) is an empirical study and does not focus on theoretical findings. Therefore, they mention only two knowledge areas, which are affected by sustainability. In contrast to that Silvius (2012d) point out, that all ten knowledge areas originally defined by the PMI (2013) are affected by sustainability.

As being highly affected from sustainability and also the most influential ones, we identified the project management areas 'Integration Management', 'Cost Management' and 'Stakeholder Management'.

All except one of the analysed publications mention that the knowledge area Integration Management is highly affected by sustainability. This project management area includes the optimal integration of all project parts, the involved persons and institutions (PMI 2013, p.63). This implies that sustainable aspects affect the complete project management process of initiating, planning, executing, controlling, and closing.

The second identified highly affected and influential area is Cost Management (PMI, 2013, p.193). As the sustainability approach is linked to project management, it can be focused on a sustainable handling of resources and a responsibility towards future generations. Therefore, costs of sustainable actions can occur in all quality issues of a project like prevention costs, appraisal costs or human resource costs. Costs can rise during the whole project through additional analyse, reviews, monitoring, controlling or similar actions due to sustainable thinking.

Stakeholder Management is quoted particularly often, too. For example, Silvius and Schipper (2014a) link sustainable development to the role of stakeholders and emphasize stakeholder participation and proactive stakeholder engagement (p.70, 77). Regarding the PMI (2013), which defines a stakeholder as an, "individual, group or organization who may affect, be affected by, or perceive itself to be affected by a decision, activity or outcome of the project" (p.563), there is a wide range of interpretation. Among Silvius et al. (2012) suggestions for typical sustainability stakeholders like environmental protection pressure groups, human rights groups, non-governmental organisations, we suggest regarding the Brundtland report to include the needs of future generations to the group of stakeholders.

Principles of Sustainable Project Management

For this category only texts that propose principles of sustainability in direct relation to project management are considered. Under this condition, we identified 30 publications.

It is remarkable that most (78%) of the texts refer to the principles of sustainable project management from the publications explicitly involving the ideas of the authors Silvius et al. (2012) and Gareis et al. (2011). 13 publications refer to the principles from the author Silvius et al. (2012), who developed their own sustainable project management principles. Twelve publications refer to the authors Gareis et al. (2011), who focus in confronting six sustainability characteristics with the project management processes and methods. All principles established so far can be found or synthesized in the nine principles from Silvius and Schipper (2016, pp.11-13) and will be briefly described in the following.

The first principle focuses on a holistic approach and can be understood as balancing or harmonise social, environmental and economic interests (Silvius & Schipper, 2016, p.11). Elkington (1997) was the first who emphasised to build a case for simultaneous and equal consideration of the three pillars of sustainability. The three pillars are interconnected and influence each other in all areas of project management. The second principle focuses on short-term and long-term orientation of project management (Silvius & Schipper, 2016, p.11). Silvius and Schipper interpret this principle in terms of considering long- and short-term effects and consequences of actions (Silvius & Schipper, 2016). In addition, there should be also considerations about intergenerational and intra-generational equity (Labuschagne & Brent, 2009, p. 4). This means that sustainable project management actions should respect current and future generations due to aspects of the Triple Bottom Line. The third principle belongs to both local and global orientation (Silvius & Schipper, 2016, p.11). Due to the globalisation, Silvius and Schipper (2016) argue that companies have been able to broaden their geographical influence. As a result, they should reconsider their national and international activities to meet the demands of stakeholders, suppliers, labours or potential customers (Silvius & Schipper, 2016). The fourth principle focus on values and ethics. For Silvius and Schipper (2016), "sustainable development is a normative concept, reflecting values and ethical considerations of society" (p.12). This means that all the activities of an organization, for example, the scope of action of a project manager and his team, should consider certain sustainable values and ethics (Silvius & Schipper, 2016). The fifth principle concentrates on transparency and accountability (Silvius & Schipper, 2016). This principle is a demandable or a desirable state, which provides free access to processes, factual projects, policies and decision-making processes of the company (Silvius & Schipper, 2016). This means that companies and their project manager have an accountability towards society and their stakeholders and should provide them with economic, social and environmental information (Silvius & Schipper, 2016). The sixth principle focuses on stakeholder participation (Silvius & Schipper, 2016). Gareis (2013) presents three possible forms of stakeholder participation. The first is to inform the stakeholder about the outcomes of the initiation process (Gareis, 2013, p.8). The second and third form of participation can be invitations to special events (Gareis, 2013). On one hand, stakeholders can participate in the evaluation and the planning of meetings and workshops (Gareis, 2013). On the other hand, stakeholders may be invited to become members of the initiation team (Gareis, 2013). The seventh principle concentrates on risk reduction (Silvius & Schipper, 2016, p.12). According to this principle, the conceivable burdens or damage to the environment or human health in advance should be avoided or minimized as far as possible (Silvius & Schipper, 2016). This serves as a risk or hazard prevention (Silvius & Schipper, 2016). When it comes to the eight principle, which is about eliminating waste, Silvius and Schipper (2016) refer to 'The Seven Wastes' (Silvius & Schipper, 2016). These are overproduction, waiting, transporting, inappropriate processing, unnecessary inventory, unnecessary or excess motion and defects (Silvius & Schipper, 2016). The ninth principle is about 'consuming income, not capital' (Silvius & Schipper, 2016, p.13). Assuming that, sustainability implies that nature generates resources or energy that should stay intact (Silvius & Schipper, 2016). This implies that activities of projects should not be designed to consume these environmental resources (Silvius & Schipper, 2016). That means that the absorptive capacity of nature of receiving waste should not be exceeded. (Silvius & Schipper, 2016). According to a social perspective, workers, or individuals, should not be mentally or physically overworked (Gilbert, Stevenson, Girardet, & Stren, 1996, p11). From an economic point of view, this means using income from previous projects or clients rather than investing the company's own capital (Silvius, 2012c, p.91).

As a result of this category, it is particularly noticeable that none of the principles of sustainable project management are empirically proven. The principles have been developed in a theoretical or conceptional way and are assumptions about a potential direction of sustainable project management.

Michaelides et al. (2014, p.5) state that sustainability has a broad scope, which also covers the basic principles of good business practice. In other words, they believe that the formulated principles like having a holistic view, considerations about long-term and global orientation, ensuring transparency and accountability or the obligation of personal values and ethics, are already components of good business practices (Michaelides et al., 2014). The essence of this argument is that in a solid business strategy those sustainable principles are already assimilated. However, the argumentation of Michaelides et al. (2014) leaves the question open what 'good business practice' is about.

Project Manager

In this category, we analysed the question how the project manager is affected by the topic of sustainability. We adopted the three dimensions of the Project Management Competence Development framework (PMCD) from the PMI as analysis criteria. In this context, Cartwright & Yinger (2007) define competencies as a cluster of related knowledge, attitude, skills, and other personal characteristics that affect a major part of one's job. We paid attention to competency requirements, which are further enhanced by the aspect of sustainability. The first dimension is called 'knowledge' and refers to the question if project manager should have a sustainable knowledge or not (Cartwright & Yinger, 2007). The second area is called 'performance' and provides information about what a sustainable project manager can do or accomplish while performing sustainable tasks (Cartwright & Yinger, 2007). The third area is called 'personal' and refers to the project manager behaviour (Cartwright & Yinger, 2007). We examined whether sustainability requires specific values or ethics from the project manager.

Overall, 39 publications attribute the project manager a significant role in the development of sustainability in project management. No assertions to the contrary can be found. In total, 22 publications make statements about the knowledge of a project manager in terms of sustainability. For example, Silvius and Schipper (2014a) emphasises that, "Integrating sustainability requires that project managers develop themselves as specialists in sustainable development" (p.79). Joseph and Marnewick (2016) underline, that project manager should have knowledge of sustainability to ensure that the principles of sustainability are applied to the project" (p.536). For all these texts, the context is quite clear: project managers are responsible for sustainability. This implies the existence of knowledge about sustainability.

When it comes to the area of performance, 20 publications provide information about what a sustainable project manager can do or accomplish while performing sustainable tasks. Six statements from authors or author groups can be summarised under the aspect of complexity (e.g. Daneshpour, 2015, p.321; Marcelino-Sádab, González-Jaen, Pérez-Ezcurdia, 2015, p.13). This implicates that the idea of the integration of sustainability into project management increases the range of tasks for a project manager. We want to provide some examples. Agarwal and Kalmár (2015) argue that the sustainable principles of transparency force the project manager reveal information about all decisions, relevant events and impact to stakeholders (p.13). Silvius (2012a) reminds that project managers give account for their actions and decisions in progress reporting's. Therefore, project managers should also consider the three dimensions of sustainability (Joseph & Marnewick, 2016, p.537). Oehlmann adds (2010), "The project manager should find a good balance between these three aspects because currently the focus tends to be placed on the 'Profit' value" (p.1). Marcelino-Sádaba et al. (2015) conclude that, "the challenge for project managers, designers and other stakeholders in the project is to identify and justify the use of sustainability elements that do not influence the cost or that even save costs" (p.8). Furthermore, Kirchhof and Brandtweiner (2011) give an example for the social perspective and argue that, "project managers have to ensure that each member of project team is acting in accordance with the established sustainability principles" (p.533).

When it comes to the third area, the behaviour dimension, it can be summarised, that 16 publications agree that sustainable values and ethics influence the project manager behaviour. Marcelino-Sádaba et al. (2015) report, "No sustainable project can exist without calling on the ethical aspect of the project manager and his team" (p.12). In line with that, Silva (2015) argues, "to incorporate principles of sustainability at the heart of a project inception is key as part of the responsibilities of a professional project manager" (p.4).

It should be emphasised that the authors Silvius et al. (2013) investigate the issue of sustainable competencies of the project manager in greater detail. For their analysis, they confronted the International Competence Baseline Version 3.0, which is one of the most widely used frameworks for project management competences standards, with their own developed principles of sustainability (Silvius, Schipper, & Nedeski, 2013, p.64-71). The ICB framework divides project management competencies into three areas: contextual competences, which describes the involvement of the project within its context (project, programme, portfolio and organisation), technical competencies, which belong to the project management processes, and the behavioural competencies, which cover the skills and attitudes of the project manager itself (IPMA, 2006, pp.38, 83, 125). Based on a theoretical analysis, Silvius et al. (2013, pp.69-70) classify the impact of sustainability on all three competences as substantial. Moreover, they discovered the following missing competencies in the ICB Version 3.0 (Silvius et al., 2013, pp.70-72).

A project manager needs consulting competency to influence the stakeholders and the project team in order to make an organisation more sustainable (Silvius et al., 2013, p.69). Knowledge about sustainability in general is essential for a project manager (Silvius et al., 2013). On a more cognitive level, this implies competency of sustainability knowledge (Silvius et al., 2013). In addition, sustainable thinking entails balancing economical, social and environmental aspects in the project (Silvius et al., 2013, p.70). In this context, project management becomes more versatile and requires competency in handling complexity (Silvius et al., 2013).

CONCLUSION

To comprehend the essence of the topic on sustainable project management a literature review according to Cooper (1989) was conducted. Cooper's taxonomy was used to set a main substantive focus with certain limitations (Cooper et al., 2009). Relevant literature was identified using the database of Google Scholar. In order to analyse the selected literature, a bibliometric analysis and a qualitative content analysis were adopted. From the bibliometric analysis, it can be concluded that the research field of sustainable project management is still evolving. There are only a few empirical studies on this topic. Most ideas of sustainable project management are conceptual and not proven empirical.

To deal with the central research question "What are connections between sustainability and project management?", we split it up into three sub-questions. The first sub-question relates to the definitions of project management, sustainability and sustainable project management. Therefore, we investigated the selected literature for these definitions. As the analysis and interpretation have shown, a consensus is about the definition of project management. Similarly, it was noticeable that the topic of sustainability has an agreed standard definition based on the Brundtland (1987, p.41) report and a common understanding relating to the Triple Bottom Line approach. However, it should be emphasised, that due to the complexity of the concept of sustainability there are many different interpretations. When it comes to the definition of sustainable project management, it can be summarised, that there is a lack of qualified definitions in the chosen literature. Only Silvius and Schipper (2014a, p.79) propose a solid definition of the term.

The second sub-question refers to sustainability affected and influential project management areas. The selected publications were scanned in relation to the ten knowledge areas defined by the PMI (2013). It follows that all ten areas by the PMI are affected because of the holistic and multidimensional impact of sustainability. Moreover, we identified the following areas as highly affected and influential: Integration Management, Cost Management and Stakeholder Management.

The last sub-question deals with related topics of sustainable project management. The project manager plays a key role in sustainable project management. The requirements have increased from a traditional project manager to a sustainable project manager. Silvius, the most productive author on this research field and his co-authors tried to integrate several sustainable principles within project management in order to evolve the profession of sustainable project management.

We showed that the 46 identified publications only allow a vague interpretation of the concept sustainability. A future challenge is to develop a uniform scientific understanding about the term sustainability in both science and practice. Furthermore, it remains open how to operationalise the concept of sustainability in the discipline of sustainable project management. Thus, we recommend an explanatory research on this operationalisation.

As a result of our research, all ten knowledge areas from the PMI (2013) are identified as affected by sustainability. In addition, further aspects of project management with are influenced by sustainability can be identified. Further investigation seems to be necessary due to increasing the relevance of the topic sustainable project management.

Approval is given to the developed principles from Silvius at al. (2012). These principles propose a way to incorporate sustainability into project management. As the next step for further research, it is suggested to focus on the empirical evaluation of these principles.

In summary, we suggest further research into the practical implementation of the theoretical sustainable project management understanding. Empirical evidence is necessary to evaluate, specify, and manifest interpretations of sustainable project management due to the evolving of this potentially new discipline.

REFERENCES

Agarwal, S. R., & Kalmár, T. (2015). *Sustainability in project management: Eight principles in practice* (Master's thesis). Umeå School of Business and Economics, Sweden. Retrieved from http://umu.diva-portal.org/smash/get/diva2:899231/FULLTEXT01.pdf

Aguilar-Fernandez, M. E., Otegi-Olaso, J. R., & Cruz-Villazón, C. (2015). Analysing sustainability in project life cycle and business models from the perspective of the sustainable innovation drivers. *Proceedings of the 8th International Conference on Intelligent Data Acquisition and Advanced Computing Systems*. 10.1109/IDAACS.2015.7341354

Albarosa, F., & Musura, R. E. V. (2016). *Social Sustainability Aspects of Agile Project Management* (Master's thesis). Umeå School of Business and Economics, Sweden. Retrieved from https://umu.diva-portal.org/smash/get/diva2:1070296/FULLTEXT01.pdf

Andres, A. (2012). *Measuring Academic Research: How to Undertake a Bibliometric Study*. Cambridge, UK: Chandos Publishing.

Association for Project Management. (n.d.). *APM supports sustainability outlooks*. Retrieved July 13, 2006, from: http://www.blackpool.ac.uk/sites/default/files/documents /apm_supports_sustainability_oultooks.pdf

Australian Institute of Project Management. (n.d.). *AIPM website*. Retrieved December 11, 2017, from http:// www.aipm.com.au/

Axelos. (2017). *Projects in Controlled Environments* (PRINCE2). Norwich: The Stationery Office.

Ball, R., & Tunger, D. (2005). Bibliometrische Analysen - Daten, Fakten und Methoden. Jülich, Germany: Forschungszentrum Jülich.

Brookes, B. C. (1990). Biblio-, sciento-, infor-metrics?? what are we talking about? In L. Egghe & R. Rousseau (Eds.), *Informetrics, 89/90* (pp. 31–43). London, Ontario, Canada: Elsevier.

Brundtland, G. H. (1987). *Our common future: World commission on environment and development*. Oxford, UK: Oxford University Press.

Cartwright, C., & Yinger, M. (2007). *Project management competency development framework*. Paper presented at PMI Global Congress (EMEA 2017), Budapest, Hungary.

Carvalho, M. M., & Rabechini, R. Jr. (2017). Can project sustainability management impact project success? An empirical study applying a contingent approach. International Journal of Project Management. *International Journal of Project Management, 35*(6), 1120–1132. doi:10.1016/j.ijproman.2017.02.018

Christen, M., & Schmidt, S. (2012). A Formal Framework for Conceptions of Sustainability - a Theoretical Contribution to the Discourse in Sustainable Development. *Sustainable Development, 20*(6), 400–410. doi:10.1002d.518

Christensen, C. M. (2006). The ongoing process of building a theory of disruption. *Journal of Product Innovation Management, 23*(1), 39–55. doi:10.1111/j.1540-5885.2005.00180.x

Cooper, H. (1989). *Integrating research* (2nd ed.). London: Sage.

Cooper, H., Hedges, L. V., & Valentine, J. C. (2009). *The handbook of research synthesis and meta-analysis* (2nd ed.). New York, NY: Russell Sage Foundation.

Daneshpour, H. (2015). Integrating Sustainability into Management of Project. *International Journal of Environmental Sciences and Development, 6*(4), 321–325. doi:10.7763/IJESD.2015.V6.611

Deland, D. (2009). Sustainability through project management and net impact. In *Proceedings of the PMI Global Congress 2009*. Philadelphia, PA: Project Management Institute.

Ebbesen, J. B., & Hope, A. (2013). Re-imagining the Iron Triangle: Embedding Sustainability into Project Constraints. *PM World Journal, 2*(3), 1–13.

Elkington, J. (1997). *Cannibals with Forks: The Triple Bottom Line of 21st Century Business*. Oxford, UK: Capstone Publishing.

Farley, H. M., & Smith, Z. A. (2014). *Sustainability: If It's Everything, Is It Nothing?* New York: Routledge.

Gareis, R. (2013). Re-Thinking Project Initiation and Project Management by Considering Principles of Sustainable Development. In A. G. Silvius & J. Tharp (Eds.), *Sustainability Integration for Effective Project Management* (pp. 129–143). Hershey, PA: IGI Global. doi:10.4018/978-1-4666-4177-8.ch008

Gareis, R., Heumann, M., & Martinuzzi, A. (2010). Relating sustainable development and project management: a conceptual model. In *Proceedings of the PMI Research Conference 2010*. Newtown Square, PA: Project Management Institute.

Gareis, R., Heumann, M., & Martinuzzi, A. (2011). What can project management learn from considering sustainability principles? *Project Perspectives*, *33*, 60–65.

Gilbert, R., Stevenson, D., Girardet, H., & Stren, R. (1996). *Making cities work: The role of local authorities in the urban environment*. London: Earthscan.

Goedknegt, D. (2012). Sustainability in project management: A case study at University of Applied Sciences Utrecht. *PM World Journal*, *1*(4), 1–18.

Goedknegt, D., & Silvius, A. J. G. (2012). *The implementation of sustainability principles in project management*. Paper presented on the 26th IPMA World Congress, Creta, Greece.

Hope, A. J., & Moehler, R. (2014). Balancing Projects with Society and the Environment: A Project, Programme and Portfolio Approach. *Procedia: Social and Behavioral Sciences*, *119*, 358–367. doi:10.1016/j.sbspro.2014.03.041

Howarth, R. B. (1997). Defining Sustainability: An Overview. *Land Economics*, *73*(4), 445–457.

International Association of Project Managers. (2010). *PM Guide 2.0: Guideline for the Certification of Project Managers*. Liechtenstein: Author.

International Project Management Association. (2006). *IPMA Competence Baseline, Version 3.0*. Author.

International Union for Conservation of Natural Resources. (1991). *Caring for the Earth: A strategy for sustainable living*. Sterling, VA: Earthscan.

Joseph, N., & Marnewick, C. (2016). Incorporating the dimensions of sustainability into information systems projects. *Southern African Business Review*, *20*(1), 530–556. doi:10.25159/1998-8125/6062

Keeys, L. A. (2012). Emerging sustainable development strategy in projects: A theoretical framework. *PM World Journal*, *1*(2), 1–15.

Kirchhof, S., & Brandtweiner, R. (2011). Sustainability in projects: An analysis of relevant sustainability aspects in the project management process based on the three pillars model. In C. A. Brebbia & E. Beriatos (Eds.), *Sustainable Development And Planning* (pp. 527–535). Southampton, UK: WIT Press. doi:10.2495/SDP110441

Kivilä, J., Martinsuo, M., & Vuorinen, L. (2017). Sustainable project management through project control in infrastructure projects. *International Journal of Project Management, 35*(5), 1167–1183. doi:10.1016/j.ijproman.2017.02.009

Labuschagne, C., & Brent, A. C. (2004). *Sustainable project life cycle management: Aligning project management methodologies with the principles of sustainable development.* Paper presented at the Project Management South Africa International Conference, Johannesburg, South Africa.

Machi, L., & McEvoy, B. (2017). *The Literature Review: Six Steps to success* (3rd ed.). London: Corwin.

Marcelino-Sádaba, S., González-Jaen, L. F., & Pérez-Ezcurdia, A. (2015). Using project management as a way to sustainability: From a comprehensive review to a framework definition. *Journal of Cleaner Production, 99*, 1–16. doi:10.1016/j.jclepro.2015.03.020

Marnewick, C. (2017). Information system project's sustainability capability levels. *International Journal of Project Management, 35*(6), 1151–1166. doi:10.1016/j.ijproman.2017.02.014

Martens, M. L., & Carvalho, M. M. (2013). An exploratory study of sustainability evaluation in project management. *Product: Management & Development, 11*(2), 111–117. doi:10.4322/pmd.2013.019

Martens, M. L., & Carvalho, M. M. (2015). The challenge of introducing sustainability into project management function: Multiple-case studies. *Journal of Cleaner Production, 117*, 29–40. doi:10.1016/j.jclepro.2015.12.039

Mayring, P. (2015). *Qualitative Inhaltsanalyse: Grundlagen und Techniken* (12th ed.). Weinheim, Germany: Beltz.

Michaelides, R., Bryde, D., & Ohaeri, U. S. (2014). Sustainability from a project management perspective: are oil and gas supply chains ready to embed sustainability in their projects? In *Proceedings of the Project Management Institute Research and Education Conference*. Newtown Square, PA: Project Management Institute.

Monto, M., Ganesh, L. S., & Varghese, K. (2005). *Sustainability and Human Settlements: Fundamental Issues, Modeling and Simulations*. New Delhi, India: Sage Publications.

Morris, P. W. G., Pinto, J. K., & Söderlund, J. (2012). *The Oxford Handbook of Project Management*. New York: Oxford University Press.

Nishida, A., Koshijima, I., & Umeda, T. (2014). The deployment of sustainable P2M. In *Proceedings of International Conference on Engineering*. Bergamo, Italy: Institute of Electrical and Electronics Engineers.

Oehlmann, I. (2011). *The sustainable footprint methodology*. Cologne, Germany: Lambert Academic Publishing.

Okland, A. (2015). Gap Analysis for Incorporating Sustainability in Project Management. *Procedia Computer Science, 64*(1877), 103-109.

Otegi-Olaso, J. R., Aguilar-Fernández, M. E., & Cruz-Villazón, C. (2015). Towards sustainable project management: A literature review. In *Proceedings of the 19th International Congress on Project Management and Engineering*. Granada, Spain: International Project Management Association.

Pritchard, A. (1969). Statistical Bibliography or Bibliometrics. *The Journal of Documentation, 25*, 348–349.

Project Management Institute. (2008). *A Guide to the Project Management Body of Knowledge (PMBOK guide)* (4th ed.). Newtown Square, PA: Project Management Institute.

Project Management Institute. (2013). *A Guide to the Project Management Body of Knowledge (PMBOK guide)* (5th ed.). Newtown Square, PA: Project Management Institute.

Sánchez, M. A. (2015). Integrating sustainability issues into project management. *Journal of Cleaner Production, 96*, 319–330. doi:10.1016/j.jclepro.2013.12.087

Siew, R. Y. J., Balatbat, M. C. A., & Carmichael, D. G. (2016). Measuring project sustainability maturity level – a fuzzy-based approach. *International Journal of Sustainable Development, 19*(1), 76–100. doi:10.1504/IJSD.2016.073680

Silva, M. (2015). Future-Proof: Foresight as a Tool towards Project Legacy Sustainability. *Project Management World Journal, 4*(5), 350–362.

Silvius, A. J. G. (2012a). *The role of Organizational Change in Green IS: Integrating Sustainability in Projects.* Paper presented at International Conference on Information Resources Management (Conf-IRM), Vienna, Austria.

Silvius, A. J. G. (2012b). Change the game: Sustainability in projects and project management. In S. Seidel, J. Recker, & J. Brocke (Eds.), *Green BPM - Towards the Environmentally Sustainable Enterprise* (pp. 161–177). Berlin, Germany: Springer. doi:10.1007/978-3-642-27488-6_10

Silvius, A. J. G. (2012c). *Sustainability in project management: Vision, mission, ambition.* Paper presented at the PM Summit 2012, Istanbul, Turkey.

Silvius, A. J. G. (2016). Sustainability as a competence of Project Managers. *PM World Journal, 5*(4), 1–13.

Silvius, A. J. G., & Schipper, R. (2010). A maturity model for integrating sustainability in projects and project management. In *Proceedings of the 24th World Congress of the International Project Management Association.* Istanbul: International Project Management Association.

Silvius, A. J. G., & Schipper, R. (2012). *Sustainability in Project Management Competences.* Paper presented on the 26th IPMA World Congress, Creta, Greece.

Silvius, A. J. G., & Schipper, R. (2014a). Sustainability in project management: A literature review and impact analysis. *Social Business, 4*(1), 63–96. doi:10.1362/2 04440814X13948909253866

Silvius, A. J. G., & Schipper, R. (2014b). Sustainability in Project Management Competencies: Analyzing the Competence Gap of Project Managers. *Journal of Human Resource and Sustainability Studies, 2*(2), 40–58. doi:10.4236/jhrss.2014.22005

Silvius, A. J. G., & Schipper, R. (2015). A Conceptual Model for Exploring the Relationship between Sustainability and Project Success. *Procedia Computer Science, 64*, 334–342. doi:10.1016/j.procs.2015.08.497

Silvius, A. J. G., & Schipper, R. (2016). Exploring the relationship between sustainability and project success -conceptual model and expected relationships. *International Journal of Information Systems and Project Management, 4*(3), 5–22.

Silvius, A. J. G., Schipper, R., & Nedeski, S. (2013). Sustainability in Project Management: Reality Bites. *PM World Journal, 2*(2), 1–183.

Silvius, A. J. G., Schipper, R., Planko, J., van den Brink, J., & Köhler, A. (2012). *Sustainability in project management.* London: Gower Publishing.

Silvius, A. J. G., & Tharp, J. (2013). *Sustainability Integration for Effective Project Management.* Hershey, PA: IGI Global. doi:10.4018/978-1-4666-4177-8

Silvius, A. J. G., van den Brink, J., & Köhler, A. (2012). The impact of sustainability on project management. In H. Linger & J. Owen (Eds.), *The Project as a Social System* (pp. 183–200). Victoria, Australia: Monash University Publishing.

Talbot, J., & Venkataraman, R. (2011). Integration of sustainability principles into project baselines using a comprehensive indicator set. *International Business & Economics Research Journal, 10*(9), 29–40.

Tam, G. C. K. (2010). The program management process with sustainability considerations. Journal of Project. *Program & Portfolio Management, 1*(1), 17–27. doi:10.5130/pppm.v1i1.1574

Tufinio, S. P., Mooi, H., Ravestijn, W., Bakker, H., & Boorsma, M. (2013). Sustainability in Project Management. *International Journal of Engineering, 6*(1), 91–101.

Section 4
Global Responsible Governance and Regulation of Digitalization and Potentially Disruptive Technologies

Chapter 7

Governance and Public Policy Challenges in Managing Disruptive and Innovative Technologies

Henry Frank Wissink
https://orcid.org/0000-0002-7149-1041
University of KwaZulu-Natal, South Africa

ABSTRACT

This chapter is an effort to promote and guide thinking about the global and local challenges in how governments respond to innovative and disruptive projects and technologies. The chapter is based on the considerations of and concerns regarding the challenges and changes that we face on a global scale and how it impacts on the notion and need for innovation. Not all inventions or innovations are disruptive or serve the interest of the public at large, and some even may have serious harmful consequences or impacts. These may be unforeseen or sometimes deliberately obscured and perhaps just serve the narrow interests of profiteers. Governments are required to consider their roles and plan to be responsible and proactive to ensure that the best interests of both the business and public sector are pursued for the purposes of long-term sustainability.

DOI: 10.4018/978-1-5225-7638-9.ch007

Copyright © 2019, IGI Global. Copying or distributing in print or electronic forms without written permission of IGI Global is prohibited.

INTRODUCTION

During the past few decades there has been a rapid increase in many innovative and disruptive technologies being introduced to address problems and issues emanating from the growing demands for improved quality of life, and those resulting from new trends and societal changes observed regionally and globally. In particular, innovations and new technologies developed in response to addressing demands for cost effectiveness, efficiency and productivity in industry and public service delivery (Ahlstrom, 2010; McKinsey, 2013). Most institutions are challenged to intervene in ensuring that such innovations and new technologies are wisely evaluated and considered as responsible, responsive and sustainable solutions to many vexatious problems and challenging conditions and changes in society. Governments in particular have an important role to play to ensure good governance and policy management of such innovations and new technologies.

BACKGROUND

Apart from evolutionary innovations such as those we often come across in areas such as public transportation systems, medical science, and information technology, we have also seen radical and disruptive technologies introduced, such as UAV's, Open Source Intelligence, Intelligent Sensor Monitoring, Uber Taxis, Airbnb, novel energy generation systems, water purification systems, and online education, to mention a few. The experience has been that many of these disruptive and innovative technologies are initiated in the private sector, with the role of government limited to broad oversight and by providing policy responses that were reactive, and not proactive (Lynch, 2017; Kaal & Vermeulen, 2017).

Limited literature and research is currently available on how governments should respond to these issues, and the innovations and new technologies that are developed in response to the pressing needs, changes and challenges as described in this chapter. In addition to review much of the literature that has been developed, and which mainly focuses on this phenomenon, this chapter will also propose a framework or model for the governance and management by government.

METHODOLOGY AND FOCUS

This chapter proposes to look at existing literature generated by scholars who have approached the subject from a management science point of view, and in particular valuable work done and published in the fields of innovation. The author uses journal publications, and in some cases institutional and news publications (secondary research), and in particular the most recent publications in the fields of responsible and sustainable management of innovation and new technologies. It is the intention to challenge scholars in governmental sciences and public policy, as well as those industries and enterprises that function in relationship with governments from a policy dependence position. The proposal is that stakeholders consider various proposed approaches and policy considerations in response to the challenges posed by changing global environments, as well as concomitant disruptive innovations. An awareness, that governments also need to be innovative and smart about the challenges that these trends and changes pose, must be developed. This chapter will focus on the question of how governments can respond to these challenges, within a proposed model derived from existing literature. This model would propose to assist all the major actors in the state to become responsive and responsible innovators, with a focus on sustainability, as they proceed with such developments.

FACTORS AFFECTING GLOBAL CHANGES AND NEEDS FOR INNOVATION

According to Lynch (2017, para.1), "We are in the midst of a fourth industrial revolution, driven by disruptive technological change. These technologies, such as big data, machine learning, artificial intelligence, quantum computing and block chain are intersecting and combining in extraordinary ways to create a 'technology 4.0 world'. Few revolutions unfold without upheaval, uncertainty and swaths of winners and losers, however, this one is no different. Its impact will be felt well beyond commerce – in how we communicate, interact, date, learn, gather news and govern ourselves". Apart from the growing needs and demands to produce an information driven technological revolution, generally referred to as the Fourth Industrial Revolution (World Economic Forum, 2019), we are also faced with many changes contributing to these demands, both globally, but also regionally. This section provides an overview of these changes and challenges.

Population Growth Patterns

Population growth has changed dramatically, from 1760, when the world population statistic measured 1.7 billion people, to 1950 when the number was 3 billion, to 2017 when it measured 7.4 billion+. Growth rates have started declining since the seventies, and are currently around 1%, but overall growth is projected to taper toward the end of the century to a figure of about 11-12 billion people (Roser & Esteban, 2018). The population figure, however, is probably the most important factor influencing our lives on a global scale. On the one hand it creates many problems regarding limited resources; on the other hand the synergistic and compound effect of demand and production creates many more opportunities for people to engage in such dynamic and rapidly growing economies. This is known as the "strength in numbers approach"[1], where large urban centres allow for innovation and increased economies of scale.

Rapid Urbanization

Urbanisation throughout the world is taking place at an unprecedented pace. In 1950, the pace of urbanization was 30%. In 2050, 66% of people on the globe will be living in cities or metropolitan spaces (World Bank, 2018). Rapid urbanization and globalisation created the need for improved and more efficient transportation systems, and in particular the need for effective and efficient urban transportation. Increasingly the concept of urban hubs and aerotropolis developments are being considered as a way of improving the efficient movement of goods and people between cities and strategic hubs. The expanding need for travel, and in particular tourism related travelling, has resulted in the growing demand to create rapid transportation systems (RTS) and autonomous aerial vehicles (UAVs) within the notion of modernistic smart cities (Bonte, 2018).

Poverty, Food Insecurity, and Global Health

The employment of agricultural development is regarded as one of the more successful instruments to manage poverty, increase economic prosperity and provide food security to approximately 9.7 billion people by 2050 (World Bank, 2018). Furthermore, the improvement of agriculture, as opposed to other economic sectors to increase the income of the poorest of the poor, is said to be 2-4 times more effective. According to the World Bank (2018), a 2016 study proved that 65% of poor working adults made a living through agriculture. In 2014, its contribution to the global gross-domestic product (GDP) was 33%. Agriculture-based growth, poverty reduction, and food security are at risk. The current food consumption trends threaten the health of people. Approximately three billion people are malnourished or are ill informed about diets, resulting in illnesses and a global health crisis. According to the World Bank (2018) a report in 2016 found that 815 million people worldwide experience hunger. In 2014, those suffering from obesity were 2.1 billion (62% from developing nations). Globally, the current health risks associated with poor diets have become major reasons for premature death. Furthermore, it is reported that non-communicable diseases such as cardiovascular disease, a variety of cancers, hypertension, diabetes and mental health, are on the increase and contribute to 70%

of deaths on a global scale, and are the dominant occurrence, prevalent in low- and middle-income countries.

Changing Notions of Economic Opportunities

In 2013, the global technology market grew by 8%. The latter is purported to be creating jobs, and broadening the provision of services and new products. According to Kvochko (2013) in 2011, Facebook applications were instrumental in creating 182,000 new jobs, and that the total value of this economy alone exceeded $12 billion. The growth of entrepreneurship, can probably also be linked to the growth of Information and Communication Technologies (ICT), facilitating start-ups to promote best practices, associated policies (legal and regulatory frameworks), as well as marketing and potentially lucrative investment opportunities. According to Kvochko (2013), in a publication by the Organisation for Economic Cooperation and Development (OECD), in these associated countries, 95% of businesses are online, providing them with alternative ways to access customers and to compete for a share in the marketplace. This includes online trading/banking and even new crypto-currencies (OECD, 2012).

Changing Notions of Democracy

The common notion, that as long as there are free and fair elections, democracy is practiced efficiently, should be questioned. In essence, certain democracies could still lead to very corrupt, irresponsible, self-serving, and inefficient governments. Zakaria (2016) argues that "they have become strong on the basis that they are logically democratic, but may be posing a threat to the maintenance of democratic governance." He continues to argue that democracy practiced without constitutional liberalism is dangerous and inherently flawed, as it promotes ethnic division, erodes liberty, and promotes abuses of power, and ultimately conflict and violence. This century should be focused on making democracies work towards a free world; and safer citizenship ought to be one of the major issues to promote. According to Moller (2008), Zakaria's notion that illiberal or intolerant democracies have gained ground is without grounds, and he suggests that this may be the case with some, but that it is not an overwhelming trend. What is concerning though, is to see such trends among some of the biggest and most influential democracies in the world, and in particular, the First World countries. Recently, as can be seen in the "Revolutionary Spring Awakenings", the particular role of social media and global Internet based communication systems should be noted when they reported on, and evaluated the nature of government actions in suppressing protests against illiberal and intolerant state actions.

According to Schneidewind and Augenstein (2016: pp. 1-5), three schools of transformation can be distinguished and to explain and analyse transformation in societies. According to them we have to understand basic ideas – "cultural values, dominant dogmas and world views – and how they impact societies. For a transition to sustainability to be achieved, the necessary societal change processes must develop as the result of powerful ideas and discourses". Schneidewind and Augenstein (2016) continue to argue that societies are driven by three conceptions of mankind that lead to specific related drivers of civilisation. Their concepts, and in combination with the notions of liberal or populist decision-making, can be used to explain why, in some societies and countries, decisions regarding the acceptance and implementation of innovations and new technologies fail or are made in a manner that either leads to failure, successes, rejection or poor implementation without much regard for responsibility. Schneidewind et al. (2016) suggest that the idealist based society will have a leaning towards accepting the guidance of authoritative drivers or leaders (often populist drivers), whereas in other cases the institutions of society (political and administrative structures – parliament, commissions, courts) are trusted. Finally, some societies will be driven by the hope and trust in technological advancements and innovation. Often the immediate urgency and "hype" and short term benefits that emanate from such technologies are very appealing.

The Information Revolution: Growth of ICT's

There are many recent findings that illustrate the positive effect of ICT on growth and development of the economies of many countries. According to Minges (2016), a 10% increase in broadband supply has resulted in a 1.4% increase in the GDP growth of emerging markets. In China for instance, 2.5% growth has been achieved. When mobile data (3G connections) is doubled, it results in an increase in global GDP per capita growth rate by 0.5%. Overall, the Internet results in an increase of 3.4% of GDP in many economies (MGI, 2018; OECD, 2014). Most of this effect is driven by e-commerce – people advertising and selling goods online. According to Hopp, Antons, Kaminski and Salge (2018, para. 1) "…the second wave of digitisation is set to disrupt all spheres of economic life. As venture capital investor Marc Andreesen pointed out, 'software is eating the world'. Yet, despite the unprecedented scope and momentum of digitisation, many decision makers remain unsure of how to cope, and turn to scholars for guidance on how to approach disruption."

INNOVATIVE AND DISRUPTIVE TECHNOLOGIES

The impact of innovative and disruptive technologies in itself impacts society, and is changing the nature of the world we live in a very significant manner. The meteoric rise and growth of these innovative technologies as described by Christensen and Bower (1995, p.10), see disruptive technology as "innovations that create an entirely new market through the introduction of a new kind of service or product".

Already there is a multitude of innovative and disruptive technologies in place or in the process of being tested for implementation, for example:

- Autonomous-driving trucks carrying goods on a highway
- The use of nano-robots to make repairs at the cellular level like nanoparticles delivering specialised chemotherapy drugs to cancer cells
- Google autonomous cars driving passengers between destinations
- Drones delivering goods and/or meals
- AI robots performing and analysing X-rays and presenting diagnoses and prognoses
- Algorithms providing retirement and investment advice
- Artificial intelligence systems set up to progressively allow robotic computers to rapidly learn, infer and predict trends
- Employment of block-chain technologies in modern transactional analyses and banking systems

These kinds of innovations and disruptive technological processes are often aimed at improving productivity and quality of life. However, sometimes they are also instrumental in disrupting the way we live, thereby being responsible for the displacement of many jobs in favour of new and technology based alternative skillsets. If governments do not anticipate such changes in the reshaping of the way we choose to live and work and are pro-active in their approach, we will certainly be facing more acute problems, "…an imminent quandary for policymakers is a certain outcome" (Lynch, 2017, para. 3). A significant part of the problem is: "the growing gap between the scale, scope and speed of these transformations and the capacity of government to implement timely and effective policy changes. Put simply, in today's dynamic world, last-generation governance and policy processes are a poor match for next-generation disruptive trends, and trust in government is an early casualty" (Lynch, 2017, para. 3).

DISRUPTIVE, SUSTAINING AND RADICAL TECHNOLOGICAL INNOVATION

Walsh and Kirchhoff (2000, p.321) provides insight into the notion of disruptive technologies, and disruptive technology versus sustaining technology. Disruptive technology has the ability to arrest technologies currently used within organisations and elsewhere. The original idea of disruptive technology may have originated from the innovations in information technologies used for critical functions in organisations. If the market or environment generally sees the potential of disruptive technology, it may replace existing practices or technology quite rapidly (Walsh & Kirchhoff, 2000, p.323). The difference then between disruptive technology and sustainable technology is often viewed as follows: Disruptive technology, on the one hand, can rapidly destroy or replace sustaining technology, whilst sustainable technologies, on the other hand, will or can be enhanced by producing version upgrades as a response to needs for systematic improvement of the system.

According to Walsh and Kirchhoff (2000, p.324) it is difficult to identify an innovation as disruptive technology before implementation or use by various users, and it is often difficult to forecast the effect of disruptive technology on society, and which sectors disruptive technologies may impact on most.

CHARACTERISTICS OF DISRUPTIVE TECHNOLOGIES

Disruptive innovations and technologies are not easy to anticipate. According to Jones, 2005: p.19) disruptive technologies are usually only recognised once their benefits have been demonstrated and the technology has found a firm place in industry or society. In this case hindsight becomes the best science, as the old adage states. In addition, Walsh and Kirchhoff (2000: p.323) and Christensen (2000), believe that disruptive technologies, despite having great potential, still need to mature by growing from an innovative idea to a valuable and demand driven product. Christensen and Bower (1995: p.10) also argue that disruptive technologies are mostly innovations, but not every innovation ends up being disruptive technology.

Rayport and Jaworski (2004: p.81) argue that to understand the characteristics of disruptive technologies, the various types of innovation can be viewed as follows:

- **Innovation as User-Driven:** This enhancement usually requires a low-cost input, and progresses from a "value added technology" towards a more sustaining technology which requires low risk (e.g. Netflix).

- **Innovation as a Developer-Based Development:** Implies that limits of current technology requires the consideration of a new solution, according to analysis of the user's needs. (e.g. Uber or Air B&B).
- **Innovation as a Brand New Application or Alternatively Combining Previous Technologies:** This may imply a technology developed for a unique context, which could be applied to many other industries (e.g. Drones or UAVs).
- **Innovation as Technology/Market Combined Development:** Innovations that promote new businesses/economic activities through solutions for markets that may be emerging but which do not yet exist (e.g. Driver monitoring systems that regulate insurance pricing/health monitoring systems – based on exercise regimes).

By implication, when an innovation responds to a new industry or an emerging market, it becomes a disruptive technology. Christensen (2000: p.xviii) raises the requirements for disruptive technologies (DTs). DTs are cheaper when procuring and implementing; simple to use without intensive training; smaller in scale than normally expected (Nano-technological advancement); more convenient to use, or reducing the effort; may not necessarily produce larger profits, but adds much more value to lower margins, and can be regarded as "radical change" or requiring radically different technological capabilities.

When a new innovation is implemented, and the new innovation or technology reduces the value of existing competencies and settled jobs. The innovation or new technology could have an extensive negative impact on the organisation or society. Alternatively when new technology enriches the value of competencies and/or creates more jobs, the implementation of the new technology may be more viable or successful.

When new technology originates from outside the existing industry, it is known as an "exogenous effect" (Walsh & Kirchhoff, 2000: p.321). This implies that the disruption was not generally expected; implying an inability to predict "how and where" the innovation technology will be implemented. According to Jones and Smith (2005: p.19) it may sometimes also problematic for users to know that a need even exists for a particular disruptive innovation or technology.

Unpredictable characteristics of disruptive technologies are inter-alia viewed as "scientific discoveries" that challenge or replace the original product or technological solution, and alters the approach to DTIs that modifies the behaviour of and benefits to clients (Kassicieh et al., 2002: p.340). For example nanotechnologies used for medical purposes, synthetic biology, gene editing, and brain science regenerative medicines.

Risks are always involved in disruptive technologies because of unpredictability. Large organisations are generally customer-sensitive, and prefer the "sustaining technology" approach. The story of the slow but sustaining development of the micro-computer serves as an example here.

When it fails to promise lucrative profits, many organisations will not proceed to invest until profit margins and business growth are proven, as these are the major considerations for adoption. The profitability and growth of battery operated cars have been an issue for many years. Even though the technology is now quite well developed and it has the potential to be quite disruptive, it still may be too expensive and ultimately not profitable to launch as a major alternative to combustion based mobility.

Understanding the nature of a particular disruptive technology may be a pre-requisite to understanding why existing arrangements or technologies have been replaced by disruptive technologies. Generally, disruptive technologies are often implemented in emerging markets and smaller organisations where there are less risks, and minimal profit losses. Online and phone application based small loan companies are challenging the major banks, making it possible for the small entrepreneur to access funds. According to Lynch (2017), there are considerable gaps between the rapid development and growth of disruptive solutions and technologies, and our ability to respond from a governance point of view. He reiterates that there are specific causes for this governance gap. Firstly, the increasing pace of technical compared to the pace at which governments can respond to adoption, policy-making and regulatory demands. He uses the example of the game "Angry Birds" that accrued 50-million clients within 35 days following the launch; and companies like Facebook, Snapchat, Netflix, Spotify and Google that develop new platforms at great pace. Governments are simply not geared to respond to the pace of disruptive events (Lynch, 2017).

Secondly, the latitude of innovation and technological change is extensive. When compared to the possibility of government policy analysis and policy making on such matters, where officials are often confined within their individual silo it makes responses very difficult. Technological innovations often do not reflect departmental parameters and concomitant regulatory powers, and it is maintained that government departments are generally not geared for the "hyper-connected" world of information technology, as many of these innovations span several areas and authorities (WEF, 2019).

Thirdly, disruptive innovation is intrinsically risk-based, as opposed to governments that are commonly risk-averse. This phenomenon of "risk averse cultures" intensifies the chasm between innovation and disruptive technology and the capacity of government to rapidly respond with appropriate policy frameworks (guides, rules and regulations) aimed at risk-management models and associated behaviour.

Fourthly, disruptive innovations often are not confined to boundaries, unlike governments who still believe that their borders define their authority and sovereignty. The 2008 global financial crisis also revealed the difference between "new" financial tools and products designed to be employed globally, and the inability of national regulations and regulators, with an inability to effect cross-border co-operation. The impact of Uber also illustrates this point. Very few national and local governments were geared to deal with the effect of the Uber innovation on the taxi industry and the economy. Another example of cross border disruptive innovation was the introduction of block-chain technology and cryptocurrencies.

Fifthly, disruptive and innovative technologies are more often computer or IT based, "…with non-linear scalability and near-zero marginal costs" (WEF, 2019). Governments and resultant policy responses are geared toward incremental changes, because less taxing and easier to gain political and public support for modifying the status quo than creating alternative or new policies.

Finally, disruptive innovations are said to grow and develop through a process of trial and error, unlike the ability of governments to respond which is constrained by uncertainty, a lack of knowledge, and internal skills. Consequently, premature policy responses can hamper innovation as well as allow fair competition to take its normal course. Alternatively, responses that become too delayed can give rise to the build-up of systemic risks. Taxi violence against Uber drivers in South Africa and elsewhere, is an example of the latter. The disruption of traditional media on an unprecedented scale by social-media platforms, allowing the evolution of virtual communities that create and drive unfiltered news, while government's policy analysis and responses are too often the of the imminence and domination of platforms like Facebook, WhatsApp, and Twitter.

HOW SHOULD GOVERNMENTS RESPOND TO DISRUPTIVE, SUSTAINING AND RADICAL INNOVATIONS IN A RESPONSIBLE MANNER?

How do governments assess and respond to these challenges? Change, the pace of life, and the rate at which we see and experience the way in which we live and relate to this changing world, is happening at an alarming pace. This is all affected by the rapid development of innovative and new technologies as explained above, of which most tend to disrupt the manner in which we access and experience new goods and services that affect the quality of our everyday life.

During this new era of disruption, it is required that policy responses shift from being reactive to pro-active, with increased elasticity and readiness to embrace change. It will require the need to improve the use of information technologies, and to assist governments in gaining insights from public mass meetings or responses generated from social media. Communications should avoid short-term perspectives and offer a longer-term focus, as well as consider adopted liberal values, especially if they are enshrined in constitutional precepts.

An important part of a government's response is that policy-making must become more innovative, and should consider the notion of being more "risk-tolerant", but not "risk ignorant". In other words, not responding bureaucratically or legalistically, but by allowing a process to inform and unfold, to allow for some risk taking in order to allow innovations and new technologies an opportunity to prove what they believe to benefit society (Lynch, 2017).

According to Baker et al (2013: p. 4-5), most innovations, despite being radical or sustaining, generally provide industry or governments with less for more. When innovation is considered, if it is not of a disruptive nature, defined as more for less, the innovation costs will typically rise more than the rate of inflation. So apart from being willing to consider change and innovative processes and technologies, if it does not provide the possibility of "more for the same or even less (inputs/costs)", then it should be seriously questioned.

According to Baker et al (2013: p.10) most innovations drive up annual costs by 6-12%, and the breaking of "trade-offs" must be of such a nature that it actually reduces the cost and increases performance and access. "Disruptive innovation comes from a very different mould. These innovations can provide a whole new population of consumers 'underserved' access to a product or service that was previously available to only a few."

RESPONSIBILITY, CARE, RESPONSIVENESS AND SUSTAINABILITY OF INNOVATIONS AND DISRUPTIVE TECHNOLOGIES

This rise in technological advancement and its concomitant effects and power is driven by accelerating globalisation. Pavie (2014: p.210) believes that innovators will have to become more concerned about the impact they have on the world. Therefore, it is appropriate to consider "responsible-innovation" as a pre-emptive precept that requires policy-makers to first take care for humanity and its future. Sadly, this is not yet the case, and as a result, governments need to become geared to anticipate the impact and make wise decisions to accept, reject and possibly to regulate innovations. According to Pavie (2014: p.210) François Rabelais in the sixteenth century wrote the famous remark that "science without consciousness is nothing but the death of the soul", and raises an issue today, which remains a critical question. He uses the Greek term *deinon*, celebrated for a multitude of meanings, and being difficult to translate quotes Sophocles in saying that "both these ideas of the terrible and of the admirable which unite to imply the power of opposites. Sophocles in *Antigone* illustrated this idea by using the example of a man who has resources, whose ingenuous skill is above all expectations, who moves sometimes towards evil, sometimes towards good".

According to Stilgoe, Owen, and Macnaghten (2013: p.1569) the current research in science and technology points toward the fact that notions of responsibility should be based on the premise that "science and technology are not only technically but also socially and politically constituted". Callon et al (2009) suggest that science and technology can ironically also create a sense of ignorance and uncertainty, as they generally tend to make people more dependent on these innovations, in addition to becoming attached to "things" and "people" at a growing scale, there is a sense of an increasing degree of intimate attachment to these innovative technologies. Consequently, unforeseen consequences, whether transformative or harmful, will not just be possible but will most likely be probable. The ongoing debate and unconfirmed concerns about the harmful effects of cellular or mobile phones on neuro-functions is a good case in point. The notion that governance has primarily responded to these challenges by virtue of "post-hoc" and often risk-intolerant based regulatory action. These responses are inherently limited, in that we face the problem of knowledge and control, lacking the evidence to form the basis on which we can "govern technologies before they turn into pathologies". Even though we may have foreseen potential risks, in many cases they are ignored, because the notion of "formal risk assessment" often fails to deal with the negative impacts such as the product innovations associated with the 2008 financial crisis.

Callon et al., (2009) believe that public concerns and questions regarding these matters cannot be reduced to risk only, but raises concerns about the motivation or initial purpose of the research. According to Stilgoe et al., (2013) the alternative approach is that governments often succumb to what is referred to as "moral luck" or " hope that an appeal to unpredictability and an inability to 'reasonably foresee' will allow us to escape moral accountability for our actions." The general consensus is that these two approaches cannot suffice, and it has shifted our focus from normal accountability, legal and other forms of liability and evidence towards principles of *responsibility, care and responsiveness*. The latter provide a better opportunity to manage uncertainty and focus on responsibility, care and responsiveness and allow reflection on purposes and values.

Emerging technologies are often regarded as an "institutional void". Many governments do not have appropriate structures or rules that govern them and characteristically cannot be governed by old forms of governance anymore, but by models that are more decentralised and open-ended, and governed by partnerships networks, markets, as well as modern evidence based politics and policies (Stilgoe et al., 2013, Dreyer et al., 2017). They consequently developed what is referred to as the Dimension Model of Responsible Innovation. Broadly speaking this model considers dimension, coupled with indicative techniques and approaches, and related factors for every dimension that affects or may affect their effective implementation (see figure 1).

Firstly, the dimension of Anticipation in the RRI Model, requires governments to consider questions such as "what if", and to consider "what is known", "what is likely", "what is plausible" and "what is possible". Anticipation is aimed at the idea of improving resilience, and simultaneously creating new and novel opportunities for innovation and creating new agendas and possibilities for socially-robust, risk based research and innovation projects. This process usually follows the line of asking pertinent questions about products, processes and purpose.

Secondly, the dimension of Inclusiveness requires interactive forums and engagements on issues of science and innovation, and going beyond just engagement with so called stakeholders. It also requires the inclusion of members of the wider public to ensure expanded dialogues with other members within the broader context. In fact, it involves mapping out certain groups and members of the public to target for their direct involvement in order to provide diverse inputs and delivery of responsible governance (Andoni, et al., 2017). This approach implies and echoes the paradigm shift from representative government to participatory government and governance.

Thirdly, the model allows for Reflexivity, or the inclusion and consideration of a variety of dimensions of ethical considerations, codes of conduct and core values.

Figure 1. Dimension Model for Responsible Innovation
Source: (Stilgoe et al., 2013: p.1573)

RRI Dimension	Possible Tools
Anticipation	Scenario Building
	Scenario Workshops
	Foresight Studies
	Technology Assessment
	Life Cycle Assessment
Inclusiveness	Stakeholder Mapping
	Stakeholder Engagement Strategies
	Stakeholder Dialogues
	Public Dialogues
	User-Centered Design
Reflexivity	Codes of Conduct
	Core Values
	Embedded Ethicists
Responsiveness to Values and Needs	Value Sensitive Design
	Stage-gate Approaches
	Sustainable Design
Responsiveness to New Developments	Monitoring
	Gradual Scaling-up
	Adaptive Risk Management
	Living Labs and Social Experimentation
	Flexible and Adaptive Design

Fourthly, the dimension of Responsiveness to Values and Needs, requires a systematic consideration of value sensitive design, so called "stage-gate approaches"[2] and designing innovation with a view to sustainability and with that purpose in mind.

Fifthly, the dimension of Responsiveness to New Developments implies monitoring the innovations and their implementation, their gradual scaling up, and ensuring that adaptive risk management is employed. The implementation of so-called "living laboratories" and "social experimentation" tools are important in this dimension, as well as nurturing the notion of remaining sustainable at all times.

Finally, the most critical and most debated concept in all the sciences, is the notion of sustainability in all our actions. This, by implication, applies in particular to the manner in which we develop and assess or evaluate the value of long-term outcomes and impacts of innovative and new technologies. This has been reiterated by many of the authoritative authors in this field (Adams, et al., 2016; Blok, et al, 2017; Christensen, et al, 2003; Hölsgens, et al., 2017; Lubberink, et al., 2017; Popper, et al., 2017). The main idea is to simply ensure that these innovations and technologies are introduced into society and the economy; to minimize the negative impacts on the system and other significant competitors; and to maximize the medium to long term benefits for the majority without harming or disadvantaging anyone. Off course this is an ideal situation. Lubberink, et al., (2017: p181) speaks of this situation, and argues that "…responsible innovation differs from social- and sustainable innovation as it…also considers possible detrimental implications of innovation… includes a mechanism for responding to uncertainties associated with innovation and achieves a democratic governance of the innovation." One of the recent and valuable contributions to the process of assessment and management of sustainable innovation is the CASI-F (Common Framework for the Assessment and Management of Sustainable Innovation) model (Popper, et al., 2017). CASI-F was developed as a project including CASI partners, stakeholders involved in work, research, pilot projects, workshops and mutual learning events in the field of sustainable innovation. (Popper, 2017: pp. 7-11). It is hoped that much will still emanate from the work of the CASI-F research. According to Popper (2017b, p.1) "…CASI-F was envisaged as a holistic tool to support forward-looking decision-making at strategic, tactical and operational levels for government, business, civil society and research and education actors. Moreover, CASI-F is a living 'knowledge co-creation, co-assessment and co-management tool' aiming to improve the economic, social and environmental sustainability of the following seven types of innovations: product, service, social, organisational, governance, system and marketing". This new approach can make a valuable contribution towards analysing, and managing tough issues in this field and towards this ideal of sustainable innovation.

TOWARDS DEVELOPING A MODEL FOR THE GOVERNANCE OF INNOVATION AND NEW TECHNOLOGIES

According to Lynch (2017), important questions arise and pose broader concerns and political challenges, for instance:

- The manner in which societies and economies respond to disruption on a large scale. In particular, disruptions that have the potential to radically affect and transform economies and societies, have to be considered. How will we respond to the transition to an electric car that will, from an environmental and economic point of view, completely outweigh current combustion based technologies?
- What jobs will technological change create or destroy? What skills will be required? Will it be possible to devise strategies to reskill new incumbents or and retrain retrenched workers? How do governments protect the labour sector and manage the potential disasters of unemployment when current skills become redundant by robots and global automated supply chains? There is a growing awareness regarding the increasing problems of income inequality and decreased equality of opportunity.
- Can both the benefits and costs of this technological change be shared and will they be shared? How do governments create opportunities to stimulate growth and support the subsequent challenges? How do they facilitate appropriate adjustments to these innovative, technological challenges and changes?
- Can populist approaches – as has recently been demonstrated by nationalism and protectionism - where there is movement from the "distrust of institutions" to "anger based approaches", be managed?
- How do governments get ahead of the "disruption curve" in policy planning and analysis and display clear leadership in innovative technology management?

For government to play this proposed role, it needs to consider its role as enabler, advocate, producer, and controller of disruptive and innovative technologies. This approach, the Strategy Process and Instruments Model (SPI), is proposed by the author as a model or framework that governments can use to respond to disruptive, innovative technologies (DITs) (see figure 2).

Figure 2. SPI Model for Innovation Governance
Source: Author and adapted from: Baker et al (2012)

Strategic Role	Process	Instruments for Intervention
• Enabler	• Focus and evaluate the RRI dimensions	• Level the playing fields
• Advocate	• Shape	• Change regulations and laws
• Producer	• Grow	• Sunset existing programmes • Promoting and fostering partnerships
• Controller	• Monitor and evaluate outcomes and impact	• Multicriteria policy analysis • Assessment for effectiveness and sustainability

THE STRATEGIC ROLE OF GOVERNMENT

In line with the ideas from Baker et al., (2012) the SPI model is proposed for managing the process of innovation and disruptive technologies. Governments have to consider and focus on what they need or what they are faced with in terms of DITs. They have to choose strategic roles to play and proceed to shaping the future and the benefits that can be derived, as well as playing a role in growing the process and actions towards the ideal future. Governments also have to consider instruments that will facilitate the process, and methods of intervention to ensure the successful implementation. The playing fields for new entrants have to be levelled, laws and regulations need to change, programme support has to be managed; "sunset clause" provisions have to be made, and partnerships between multiple levels and different layers of role players facilitated, as well as ensuring sustainability as the processes unfold.

MANAGING THE PROCESS

According to Ernest and Young (2018), the Wallcot and Lippitz model provides an indication of the role that governments can play in fostering and ensuring innovation takes place. The idea of playing different roles such as that of enabling, versus the advocacy role, and even the role of producing innovation could be just as relevant for the public sector as it is for the private sector.

Focus on the Ideal Outcome and Apply the RRI Dimensions

What needs to be accomplished? Here it is important to consider short, medium and long-term outputs and impacts. It requires governments to consider exactly what the ideal outcome needs to be (Andoni, et al., 2017; Blok, et al., 2017). This includes the actual process, specific milestones, as well as the necessary tasks to be undertaken to reach every milestone. To what extent does the notion of responsive and responsible innovation determine how and what will be embraced? In addition, it also requires introducing and embracing trade-offs[3], which are always part and parcel of the process. When calculating trade-offs, they should first be identified in order to ensure that the values are correctly and effectively compared. Legitimately, the question may be raised: When is it necessary to consider breaking these trade-offs and how can it best be done? The debate regarding the "trade-off" between improving the quality of education from overcrowded classes to smaller classes (teacher/pupil ratio) with better equipped classrooms and spending more resources on good content, serves to illustrate. The cost-effectiveness (quantity served/per input costs) declines, but the cost-efficiency (quality) increases. At the same time this trade-off can be broken by considering online education which introduces a marginal increase of costs with the same quality of outcomes.

Shaping the Proposed Innovations

It should be decided how and where the best way would be to initiate the disruption. As previously stated, generally, DTIs may be evident in an area or space that is either overserved, or alternatively not served at all current models of delivery. The timing of its implementation is critical, as disruptive innovations are often unique, unprotected ideas driven by entrepreneurs and innovators who want to surprise the market. However, with more protected innovations, and those requiring major capital and financial inputs, the timing is less important, but breaking "trade-offs" become more critical. Ideally, innovations should be required to provide "more for less/or the same input".

Growing and Nurturing the Proposed Innovations

Governments should develop tools and instruments that can be used to foster the growth of innovative and DTIs. Tools and instruments include the design of legislation, budget manoeuvres and special funding tools. It is often necessary to protect and nurture innovations until they are regarded as mature in bearing the expected benefits.

Controlling the Outcomes and Impacts of Innovations and DITs

Apart from the importance, that government is also responsible for ensuring fairness and equity in the manner in which innovations are supported and regulated. Based on the understanding of the nature of innovation and new technologies, the importance and application of RRI, the framework for the assessment and management of sustainable innovation (CASI-F), as well as other considerations as listed above from recent literature is critical. When the outcomes and impacts of innovations are assessed, they need to be aligned with the agreed on objectives, values and principles designed at their inception (Cloete et al., 2018). Assessing the outcomes and impacts applying the process of monitoring and evaluation (M&E), is one of the most important approaches to ensure that sustainability is achieved.

SELECTING THE POLICY INSTRUMENTS ARE PROPOSED FOR SHAPING AND GROWING INNOVATIONS

Level the Playing Field

On the one hand by altering and/or removing the special subsidies, regulations and contracts that allow a few dominant role players and stakeholders to dominate a market space, will allow for new competitors who can produce innovations and/ or even import new technologies to provide real economic growth opportunities in regions. On the other hand, however, it still remains important to regulate this space. Kaal and Vermeulen (2017) emphasise the importance of regulation, whether it is for the sake of levelling the playing field, or recreating the playing fields altogether. The next rubric and policy action speaks to this requirement.

Ensuring Laws and Regulations are Changed or Introduced

Legal and specific regulatory changes are often required before they can survive or even thrive in a specific market. Lynch (2017); Kaal and Vermeulen (2017) and Buri (2017), refer to this requirement, and often the challenge is to ask the following questions. "Why should regulators be proactive; when should regulators respond; what should regulators respond to, and how should regulators respond?" (Kaal and Vermeulen, 2017: p.169).

Often these requirements for new regulations and laws cannot be foreseen, until the unforeseen effects or consequences of a particular innovation or new technology is implemented. The reference to the Uber dilemma in South Africa below, as well as certain requirements in other countries to regulate Uber or, as in Seattle where there have been calls to unionise their members, are classic cases of not anticipating the unforeseen legislative or regulatory demands (Groover, 2016).

Allowing for Sunset Programmes and Legislation to be Relaxed or Amended

When it is evident that an innovation or DTI is aligned for future success, the financial support or funding can be phased out. Allowing for the spontaneous development of further growth, expansion of an innovation in the market, it has to happen without undue intervention or support from government that may only benefit a small sector. Governments need to allow for maximizing benefits used; particularly tax benefits - in a Pareto Optimality[4] fashion. When certain technologies have been given government support, for the purpose of the greater good, it is critical that this support is re-evaluated at some point, allowing for new entrants (innovations and new technologies) into the space. The current case of South African state owned enterprises is a case in point, where the withdrawal of unequal or excessive government support in the energy sector and other critical high technology areas is long overdue (Mfeka, 2018).

Fostering Partnerships and Internal Capacity

The introduction of "public-private partnerships" can assist to scale the innovation, in addition to playing the role of facilitating cooperation and partnerships in order to promote innovation and collaboration. A classic case would be facilitating discussions between new technologies such as Uber, Taxify, Lyft and the mainstream or settled industries (taxi cabs). It must, however, be ensured that policy-makers and internal policy analysts are well informed and skilled in the fields of innovation and technology management. The task of governments is to facilitate the balancing of interests and conflict that may arise from new innovations and technologies. Another relevant and classic example is the growing fear in formal accommodation establishments such as hotels, guest houses and bed-and-breakfasts that the Airbnb industry is creating by grabbing a massive market share of what has previously been regarded as formal establishments. This has led to disruptions in the industry, and suggestions to regulate these new industries from a tax collection point of view. The innovative businesses will now have to be monitored and new regulations; and in some cases legislation, will need to be drafted. A lot more research needs to be done to look at the impact and outcomes of technologies. It is not clear what the real effects are when evaluating recent research done in this field (Blal, Singal, & Templin, 2018).

Applying Multi-Criteria Driven Policy Analyses

Apart from ensuring that they make rational and evidence based policies and decisions to determine what and how innovations will be supported, governments must be driven by the idea that apart from economic variables and criteria such as relevance, desirability, effectiveness, efficiency, equitability or adequacy, there are political, social, cultural, legal and environmental factors that drive important policy decisions and government support. This makes their role complex, but ensures that there is fairness all round, including the different sectors, in deciding to support innovation and new technologies (Blok, et.al., 2015; Cloete, et al., 2018: pp.186-188, pp. 275 & 361).

Assessment for Effectiveness and Sustainability

In the final instance, it requires that governments should be concerned about the overall effectiveness of new technologies or innovations, as well as the sustainability of such technologies and innovations. Even though some of these technologies or innovations have been successfully implemented in some countries, or different contexts, it may not apply elsewhere. For instance, we have seen sharing economy innovations like Uber being implemented in South Africa, which has created quite a disruption in the taxi industry, not only in South Africa, but on a global scale (Groover, 2016; Whittles, 2019).

It would appear that some of the socio-economic contexts and safety-security issues are raising serious concerns about the sustainability of this innovation. Governments in many countries are faced with the task of renewed regulation of the taxi industry, as well as intervening from a safety and security point of view. According to Whittles (2019) who reported on this situation: "…Uber said it had received more than 200 complaints of violence against its drivers since July, and hundreds more unresolved complaints have been lodged over the past year. Drivers contracted to Uber and Taxify have launched a fight-back against what they say is persistent victimisation by metered taxi drivers".

It is clear from the existing literature that many innovations may not be as effective as was initially intended. Ultimately this would also have an effect on sustainability issues. It does not only pertain to the sustainability of the actual technology or innovation, but also to the effect it may have on the sustainability of livelihoods, flexibility on working conditions and sustained employment, to mention just a few. Some evidence based policy analysis and other models such as CAFI-I will clearly be applied and necessary to assess the overall effectiveness of such innovations and new technologies (Cloete, 2018; Popper, 2017).

CONCLUSION AND RECOMMENDATIONS

It is concluded from the above analysis that governments need to create policy environments that are focused on the growth and development of regions and countries. Applying the precepts as described in the RPI model as proposed in the chapter means governments also have to:

Ensure that innovations are appropriate and responsible in terms of maintaining sustainable economic development and growth, through channelling resources and creating appropriate and responsible strategies to support the strategic priorities of the region and the globe.

Provide support through infrastructure development to support modern technologies, and to create opportunities through special and strategic projects and disruptive and innovative technologies (DITs).

Provide incentives for government, business and research in technological innovation, especially in regions and areas where they want to stimulate growth and development.

Ensure responsible management of innovation and disruption (evaluating both the economics and ethics of innovations). The problems between Uber and the survival of the traditional taxis in many countries and the impact of gene manipulation to cure ailments and diseases, and making it affordable, serve as examples. It will also challenge governments to manage potentially dangerous technologies based on unpredictable long term effects or unforeseen consequences such as atomic or nuclear power and chemical weapons.

It will also require governments, to manage potential conflict between important role players, such as local and regional governments/consultants/corporates, and ensure that innovations and their possible unforeseen consequences are analysed and managed, to determine their longer term impacts (drones/nanotechnologies). Here the opportunity exists to engage with top policy stakeholders, researchers and practitioners in order to practice good policy analyses in order to optimise outcomes to manage DITs (Cloete, et al., 2018).

SUMMARY

This chapter focused on the nature of disruptive and innovative technologies and the questions raised regarding the role and responsibility of government in responding to these innovations from a policy and governance point of view. Governments are generally reactive, and not able to effectively and timeously respond to these innovations. Often these innovations are disruptive in nature, and give rise to many unforeseen consequences or ripple effects that may not be advantageous. Generally, the greatest concern in the management and governance of innovations, is that there should be a prime concern for responsible governance of innovation. The most important consideration is that these innovations are well managed in order to ensure that all sectors of society are benefitting, or that the majority benefit, with minimal negative consequences or disadvantages to society. Governments need to gear up and ensure that they are prepared to consider their respective roles in fostering and facilitating innovations and new or disruptive technologies. Choosing a role to play within a particular context is going to be critical in future considerations of maximizing and embracing innovations and new or disruptive technologies. Moreover, ensuring that the outcome and impact of introducing these innovations and new technologies are sustainable will be critical. It is proposed that once governments have considered these dimensions, the SPI model can be applied to ensure the appropriate management and governance of innovations is pursued. Worst-case scenario, some of these effects - which are difficult to forecast at the time of the innovation - if not well managed and governed, could have long term negative effects on society or the physical environments.

REFERENCES

Adams, R., Jeanrenaud, S., Bessant, J., Denyer, D., & Overy, P. (2016). Sustainability-oriented innovation: A systematic review. *International Journal of Management Reviews*, *18*(2), 180–205. doi:10.1111/ijmr.12068

Ahlstrom, D. (2010). *Innovation and Growth: How Business Contributes to Society, 2010.* Retrieved October 19, 2018, from SSRN: https://ssrn.com/abstract=2643390

Andoni, E., Hannot, R., & Andoni, E. (2017). Politicising Responsible Innovation: Responsibility as Inclusive Governance. *IJIS*, *1*(1), 20–36. doi:10.3724/SP.J.1440.101003

Baker, L., Eggers, W., Gonzalez, R., & Vaughn, A. (2012). *Public sector, disrupted. How disruptive innovation can help government achieve more for less.* Deloite Govlab Study. Deloitte Development LLC.

Blal, I., Singal, M., & Templin, J. (2018). Airbnb's effect on hotel sales growth. *International Journal of Hospitality Management, 73*, 85–92. doi:10.1016/j.ijhm.2018.02.006

Blok, V., Hoffmans, L., & Wubben, E. F. M. (2015). Stakeholder engagement for responsible innovation in the private sector: Critical issues and management practices. *Journal on Chain and Network Science, 15*(2), 147–164. doi:10.3920/JCNS2015.x003

Blok, V., Tempels, T.,Pietersma, E. & Jansen, L. (2017). *Exploring Ethical Decision Making in Responsible Innovation: The Case of Innovations for Healthy Food.* doi:10.1007/978-3-319-64834-7_12

Bonte, D. (2018). *The Role of Smart Cities for Economic Development.* New York: ABI Research.

Burget, M., Bardone, E., & Pedaste, M. (2017). Definitions and conceptual dimensions of responsible research and innovation: A literature review. *Science and Engineering Ethics, 23*(1), 1–19. doi:10.100711948-016-9782-1 PMID:27090147

Burri, M. (2017). *Current and Emerging Trends in Disruptive Technologies: Implications for the Present and Future of EU's Trade Policy.* doi:10.2861/96860

Callon, M., Lascoumes, P., & Barthe, Y. (2009). *Acting in an Uncertain World: An Essay on Technical Democracy.* Cambridge, MA: MIT Press.

Christensen, C. M. (2000). *The innovator's dilemma.* New York: Harper Collins Publishers.

Christensen, C. M., Baumann, H., Ruggles, R., & Sadler, T. M. (2006). Disruptive Innovation for Social Change. *Harvard Business Review.* Retrieved from http://hbr.org/2006/12/disruptive-innovation-for-social-change/ar/1

Christensen, C. M., & Bower, J. L. (1995, January). Disruptive technologies: Catching the wave. *Harvard Business Review*, 43–53.

Christensen, C. M., & Overdorf, M. (2000, March). Meeting the challenge of disruptive change. *Harvard Business Review*, 66–76.

Christensen, C. M., & Raynor, M. (2003). *The Innovators Solution: Creating and Sustaining Successful Growth.* Cambridge, MA: Harvard Business School Press.

Clark, P. (2003). *Organizational innovations*. London: SAGE Publications.

Cloete, F., De Coning, C., Wissink, H. F., & Rabie, B. (2018). *Improving Public Policy for Good Governance* (4th ed.). Pretoria: Van Schaik.

Dreyer, M., Chefneux, L., Goldberg, A., Von Heimburg, J., Patrignani, N., Schofield, M., & Shilling, C. (2017). Responsible innovation: A complementary view from industry with proposals for bridging different perspectives. *Sustainability*, *9*(10), 1719. doi:10.3390u9101719

Ernest and Young. (2017). *Public Sector Innovation: From Ideas to Actions*. Retrieved from http://www.ey.com/ca/en/industries/government---public-sector/ey-public-sector-innovation-ideas-actions

Groover, H. (2016). As Seattle Uber Drivers Try to Unionize, the Company Doubles Down on a Scare Campaign. *The Stranger*. Retrieved from https://www.thestranger.com/news/2016/12/07/24731875/can-uber-convince-its-drivers-they-dont-need-a-union

Hölsgens, R., Schultze, J., Anttila, V., Kozarev, V., Linford, S., Martin, L., ... Popper, R. (2017). Lessons from a multi-level/stakeholder approach to sustainable innovation actions analysis. In R. Popper & G. Velasco (Eds.), *Sustainable Innovation Policy Advice* (pp. 76–86). Brussels, Belgium: European Commission.

Hopp, C., Antons, D., Kaminski, J., & Salge, T. O. (2018). What 40 Years of Research Reveals About the Difference Between Disruptive and Radical Innovation. *Harvard Business Review*. Retrieved from https://hbr.org/2018/04/what-40-years-of-research-reveals-about-the-difference-between-disruptive-and-radical-innovation

Kaal, W. A., & Vermeulen, E. P. M. (2017). How to Regulate Disruptive Innovation—From Facts to Data. *Journal of Jurimetrics*, *57*, 169–209.

Kaplan, S. M. (1999). Discontinuous Innovation and the growth paradox. *Strategy and Leadership*, *27*(2), 16–21. doi:10.1108/eb054631

Kassicieh, S. K., Kirchhoff, B. A., Walsh, S. T., & McWhorter, P. J. (2002). The role of small firms in the transfer of disruptive technologies. *Technovation*, *22*(2), 667–674. doi:10.1016/S0166-4972(01)00064-5

Kupper, F., Klaassen, P., Rijnen, M., Vermeulen, S., & Broerse, J. (2015). *Report on the Quality Criteria of Good Practice Standards in RRI, Deliverable 3.1 RRI Tools*. Amsterdam: Athena Institute, VU University Amsterdam.

Kvochko, H. (2013). Five ways technology can help the economy. *World Economic Forum*. Retrieved October 19, 2018, from https://www.weforum.org/agenda/2013/04/five-ways-technology-can-help-the-economy

Lubberink, R., Blok, V., Van Ophem, J., & Omta, O. (2017). Lessons for Responsible Innovation in the Business Context: A Systematic Literature Review of Responsible, Social and Sustainable Innovation Practices. *Sustainability, 9*(5), 721. doi:10.3390u9050721

Lubberink, R., Blok, V., Van Ophem, J., Velde, G., & Omta, O. (2017). Innovation For Society: Towards a Typology of Developing Innovations by Social Entrepreneurs. *Journal of Social Entrepreneurship*, 1–27. doi:10.1080/19420676.2017.1410212

Lynch, K. (2017). How disruptive technologies are eroding our trust in government. *The Globe and Mail*. Retrieved from https://www.theglobeandmail.com/opinion/how-disruptive-technologies-are-eroding-our-trust-in-government/article34857043/

McKinsey Global Institute (MGI). (2013). *Disruptive technologies: Advances that will transform life, business, and the global economy*. Retrieved February 19, 2019, from https://www.mckinsey.com/~/media/mckinsey/business%20functions/mckinsey%20digital/our%20insights/disruptive%20technologies/mgi_disruptive_technologies_full_report_may2013.ashx

McKinsey Global Institute (MGI). (2018). *Notes from the AI Frontier. Insights from Hundreds of Use Cases*. McKinsey and Company. Retrieved October 19, 2018, from https://www.mckinsey.com/~/media/McKinsey/Global%20Themes/Artificial%20Intelligence/Notes%20from%20the%20AI%20frontier%20Applications%20and%20value%20of%20deep%20learning/MGI_Notes-from-AI-Frontier_Discussion-chapter.ashx

Mfeka, B. (2018). Rationalisation of state-owned enterprises has become inevitable. *BusinessDay*. Retrieved from https://www.businesslive.co.za/bd/opinion/2018-12-05-rationalisation-of-state-owned-enterprises-has-become-inevitable/

Minges, M. (2016). Exploring the Relationship between Broadband and Economic Growth. Background Chapter – Digital Dividends. *World Development Report*. Retrieved October 19, 2018, from http://pubdocs.worldbank.org/en/391452529895999/WDR16-BP-Exploring-the-Relationship-between-Broadband-and-Economic-Growth-Minges.pdf

Moller, J. (2008). A Critical Note on 'The Rise of Illiberal Democracy'. *Australian Journal of Political Science, 43*(3), 555–561. doi:10.1080/10361140802267316

OECD. (2003). *ICT and Economic Growth.* Paris: OECD Publishing. Retrieved October 28, 2013, from http://www.cla.org.pt/docs/OCDE_TIC.PDF

OECD. (2014). *Recommendation of the Council on Digital Government Strategies.* OECD Publishing. Retrieved October 28, 2013, from http://www.oecd.org/gov/digital-government/Recommendation-digital-government-strategies.pdf

OECD&ITU.(2011).*M-Government:MobileTechnologiesforResponsiveGovernments and Connected Societies.* Paris: OECD Publishing. doi:10.1787/9789264118706-en

Owen, R., Stilgoe, J., Macnaghten, P., Gorman, M., Fisher, E., & Gustion, D. (2013). A Framework for responsible innovation. In R. Owen, J. Bessant, & M. Heintz (Eds.), *Responsible innovation* (pp. 27–50). London: Wiley. doi:10.1002/9781118551424.ch2

Parry, M. E., & Kawakami, T. (2016). The Encroachment Speed of Potentially Disruptive Innovations with Indirect Network Externalities: The Case of E-Readers. *Product Development & Management Association, 34*(2), 141–158. doi:10.1111/jpim.12333

Pavie, X. (2014). The Importance of Responsible Innovation and the Necessity of 'Innovation-*Care*'. *Philosophy of Management, 13*(1), 21–42. doi:10.5840/pom20141313

Popper, R., Popper, M., & Velasco, G. (2017a). Towards a more responsible sustainable innovation assessment and management culture in Europe. *Engineering Management in Production and Services, 9*(4), 7–20. doi:10.1515/emj-2017-0027

Popper, R., Velasco, G., & Popper, M. (2017b). *CASI-F: Common Framework for the Assessment and Management of Sustainable Innovation, CASI project report.* Deliverable 6.2. Retrieved from http://www.futuresdiamond.com/casi2020/casi-f/

Popper, R., Velasco, G., & Ravetz, J. (2016). *State-of-the-art of Sustainable Innovation: Climate action, environment, resource efficiency and raw materials.* Brussels, Belgium: European Commission.

Roser, M., & Esteban, O. (2018). *World Population Growth.* Retrieved October 28, 2018, from https://ourworldindata.org/world-population-growth

Schneidewind, U., & Augenstein, K. (2016). Three schools of transformation thinking: The impact of ideas, institutions, and technological innovation on transformation processes. *GAIA – Ecological Perspectives for Science and Society, 25*(2), 88-93. doi:10.14512/gaia.25.2.7

Stilgoe, J., Owen, R., & Macnaghten, P. (2013). Developing a framework for responsible innovation. *Research Policy, 42*(9), 1568–1580. doi:10.1016/j.respol.2013.05.008

Walsh, S., Kirchhoff, B., & Newbert, S. (2000). Differentiating market strategies for disruptive technologies. *IEEE Transactions on Engineering Management, 49*(4), 341–351. doi:10.1109/TEM.2002.806718

Whittles, G. (2019). Uber drivers fight back with spotters. *Mail and Guardian.* Retrieved from https://mg.co.za/article/2017-09-15-00-uber-drivers-fight-back-with-spotters

Windell, A. C. (2007). *The impact of disruptive technologies on designated organisations within the IT industry in South Africa* (Unpublished Masters Dissertation). University of Pretoria.

World Bank. (2018). *World Bank Open Data - 2018 update of World Development Indicators available.* Retrieved October 28, 2018, from https://data.worldbank.org/

World Economic Forum (WEF). (2019). *The Fourth Industrial Revolution.* Retrieved February 28, 2019, from https://www.weforum.org/focus/fourth-industrial-revolution

Zakaria, F. (2016). America's democracy has become illiberal. *Washington Post.* Retrieved October 28, 2018, from https://www.washingtonpost.com/opinions/america-is-becoming-a-land-of-less-liberty/2016/12/29/2a91744c-ce09-11e6-a747-d03044780a02_story.html?noredirect=on&utm_term=.0f4e78bc5557

KEY TERMS AND DEFINITIONS

CASI-Framework: This refers to a common framework for the assessment and management of sustainable innovation, directed at assisting academics and practitioners to assess and manage the more intangible, but important elements that are important for sustainable innovation in order to facilitate "socio-technical" system adoption and implementation.

Disruptive Innovations: Innovations that create entirely new markets through the introduction of a new service or product, that tends to disrupt some of the existing systems or established methods or products in favor of an alternative, emerging as a result of innovative thinking and often the production of new or smart information technologies.

Governance: General approach to the management of services that include the overall management of all of the processes by the government or by the private sector and their associated networks either through the laws, norms, power structures, or language, culture, and traditions of an organized society in order to ensure a healthy and economically viable state.

Innovation: New or novel approaches to the way we work, systems are designed, redesigned to meet rapidly changing and growing needs in society. Often viewed as how problems are resolved in order to produce better and often creative outcomes; and are often a result of new and more effective, efficient, and productive solutions to both the inputs as well as throughput operations in a system.

Public Policy Analysis: Process of generating policy relevant information, and applied for, or used to generate policy solutions, plans for implementation, and proposals for evaluation, and ensuring the success of policy intentions.

Public Policy Frameworks: Framework (usually legal in nature) to provide the basis on which policy decisions can be made, and actions can be taken to give effect to policy goals and objectives agreed on within the political or organizational system.

RPI Model for Governance: Refer to the application of the concepts of strategic roles, processes, and instruments for good innovation governance.

RRI Dimensions: This term refers to the general application of responsible, responsive actions to manage innovation.

Sustainable Innovation: Is an approach that applies in particular to the manner in which we develop and assess or evaluate the value of innovations that are supported to ensure positive and lasting long-term outcomes and impacts of innovative and new technologies.

ENDNOTES

[1]   This idea supports the notion that rapid economic growth does not only pose challenges and problems, but can also assist in creating a dynamic for economic growth and new markets.

[2]   A phase-gate process (also known as a stage-gate process or a waterfall process), is a project management technique in which an initiative or process is divided into distinct *stages* or *phases*. This process is marked by decision points (known as *gates*). These gates are prerequisites for continued progress of the project.

[3]   A balance achieved in negotiations between parties, and involves two desired or ideal outcomes, but with incompatible features; or often viewed as a compromise.

[4]   Pareto efficiency or Pareto optimality is an economic theory or paradigm of allocating resources to make any one individual or specific preference better off without making at least one individual or preference worse off.

Chapter 8
Blockchain Technology in International Trade in Goods

Dagmar Gesmann-Nuissl
Chemnitz University of Technology, Germany

ABSTRACT

No other technology has been mentioned as frequently as blockchain technology. No less than a technical revolution should go along with it. In addition to a brief introduction to the functionality of the blockchain technology, this chapter will also highlight various fields of application and the related legal challenges in international trade. The transport industry may be mentioned as an example. Especially in the transportation of goods, a large number of documentation obligations must be adhered to and permits must be obtained. Packing lists, export licenses, and product certificates are examples of this. All mentioned documents are based on the same data set, namely the details of the type, origin, and quantity of the goods. Large parts of these documents must be carried along with the goods and presented on instructions, which causes considerable bureaucracy and makes transportation more difficult and expensive. These documents could be displayed on the blockchain in the future.

INTRODUCTION

In the context of globally and digitally networked companies, blockchain technology will gain considerably in significance in the future. The technology is intended after the initial considerations to increase the security of digital processes, reduce data loss and increase confidence in organisational processes. The extent to which it can also accompany transactions in international trade of goods in particular in the declaration of goods and freight, which are increasingly triggered autonomously

DOI: 10.4018/978-1-5225-7638-9.ch008

Copyright © 2019, IGI Global. Copying or distributing in print or electronic forms without written permission of IGI Global is prohibited.

by cyber-physical systems in the environment of industry 4.0, will be discussed in this article.

First of all, the functionality of blockchain technology hast to be introduced. Subsequently, an outline of various fields of the application of blockchain technology in international trade will be given. The associated legal challenges in particular with reference to the International Sales and Trade Law will be highlighted. In the conclusion it will be evaluated, to what extent the blockchain technology can support the international trade under the current law.

BLOCKCHAIN AND TECHNOLOGY

Blockchain and Functionality

Increasing Importance of Blockchain Technology

In the past ten years, the blockchain technology has gained notoriety especially due to the publicity of the cryptocurrency "Bitcoin". Under the impact of the financial crisis, Satoshi Nakamoto published his white paper on a new currency concept, which was made to take place "peer to peer" and therefore without financial intermediaries. (Nakamoto, 2008, p. 2). Because of the validity of the used algorithms, whose technological foundation forms the "blockchain technology", the cryptocurrency "Bitcoin" should be trustworthy.

While the Bitcoin underlying blockchain technology would soon be relatively unnoticed and would only contribute to the operating principle of the new currency concept, it recently attracted increased attention. The interest on the blockchain technology increases exponentially due to its very special network architecture, which does not require any intermediaries. Almost every day, new ideas for possible blockchain applications are born. In addition to the payment traffic, among other things the blockchain will already be associated with the insurance industry, the healthcare sector, the energy supply or the logistics control.

How the Blockchain Technology Works

Blockchain technology is based on the "Distributed Ledger Technology (DLT)" (Kaulartz, 2017, pp. 3 ff.). DLT represents by definition a special form of electronic data booking, which is carried out by the write- and read-authorized network participants (so-called node) in a decentralized database (Distributed Ledger or shared digital account book). The special feature of the digital account book is, the continuously expandable list of entries or records for transactions (so-called blocks), which in turn are linked together by a cryptographic process. The blockchain is realized by a decentralized peer-to-peer network, in which the individual transactions are mapped, verified, validated and summarized into blocks and finally updated on an ongoing basis.

In other words, blockchain technology is a distributed database. The so-called nodes, the initiated members of the blockchain, can create a new "data block" to this database. These "blocks" can contain information, regardless of a specific content. The created "blocks" will be afterwards encrypted and broadcasted in the network, so that every party would get access, but only by using utilizing cryptography. In this way it is guaranteed, that the content of each transaction will not be made public. Other network nodes will collectively determine the validity of the block. Therefore, a pre-defined algorithmic validation method, which can be named as "consensus mechanism" is utilized. After the validating process, the new "data block" will be added to the whole blockchain. The transaction ledger is updated with the results and furthermore distributed across the blockchain network (CPMI, 2015, p. 5.).

For a better understanding, the special features of the blockchain technology will be explained in detail.

Peer-to-Peer-Network (P2P)

All blockchain systems are based on a so-called "peer-to-peer network" (P2P). This is a network, which has no longer a central organizational unit. The participants of the network (so-called "node") are directly connected with each other. They take the organization over. Each node can download the standard software and maintain a digital image of the database or transaction history on his/her own computer or server. First, this leads to a decentralized storage of the channelled information and it secondly allows each node in the network to interact in real time and to set, verify or validate information. Therefore, the main purpose of blockchain is to decentralize the trust and to allow decentralized authentication of transactions.

Concerning the nodes, a distinction is made between "client" and "miner". The client only participates in the P2P-network for example to execute a transaction, whereas the miner also creates new blocks by inserting computing power; thereby he can lengthen the blockchain actively.

Hashing

Hashing is a cryptographic technique, which can transform any information into a hash. Usually, the SHA-256 or SHA-512 method, in which the output information (input) is transformed into a 64-digit or 128-digit hash value (output), are used. The hash value represents the converted information. It forms a type of digital fingerprint of the underlying information or process, in order to make them identifiable by using the hash value.

Hashing can combine multiple datasets together into a single hash, connect multiple hashes, or represent multiple hash values along with a new dataset as a new hash value. All these hash operations have in common, that the change of the input value changes the output value. In respect of this, the simple comparison between the hash values will be enough to determine, whether the input value has recently undergone a change. Therefore, a detailed proof of tampering (who, where, when) is no longer required.

Block and Blockchain

The blockchain consists of individual linked blocks (eponymous for the technology). The first block, in which the source information is cryptographically programmed and encrypted, is called "Genesis Block". This one is followed by further blocks of information. Each additional block is formed out of a total hash value of the previous block (so-called block header). The newly added one contains new converted transaction information (the number may be arbitrary) as hash value and a randomly attached number (so-called "nonce"). The newly created block, including all of its information, can be represented by the reproduction of its own total hash value, without naming or presenting the processed information in detail. By lining up such blocks, all previously contained information is continuously processed (further); the block structure increases linearly out of the genesis block.

Asymmetric Encryption

The asymmetric encryption secures the system and creates trust. Each blockchain-user has a set of two keys: There is a private key, which is used for transactions and for creating a digital signature and a public key, which is known by everyone in the network. Each transaction is attached with a private digital signature of the sender. The recipient can authenticate the message with the sender's public key. Unlike the symmetric encryption, where only the sender and recipient know the key, in asymmetric encryption the message can be authenticated by anyone in the network. This form of encryption ensures a high integrity of the message; due to the "multi-eye principle", no changes are possible.

Function of Nodes and Consensus Mechanism

The nodes have a multifunctional role in the blockchain. They store the transaction history on their server, validate the transactions that have to be added to the blockchain, and they are able to create new blocks by passing a mathematical hash puzzle and forwarding them to the other nodes.

In general, any member of a blockchain network (node) is able to propose new content / information, which should be added to the blockchain. However, the validation of this addition of content must be proven by an agreement, which is reached by the other nodes before. One example for new information on the blockchain might be a transaction record. A "consensus mechanism", which is a cryptographic validation method working in a predefined specific manner, is used to make the mentioned agreement, which will be used by any node at the end. Exactly this method ensures at the end a correct and proper classification of the proven transactions on the blockchain network. The two best-known are the "Proof of Work" (PoW) and the "Proof of Stake" (PoS) (Houben, R. & Snyers, A., 2018, p. 18):

1. **Proof of Work:** In a PoW system, network participants have to solve so-called "cryptographic puzzles" in order to be allowed to add new "blocks" to the blockchain. Exactly this process is well known as "mining". These "cryptographic puzzles" include all previously recorded content / information on the blockchain network. In the next "block" new information about the new transactions have to be included. At the end, the stored information of each "cryptographic puzzle" becomes larger and therefore each further calculation would be more and more complex. For that reasons one requirement for the mechanism "Proof of Work" is a vast amount of computing resources. In conclusion, also electricity is needed in a significant amount. In other words, PoW mechanism works in that way, that a member of the network – a node – has to solve a "cryptographic puzzle" at first. After he or she did it, exactly that procedure proves the completion of his or her work and he or she will be rewarded with a value, which is provided in a digital form and at the same time an incentive for each participant to uphold the blockchain network. (Houben, R. & Snyers, A., 2018, p. 18).

2. **Proof of Stake:** A transaction validator / network node must deliver a proof of his or her ownership with regard to a certain asset in a Proof of Stake (PoS) system. Otherwise, it is not possible to participate in the validation process of transactions. Instead of the "mining" in the Proof of Work system, these validating transactions are called "forging". This means in the case of cryptocurrencies, that the network node (transaction validator) must be able to prove his or her ownership of the certain amount of all existing coins in order to do transactions. Only if there is a proof of his or her "share" / "stake" of all coins it is allowed to do the validated transaction. If he or she has a huge amount of coins, the chance is quite high to be responsible for the validation of the next block. This is because of the fact of greater seniority within the cryptocurrency blockchain network, which will give him or her a more trusted position in the network. For this transaction process all parties, which are transact within the network,

have to pay a transaction fee. These fees are covering the validation service, which is offered of the transaction validator. (Houben, R. & Snyers, A., 2018, p. 19).

In both variants, the particularity is that only when the majority of the nodes have authenticated and validated the new information or the block they will be included in the chain. If an information or a block contradicts the data set, the validation would fail and the nodes would refuse the inclusion of the information or the block.

Chaining of Blocks and Irreversibility of the Data Set

The blocks are – as already mentioned – closely linked with each other. Information, which is stored in the blockchain, can be removed extremely difficult from the blockchain. If only a single block information is changing, the hash puzzle would have to be redissolved, which changes the total-hash of the block. Because the total-hash value of the block is also relevant for all other blocks, the hash puzzle would have to be solved for all other blocks based on it, and their total hashes would have to be changed – an iterative and expensive process in the chain. Any change to the block information is costly and virtually impossible due to this "yo-yo effect" ("mathematical chaos"). In addition, all nodes where the blockchain is stored would need to validate and support each of these changes, which also means an unrealizable effort.

Final Illustration Example

How the blockchain works is illustrated with a simple example in Figure 1: Suppose A wants to transfer information or a data set (a value, a document) to B via blockchain. First, A has to sign digitally this transaction using his private key (which is only known to him). After that, he will have to address the transaction to B´s public key – B´s address on the network. Afterwards the nodes within the blockchain network have to verify the transactions, which are collected into the "transaction block". Therefore, all nodes check the data or the data set to see, if A is the owner of the data set and if the transaction will not conflict with other information in the block. If the majority of the nodes confirm the data or the data set, the network will process the transaction; the transaction will be included into a block by fixing their hash value. If the maximum number of block information is reached (this has been previously set), the nodes attempt to resolve the so-called "hash puzzle" to close the block. Once a node has solved the puzzle, it sends its result to all other nodes, who check the result of the calculation. If the majority of nodes consider the result as correct, the total hash value of the block is fixed and the block – including all

Figure 1. How a blockchain works
Source: (as cited in Houben, R. & Snyers, A., 2018, p. 17)

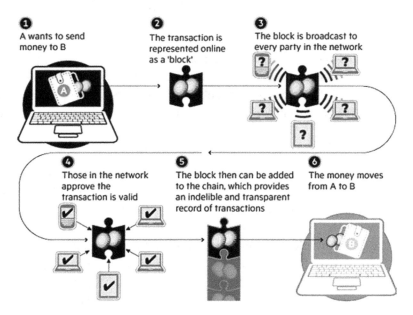

information – is added to the chain; a correction is practically impossible. Now, B can accept and use the data set for itself.

Possible Network Architectures of Blockchain

In practice, blockchain is a technology with many "faces". The network architecture differs depending on the purpose and can range from being fully open to completely limited (Drescher, 2017, p. 124).

"Open, permissionless blockchains" are fully open. That means that everyone can join or not join the network at will. There is especially no central entity, which approves or preapproves prospective members of the blockchain network (World Bank Group, 2017, pp. 4 ff.; Laschewski, 2017, pp. 359, 362). The only requirement, which has to be fulfilled for joining the blockchain network and for adding more transactions to the distributed transaction ledger, is a computer and the installed relevant blockchain software. In the blockchain network, all the identical copies of the ledger are distributed to all the blockchain members (nodes). For this reason, there is no central blockchain network owner and no owner of the blockchain software. (Houben, R. & Snyers, A., 2018, p. 15).

However, a "permissioned blockchain" works different. On such a blockchain, a network administrator pre-selects the transaction validators / nodes. He or she defines the requirements and the rules for the transaction ledger. Therefore, prospective nodes have to agree with these rules, if they would like to join the network. All "permissioned blockchains" grant permissions to each node / blockchain member. They decide for each participant, which special permission he or she will get. It depends on the specific functions, which should be performed. For example, one node is able to read and access. Another one is able to write information on the "permissioned blockchain" (Shobhit, 2018; Laschewski, 2017, pp. 359, 362). This allows, amongst others, the easy verification and identification of the network participants (World Bank Group, 2017, p. 6). Regardless of this procedure, in a "permissioned blockchain" each network participant has to trust in the mentioned central organized coordinating entity. He or she decides about selecting trustworthy network nodes.

Furthermore, "permissioned blockchains" mostly divided into two subcategories. "Public permissioned blockchains" – sometimes also called "open permissioned blockchains" – are open for anyone, which means that anyone has reading rights and can access and view the content of the blockchains. However, on open permissioned blockchains only authorised network members can establish or generate transactions. Only these authorised nodes can at the end update the state of the ledger, in other words only they have reading rights. (Witzig & Salomon, 2018/E, p. 6). "Closed permissioned blockchains" on the other hand – sometimes also called "enterprise permissioned blockchains" (Jayachandran, 2017; Sohbhit, 2018; Witzig, Salomon & Cutting, 2018/E, p. 7) or "private blockchains" (Houben, R. & Snyers, A., 2018, p. 16) – are strongly restricted, wherein access is strongly restricted and only certain participants are allowed to access. They are additionally equipped with previously, precisely, well-defined and restricted rights (e.g. writing access).

Advantages and Disadvantages of the Blockchain Technology

The greatest advantage of the technology is that no intermediary or conveyor is required who could falsify the data set. The transparency and consensus mechanism also allows a high degree of confidence in the validity of the data set, which has to be transported. In addition, the irreversibility of the data set protects the belief in its accuracy and correctness.

However, a disadvantage is that the proof-of-work procedure causes considerable electricity costs. In the currently largest blockchain network, the Bitcoin blockchain, a transaction consumes as much electricity as an average German household needs in 36 hours. Only if less complicated hash puzzles will be used, power consumption can be reduced significantly. The latter is probably only possible in private/permissioned or private/permissionless blockchains, when the parties know each other as described above and therefore the irreversibility or the security of the integrity of the data set can fade into the background.

Application Areas of the Blockchain

The applications, in which blockchain technology could be used, are numerous and diverse. In 2015, the World Economic Forum estimated that ten percent of the gross domestic product would be managed on the blockchain by 2027 (World Economic Forum, 2015, September).

The use of the blockchain is ideal wherever a large number of fixed information needs to be managed in a tamper-proof manner and the uniqueness of the information should remain constant. It is not suitable for situations which may experience a retrospective change (such as a contract for the purchase of an item or the creation of a work), because the reversal of prior entries would cause a "mathematical chaos".

The blockchain – based on the model of bitcoin – is primarily linked to financial transactions, whereby besides the mere booking of a monetary value, the subsequent transaction processing could also be included (Tobias, 2016, pp. 37 f.). It can already be seen as a viable tool to enhance investor protection in OTC and securities in trading, particularly in matching[1], settlement[2] and clearing[3]. Since data about the identity, the property or verifications can be mapped tamper-proof and counterfeit-proof in the blockchain, it is also discussed to use it as a support for the public administration. Especially in any form of registry administration, like land registration, register of birth and marriage[4], the management of identity card data, the vehicle tax but also in the management of patient records (Dapp, Balta & Krcmar, June 2017, p. 5; Voshmgir, 2016, p. 21).

Goods and Transport Documents in International Trade

One area, that has received little attention so far, is the international cross-border trade in goods and the logistic-process (merely Stahlbock, Heilig & Voß, Dec. 2018, pp. 1185 ff.; Dobrovnik, Herold, Fürst & Kummer, July 2018), which are accompanied by a large number of documents and approvals – particular transport documents. Most of these documents are based on the same data set, with statements to the type, origin, quality and quantity of the goods.

Most of these documents must be brought together with the goods and presented to various supervisory authorities on instructions, which leads to a considerable bureaucracy, increases the risk of manipulation and sometimes delays the transport of the goods. These enclosed documents include, documents, which certify the ownership of the goods, as a bill of lading, consignment bill or warehouse receipt, but also other accompanying and transport documents.

Bill of Lading

The bill of lading is the document for a concluded sea freight contract; the consignment bill is the document for an inland freight contract. Both of them are receipts and hand-over documents. The carrier – regularly the seller – issues both documents. They contain various information about the carrier and the goods, et al the date of issue, name and place of the carrier residence, information about sender and recipient, place of delivery and nature of goods. By means of the documents, the embodied goods can be traded and resold even during transport, which simplifies the tradability of the goods. The documents are regularly used for third-party transactions (drop shipment deliveries).[5] The legal owner of the document obtains a direct right of restitution against the carrier or other owner of the goods – the documents thus represent a right of surrender.

Warehouse Receipt

The warehouse receipt is a document in which the warehousekeeper confirms that he has received the goods for storage and in which he commits himself to hand them over to the authorized person upon presentation of the warehouse receipt. It is a proof of ownership of such commodities, which are stored in the mentioned warehouse. Warehouse receipts may be negotiable or non-negotiable. In the first case they allow, that the ownership of the commodities will be transferred without delivering the commodities in a physical way (BAFT, EBA, FCI, ICC & ITF, 2016, p. 91). There are three variants:

1. **Warehouse Receipt:** Legitimization paper, in which the warehousekeeper certifies the receipt of the goods and agrees to hand them over to the one, who identifies himself as the recipient (take-back obligation).
2. **Negotiable Warehouse Receipt:** Disposition paper, which is issued "to order". The paper includes the right to surrender and ownership of the goods. If the stored goods should be resold during storage, the previous owner must hand the order storage certificate over to the buyer with a confirmation (endorsement). The issue of the warrants "to order" is reserved for state authorized warehouses only.
3. **Warehouse Receipt to Name:** Here, the warehouse receipt is issued in the name of the depositor of the goods (rectal paper). An assignment can only be made by assigning the name-holder. If the name certificate is pledged for financing purposes, the warehouse keeper must be notified.

Accompanying Documents

Accompanying documents are the documents attached to the goods in order to specify them or to explain their use, such as packing lists, certificates of origin, certificates of analysis, insurance policies, commercial invoices, customs duties, and even operating costs instructions and manuals.

Transport Documents

Transport documents are the documents that concern the means of transport. For example, in the transportation sector there must be registration certificates, emission certificates, logbooks and qualification certificates relating to the driver.

While the accompanying and transport documents are sometimes required to be carried by law (such as certificates of origin, customs documentation, and logbook), the provision or forwarding of other documents is usually agreed between the parties (e.g. a loading slip, operating instructions, and manuals). Especially in the context of international sales contracts such documentation obligations between the parties are formulated directly or in terms and conditions. In this case, the seller is obligated to hand over the documents in the manner stipulated in the contract – this is part of the delivery obligation (see Articles 25, 30, 34 CISG). The documents and records must be handed over regularly and unchanged from one party to another, even if they often go a long way through various regulatory institutions. It must also be ensured that they are faultless and that the documents remain reliable. If the seller does not provide the documents in time to the buyer or with errors, certain warranty rights become valid – i.a. the possibility to terminate the contract[6] – (see Art. 49 CISG). The reason for this is a contrary to contract.

This can be very unsatisfactory for the seller, who is suddenly confronted with a contract termination because of the faulty documents. The product can be returned, even though he is not responsible for the loss or manipulation of documents and records. This is the responsibility of a third party (such as an agency). Certainly, there will be claims for damages against the authority. However, those measures mean a lot of work and the disappointed buyer will be lost for a long time, which can do much more damage.

Insufficient Measures by UNCITRAL

The United Nations Commission on International Trade Law (UNCITRAL)[7] has recognized this problem. Since the transmission of paper documents has generally a high error rate, the organization has recently decided upon a model law on electronically transferable documents (MLETR), which provides paperless electronic commerce in addition to the existing electronic commerce agreements[8]. In addition to the already possible electronic contracts and declarations of intent, electronic records such as promissory notes, bills of exchange, bills of lading, warehouse receipts or other accompanying trade documentation have to be included. The MLETR defines the requirements for the use of an electronic transferable record.

However, the model law primarily contains rules on the circumstances in which an electronically transferrable record can be regarded as legally valid and enforceable on a cross-border basis. It sets rules for functional equivalence (see chapter II of the Model Law), but – because of the self-imposed technical neutrality – there are no indications of which instruments could be used to establish or ensure this equivalence. It only mentions "electronic protocols" and "electronic records" (article 6) and the requirement of a "reliable media change" to overcome compatibility problems with country-specific electronic systems (article 18), but refrains from making recommendations on the applicable technology.

Useful Addition by Blockchain Technology

For this, the blockchain technology could be used. In particular, the guarantee of uniqueness of the blockchain could be an attractive tool by supporting the international trade, especially when sending electronic documents.

All the documents might be illustrated on the blockchain. The charge would be always represented by a "token"[9], which could contain all necessary information. It is suitable to base an electronic bill of lading on the token model, because an electronic token is susceptible to immediate visual verification on the spot, like a tangible paper document. The identification of the holder of an electronic token is done by the token itself. As a result, the holder can prove an entitlement or right to the possessory interest. Accordingly, the holder can assert this right, enforce his interest, and defence himself by claiming remedies for illegal interference with goods.

The network structure of the private permissioned blockchain could be selected for the accompanying papers (e.g. packing lists, export licenses, certificates), in which all parties, which are involved in the transport, as well as the responsible authorities could act as a node. In this way, all involved parties would automatically be informed at any time about the condition of the load, without the need to produce a paper document. Checks and inspections could be avoided. Approvals could be extended automatically if necessary. In addition to that, it would be ensured that manipulations wouldn´t been made. As always, the majority of nodes would have to agree to a change. The permissioned architecture could also prevent that official information reach private actors and would be changed there.

For the documents of title to goods (bill of lading, loading and warehouse vouchers) the so-called asset back token can be used (efficiently). The claims to return could be represented on the blockchain by the token. To transfer the ownership of the goods, it would be sufficient, to pass on the token in the blockchain from the seller to the buyer; the functional equivalence would be given. The use of such an asset back token is particularly suitable for a bill of lading in overseas trade. In this way, all involved persons of the transport, as well as the parties of the payment transactions (usually advised credit) or of the insurance could become nodes of the blockchain. This would not only make the transport much more efficient, but also solve the problems, which are caused by a delivery without or incorrect submission of the bill of lading (for example, interim storage, return, etc.) (Jessen, 2011, pp. 405 ff.).

It becomes clear that the Blockchain is quite suitable to simplify the international movement of goods and in particular, make the exchange of transport accompanying documents legally secure. The advantage is a saving of time and money compared to the usual use of analogue, paper-bound courier mail. Everyone involved has immediately the required most up-to-date information, so that work steps can be carried out more quickly. The blockchain technology guarantees the authenticity of the digital documents and is the central point of trust and truth ("Single Point of Truth"). Individual companies seem to recognize the benefits and embark on the blockchain adventure. For example, IBM recently formed a joint venture with Maersk, the world's largest container ship operator, to make the transport of goods from Europe to the United States more efficient and secure. A number of companies including Dupont, Dow Chemical, Tetra Pak and the port operators of Houston and Rotterdam have already tried the joint venture platform ("Maersk and IBM Introduce TradeLens Blockchain Shipping Solution", August 2018).

Challenges for Businesses

Blockchain technology is a young technology that has not yet proven itself over many years in widespread practical use. The previous knowledge about risks and weak points of the blockchain is therefore still low. Because of this, the integration of a blockchain into a proven supply chain could be problematic, especially in retail systems and logistics processes. The challenge of integrating a new technology into logistics processes should therefore not be underestimated. Technical as well as organizational aspects are important.

Scalability is also a significant part. It is seen as one of the greatest limitations of a blockchain, so that there is also a need for further discussion and research with regard to increasing performance (Mougayar, 2011). Especially in the context of enterprise resource planning, scalability is an important building block, as the number of transactions to be validated can be significant and a smoother and more efficient process should be guaranteed. Depending on the economic situation or the time of day, this number can also vary considerably. Scalability should therefore be limited by validation/consensus mechanisms.

Moreover, the other core conflicts have to be resolved regarding the enforcement of the global block-chain-based processes: In global competition, the open structure of a block chain would have to be accepted. In addition, many supply chain actors would have to be part of the network for the blockchain network to be worthwhile. Furthermore, the existing IT infrastructure and networking in the company would have to be adapted into the required IT infrastructure for the blockchain. The expected reduction in communication and transaction costs would only be achieved if initial investments were made in the development of the IT infrastructure, i.e. its implementation and integration. Finally, since the desired benefits of the largest possible global blockchain network could lead to problems within the required storage space, which would impair communication within the network, an adequate solution has to be found ultimately.

Challenges for Law

The legal challenges associated with blockchain technology should also be highlighted, even if they are not directly related to documentation requirements.

Primarily it is the irreversibility of a blockchain, which causes problems when contractual relationships would be challenged or reversed. The contesting leads from the beginning to nullity, the rescission to a reversal contract. In this respect, all actions and services should be returned to their original state. The reversal of a contract is therefore in contradiction with the objective of the blockchain, which goal is precisely to save the data in such a way that the subsequent change is no longer possible. The reversal of a contract cannot be realized in the blockchain or only via specific technical delays (e.g. time-lags). However, this shortcoming initially applies only to the contractual relationship itself. Concerning the documents, a contestation or reversal of the contract would only require the return of the documents, which could be done in the same way as they were sent. This wouldn´t cause any problems.

Another question that arises in the context of the blockchain is to whom the individual information of the network can be assigned. Due to the fact that each node is the owner of the entire data set, it is natural to assign the entire data set to everybody as well. Thus, each node would be responsible for violations in the blockchain (e.g. falsification of the dataset). Even this unsolved problem has no relevance for goods and transport-accompanying documentation, because with the selection of the blockchain type a small number of write-authorized nodes can be selected. Therefore, the risk of manipulation would be reduced significantly. In any case, this is necessary in the interests of the parties.

SUMMARY AND OUTLOOK

It can be summarized, that the blockchain technology is excellently suited to facilitate and speed up processes in the international trade in goods. The blockchain technology ensures permanent, attack-proof and thus sustainable documentation of goods traffic. UNCITRAL has already taken a step in the right direction by enabling electronic transport and accompanying documents, which could be technologically supported by the blockchain instrument in future. Due to its technological background, the blockchain technology can also be optimally integrated into the digital business models of industry 4.0.

REFERENCES

Bankers Association for Finance and Trade (BAFT), Euro Banking Association (EBA), Factors Chain International (FCI), International Chamber of Commerce (ICC), & International Trade and Forfaiting Association (ITFA). (2016). Standard Definitons for Techniques of Supply Chain Finance. *Global Supply Chain Finance Forum.* Retrieved from https https://www.tradefinance.training/library/files/Standard%20 Definitions%20for%20Techniques%20of%20Supply%20Chain%20Finance.pdf

Committee on Payments and Market Infrastructures (CPMI). (2015). Digital currencies. *Bank for International Settlements.* Retrieved from https://www.bis. org/cpmi/publ/d137.pdf

Dapp, M., Balta, D., & Krcmar, H. (2017). Blockchain - Disruption der öffentlichen Verwaltung? Eine Technologie zur Neugestaltung der Verwaltungsprozesse. *Konrad Adenauer Stiftung.* Retrieved from http://www.kas.de/wf/doc/kas_49305-544-1-30. pdf?170622171027

Drescher, D. (2017). *Blockchain-Basics.* Springer Berlin APress.

Dobrovnik, M., Herold, D., Fürst, E., & Kummer, S. (2018). Blockchain for and in Logistics: What to Adopt and Where to Start. *Logistics 2018, 2*(3), 18. Retrieved from https://www.mdpi.com/2305-6290/2/3/18

Houben, R., & Snyers, A. (2018). *Cryptocurrencies and blockchain: Legal context and implications for financial crime, money laundering and tax evasion.* European Parliament. Policy Department of Economic, Scientific and Quality of Life Policies. Retrieved from http://www.europarl.europa.eu/cmsdata/150761/TAX3%20Study%20 on%20cryptocurrencies%20and%20blockchain.pdf

Jayachandran, P. (2017). The difference between public and private blockchain. *IBM-Research*. Retrieved from https://www.ibm.com/ blogs/blockchain/2017/05/ the-difference-between-public-and-private-blockchain/

Jessen, H. (2011). Die Auslieferung von Gütern ohne Vorlage eines Konnossements: Neuere Empfehlungen für die Praxis bei der Verwendung des "Letter of indemnity." TranspR.

Kaltofen, T. (2016, Oktober 18). Blockchain im Einsatz. *Computerwoche*. Retrieved from https://www.computerwoche.de/a/blockchain-im-einsatz,3316539

Kaulartz, M. (2016). Die Blockchain-Technologie. *Computer und Recht, 7*.

Laschewski, C. (2017*). Der Blockchain-Algorithmus*: *Eine GoB-konforme digitale Buchführung?* Retrieved from https://www.maersk.com/news/2018/06/ 29/maersk-and-ibm-introduce-tradelens-blockchain-shipping-solution

Mougayar, W. (2011). *The business blockchain: promise, practice, and application of the next internet technology*. Hoboken, NJ: John Wiley & Sons.

Nakamoto, S. (2018). *Bitcoin: A Peer-to-Peer Electronic Cash System*. Retrieved from https://bitcoin.org/bitcoin.pdf

Shobhit, S. (2018, April). Public, Private, Permissioned Blockchains Compared. *Investopedia*. Reviewed from https://www.investopedia.com/news/public-private-permissioned-blockchains-compared/

Stahlbock, R., Heilig, S., Voß, S. (2018, December). Blockchain in der maritimen Logistik. *HMD Praxis der Wirtschaftsinformatik, 55*(6).

Tobias, J. (2016, August 1). *Blockchain in der Finanzbranche: eine disruptive Technologie?* Bank und Markt.

Voshmgir, S. (2016). Blockchains: Smart Contracts und das Dezentrale Web. *Technologiestiftung Berlin*. Retrieved from https://www.technologiestiftung-berlin. de/fileadmin/daten/media/publikationen/170130_BlockchainStudie.pdf

Witzig, P., & Salomon, V. (2018). *Cutting out the middleman: a case study of blockchain-induced reconfigurations in the Swiss Financial Services Industry*. Working Paper 1. Université de Neuchâtel. Retrieved from http://www.unine.ch/ files/live/sites/ maps/files/shared/documents/wp/WP-1_2018_Witzig%20and%20 Salomon.pdf

World Bank Group. (2017). Distributed Ledger Technology (DLT) and blockchain. *FinTech note, 1*. Retrieved from http://documents.worldbank.org/curated/en/177911513714062215/pdf/122140-WP-PUBLIC-Distributed-Ledger-Technology-and-Blockchain-Fintech-Notes.pdf

World Economic Forum. (2015, September). Deep Shift - Technology Tipping Points and Societal Impact. *Survey Report*. Reviewed from http://www3.weforum.org/docs/WEF_ GAC15_Technological_Tipping_Points_report_2015.pdf

ADDITIONAL READING

Chistidis, K., & Devetsikiotis, M. (2016). Blockchains and Smart Contracts for the Internet of Things. *IEEE Access 2016*. Retrieved from https://ieeexplore.ieee.org/stamp/stamp.jsp?tp=&arnumber=7467408

Girasa, R. (2018). *Regulation of Cryptocurrencies and Blockchain Technologies: National and International Perspectives*. Palgrave Studies in Financial Services Technology. doi:10.1007/978-3-319-78509-7

Herian, R. (2018). *Regulating Blockchain: Critical Perspectives in Law and Technology*. Open University UK. doi:10.4324/9780429489815

Ishmaev, G. (2017). Blockchain technology as an institution of property. *Metaphilosophy*, 48(5), 666–686. doi:10.1111/meta.12277

Sulkowski, A. (2018). *Blockchain, Law, and Business Supply Chains: The Need for Governance and Legal Frameworks to Achieve Sustainability*. Retrieved from SSRN https://ssrn.com/abstract=3205452

Treibelmaier, H., & Beck, R. (2018). Business Transformation through Blockchain: Volume I and Volume II. Palgrave Macmillan.

World Trade Organization. (2018). *Can Blockchain Revolutionize International Trade?* Retrieved from https://www.wto.org/english/res_e/booksp_e/blockchainrev18_e.pdf

KEY TERMS AND DEFINITIONS

Blockchain: A blockchain is a continuously expandable list of data records, which are linked together by cryptographic methods.

CISG: United Nations Convention on Contracts for the International Sale of Goods.

Cyper-Physical System (CPS): CPS refers to the combination of informatic, software-technical components with mechanical and electronic parts that communicate via a data infrastructure such as the internet.

International Trade: International trade is the exchange of goods, services, and capital across international borders or territories.

Transport Documents: Transport documents accompany the goods on their way to the customer. This includes documents which certify the ownership of the goods (bill of lading, consignment bill, or warehouse receipt) but also other accompanying documents.

UNICTRAL: United Nations Commission on International Trade Law.

ENDNOTES

1   "Matching" in the financial sector means the clearing of receivables and liabilities.
2   "Settlement" means the conclusion of transactions in the field of securities trading.
3   "Clearing" means the settlement, in particular of futures, options and swaps.
4   In October 2014, the first couple in the US were married using a QR code (Kaltofen, Oct. 2016).
5   A from Germany sells to B in the US and B sells to C in Canada.
6   The cancellation of the contract requires a "fundamental breach of contract". The assessing of "materiality" differentiate according to the nature of the document. If the seller does not deliver documents that entitle the user to dispose of the goods (e.g. bills of lading, loading or warehousing bills) or if these are not in conformity with the contract, in any case an objectively serious defect entitles the customer to contract. For other documents (e.g. insurance policy, certificate of analysis, customs and origin certificate) the assessment of the defect depends on whether the buyer is restricted in the use of the goods or whether he can easily obtain the documents again. However, the latter would entitle the purchaser to a reduction (Article 50 CISG) or claims for damages (Article 74 CISG).

[7]   On 17 December 1966 the United Nations Commission on International Trade Law (UNCITRAL) was established by the United Nations General Assembly. As principal legal body of the United Nations it deals with international trade law and is responsible for modernising and harmonising rules of international trade to facilitate trade and investment and counts preparation and promotion of use and adoption of model laws amongst these legislative techniques to achieve this objective.

[8]   UNCITRAL Model Law on Electronic Commerce (1996), UNCITRAL Model Law on Electronic Signatures (2001) and UNCITRAL Model Law on Electronic Transferable Records (2017). Retrieved from http://www.uncitral.org/uncitral/en/uncitral_texts/electronic_commerce.html.

[9]   A "token" may represent any asset.

Section 5
Applications and Reflections of Innovative Technologies and Global Responsible and Sustainable Management

Chapter 9
Responsible and Sustainable Business Model Innovation in the Textile Industry:
Exploring Approaches to Social Sustainability

Katja Schneider
Chemnitz University of Technology, Germany

Marlen Gabriele Arnold
Chemnitz University of Technology, Germany

ABSTRACT

The global textile industry offers huge potentials regarding the transformation towards sustainability. These improvements require a facilitation of business model innovations embedding shifting consumer demands. How can the textile industry drive responsible and sustainable business practices in terms of social sustainability? Tackling this question, a qualitative content-based analysis of current literature conducted highlights main themes and concepts on business model innovations, textile industry, and social sustainability. In addition, an exploratory multiple case study design was used. Results show social sustainability patterns are seldom and often linked to external pressures. This chapter proposes a reorientation towards stronger holistic and inclusive approaches for sustainability and reflects on socio-cultural aspects linked to sustainable textile business models. Progressing sustainability in the textile industry needs both a single consideration of environmental and social issues as well as an integrative and systemic perspective in academia as well as in practice.

DOI: 10.4018/978-1-5225-7638-9.ch009

Copyright © 2019, IGI Global. Copying or distributing in print or electronic forms without written permission of IGI Global is prohibited.

INTRODUCTION

The textile industry with its global reach and interconnectedness provides huge potentials regarding the development towards more ecological, social and economic sustainability (Barnes & Lea-Greenwood, 2006; Franco, 2017; Börjeson & Boström, 2018). Yet, according to *Köksal et al. (2017),* textile value and supply chains are increasingly complex, globally dispersed and highly dynamic. Further, they are long and involve multiple partners with often conflicting objectives (Börjeson & Boström, 2018). Changes in consumer attitudes and consumption patterns reinforced by fast-paced trends in fashion and product design (Niinimäki & Hassi, 2011) are seen to apply massive pressure on the various actors resulting in severe environmental damages and questionable social practices (Köksal et al., 2017; Lueg et al., 2015). These challenges have been persistently highlighted in prior studies on the textile industry (Gardetti & Torres, 2012; Franco, 2017).

Against this background, research on the responsibilities of the textile industry has emphasized the strategic necessity of companies to maintain their competitive advantage by incorporating concerns related to environmental performance (Börjeson & Boström, 2018). In this regard, environmental risk management with regard to the management of hazardous chemicals in textile products, production and distribution channels have achieved considerable attention in the last decade, both among practitioners and scholars. However, the featuring elements of the contemporary textile industry conflict with the long-term orientation of sustainable development (Köksal et al., 2017). At the same time achieving sustainability seems to be a greater challenge for textile companies.

In this chapter we argue that sustainability in the textile industry does not only mean to integrate environmental concerns into a firm's strategy and business model, but also needs to be reflected by the adequate management and incorporation of social values and responsibilities in a company's business model. The impact of social issues on operational and reputational risk management has repeatedly been highlighted in prior research on global supply and value chains (e.g., Klassen & Vereecke, 2012; Lund-Thomsen & Lindgreen, 2014). Social issues affecting global supply and value chains of companies comprise multiple aspects such as labor practices in less affluent countries, public concerns related to human rights abuses, management of cultural differences or one-sided power relationships (Klassen & Vereecke, 2012; Eriksson & Svensson, 2015; Khurana & Ricchetti, 2016; Pedersen et al., 2018).

Against this background, a fundamental re-thinking of existing business models, structures and practices is of prime importance (Arnold, 2017a). Indeed, changes and adjustments to existing business model conceptualizations are seen to provide alternative solutions and foster sustainability-oriented innovations and transformations

(Evans et al., 2017; Bocken et al., 2014; Dickson & Chang, 2015). By integrating sustainable values into a company's business model and identifying all value flows among the involved stakeholders, business model innovations aim at a more holistic approach and integrated thinking (Evans et al., 2017).

However, research particularly on social and cultural aspects or effects regarding the imagination, creation and implementation of sustainable business models in the textile industry appears to be doomed rather sidelined. Yet, in this chapter we suggest that in the textile industry social sustainability is linked to "the importance of our cultural and emotional connection with clothes" (Gardetti & Torres, 2012: p. 6). This view also extends to the inclusion of aspects related to social sustainability in various business models in the textile industry. In this regard, also CSR is considered to play an increasingly important role (Todeschini et al., 2017; Dickson & Chang, 2015; Lueg et al., 2015). Textile companies are striving to meet the above-mentioned challenges by fostering transparent communication and increasing positive impacts on local communities and development. The following three research questions frame the focus of our study:

- *How are components of business models in sustainability-driven companies in the global textile industry shaped in terms of social sustainability?*
- *Which social aspects are considered in these business models?*
- *How do they meet the above-mentioned challenges of the textile industry and drive responsible and sustainable business practices?*

This chapter aims to fill in the gap by exploring approaches to social sustainability and responsibility in business models in the global textile industry. We shed light on the social dimension of sustainable business models and responsible management practices in the textile industry by drawing on a critical appraisal of earlier research on sustainable business models and by combining these results with empirical findings of selected real-world cases. The methodological section of the chapter adopts a qualitative content-analysis of academic publications on business models and business model innovations for sustainability, textile industry and social sustainability by means of the content analysis and text mining software *Leximancer™*. In addition to this, an exploratory multiple case study design was used to gain exemplary insights into practical approaches on social sustainability (Bryman, 2015).

The present chapter is structured as follows: First, the relevant literature on business models and business model innovations for (social) sustainability is briefly reviewed to underpin our research. Following this, the methodological procedure, like data collection and analyses, is presented. The section on solutions and recommendations synthesizes our findings of the qualitative content-analysis of academic publications with the empirical analysis of four sustainability-oriented companies in the textile industry located in different parts of the world. After that we suggest several propositions and avenues for future research directions based on our research questions. The chapter ends with a summary of theoretical, methodological and practical implications.

BACKGROUND AND THEORETICAL UNDERPINNING

To underpin our research, earlier literature on business models, business model innovations and social sustainability is briefly reviewed. By highlighting key themes and aspects of these different streams of research, the intent here is to provide a basic frame of reference for our study.

Studies on Business Models and Business Model Innovations for Sustainability

As *Rauter et al. (2017)* recently have highlighted the topic of business models seems to be one of the most appealing research themes to management scholars. Multiple studies have focused on the objectives, elements and success factors of business models (e.g., Zott et al., 2011; Shafer et al., 2005; Lambert, 2015; Osterwalder et al., 2005; Long et al., 2018). Although the literature identifies substantial deficits regarding the definitional, theoretical and conceptual foundations as well as the implementation of business models (Joyce & Paquin, 2016; DaSilva & Trkman, 2014; Teece 2010; Magretta, 2002), they seem to be a crucial component of competitive market economies and a necessary condition for the profitability and survival of companies. This has been accompanied by a broad application of these models in practice spurring interdisciplinary issues (Teece 2010; DaSilva & Trkman, 2014; Beattie & Smith, 2013). In order to address these gaps and criticisms, recent literature has made efforts to develop new approaches for categorisation and to theoretically ground explanations of business models (Fjeldstad & Snow, 2018; Lambert, 2015; DaSilva & Trkman, 2014).

Traditionally understood business models are strongly based on the firm's value proposition, creation and delivery to the customer (Bocken et al., 2014; Schaltegger et al., 2016). Albeit there may be an inherent tension between value capturing and value creation (Howell et al., 2018), a conventional business model combines strategic and tactical considerations aimed at large scale and profit generation for the company. Assuming the 'deep truth' of fundamental needs and future behavior of consumers and competitors are, among others, crucial elements when designing business models (Teece, 2010). The literature has suggested multiple types and conceptualizations of business models (e.g., Bocken et al., 2014; Joyce & Paquin,

2016; Boons & Lüdeke-Freund, 2013). In this regard, research has also pointed to the fact that the suitability of a particular business model and its design must be evaluated in light of the business ecosystem, context and likely interactions (DaSilva and Trkman, 2014; D'Souza et al., 2015; Howell et al., 2018).

In recent years, a challenge for business models has arisen from an increased awareness regarding sustainability-related aspects stipulating business model innovations. Such innovations may be reflected twofold, depending on the nature of the firm. Business model innovations in already existing companies may be achieved by a shaping and transition of conventional business models, whereas within newly established ventures a design of new business models is pursued (Baldassarre et al., 2017). The wide range of studies on business model innovations for sustainability reflect on a variety of approaches, industries and sustainability-related benefits (e.g., Bocken et al., 2014; Dickson & Chang, 2015; Schaltegger et al., 2016; Yang et al., 2017). Including environmental and social values in the value creation and delivery to the customer constitutes an essential characteristic of innovative sustainable business models (Yang et al., 2017; Bocken et al., 2014). In this regard, the understanding of a sustainable value proposition as well as its holistic and balanced capturing becomes a critical component when designing a sustainable business model (Baldassarre et al., 2017; Rauter et al., 2017). A sustainable value is seen to reflect the triple bottom line of sustainability, namely incorporating not only issues related to environmental sustainability, but also to economic and social sustainability (Evans et al., 2017). Furthermore, the sustainable value proposition is also considered to be measurable, both in terms of economic as well as ecological and social value (Bocken et al., 2014). At the same time, the different meanings of the word 'value' as emphasized by *Evans et al. (2017)* set up even further challenges when designing a sustainable business model.

As a result, conceptualizing business model innovations for sustainability requires a holistic perspective and integrated thinking. This particularly holds true for addressing interrelated sustainability objectives in global supply and value chains (Khurana & Ricchetti, 2016). The change, innovation and adjustment of conventional business models allowing shifts to sustainable innovations and sustainable development also implies a reconfiguration of management and business aspects. These include issues such as capability and stakeholder relationship management, knowledge management, the role of leadership and cultural management (Evans et al., 2017; Rauter et al., 2017). Exemplarily, the increasing necessity of collaborative and inclusive approaches, multi-stakeholder engagement as well as complex interactions with the organization's business environment require additional efforts. Thus, in order to enhance sustainability-oriented concepts and innovations, participation and interaction between all stakeholders are essential, which also needs to be reflected in more inclusive business models (Arnold 2017a; Arnold 2010; Evans et al., 2017).

However, in light of this, designing and securing the sustainable value proposition may become even more challenging (Evans et al., 2017). Addressing these issues policy is also required to derive solutions (Allievi et al., 2015). There are differences in current literature streams discussing sustainable business models and business models towards sustainability (Evans et al., 2017; Schaltegger et al., 2016). However, we do not distinguish between sustainable business models and business models towards sustainability, but stress the integration of all three sustainability strategies 'sufficiency', 'efficiency' and 'consistency' while developing and establishing business models.

Specific types of business model innovations for sustainability are derived by social business models or social enterprises. Though there is still debate on defining and classifying these different phenomena; literature agrees on the fact social business model innovations relate to different elements of the conventional business model. At the same time, social business models and social enterprises are seen to feature an explicit social impact approach or inclusivity (Howell et al., 2018). In this regard, the concept of 'shared value' may be of particular importance. Exemplarily, relating to the business model component 'value creation', the notion of shared value implies a deeper understanding of the interrelatedness between business and society. Therefore, the way of overall (economic) value creation must be extended to value creation for society (Evans et al., 2017; Schmitt & Renken, 2012). As a result, society becomes a crucial and primary stakeholder in business model innovations for sustainability. *Howell et al. (2018)* introduce the notion of business model intimacy, reflecting the embedding of a business model in a particular community. Sharing value between the company and its external environment may result in a deeper value beyond that of mere product consumption. At the same time, it reinforces the featuring element of business models as being flexible and interactive in as much as the business model needs to be adapted to contextual challenges and the whole ecosystem (e.g., institutional voids and market failure in emerging economies).

Business Model Innovations in the Textile Industry

In order to meet the challenges in the textile industry as overviewed above, also managers and entrepreneurs are encouraged to develop and implement sustainable business models as these are crucial in order to survive in a competitive environment and to achieve business success. However, rethinking innovative and sustainable business models in this particular industry is still in its infancy (Todeschini et al., 2017; Kudłak et al., 2015). With regard to the textile industry, we find that only single studies refer to sustainability-related changes and innovations in business models (Dickson & Chang, 2015; Franco, 2017; Niinimäki & Hassi, 2011). Examples included are often based on singular company presentations (Fischer & Pascucci, 2017; Franco, 2017; Todeschini et al., 2017).

Several drivers of sustainability-related business model innovations in the textile industry have been identified of crucial importance for meeting the main socio-economic, cultural and technological challenges of future market development (Todeschini et al., 2017; Fischer and Pascucci, 2017; Franco, 2017). These drivers can be distinguished into, first, technological aspects such as necessary innovation in fibres based on renewable raw materials, enhancement of manufacturing processes or the implementation of circular economy approaches. The second group comprises social facets, namely an increasing consumer awareness regarding social and economic responsibilities of fashion production and collections.

Drivers of sustainability-related changes in business models in the textile industry focus on upcycling, recycling, fair trade, CSR and lowsumerism. According to *Todeschini et al. (2017)*, different elements and components of business models are impacted by such innovation-driving aspects including, among others, partner selection, costumer relationship and value proposition. Similar to the importance of new solutions for dealing with pressure on capital or fostering a collaborative mind-set among stakeholders research has revealed the importance of inter-firm collaborations or the facilitation of joint investments in circular textile flows (Fischer & Pascucci, 2017). Opportunities for sustainability-related innovations in the textile sector are to be detected both in mass as well as niche markets, emphasizing the heterogeneity of segments and considerable amount of relevant stakeholders in this particular industry (Barnes & Lea-Greenwood, 2006; Gardetti & Torres, 2012). Thus, the design and implementation of innovative business models for sustainability is also to reflect the diversity in this industry. Proposing the development of a number of innovative policy tools may foster transparency. Moreover, governance and institutional dimensions of transformations to sustainability as well as social and cultural values relating to sustainability by looking at the consumer side and by understanding transition factors for sustainable business model innovations have to be jointly addressed.

The Social Dimension of Sustainability in Business Models of Textile Companies

Indeed, the social dimension and related strategies for social sustainability (e.g., 'sufficiency') need to be strengthened in the re-thinking of business models and innovative practices in the textile industry. This is the more as clothing production and consumption tackle almost everybody around the globe (Gardetti & Torres, 2012). The above mentioned sustainability-related drivers are particularly enhanced by varying and likely shifting perceptions, attitudes and behaviours of consumers.

Indeed, for many scholars the consumer is fundamentally important for the design and implementation of business models (Magretta, 2002). The increasing consumer awareness is a sufficient condition for drivers for sustainability-related innovation in fashion business models (Todeschini et al., 2017) since there the customer is directly involved in determining the success and survival of a particular brand. So, the fundamental needs of the consumer as assumed by the company's management appear to play a key role in successful business model innovations especially in the textile sector.

At the same time, cultural aspects (e.g., knowledge and learning) are crucially important for successful business model innovations in the textile industry. Social value forms constitute a part of a sustainable value and have been differentiated in the literature. Typically social values encompass the following aspects: Equality and diversity, well-being, community development, secure livelihood, labour standards, health and safety as well as transparency and power relationships (Evans et al., 2017; Lund-Thomsen & Lindgreen, 2014). With particular emphasis on the textile industry, social sustainability and responsibility involves also aspects such as child labour, women workforce as well as consumer safety (e.g., Köksal et al., 2017; Khurana & Ricchetti, 2016). The latter also extends to marketing and communication aspects since glorified extremely body-shaped models showcasing collections may favour eating disorders (Khurana & Ricchetti, 2016). With regard to the management of social issues, Klassen & Vereecke (2012) point to the need of social management capabilities. They differentiate three types of capabilities, namely monitoring practices, collaborative practices as well as (social) innovation practices in order to secure competitive advantages for companies.

Furthermore, increasing educational and consciousness work means new challenges for the companies concerned in terms of greater transparency as well as improved communication and stakeholder relationship management. Transparency and improved traceability regarding socially responsible management practices and corporate actions can offer considerable benefits for various stakeholders in the global textile value and supply chains. Further, it provides a potential mechanism to enhance legitimacy in local communities. Albeit dependent on stakeholders' perceptions, presented CSR data on corporate websites concerning sensitive social and ecological problems is seen advantageous given easy accessibility of large, seamless and current data at low costs (Arnold, 2017b). In addition to the overlaps between ecological and social aspects related to sustainability (Khurana & Ricchetti, 2016), incorporating CSR activities in business model innovations of companies in the textile industry reflect the holistic approach needed for sustainable business models.

However, despite this obvious importance of the social dimension of sustainability, research on this stream has repeatedly criticized of being largely neglected (Missimer et al., 2017; Vallance et al., 2011). So far, related cultural and social facets are hardly taken into account in contemporary research studies on business model innovations in the textile industry, let alone starting points for a more in-depth analysis. The prerequisites and framework conditions required for this are accompanied by a "fundamental change in society's culture and collective consciousness that enables the creation of new collective beliefs and values" (Schaefer et al., 2015, p: 395). Since there is a difference between merely decreasing *un*sustainability and engendering sustainability (Schaefer et al., 2015), consciousness on the part of the consumer as well as other stakeholders in the textile industry is likely to promote the design of business model innovations for sustainability.

To conclude, a general lack of theoretical grounding concerning (social) sustainability in the textile industry (Todeschini et al., 2017) as well as the paucity of case research and empirical findings particularly on business model innovations for sustainability (Evans et al., 2017) call for an exploratory investigation of business model innovations towards sustainability in the global textile industry. Therefore, in this study we employ a mixture of inductive and deductive qualitative content analysis techniques (Elo & Kyngäs, 2007; Moldavska & Welo, 2017), an exploratory multiple case study as well as an innovative stepwise sequential mapping approach to systematically identify, explore and describe approaches and patterns for social sustainability in business models of textile companies more closely. The corresponding research design and methods used in our study are comprehensively presented in the next section.

METHODOLOGY AND RESEARCH DESIGN

Research Material and Methodological Procedure

In order to answer our research questions, our methodology encompasses three steps: First, a qualitative content-based analysis is taken in order to detect and highlight main themes and concepts explored within previous research on business model innovations, textile industry and social sustainability. Second, we employ an exploratory multiple case study design by focusing on four sustainability-oriented companies located in different hubs of the global textile industry and analyse their corporate websites, as statements on social missions, objectives, activities and responsibilities. Eventually, drawing on research by *Bocken et al. (2014)*, *Rosca et al. (2017)* and *Todeschini et al. (2017)* the findings of the theory-based discussion are mapped with results derived from our empirical analyses and further elaborated in the solutions and recommendations section of this chapter. Selecting the authors is justified by their ground-breaking concepts. More specifically, *Bocken et al. (2014)* identified eight main sustainable business model archetypes, clustering technological (T), social (S) and organisational (O) groupings of business model innovations: *maximize material and energy efficiency* (T), *create value from waste* (T), *substitute with renewable and natural processes* (T), *deliver functionality rather than ownership* (S), *adopt a stewardship role* (S), *encourage sufficiency* (S), *repurpose for society/environment* (O), and *develop scale up solutions* (O). *Rosca et al. (2017)* condensed the various and diverse discussed business model elements in the literature to *Target customer, Value proposition, Revenue model, Value chain* for analysing business models effectively. In addition, innovation-driving aspects particularly for the textile industry as developed by *Todeschini et al. (2017)* and described above were used for analysis. The comprehensive three steps establishing the methodological framing used in our study are also summarized in *Figure 1*.

Qualitative Content Analysis of Prior Publications

Further contributing to research on business model innovations and approaches towards social sustainability in the textile industry, a content analysis connecting the main literature streams relevant to this paper was conducted. In doing so, a literature review based on multiple criteria (e.g., Ansari & Kant, 2017; Quarshie et al., 2016) was initially performed in order to systematically and rigorously manage the diverse and fragmented body of knowledge on particularly business models and business model innovations for sustainability. The comprehensive paper search was based on multiple keywords in order to gain a sufficient and broad basis for the analysis and conducted from January to July 2018. Exemplarily, scientific articles focusing

Figure 1. Methodological framing used in this study

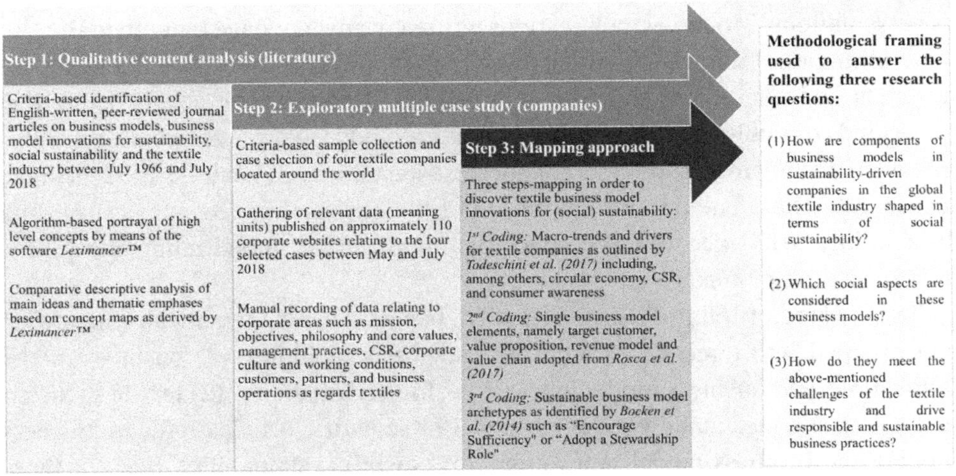

on business models for sustainability were retrieved by employing the keywords "business models for sustainability", "business models for sustainable innovation", "sustainable business models", "sustainability business models", "business model innovations for sustainability" as well as "sustainable value proposition, creation and delivery". Regarding scientific articles focusing on the textile industry a great variety of keywords and synonyms describing both, steps, processes and resources as well as relevant agents and stakeholders along textile value and supply chains was used. Albeit not a prominent objective of our procedure, we searched for scientific articles dealing with sustainability-related issues in the textile industries. Among others, the following terms and synonyms were used for literature identification: "sustainable/green fashion", "clothing design", "fair trade apparel", "garment manufacturing", "textile fibers", "ethical clothing", "circular fashion", "sustainable textile production", "organic cotton industry", "sustainable fashion consumption", "greenwashing" as well as "slow fashion retail". To identify relevant publications in the field of social sustainability a list of multiple keywords was applied, too. Among others, we used "corporate social responsibility/performance", "social sustainability" "social value (creation)", "social system/change", "beliefs", "social enterprise", "ethical responsibility" or "corporate irresponsibility" in our literature search.

Our literature base contains full-text English articles and open access articles from peer-reviewed academic journals. The used scientific search engines and academic databases are *'EBSCOhost'*, *'ScienceDirect'*, *'Academic Search Premier'*, *'EconLit with Full Text'* as well as *'Google Scholar'*. The relevance of each publication was indicated when the pre-defined keywords and synonyms could be retracted in any of the following three parts of the scientific article: title, keyword list and/or abstract. In order to refine our article selection procedure we abstained from including editorial notes, commentaries, conference and working papers, reports from consulting companies or international organizations, books, e-books and book reviews as well as presentations. Moreover, publications written in any language other than English were eliminated from our final database. Another exclusion criterion constituted abstracts and non-access to full-length articles. However, we acknowledge that these kinds of publications and types of media could also provide valuable insights in a further study to map the field of social sustainability in business models in the textile industries. The publication period of the retrieved papers spans from July 1966 to July 2018 since we followed a broad approach and aimed at mirroring shifts as well as developments.

In so doing, a total of 1.003 scientific papers were systematically identified and grouped into three broad thematic categories including (1) business model innovations and business model innovations for sustainability, (2) textile industry, and (3) social sustainability. Out of this, 194 scientific articles refer to business models and business model innovations for (social) sustainability. Each of these articles was individually screened in order to detect research specifically focusing on business model innovations for sustainability in the textile industry. Relevance was indicated if the article contained one of the following four pre-defined textile-related keywords in any of the three article sections title, keyword list and/or abstract: "textile", "clothing", "apparel" and/or "fashion". In case of doubts the entire article was read. This procedure yielded to 61 articles with references to the textile industry. Yet, among them, only 18 publications dealt exclusively with this particular industry sector. The remaining publications of the overall number of publications retrieved focus on different aspects in the textile industry as well as on social sustainability. It should be noted that a large proportion among the latter category centres around articles on CSR since research on genuinely social sustainability appears to be rather scarce.

In a next step, we examined the publications by applying the content analysis software *Leximancer*™ (version 4.50) for each of the relevant literature streams. We chose this particular software tool as it helps to automatically explore the semantic structure of themes and key concepts within the selected scientific articles (Zawacki-Richter & Latchem, 2018). The intelligent proprietary algorithms and sequential stages of this text mining software tool as described in previous studies (e.g., Sullivan et al., 2018; Thomas, 2014) have also been deployed in the present research. However, at each stage manual edits have been made regarding further data processing. Exemplarily, the list of thesaurus-based concepts directly discovered and extracted from the articles by *Leximancer*™ has been refined by the authors manually in order to eliminate inappropriate word-like or name-like concepts. Further, this program visualizes results by means of an exploratory concept map and table formats indicating the frequency and co-occurrence of concepts as well as likely relationships and overlaps (Mayner & Arbon, 2015). Considered to be highly useful especially in studies concerned with large data sets, the text mining software tool is also found to meet fundamental criteria for research quality such as reliability and validity as well as to lessen human bias in content analysis (Bedenlier et al., 2018). At the same time previous research has also emphasized the necessity and importance of analytical sensitivity and judgment when interpreting the findings, namely the concept maps (Zawacki-Richter & Latchem, 2018). With particular regard to this chapter's research questions, the different concept maps for each literature stream are illustrated in the *Figures 2 – 4* below. Further, main aspects, like thematic regions, concepts and concept paths, are descriptively presented below.

Description of Investigated Cases and Data Analysis

This chapter takes an exploratory multiple case study design in order to illustrate diverse approaches to social sustainability in the global textile industry (Bryman,

2015). This research design was considered highly appropriate for two reasons: First, the paucity of empirical research to date on business model innovations in the textile industry makes it difficult to generalise statements. Second, the intent to select cases from different parts of the world was in line with characterising elements of the textile industry, namely its global reach and suitability for holistic approaches on sustainability. Including companies located in four different countries also provide a differentiated view on the fostering of sustainability-oriented innovations and concepts in both, developed countries as well as emerging markets in the world.

The company cases were selected based on the following four selection criteria: First, the companies had to be sustainability oriented in their offerings and processes (e.g., by using sustainable materials or designing sustainable products). Second, each company had to have its own corporate website since the main focus here was to identify and analyse statements regarding business model (innovations) as well as (social) sustainability. The third selection criterion related to the preferably pioneering role of companies selected. In order to meet this criterion, each of the companies had to be included into prior academic research, either by way of referencing or inclusion into empirical enquiries and samples. The last, fourth, selection criterion comprised the necessity of each company to be awarded or having received internationally acknowledged certifications and recognitions. This criterion relates and is closely linked to the third criterion since it was set up to substantiate the needed leading role of each company in fostering the implementation of (social) sustainability in the textile industry.

The companies considered suitable and relevant for this research were retrieved by relying on multiple sources including personal networks (e.g., experts from governmental as well as non-governmental bodies as well as representatives of Western companies in the textile industry). Further, the companies selected were searched for in databases (e.g., *Google*), media documentaries as well as in textile or fashion websites and magazines. This search yielded to the following textile companies from four different countries to be included in our final sample: *soleREBELS, Hirdaramani, Globe Hope* and *Gildan* (see *Table 1*). We chose to include two smaller and two larger companies in order to find generalizable patterns. The overall sample is located in equal parts in less affluent countries in Africa and Asia as well as in western style developed countries in North America and Europe.

In our subsequent analysis we gathered data by qualitatively analysing approximately 110 corporate websites and tabs relating to the four companies included in our final sample from May 2018 until July 2018. We exclusively relied on text passages on corporate websites, including also factsheets, posters and reports published by each company. Particular attention was paid to the following aspects and themes portrayed on the corporate websites: statements concerning company mission, objectives, philosophy and core values, management practices, corporate

Table 1. Sample characteristics

	soleREBELS	Globe Hope	Hirdaramani	Gildan
Country	Ethiopia	Finland	Sri Lanka	Canada
Year of formation	2004	2003	Early 1900s	1984
Industry segment	Manufacturing	Manufacturing	Manufacturing	Manufacturing
Products	Shoes	Clothes; shoes; bags; accessories	Apparel	Apparel
Core (sustainability) values	Eco-sensibility; Community empowerment; Development of local supply chains; Usage of local and sustainable materials; Zero carbon production; 'True recycling'	Ecology (eco-friendly products; ecological design); Ethics (ethical clothes and bags); Slow fashion; Responsible Company	Committed to sustainability; Triple bottom line – People; Planet; Profit; Innovation in apparel manufacturing; Global diversified conglomerate	We act like entrepreneurs; We operate responsibly; We believe in our people
Number of employees	~ 1.200	~ 20	~ 60.000	~ 48.000
Type of business model innovation*	Newly established	Newly established	Already existing	Already existing
Academic research**	McCarthy, B. (2015). soleRebels: targeting the ethical consumer. Report. SAGE, London. (In Press)	Ketola, T. (2012). Fair business as a corporate responsibility and competitiveness factor? Fashion design company Globe Hope as an example. International Journal of Technology Management. 58(1/2), 109-128.	Ediriweera, A., Armstrong AM, A., & Heenetigala, K. (2015). Governance in family business: A literature review. Journal of Law and Governance, 10(2), 36-46.	B.-Turcotte, M.-F., de Bellefeuille, S., & den Hond, F. (2007). Gildan Inc.: Influencing corporate governance in the textile sector. Journal of Corporate Citizenship, 27, 23-36.
Awards and recognitions for sustainability and innovation initiatives***	"Most Valuable Entrepreneur" Award at 2011 Global Entrepreneurship Week	"Vision of the Year" Award from Finnish Green Association in 2005	"Garment Maker of the Year" at the World Textile Awards in 2015	"Honduran CSR Seal" Award 2017
Company website	https://www.solerebels.com/	https://www.globehope.com/en/	http://www.hirdaramani.com/	http://www.gildancorp.com/homepage

* according to *Baldassarre et al. (2017)*

** related to the third case selection criterion

*** related to the fourth case selection criterion; selection as emphasized by the authors social responsibility as well as corporate culture and working conditions, statements referring to customers, partners and the local environment as well as statements on business operations (e.g., materials, products and processes) with regard to textiles. For each company the relevant data, in the form of verbal statements, was identified, copied and stored in a separate file.

Albeit the sample is quite heterogeneous, e.g. geographic scope, size and history, offered products, segment in the textile supply and value chains as well as business operations, our method has several limitations. The number of company cases is rather small, thus causing restrictions concerning transferability and generalizing of findings. This supports the exploratory and conceptual character of the chapter. Further, the web presentations by each company differ in terms of amount and quality. This particularly holds true for aspects concerning social responsibility. So far, additional material (e.g., media coverage) was retrieved for each company, yet not explicitly included into our subsequent analysis. Among others, videos offered on corporate websites or interviews with founders or board representatives in the media could be used in future research as valuable data and complement this research. In line with this, our research reflects a snapshot. Therefore, the period of data collection could be expanded in order to investigate dynamics. Moreover, the analysis of relevant text passages is rather subjective and relative. This particularly points to the required aligning of corporate statements with theory-based aspects on social sustainability and responsibility. So, our analysis is limited to the given and presented information on the companies' websites, not allowing for conclusions regarding the covering up of activities. However, the analysis of pioneer companies as good practice cases allows the investigation of positive patterns (Bryman, 2015) for driving responsible and sustainable business practices.

Results of the Leximancer™-Based Literature Review

Figure 2 shows the overall concept map based on the computer-aided text analysis software *Leximancer*™. It visualises the analysis of all 1.003 articles retrieved on business models and business model innovations for sustainability, textile industries as well as social sustainability in order to provide an overview of main themes, concepts and relationships captured in prior research on these literature streams. The concept map reveals a great variety of thematic regions. Along with this, the map also illustrates a great diversity in terms of concepts displayed within each thematic region, both content and quantity of concepts investigated. The biggest themes are "consumers", "sustainable" and "sustainability", thus appearing to be most frequent under investigation in publications covered. They are followed by other relatively large thematic regions, namely "product", "company" and "business".

Figure 2. Overview of main themes and concepts on business models, business model innovations for sustainability, textile industries and social sustainability (N = 1.003 publications)

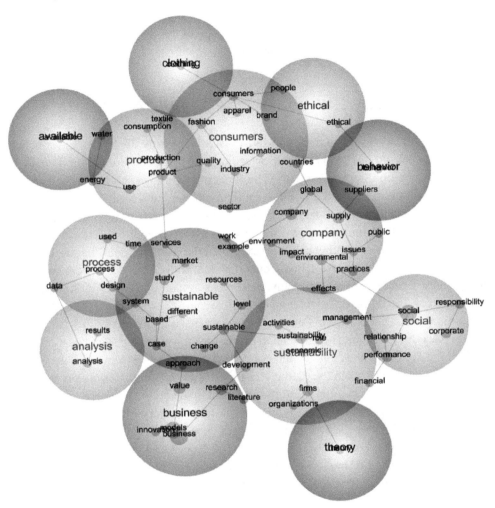

The thematic region "social" forms a single theme, albeit – compared to the above mentioned – a smaller one. It entails five different concepts, namely "social" as the largest concept as well as the concepts "responsibility", "corporate", "relationship" and "performance". Within the thematic region "social" the concept "social" is directly linked to the concepts "responsibility" as well as "performance". Further it is linked directly to the concepts "environmental" and "management" as well as "financial", thus connecting two other thematic regions, namely "company"

and "sustainability", respectively. The concept "clothing" forms simultaneously a single theme with overlaps to two other thematic regions, namely "consumers" and "product". However, the theme "clothing" does not display any other single concept. Interestingly, the concept map shows a separate thematic region "ethical" with the concepts "ethical", "people" and "brand" included. It also forms broad overlaps with the two themes "consumers" and "behaviour".

BUSINESS MODEL INNOVATIONS FOR SUSTAINABILITY

Figure 3 specifies the proceeding analysis by visualising the main themes and concepts covered in 194 (out of 1003) publications concerning business models and business models innovations for sustainability. The concept map shows the themes "business" and "system" to represent the two largest thematic regions. Similar to the concept map in *Figure 2,* a variety in terms of content-wise concepts as well as quantitative prominence within single thematic regions can also be depicted. Exemplarily, the theme "data" displays no other concept (except for the concept "data" itself), whereas the theme "system" portrays 13 concepts. Compared to *Figure 2* the concept map reveals new thematic regions, namely the themes "system", "economy", "creation" and "design" including different concepts. However, *Figure 3* does not contain the thematic regions "social" and "ethical". Nevertheless, issues related to "social" or "social sustainability" can be retraced in the themes "sustainable" and "design" such as e.g., the concept "learning" or the concept "knowledge". Moreover, the concept "social" also plays a role in the theme "business". Interestingly, it is not presented in the thematic region "creation" though there is also the concept "value" embedded. In addition, the concept "people" is situated at the periphery of the theme "system" and has no single concept path to the concept "social" or other assumingly social sustainability-related concepts such as "learning" or "knowledge".

The thematic region "business" illustrates a 'concept spider', providing links from the concept "business" to each of the following concepts: "innovation", "strategy", "strategic", "performance", and "social". In addition, in this 'concept spider' the direct links of the concept "business" span to the concepts "sustainability", "perspective", "organizational", "change", "role" and "firm" interconnecting it with three other themes, namely "sustainable", "different" and "creation". Regarding the specific focus of this chapter on business model innovations for sustainability in the textile industry the concept "fashion" is represented in the thematic region "economy". However, it is placed at the very periphery of this theme and also entails only one direct path to another concept, namely "consumption" in the theme "system", thereby linking both themes "economy" and "system".

Figure 3. Overview of main themes and concepts on business models and business model innovations for sustainability (N = 194 publications)

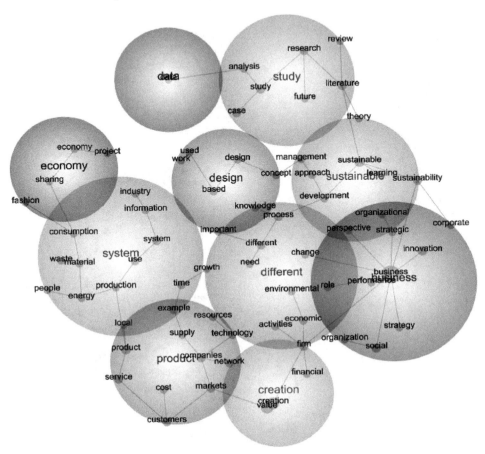

Business Model Innovations for (Social) Sustainability in the Textile Industry

Since our intent here is to streamline and synthesise research on business model innovations in the textile industry with a particular emphasis on social sustainability and social responsibility, a third analysis of publications by means of *Leximancer*™ was employed. *Figure 4* illustrates the results of this evaluation step. Specifically, it maps the analysis of 18 (out of 1003) scientific articles concerning business models innovations for (social) sustainability in the textile industry. The concept map displays 14 thematic regions of which the largest are "value", "business", "sustainability" and "customers". This finding suggests a widespread interest of

Figure 4. Overview of main themes and concepts on business models innovations for (social) sustainability in the textile industry (N = 18 publications)

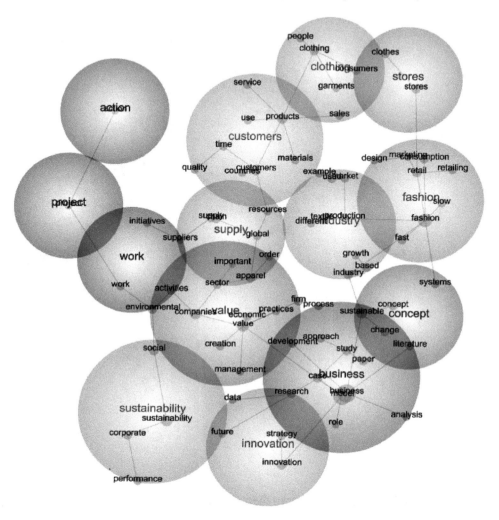

scholars in these concepts. The following concepts are mainly represented within these biggest thematic regions: "products", "customers", "companies", "value", "apparel", "management", "environmental", "business", "model", "sustainable/sustainability" as well as "corporate" and "social". Smaller themes are represented by a considerable amount of thematic regions, too. These include themes such as "work", "stores", "clothing", "industry" as well as "supply".

Similar to the concept maps in *Figures 2* and *3* quite diverse concepts and quantities within each thematic region are reflected. The amount of concepts named for each of the largest themes varies considerably. Whereas in the theme "value" 14 concepts are presented, the theme "sustainability" entails only four concepts. Moreover, in two themes, namely "action" and "project" no other single concept is shown. The concept map also shows several overlaps between single thematic regions. Exemplarily, the concept "development" is at the interface between the two themes "business" and "value"; the concept "future" is also presented at the intersection between the two themes "innovation" and "sustainability". The thematic region "value" features most overlaps as it has interfaces with the following four themes: "business", "sustainability", "work" and "supply".

As *Figure 4* shows the concept map visualises the separation of genuinely textile-related themes in two thematic regions, namely "clothing" and "fashion". Yet, several differences can be highlighted: Whereas "clothing" has some overlaps with the themes "customers" and "stores", such interface for the thematic region "fashion" cannot be retraced. Instead, the thematic region "fashion" is located at the intersection with the theme "industry". Between the two thematic regions "clothing" and "fashion" differences also exist with regard to content and quantity of concepts. In the thematic region "clothing" five concepts can be found, whereas for the thematic region "fashion" eight concepts are depicted. In addition, for the theme "clothing" aspects related to the concepts "consumer" and "people" are of prior concern whereas with regard to the thematic region "fashion" concepts like "marketing", "design" and "retail" form key issues next to "consumption".

The concept "social" is situated at the edge of the thematic region "sustainability". This concept is part of the concept path *performance – corporate – sustainability – social – environmental*. In so doing, the thematic region "sustainability" is connected with the theme "value". Other concept paths for the concept "social" cannot be retraced. In the same way the concept "social" is not visible in other thematic regions and does not exhibit any other direct link (e.g., to the concept "people"). As a consequence, the question arises whether the concept "social" is likely to play a neglected or marginalised role in relation to other thematic regions such as, among others, "customers". In line with this the concept map in *Figure 4* also illustrates that other aspects related to the terms "social" or "social sustainability" such as CSR, human rights, knowledge, learning, relationship, fair trade or sharing are obviously not portrayed.

Interestingly, similar to the concept "social", also the concept "environmental" is mirrored rather at the periphery of the theme "value". It links this thematic region with the theme "business" by means of the concept path *environmental – activities – companies – value – case – model*. However, the analysis provides a concept map that also shows multiple concept paths and forms within one thematic region. Exemplarily, with regard to one of the largest themes, namely "customers", we find a first concept path *quality – time – customers – countries*, a second concept path *quality – time – customers – products* as well as a 'concept spider' centring around the concept "products" with single links to each of the following concepts "service", "use", "customers" and "materials". The thematic region "customers" is also attached directly to two of its neighbouring thematic regions "clothing" and "supply" via the two concept paths *products – clothing* as well as *customers – resources.*

To summarise, the proceeding analysis by means of the text-mining software *Leximancer*™ helps visualising and mapping important research topics and concepts within earlier literature on business model innovations for (social) sustainability in the textile industry. At the same time, this analysis is limited since the subsequent evaluation involves a particular interpretive and subjective approach, in particular the identification of important and relevant thematic regions, concepts as well as concept paths within single themes. Despite these drawbacks, such a literature-based and software-aided analysis may lead to critically appraising existing research as well as discovering new avenues for advancing future research. Moreover, it may also support (re-)evaluating empirical findings. However, the concept maps show the limited concepts on business models innovations for social sustainability.

RESULTS OF THE EMPIRICAL INVESTIGATION

The findings from our analysis of all four cases companies included in the sample are revealed in *Tables 2 to 4*. The initial step of our investigation comprised the mapping of statements on corporate websites along macro-trends and drivers for companies operating in the textile industry. Though we acknowledge the limitations of our procedure (e.g., subjectivity and bias of statement identification and alignment; analysis bound to written statements), to our best knowledge, there has not been such a comprehensive mapping of various approaches to (social) sustainability in the textile industry based on statements of corporate websites to date. As emphasized by *Todeschini et al. (2017)*, these trends encompass the following five aspects: "circular economy", "corporate social responsibility", "sharing economy and collaborative consumption", "technological innovation" as well as "consumer awareness". Each of these trends summarises a number of single anticipated driving forces that are likely to impact on textile companies in general and their business model innovations in particular. These aspects are visualised in *Table 2* in more detail. Specifically, *Table 2* illustrates the impacts on elements and components of the conventional business model. The statements identified on each corporate website concerning primarily environmental and social sustainability were mirrored with the description of trends and drivers as outlined by *Todeschini et al. (2017).*

Overall, the results indicate that all four cases report on their websites about objectives and activities related to the macro-trends and drivers towards sustainability in the textile company. Yet, for each company a different amount of statements for each trend and driver can be revealed. This finding is in line with the service- and production-focus of the companies under investigation. Exemplarily, the drivers "vegan" and "fashion library" have not been addressed by any company since none of the four cases appears to produce textiles of animal origin or to focus on a subscription service for apparel. Each of the four companies target to communicate issues related to "fair trade", "sustainable raw materials" as well as "zero waste". Only one company, namely *Globe Hope* from Finland, reports on issues related to "second hand" as well as "wearables", "capsule wardrobe" and "lowsumerism".

Albeit of minor relevance, the majority of companies also focus on aspects related to "recycling", "locally sourced" and "collaboration". Interestingly, the two big apparel manufacturing companies included in the sample, namely *Hirdaramani* and *Gildan*, obviously cover a smaller number of aspects regarding the triple bottom line of sustainability in business models. The primary emphasis of sustainability efforts is put on issues relating to "fair trade", "collaboration" as well as "zero waste". At the same time, the analysis of the two large companies revealed that they mainly focus on organizational requirements and the firm's perspective when –at least– exploiting and communicating the sustainability pillars in their business models. In so doing, quite unexpectedly, less attention is paid towards a direct treatment and addressing to the consumer. Further, the two largest companies focus in their (social) sustainability-related statements on standards set forth by international organizations as well as aspects referring to (global as well as local) leadership and corporate culture (e.g., values such as dignity and diversity). In sharp contrast to this, the two smaller firms analysed, namely *soleREBELS* and *Globe Hope*, seem to thrive forwards a closer relationship with their mindful customers, including fostering education and raising awareness towards sustainability in textile production and consumption.

Following this first step of analysis, the statements regarding corporate activities as presented on the websites were streamlined and mapped with single elements of business models as explored in previous research by *Rosca et al. (2017)*. Particularly, we focused on four components of the conventional business model as these appear to be the central elements in the literature (e.g., Dickson & Chang, 2015): "target customer", "value proposition", "revenue model" and "value chain". Differing statements concerning single business model components on each corporate website were merged and amalgamated (*Table 3*). Further, this step helped us to summarize specific issues concerning sustainability orientation in business model elements as addressed by companies in the textile industry. This step of analysis reveals interesting evidence regarding the integration of sustainability-oriented aspects into business model innovation. In fact, as our findings reveal, strong sustainability efforts in the textile industry are apparently reflected in each of the four components of conventional business models. The element "target customer", the companies

Table 2. Mapping the trends and drivers of sustainability-related business model innovation for textile companies

Macro-Trends and Drivers*	Business Model Component Affected**	soleREBELS	Globe Hope	Hirdaramani	Gildan
Circular Economy					
Recycling	• Cost structure • Key activities • Key partners	"recycled tires" "true recycling"	"using a wide variety of recycled and left over materials" "Ecological design for us means using recycled materials and close production."	-	"look to reduce, reuse and recycle wherever possible" "86% of our total company waste was recycled or repurposed in 2016"
Vegan	• Key partners • Key resources • Channels • Value proposition	-	-	-	-
Upcycling	• Key activities • Key resources • Value proposition	"find new uses for indigenous and recycled materials comes very naturally to us"	"Through re-designing and re-sewing, left over and old materials are turned into new and unique clothes, bags and accessories." "also combine different kinds of materials, such as take pockets from old coats and attach them to a bag made from another material."	-	
Corporate Social Responsibility					
Sweatshop free	• Customer relationship • Key activities • Key resources	"wages that are on average 4 times the legal minimum wage & 3 times the industry average wage"	"production is done mainly by subcontractors (...). As ethical working conditions are a key factor for us, we have personally visited the premises of all our subcontractors." "our products are made in Finland and Estonia" "As an exception, our shoes are made in Portugal and our organic cotton T-Shirts in Turkey."	-	

continued on following page

Table 2. Continued

Macro-Trends and Drivers*	Business Model Component Affected**	soleREBELS	Globe Hope	Hirdaramani	Gildan
Fair trade	• Customer relationship • Key partners	*"1st Fair Trade footwear company"* *"100% medical coverage program covering workers and their families"* *"best investment is the one we make in our children's educational needs"* *"bring jobs to our community"*	*"want to offer consumers an ecological alternative and to encourage people to think about their environment"* *"products offer companies an opportunity to implement and communicate their commitment on sustainability through the gifts they give to their customers and other stakeholders"*	*"operates 5 Fair Trade US Certified Facilities"* *"empowering our people and communities to live a healthy and fulfilling life"* *"become a greener, more people-oriented organization"* *"wellbeing strategy"* *"Hirdaramani has been working on (...) the development of the HiGG index with several facilities participating (...)"* *"(...) provides assistance to communities and schools trying to implement green initiatives (...)"* *"providing support and security in the worst times (e.g., disaster relief and rebuilding)"*	*"providing safe and ethical work environments, empowering our employees with robust compensation and attractive benefits structures (...)"* *"supporting a diverse workplace is a business imperative (...)"* *"built a strong reputation of providing support to the communities where we operate, (...) responsibility to play an active role through humanitarian aid in times of need"* *"foster and preserve a culture of diversity and inclusion. (...) embrace and encourage the differences that each employee brings to (...) and (...) every employee should be empowered to reach their full potential"* *"(...) providing employees with ongoing education through various types of training (...)"* *"Code of Ethics addresses matters that include conflicts of interest, (...) protection of human rights, health and safety, anti-corruption laws, (...) compliance with laws and reporting of unethical or illegal behaviour."*
Locally sourced	• Customer relationship • Key partners • Value proposition	*"So every action we take is with the communities betterment in mind."*	*"the production is close"* *"To minimize transportation distances and the related pollution, we have centered our production in Finland and Estonia."*	*"empowering local farmers"*	-
Sharing Economy and Collaborative Consumption					
Fashion library	• Customer relationship • Value proposition • Revenue streams	-	-	-	-

continued on following page

Table 2. Continued

Macro-Trends and Drivers*	Business Model Component Affected**	sokeREBELS	Globe Hope	Hirdaramani	Gildan
Second hand	• Key activities • Channels • Customer relationship • Value proposition • Revenue streams	-	*"Twice Loved Hope is a second hand concept where Globe Hope-products, already made from recycled materials, can be recycled once again. The idea behind the concept is that customers can return their old, unused clothes and bags (...)"*	-	-
Collaboration	• Key activities • Key partners • Key resources • Delivery channels • Customer relationship	-	*"also work together with many companies, associations and bands to create specifically designed products for their customers, employees and fans"* *"(...) products; such as handbags, computer bags and iPhone cases in collaboration with Veikkaus Oy."*	*"developed long term relationships and partnerships with global fabric and accessory manufacturers"* *"(Environmental Sustainability Strategy) provides stakeholders with clear guidelines for Prevention, Reduction and Mitigation of any harmful effects on the environment and natural resources (...)"* *"(...) partnering with suppliers who share its sustainable values (...)"*	*"The Gildan Code of Conduct encompasses the principles set forth by the International Labor Organisation (ILO), the Fair Labor Association (FLA) and various other organisations. (...) openly communicates our commitment to employees, partners and stakeholders (...)"* *"use our visibility of the total value chain (...) to collaborate with our partners (...)"*

Technological Innovation

Macro-Trends and Drivers*	Business Model Component Affected**	sokeREBELS	Globe Hope	Hirdaramani	Gildan
Sustainable raw materials	• Cost structure • Key resources • Customer relationship	*"more sustainable materials"*	*"use organic cotton that gets hand-picked and is not sprayed with nature-harming pesticides at any stage"*	*"sourcing new sustainable fabrics"* *"(...) offer top quality organically grown eco-friendly products"* *"(...) promoting organic farming activities"*	*"cotton (...) grown (...) under strict US-EPA and OSHA regulations"*
Zero waste	• Cost structure • Key activities • Key resources	*"save the planet with zero carbon output from the making of these wondrous fabrics"*	*"When we design products we always try to use all of the material completely."*	*"develop techniques and formulas that eliminate the use of water, chemicals and reduce energy consumption"* *"using the latest technology in manufacturing together with a strong focus on R&D in fabric development"* *"ensuring that its processes prevent pollution and protect the environment and that it promotes resource efficiency and environmental enrichment"*	*"featuring sustainable solutions such as the BioTop wastewater treatment and BioMass renewable energy steam generation systems"*

continued on following page

Table 2. Continued

Macro-Trends and Drivers*	Business Model Component Affected**	soleREBELS	Globe Hope	Hirdaramani	Gildan
Wearables	• Cost structure • Key activities • Key partners • Key resources • Value proposition	-	*"(…) bag that uses solar panel technology from Finnish company Suntrican. The technology enables e.g. charging a mobile phone in the bag."*	-	
Consumer Awareness					
Capsule wardrobe	• Customer relationship • Value proposition • Revenue streams	-	*"want you to hang on to your Globe Hope-products for as long as possible"*	-	
Lowsumerism	• Customer relationship • Value proposition • Revenue streams	-	*"Buy less and choose well."* *"Consume with good conscience."*	-	
Slow fashion	• Value proposition • Customer relationship	*"sustainable production"*	*"We represent slow fashion and that is something we believe in."*	-	

* adopted from *Todeschini et al. (2017)*

** adopted from *Todeschini et al. (2017)*

Table 3. Components of business model innovations for sustainability in the global textile industry

Business Model Element*	Description**	Corporate Practices Among Sample Investigated	Business Model Innovations in the Textile Industry***	
			Drivers	Trends
Target customer	Main group of customers	✓ Transparency in working conditions (e.g., wages, medical coverage, employment opportunities, education and local empowerment)	• Sweatshop free • Fair trade • Locally sourced	• Corporate social responsibility
		✓ Offerings concerning used clothing take-back systems and concepts ✓ Information about partnerships and relationships (e.g., suppliers, other manufacturers, associations, international organizations)	• Fashion library • Second hand • Collaboration	• Sharing economy and collaborative consumption
		✓ Encouraging environmentally friendly and sustainable cultivation methods ✓ Sourcing of new, sustainable textile fabrics	• Sustainable raw materials	• Technological innovation
		✓ Promoting mindful and conscious textile consumption as well as production ✓ Fostering appreciation and long-term use of textile products	• Capsule wardrobe • Lowsumerism • Slow fashion	• Consumer awareness
Value proposition	Economic, social or environmental benefit offered by product or service	✓ Transformation of left-over, old and diverse materials into new and high-quality textile products	• Vegan • Upcycling	• Circular economy
		✓ Local textile production and minimizing environmental impacts (e.g., transportation) ✓ Transparency regarding community involvement and development	• Locally sourced	• Corporate social responsibility
		✓ Clothing return systems as opportunity for brand loyalty and customer retention as well as valuable source for (new) raw materials	• Fashion library • Second hand	• Sharing economy and collaborative consumption
		✓ Providing textile products with additional functionalities	• Wearables	• Technological innovation
		✓ Offering of high quality, durable, ethically manufactured and aesthetic products ✓ Preservation of local values, cultures and traditions	• Capsule wardrobe • Lowsumerism • Slow fashion	• Consumer awareness

continued on following page

Table 3. Continued

Business Model Element*	Description**	Corporate Practices Among Sample Investigated	Business Model Innovations in the Textile Industry***	
			Drivers	Trends
Revenue model	Revenue generation; cost drivers and profit opportunities; distribution of economic benefits among partners and stakeholders	✓ Sustainable solutions (e.g., environmental management; waste management) as integral part of revenue generation ✓ Earnings from products donated to support partners and stakeholders (e.g., international organizations; communities)	• Recycling	• Circular economy
		✓ Offering of discount vouchers in take-back concepts for used clothes that are already made from recycled materials	• Fashion library • Second hand	• Sharing economy and collaborative consumption
		✓ Commitment to environment as core corporate value ✓ Continuing technological and product quality improvements (e.g., sustainable cultivation and resource utilization; environmentally friendly manufacturing facilities and technologies) ✓ Strong focus on R&D ✓ Selling of ethically manufactured promotional gifts to business partners ✓ Promotion of paid repair services	• Sustainable raw materials • Zero waste • Wearables	• Technological innovation
		✓ Encouraging responsible operations ✓ Fostering appreciation and long-term use of textile products	• Capsule wardrobe • Lowsumerism	• Consumer awareness
Value chain	Specific and sustainability-oriented activities used for value creation	✓ Importance of sustainable solutions in all parts of the value chain (e.g., product development and design; end-to-end) ✓ Additional value creation using left-over or recycled materials for new products of superior quality	• Recycling • Vegan • Upcycling	• Circular economy
		✓ Information about manufacturing sites and working conditions (e.g., wages, medical coverage, employment opportunities, education and local empowerment) ✓ Participation in international standard setting rules and measures concerning environmental and social sustainability ✓ Building up of strong legitimacy and reputation as well as positive influence on local communities	• Sweatshop free • Fair trade • Locally sourced	• Corporate social responsibility
		✓ Information about infrastructure on clothing take-back systems and concepts ✓ Enduring cooperation with partners operating sustainably (e.g., suppliers, other manufacturers, associations, international organizations)	• Second hand • Collaboration	• Sharing economy and collaborative consumption
		✓ Commitment to environment as core corporate value involving all stakeholders (e.g., local farmers and weavers) ✓ Provision of information and guidelines on environmental damages or unethical behaviour to stakeholders in the textile supply chain	• Sustainable raw materials • Zero waste • Wearables	• Technological innovation

* adopted from *Rosca et al. (2017)*
** adopted from *Rosca et al. (2017)*
*** inspired by *Todeschini et al. (2017)*

investigated emphasize transparent information on working conditions or provide statements on partnerships and relationships with various stakeholders. Referring to the component "value proposition", the smaller companies included in the sample focus on clothing return systems as opportunity for brand loyalty and customer retention as well as a valuable source for (new) raw materials.

Further, all cases examined more or less aim at offering high quality, durable, ethically manufactured and aesthetic products. Based on our case date the revenue model of sustainability-oriented textile companies comprises issues such as the donation of earnings from products to support partners and stakeholders or, among others, the promotion of paid repair services. Concerning the "value chain" component the companies under investigation prioritize statements referring to establishing and strengthening legitimacy, corporate accountability and reputation as well as positive influence on local communities. In addition, fostering a long-term cooperation with partners such as suppliers that base their operations on sustainable values, too, seems to play a crucial role regarding business model innovations.

Next, our data also revealed that several corporate activities can be aligned twice or more to the elements of conventional business models. Exemplarily, offerings concerning used clothing take-back systems or concepts refer to both components "target customers" as well as "value proposition". This reflects the importance of perspective primarily taken (e.g., customer vs. service). Furthermore, issues relating to an increasingly needed appreciation and long-term use of textile products can be aligned to both elements "target customers" as well as "revenue model", the latter reinforcing the highly desirable shift towards different economic rationales when conceptualizing, among others, the notion of slow fashion and related business models for the textile industry. Interestingly, our analysis also stresses several drivers for business model innovations in the textile industry to be found categorized only in the literature (e.g., "vegan"; "fashion library"). However, since they are not represented by the companies under focus it likely seems to be another methodological limitation of our research (e.g., sampling) rather than a content-wise restriction.

In the last step of our empirical investigation we conflated our prior findings with selected ideas on social sustainability and corporate social responsibility. In particular, by drawing on previous research by *Bocken et al. (2014)*, we identified sustainable business model archetypes for each of the corporate sustainability-related practices presented on the corporate websites. In doing so, this step enabled us to particularly identify business model innovations related to a somewhat social category of sustainable business models as worked out by *Bocken et al. (2014)*. Consequently, this step was seen to nurture our research objective, namely exploring likely different approaches to social sustainability in the textile industry. The findings of this final evaluation step are presented in *Table 4*. As can be depicted from our results, all three groupings of sustainable business models as developed by *Bocken*

Table 4. Mapping sustainable business model archetypes for the global textile industry

Business model element*	Description**	Corporate practices among sample investigated	Sustainable business model archetype***
Target customer	Main group of customers	✓ Transparency in working conditions (e.g., wages, medical coverage, employment opportunities, education and local empowerment)	➤ "Adopt a stewardship role"
		✓ Offerings concerning used clothing take-back systems and concepts	➤ "Encourage sufficiency"
		✓ Information about partnerships and relationships (e.g., suppliers, other manufacturers, associations, international organizations)	➤ "Develop scale up solutions"
		✓ Encouraging environmentally friendly and sustainable cultivation methods	➤ "Substitute with renewables and natural processes"
		✓ Sourcing of new, sustainable textile fabrics	
		✓ Promoting mindful and conscious textile consumption as well as production	➤ "Encourage sufficiency"
		✓ Fostering appreciation and long-term use of textile products	
Value proposition	Economic, social or environmental benefit offered by product or service	✓ Transformation of left-over, old and diverse materials into new and high-quality textile products	➤ "Create value from waste"
		✓ Local textile production and minimizing environmental impacts (e.g., transportation)	➤ "Repurpose for society/environment"
		✓ Transparency regarding community involvement and development	➤ "Adopt a stewardship role"
		✓ Clothing return systems as opportunity for brand loyalty and customer retention as well as valuable source for (new) raw materials	➤ "Create value from waste"
		✓ Providing textile products with additional functionalities	➤ "Maximize material and energy efficiency"
		✓ Offering of high quality, durable, ethically manufactured and aesthetic products	➤ "Encourage sufficiency"
		✓ Preservation of local values, cultures and traditions	➤ "Repurpose for society/environment"
Revenue model	Revenue generation; cost drivers and profit opportunities; distribution of economic benefits among partners and stakeholders	✓ Sustainable solutions (e.g., environmental management; waste management) as integral part of revenue generation	➤ "Substitute with renewables and natural processes"
		✓ Earnings from products donated to support partners and stakeholders (e.g., international organizations; communities)	➤ "Repurpose for society/environment"
		✓ Offering of discount vouchers in take-back concepts for used clothes that are already made from recycled materials	➤ "Encourage sufficiency"
		✓ Commitment to environment as core corporate value	➤ "Adopt a stewardship role"
		✓ Continuing technological and product quality improvements (e.g., sustainable cultivation and resource utilization; environmentally friendly manufacturing facilities and technologies)	➤ "Maximize material and energy efficiency"
		✓ Strong focus on R&D	➤ "Substitute with renewables and natural processes"
		✓ Selling of ethically manufactured promotional gifts to business partners	➤ "Encourage sufficiency"
		✓ Promotion of paid repair services	➤ "Deliver functionality rather than ownership"
		✓ Encouraging responsible operations	➤ "Adopt a stewardship role"
		✓ Fostering appreciation and long-term use of textile products	➤ "Encourage sufficiency"
Value chain	Specific and sustainability-oriented activities used for value creation	✓ Importance of sustainable solutions in all parts of the value chain (e.g., product development and design; end-to-end)	➤ "Create value from waste"
		✓ Additional value creation using left-over or recycled materials for new products of superior quality	➤ "Maximize material and energy efficiency"
		✓ Information about manufacturing sites and working conditions (e.g., wages, medical coverage, employment opportunities, education and local empowerment)	➤ "Adopt a stewardship role"
		✓ Participation in international standard setting rules and measures concerning environmental and social sustainability	
		✓ Building up of strong legitimacy and reputation as well as positive influence on local communities	➤ "Repurpose for society/environment"
		✓ Information about infrastructure on clothing take-back systems and concepts	➤ "Create value from waste"
		✓ Enduring cooperation with partners operating sustainably (e.g., suppliers, other manufacturers, associations, international organizations)	
		✓ Commitment to environment as core corporate value involving all stakeholders (e.g., local farmers and weavers)	➤ "Adopt a stewardship role"
		✓ Provision of information and guidelines on environmental damages or unethical behaviour to stakeholders in the textile supply chain	

* adopted from *Rosca et al. (2017)*

** adopted from *Rosca et al. (2017)*

*** inspired by *Bocken et al. (2014)*; *Groupings of business model archetypes: green = technological; yellow = social; blue = organizational*

*For a more accurate representation see the electronic version.

et al. (2014) – technological, social and organizational – are mirrored by the cases investigated. In order to provide for better clarity and developing distinct profiles each of the three higher order groupings as outlined by *Bocken et al. (2014)* is marked in a different colour. The green category encompasses the technical grouping of business models for sustainability with prevailing technological and technical innovation components. The higher order grouping marked in blue colour includes business model archetypes with a dominant organizational innovation change component. The remaining yellow-marked grouping encompasses social business model innovation archetypes and highlights social innovation components (Bocken et al., 2014). Since our focus here was to capture aspects relating to social sustainability in business model innovations in the textile industry the following sustainable business model archetypes with regard to social sustainability are represented among the sample: "Adopt a stewardship role", "Encourage sufficiency" as well as "Deliver functionality rather than ownership".

Albeit all three archetypes relating to social sustainability as identified by *Bocken et al. (2014)* can be retraced among the companies analysed, the extent differs, however. Whereas the archetype "Deliver functionality rather than ownership" is to be characterized only once in our sample, both "Adopt a stewardship role" as well as "Encourage sufficiency" are mirrored more than five times by respectively aggregated data on corporate statements. Nevertheless, the exemplar archetypes derived prior in literature unfortunately do not fully reflect aspects that are central to some of the four companies analysed and their efforts in addressing societal aspects and values. Though relating to social sustainability and (corporate) social responsibility, the following issues cannot be aligned with earlier academic research on business model innovations for sustainability, pointing to a gap between practice and research. Among them, statements regarding corporate leadership, information about corporate culture (e.g., employee and supervisor training) and values (e.g., diversity), statements regarding community support and development (e.g., regarding disaster recovery and relief; educational support) as well as statements on shared values are found to be neglected.

In addition to this, the archetypes worked out by *Bocken et al. (2014)* do little distinguish between single agents along the value and supply chains. This seems highly problematic due to the given considerable amount of actors in the textile industry as well as their likely varying objectives and interests. So, the alignment of corporate statements from our four cases analysis becomes limited since different worldviews and perspectives between e.g., suppliers, managers and customers concerning social sustainability related efforts are not exhaustive.

SOLUTIONS AND RECOMMENDATIONS

Combining our findings from the preceding empirical investigation with the *Leximancer*™-based content analysis as described above, the following results can be summarised: In accordance with the analysis of earlier literature on business models, business model innovations for sustainability, textile industry as well as social sustainability, our empirical data stresses concepts - such as "value", "business", "customer" and "sustainability" - playing an important role in statements on corporate websites of textile companies, independent of the geographic region or textile segment the company is operating in. However, depending on the size of the company and –likely– the emphasis on sustainability in the genuine business model, the concept of the "customer" is more or less directly considered and addressed. Exemplarily, as revealed by our empirical analysis, the two large apparel manufacturing companies involved in our sample do not directly address issues relating to consumer awareness on their corporate websites. Thus, their business models and in particular the three related business model elements 'customer relationship', 'value proposition' and 'revenue streams' apparently involve less aspects related to increasing shifts of consumer perspectives towards sustainability and ethics in textile production and consumption emphasized in academic research (Lueg et al., 2015). Based on our data analysis we find that companies already established in the global textile value chain over several decades primarily align their business models towards social sustainability by highlighting almost exclusively corporate social responsibilities, like local sourcing and production as well as compliance with fair trade principles on their corporate websites. Thus, social value forms as highlighted in prior research (e.g., Evans et al., 2017) are not exhaustively covered by already established business models. At the same time, this spurs the need for developing genuinely 'true' social business model innovations for the textile industry.

Moreover, all four textile companies included in this research highlight issues relating to the concepts "products" as well as "environmental". This seems to emphasize the presumption that business model innovations for the textile industry – independent of their inclusion of social facets – prioritise sustainable products or materials. In line with this, the increasing introduction of environmentally friendly technologies or manufacturing facilities, especially in the two larger companies, seem to confirm this priority of environmental management and objectives. Thus, this might spur further debates on whether larger companies address a wider range of sustainability issues compared to smaller ones due to different organizational capabilities (Weissbrod & Bocken, 2017).

In addition, several themes and concepts as identified by means of the *Leximancer*™-based content analysis are of only little relevance to the practitioners. These include, among others, issues related to "project" and "action". The content analysis also revealed several thematic and conceptual intersections, as business model innovations for (social) sustainability in the textile industry. Exemplarily, the intersections between the themes "business" and "value" as well as "innovation" and "sustainability" were built by the concepts "development" and "future" respectively. The question is whether these aspects are inherently linked to promoting real-world cases of 'truly' innovative and sustainable business models in the textile industry in order to gain long-term competitiveness.

The analysis of earlier research by means of the text-mining software also confirmed a distinguishing between the two thematic regions "clothing" and "fashion". Two large apparel manufacturers of global reach and two smaller companies focusing on sustainable shoes or bags and accessories were included. Thus, the sample involved less typical cases compared to fast fashion companies. However, fashion and clothing by definition involve different ways of systemic thinking and economic priorities as well as (cultural and emotional) values (Armstrong et al., 2015). This might stipulate further research streams in two directions, namely business model innovations for social sustainability in the clothing as well as in the fashion industry.

Another finding, as the content analysis of previous research, indicates the concept "social" to be situated at the edge of the thematic region "sustainability". Further, as part of the concept path *performance – corporate – sustainability – social – environmental*, the two themes "sustainability" and "value" became connected.

Similar to this, the analysis of corporate websites reveals a high interrelatedness between social and environmental aspects. Indeed, sustainable materials, products or manufacturing technologies are linked to genuinely social aspects such as working conditions or labour rights. By contributing to the overall philosophy and (long-term economic) performance, these aspects are seen to be highly relevant for a company's strategy as well as subsequent changes to business models (Dickson & Chang, 2015; Haubro et al., 2015). However, the alignment of corporate strategy and business model innovations might also oppose efforts towards increasing sustainability. Exemplarily, one of the smaller companies, included in our sample directly, addresses the re-orientation towards, among others, international expansion in statements on its website. This, however, may be followed by multiple consequences including positive and negative (social) sustainability impacts. Though they might expand their client base as environmentally conscious consumers worldwide, they also might lose their initial claims and values like slow fashion. So, consequently, business model innovations for social sustainability are at risk by an increase in growth-focused forms and patterns of conventional textile production and consumption (Fletcher, 2010). A deeper exploration of associated trade-offs, paradoxes and contradictions in business model innovations for social sustainability could be a valuable path for future research.

The concept "social" was not visible in other thematic regions of the concept maps displayed by *Leximancer*™. Further, direct links to other somehow related concepts such as "people" were not uncovered. This proves also true for similar aspects relating to the notions of "social" or "social sustainability" including CSR, human rights, knowledge, learning, relationship, fair trade or sharing. This is partly also reflected by our empirical analysis where issues central to business model innovations, yet rooted in managerial or organizational capabilities are reflected in corporate statements, but cannot be aligned to existing models and frameworks for sustainable business models or innovations developed or dealt with in previous literature (e.g., Bocken et al., 2014). A recent effort in tackling the relationship between business model innovation and corporate sustainability by including organizational values explicitly, however, has been made by *Pedersen et al. (2018)*.

FUTURE RESERACH DIRECTIONS

The purpose of this paper was to answer the above stated research questions based on a content analysis of prior research as well as an empirical investigation of four textile companies located in different parts of the world. Although all elements of conventional business models are addressed and shaped by sustainability-oriented textile companies, further research is necessary. Based on the above presented theoretical background and our findings of the empirical analysis, the following research propositions concerning social sustainability in business model innovations for the global textile industry can be derived:

Proposition 1: *Precise social value is inadequate and unclear embedded in business models in the textile industry and needs further evaluation in terms of theoretical conceptualization, focus and practical impact (e.g., consumer education; community involvement).*

Proposition 2: *Addressing the social dimension in business model innovations in the globally interrelated textile industry needs a stronger inclusion of company-related organizational and cultural values towards (social) sustainability (e.g., managerial mind-sets).*

Proposition 3: *A proactive realigning of existing business model innovations to radically new business models in terms of social sustainability is often subordinated by components and pressure on the companies' embedment in their external environment, e.g. macro-trends (e.g., CSR) and sufficiency; thus, proactive social business model innovations for the textile industry are pivotal, but mainly neglected.*

Proposition 4: *The strong intersections between environmental and social sustainability result in an increasingly purely ecological and economic orientation as well as a high fragmentation of sustainability initiatives; in the long-term, the social dimension is threatened by the traditional logics and paradoxes of the textile industry due to competitiveness (e.g., desire and pressure for sales growth and international expansion).*

CONCLUSION

The purpose of this paper was to explore approaches to social sustainability in business model innovations. We focused our analysis on the global textile industry since this particular sector is well-known for its considerably negative environmental and social impacts. Our study contributes to existing literature on business models, business model innovations, textile industry as well as social sustainability. In line with this, a qualitative content analysis by using the innovative text-mining software *Leximancer*™ was applied. Furthermore, exploratory multiple case study approach advances the generally acknowledged gap of empirical research in the field of sustainable business models.

Our research has implications for practitioners in the textile industry as well as for further scholarly endeavours. First, it reinforces a stronger inclusion and consideration of social sustainability-related aspects in textile operations including a more holistic communication of working conditions. Second, it emphasizes a stronger approach towards aligning the thinking and designing of sustainable business models with aspects relating to organizational culture and managerial values. Third, it calls for a stronger separation of environmental and social sustainability in terms of analysis and business model integration. Ideally, both is stressed, a single consideration of environmental and social issues and an integrative and systemic perspective. Though indispensably linked, in practice both dimensions are often covered up by solely focusing on environmental aspects, thus neglecting societal impacts of global textile production and consumption. Such a deeper understanding of social aspects regarding business operations in the textile sector also expands to an increasing responsibility of especially large companies, among others consumer education and raising awareness. In this respect, however, the relevant business model innovations and their components still have to be more clearly explored and characterised by academic research.

REFERENCES

Allievi, F., Vinnari, M., & Luukkanen, J. (2015). Meat consumption and production: Analysis of efficiency, sufficiency and consistency of global trends. *Journal of Cleaner Production, 92*(1), 142–151. doi:10.1016/j.jclepro.2014.12.075

Ansari, Z. N., & Kant, R. (2017). A state-of-art literature review reflecting 15 years of focus on sustainable supply chain management. *Journal of Cleaner Production, 142*, 2524–2543. doi:10.1016/j.jclepro.2016.11.023

Armstrong, C. M., Niinimäki, K., Kujala, S., Karell, E., & Lang, C. (2015). Sustainable product-service systems for clothing: Exploring consumer perceptions of consumption alternatives in Finland. *Journal of Cleaner Production, 97*, 30–39. doi:10.1016/j.jclepro.2014.01.046

Arnold, M. (2010). Stakeholder dialogues for sustaining cultural change. *International Studies of Management & Organization, 40*(3), 61–77. doi:10.2753/IMO0020-8825400304

Arnold, M. (2017a). Fostering sustainability by linking co-creation and relationship management concepts. *Journal of Cleaner Production, 140*(Part 1), 179–188. doi:10.1016/j.jclepro.2015.03.059

Arnold, M. G. (2017b). Corporate social responsibility representation of the German water-supply and distribution companies: From colourful to barren landscapes. *International Journal of Innovation and Sustainable Development*, *11*(1), 1–22. doi:10.1504/IJISD.2017.080655

Baldassarre, B., Calabretta, G., Bocken, N. M. P., & Jaskiewicz, T. (2017). Bridging sustainable business model innovation and user-driven innovation: A process for sustainable value proposition design. *Journal of Cleaner Production*, *147*, 175–186. doi:10.1016/j.jclepro.2017.01.081

Barnes, L., & Lea-Greenwood, G. (2006). Fast fashioning the supply chain: Shaping the research agenda. *Journal of Fashion Marketing and Management: An International Journal*, *10*(3), 259–271. doi:10.1108/13612020610679259

Beattie, V., & Smith, S. J. (2013). Value creation and business models: Refocusing the intellectual capital debate. *The British Accounting Review*, *45*(4), 243–254. doi:10.1016/j.bar.2013.06.001

Bedenlier, S., Kondakci, Y., & Zawacki-Richter, O. (2018). Two decades of research into the internationalization of higher education: Major themes in the *Journal of Studies in International Education* (1997-2016). *Journal of Studies in International Education*, *22*(2), 108–135. doi:10.1177/1028315317710093

Bocken, N. M. P., Short, S. W., Rana, P., & Evans, S. (2014). A literature and practice review to develop sustainable business model archetypes. *Journal of Cleaner Production*, *65*, 42–56. doi:10.1016/j.jclepro.2013.11.039

Boons, F., & Lüdeke-Freund, F. (2013). Business models for sustainable innovation: State-of-the-art and steps towards a research agenda. *Journal of Cleaner Production*, *45*, 9–19. doi:10.1016/j.jclepro.2012.07.007

Börjeson, N., & Boström, M. (2018). Towards reflexive responsibility in a textile supply chain. *Business Strategy and the Environment*, *27*(2), 230–239. doi:10.1002/bse.2012

Bryman, A. (2015). *Social research methods* (5th ed.). Oxford, UK: Oxford University Press.

D'Souza, A., Wortmann, H., Huitema, G., & Velthuijsen, H. (2015). A business model design framework for viability; a business ecosystem approach. *Journal of Business Models*, *3*(2), 1–29.

DaSilva, C. M., & Trkman, P. (2014). Business model: What it is and what it is not. *Long Range Planning*, *47*(6), 379–389. doi:10.1016/j.lrp.2013.08.004

Dickson, M. A., & Chang, R. K. (2015). Apparel manufacturers and the business case for social sustainability: 'World class' CSR and business model innovation. *Journal of Corporate Citizenship, 57*(57), 55–72. doi:10.9774/GLEAF.4700.2015.ma.00006

Elo, S., & Kyngäs, H. (2007). The qualitative content analysis process. *Journal of Advanced Nursing, 62*(1), 107–115. doi:10.1111/j.1365-2648.2007.04569.x PMID:18352969

Eriksson, D., & Svensson, G. (2015). Elements affecting social responsibility in supply chains. *Supply Chain Management, 20*(5), 561–566. doi:10.1108/SCM-06-2015-0203

Evans, S., Vladimirova, D., Holgado, M., Van Fossen, K., Yang, M., Silva, E. A., & Barlow, C. Y. (2017). Business model innovation for sustainability: Towards a unified perspective for creation of sustainable business models. *Business Strategy and the Environment, 26*(5), 597–608. doi:10.1002/bse.1939

Fischer, A., & Pascucci, S. (2017). Institutional incentives in circular economy transition: The case of material use in the Dutch textile industry. *Journal of Cleaner Production, 155*, 17–32. doi:10.1016/j.jclepro.2016.12.038

Fjeldstad, Ø. D., & Snow, C. C. (2018). Business models and organization design. *Long Range Planning, 51*(1), 32–39. doi:10.1016/j.lrp.2017.07.008

Fletcher, K. (2010). Slow fashion: An invitation for systems change. *Fashion Practice, 2*(2), 259–266. doi:10.2752/175693810X12774625387594

Franco, M. A. (2017). Circular economy at the micro level: A dynamic view of incumbents' struggles and challenges in the textile industry. *Journal of Cleaner Production, 168*, 833–845. doi:10.1016/j.jclepro.2017.09.056

Gardetti, M. A., & Torres, A. L. (2012). Introduction. *Journal of Corporate Citizenship, 45*(45), 5–15. doi:10.9774/GLEAF.4700.2012.sp.00003

Haubro, A. P., Lomholt, H. A., Lueg, R., Nielsen, S. V., & Knudsen, U. (2015). Tactical and strategic choices in business models: Evidence from a Danish fashion outlet. *Journal of Fashion Marketing and Management, 19*(3), 274–289. doi:10.1108/JFMM-07-2014-0056

Howell, R., van Beers, C., & Doorn, N. (2018). Value capture and value creation: The role of information technology in business models for frugal innovations in Africa. *Technological Forecasting and Social Change, 131*, 227–239. doi:10.1016/j.techfore.2017.09.030

Joyce, A., & Paquin, R. L. (2016). The triple layered business model canvas: A tool to design more sustainable business models. *Journal of Cleaner Production, 135*, 1474–1486. doi:10.1016/j.jclepro.2016.06.067

Khurana, K., & Ricchetti, M. (2016). Two decades of sustainable supply chain management in the fashion business: An appraisal. *Journal of Fashion Marketing and Management, 20*(1), 89–104. doi:10.1108/JFMM-05-2015-0040

Klassen, R. D., & Vereecke, A. (2012). Social issues in supply chains: Capabilities link responsibility, risk (opportunity), and performance. *International Journal of Production Economics, 140*(1), 103–115. doi:10.1016/j.ijpe.2012.01.021

Köksal, D., Strähle, J., Müller, M., & Freise, M. (2017). Social sustainable supply chain management in the textile and apparel industry: A literature review. *Sustainability, 9*(100), 1–32.

Kudłak, R., Martinuzzi, A., Schönherr, N., & Krumay, B. (2015). Quo vadis responsible fashion? Contingencies and trends influencing sustainable business models in the wearing apparel sector. *Journal of Corporate Citizenship, 57*(57), 33–54. doi:10.9774/GLEAF.4700.2015.ma.00005

Lambert, S. C. (2015). The importance of classification to business model research. *Journal of Business Models, 3*(1), 49–61.

Leximancer Pty Ltd. (2018). *Leximancer*™ (Version 4.50). Author.

Long, T. B., Looijen, A., & Blok, V. (2018). Critical success factors for the transition to business models for sustainability in the food and beverage industry in the Netherlands. *Journal of Cleaner Production, 175*, 82–95. doi:10.1016/j.jclepro.2017.11.067

Lueg, R., Medelby Pedersen, M., & Clemmensen, S. N. (2015). The role of corporate sustainability in a low-cost business model: A case study in the Scandinavian fashion industry. *Business Strategy and the Environment, 24*(5), 344–359. doi:10.1002/bse.1825

Lund-Thomsen, P., & Lindgreen, A. (2014). Corporate social responsibility in global value chains: Where are we now and where are we going? *Journal of Business Ethics, 123*(1), 11–22. doi:10.100710551-013-1796-x

Magretta, J. (2002). Why business models matter. *Harvard Business Review*. Available at: https://hbr.org/2002/05/why-business-models-matter

Mayner, L., & Arbon, P. (2015). Defining disaster: The need for harmonisation of terminology. *Australasian Journal of Disaster and Trauma Studies, 19*, 21–26.

Missimer, M., Robèrt, K.-H., & Broman, G. (2017). A strategic approach to social sustainability – Part 1: Exploring the social system. *Journal of Cleaner Production, 140*, 32–41. doi:10.1016/j.jclepro.2016.03.170

Moldavska, A., & Welo, T. (2017). The concept of sustainable manufacturing and its definitions: A content-analysis based literature review. *Journal of Cleaner Production, 166*, 744–755. doi:10.1016/j.jclepro.2017.08.006

Niinimäki, K., & Hassi, L. (2011). Emerging design strategies in sustainable production and consumption of textiles and clothing. *Journal of Cleaner Production, 19*, 1876–1883.

Osterwalder, A., Pigneur, Y., & Tucci, C. L. (2005). Clarifying business models: Origins, present, and future of the concept. *Communications of the Association for Information Systems, 16*, 1–25. doi:10.17705/1CAIS.01601

Pedersen, E. R. G., Gwozdz, W., & Hvass, K. K. (2018). Exploring the relationship between business model innovation, corporate sustainability, and organisational values within the fashion industry. *Journal of Business Ethics, 149*(2), 267–284. doi:10.100710551-016-3044-7

Quarshie, A. M., Salmi, A., & Leuschner, R. (2016). Sustainability and corporate social responsibility in supply chains: The state of research in supply chain management and business ethics journals. *Journal of Purchasing and Supply Management, 22*(2), 82–97. doi:10.1016/j.pursup.2015.11.001

Rauter, R., Jonker, J., & Baumgartner, R. J. (2017). Going one's own way: Drivers in developing business models for sustainability. *Journal of Cleaner Production, 140*, 144–154. doi:10.1016/j.jclepro.2015.04.104

Rosca, E., Arnold, M., & Bendul, J. C. (2017). Business models for sustainable innovation: An empirical analysis of frugal products and services. *Journal of Cleaner Production, 162*, S133–S145. doi:10.1016/j.jclepro.2016.02.050

Schaefer, K., Corner, P. D., & Kearins, K. (2015). Social, environmental and sustainable entrepreneurship research: What is needed for sustainability-as-flourishing? *Organization & Environment, 28*(4), 394–413. doi:10.1177/1086026615621111

Schaltegger, S., Hansen, E. G., & Lüdeke-Freund, F. (2016). Business models for sustainability: Origins, present research, and future avenues. *Organization & Environment, 29*(1), 3–10. doi:10.1177/1086026615599806

Schmitt, J., & Renken, U. (2012). How to earn money by doing good! Shared value in the apparel industry. *Journal of Corporate Citizenship, 45*(45), 79–103. doi:10.9774/GLEAF.4700.2012.sp.00007

Shafer, S. M., Smith, H. J., & Linder, J. C. (2005). The power of business models. *Business Horizons*, *48*(3), 199–207. doi:10.1016/j.bushor.2004.10.014

Sullivan, K., Thomas, S., & Rosano, M. (2018). Using industrial ecology and strategic management concepts to pursue the Sustainable Development Goals. *Journal of Cleaner Production*, *174*, 237–246. doi:10.1016/j.jclepro.2017.10.201

Teece, D. J. (2010). Business models, business strategy, and innovation. *Long Range Planning*, *43*(2-3), 172–194. doi:10.1016/j.lrp.2009.07.003

Thomas, D. A. (2014). Searching for significance in unstructured data: Text mining with Leximancer. *European Educational Research Journal*, *13*(2), 235–256. doi:10.2304/eerj.2014.13.2.235

Todeschini, B. V., Cortimiglia, M. N., Callegaro-de-Menezes, D., & Ghezzi, A. (2017). Innovative and sustainable business models in the fashion industry: Entrepreneurial drivers, opportunities, and challenges. *Business Horizons*, *60*(6), 759–770. doi:10.1016/j.bushor.2017.07.003

Vallance, S., Perkins, H. C., & Dixon, J. E. (2011). What is social sustainability? A clarification of concepts. *Geoforum*, *42*(3), 342–348. doi:10.1016/j.geoforum.2011.01.002

Weissbrod, I., & Bocken, N. M. P. (2017). Developing sustainable business experimentation capability: A case study. *Journal of Cleaner Production*, *142*, 2663–2676. doi:10.1016/j.jclepro.2016.11.009

Yang, M., Evans, S., Vladimirova, D., & Rana, P. (2017). Value uncaptured perspective for sustainable business model innovation. *Journal of Cleaner Production*, *140*, 1794–1804. doi:10.1016/j.jclepro.2016.07.102

Zawacki-Richter, O., & Latchem, C. (2018). Exploring four decades of research in computers & education. *Computers & Education*, *122*, 136–152. doi:10.1016/j.compedu.2018.04.001

Zott, C., Amit, R., & Massa, L. (2011). The business model: Recent developments and future research. *Journal of Management*, *37*(4), 1019–1042. doi:10.1177/0149206311406265

Chapter 10
Factors Influencing Port Terminal Automation in the Fourth Industrial Revolution:
A Case Study of Durban

Indira Padayachee
University of KwaZulu-Natal, South Africa

John Mukomana
 https://orcid.org/0000-0002-2390-8893
University of KwaZulu-Natal, South Africa

ABSTRACT

Port terminals play an integral role in the transportation logistics chain by providing cargo handling, storage, and warehousing services to a range of shipping lines, freight forwarders, and cargo owners. This chapter reports on a case study aimed at determining the challenges and limitations experienced with the current information and communication technology used in port terminals in Durban and examines how technological, organizational, and environmental factors influence port automation. A quantitative approach was adopted, and a questionnaire was designed to collect data. The findings revealed that adequate technology needs to be acquired, and the compatibility and complexity of the technology have the biggest influence on the automation of terminal ports in Durban. Communication with stakeholders and IT skills retention were found to be the most important organizational factors and customer readiness emerged as an important environmental factor influencing the automation of port terminals in Durban.

DOI: 10.4018/978-1-5225-7638-9.ch010

Copyright © 2019, IGI Global. Copying or distributing in print or electronic forms without written permission of IGI Global is prohibited.

INTRODUCTION

The global financial crisis of 2007–2008, which caused a decline in economic activity leading to the 2008–2012 global recession (Eaton, Kortum, Neiman & Romalis, 2010) has intensified competition between ports worldwide. This has led to the need for implementing performance improvement techniques and effective cost reduction mechanisms in the operation of port terminals, to sustain development activities and improve their governance (Verhoeven, 2010). These factors have steered port terminals worldwide to implement the latest technology to increase productivity in their processes and grow their market share (Tongzon, 2001). The Fourth Industrial Revolution, sometimes called Industry 4.0 or 4IR, which embraces technologies such as artificial intelligence (AI), autonomous vehicles and drones, the internet of things (IoT), and advanced materials is set to have a major impact on automation of port terminal operations. This chapter aims at determining the challenges and limitations experienced with the current technology used for port terminal operations in the port of Durban and examines how technological, organizational and environmental factors influence the automation of port terminals.

BACKGROUND

A port terminal is a place on the edge of the earth called a coastline with seafronts deep enough for ships to dock, so that goods and people can enter into ships for transportation through the sea (Verhoeven, 2010). Port terminals have been used from many centuries back as the points of entry, mainly for goods meant for trading purposes from one continent to another (Roso, Woxenius & Lumsden, 2009). Port terminals play an integral role in the transportation logistics chain by providing cargo handling, storage and warehousing services to a wide range of shipping lines, freight forwarders and cargo owners (Pettit & Beresford, 2009). Port terminal operations are divided into four major business segments, namely containers, bulk, break-bulk (multi-purpose) and automotive as depicted in Figure 1.

The operations of a port is a large process in which the final element is not a tangible product but rather a specified service (Homayouni & Tang, 2015). The service referred to is the handling and storage of the containerized merchandise for customers through the reception terminals (import and export) or transhipment terminals, where merchandises are transferred from one vessel to another. This service needs to be performed on the date agreed with the customer, and in accordance with the conditions that the seller, exporter and loader has contracted with the customer (Yu & Qi, 2013). The basic objective is to carry out the operations as rapidly as possible, to enable the vessel to spend the minimum time necessary in port and,

Figure 1. Types of port terminals
(overendstudio, n.d.)

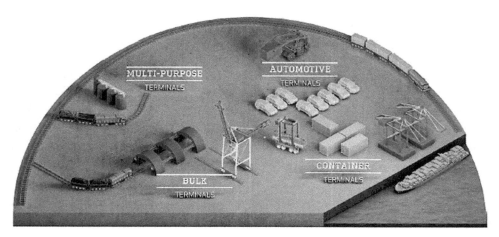

consequently, to obtain maximum economic utilization, reduce energy consumption and improve environmental efficiency.

The environment in which these ports operate has changed as it has become increasingly competitive. It is no longer sufficient for organisations to have only the right equipment and systems but rather it needs organisations with the ability to integrate systems and analyse the available data in order to predict future trends and plan efficient ways to accomplish these predicted activities (Felício & Caldeirinha, 2013).

Automation is the most effective way to move cargo quicker (Maturana, 2004) as it will reduce delays and sluggish times. The automation of port terminals can make them efficient in running their operations (Zehendner & Feillet, 2014) by enabling implementation and utilisation of business intelligence (Lokuge & Alahakoon, 2007).

The port of Durban is currently the largest and considered one of the busiest ports in Africa, which handles approximately 80 million tons of cargo a year and clears 60% of all imports and exports through its port (TransnetPortsAuthority, 2019). Increased port automation is a necessary and evolutionary step towards improving performance at the port terminals in Durban. The envisaged benefits of port automation include among others lower operational costs, increased terminal productivity, improved capacity, enhanced safety and security. (Naicker & Allopi, 2015). It is against this background that the current study undertakes to ascertain factors influencing port automation in Durban.

LITERATURE REVIEW

Challenges and Limitations Faced by Port Terminals

Port terminals in Africa are currently facing several challenges and limitations in their day-to-day operational activities. Congestion at seaports in Durban and South Africa has been the greatest challenge. Until recently, there were no attempts to automate processes at port terminals resulting in inefficiency and huge delays in the transportation of commodities. Raw materials lost their freshness and cargo distribution to industries became increasingly expensive. As a result, the country is not competitive with the rest of Africa or the rest of the world and it is beginning to lose business to new fully automated seaports, which are emerging in nearby countries such as Mozambique, Namibia and Tanzania (Ndlovu, 2007). Challenges range from technological and organisational to environmental issues (Trujillo, González & Jiménez, 2013).

Technology Issues

In order for a maritime transportation system to function optimally, it requires reliable information and communication technology (ICT) to track vessels, monitor cargo loading and unloading times, and trace truck movements. Customers also need access to timely information and speedy transactions. Lack of an adequate ICT infrastructure to support marine transportation will limit growth and negatively affect a country's ability to compete on a global scale (Kahyarara, 2018). Ruto & Everlyn (2015) recommended an improvement in ICT infrastructure to improve port performance. These point to the need for Maritime Management Information Systems, encompassing an Automatic Identification Systems (AIS), Vessel Traffic Management System (VTMS) and Port Operating Systems (POS), as well as a Port Community System to achieve efficiency and productivity gains in port operations. Kahyarara, (2018) noted challenges relating to infrastructure across subsectors in East Africa, namely inadequacies in human resource and ICT systems, which hampered port administration, competition and performance. He further reported that the ICT sector in East Africa showed high costs and low penetration. A report by the African business communities stated that ports in Africa are facing major challenges of inadequate infrastructure and unproductive operations, thereby resulting in substantial loss of potential future revenue (Africabusinesscommunities, n.d.). Narsoo, Muslun & Sunhaloo, (2009), emphasize the importance of the efficient use of ICT to achieve organisational competitiveness and enable smooth information and knowledge transfer.

Organisational Issues

The challenges encountered by port terminals in Africa are affecting business operation. These challenges include non-alignment of business process with the computer systems currently used for operations, lack of support from top management in terms of finance to invest in new IT initiatives and lack of willingness to change and adopt new ways of doing business (Ndlovu, 2007). There is also a big issue concerning lack of critical IT skills and their retention (Trujillo, González & Jiménez, 2013). According to Chu, Gailus, Liu & Ni (2018), ports are experiencing challenges of acquiring the needed capabilities, such as specialist engineer positions, as well as planning and implementation expertise.

As current business processes in port terminals do not match computer system functions, some tasks are performed manually, thereby leading to inefficiencies. There is a need for business process engineering to align port terminal processes to acceptable standards of port terminal operations. Most reporting is performed manually as systems are not being integrated leading to inadequate information being provided for decision-making (Ndlovu, 2007).

Communication is another challenge encountered at port terminals in Durban. There seems to be no clear communication between top-level management and operational employees working at the bottom of the hierarchy (Ndlovu, 2007). There is need to develop a clear model of communication, which will enable management to inform employees of the company's overall strategy, target goals for each year and identify activities to concentrate on at each particular moment (Hall & Jacobs, 2010). The communication model should also empower employees to raise to management the challenges they are facing in completing assigned activities, meeting the expected targets and achieving the organisation's overall objectives.

Information technology skills retention is another huge challenge the organisation is facing, because of the high demand for people with critical IT skills worldwide (Horwitz, 2013). Currently the organisation is not able to attract skilled and experienced people with critical IT skills as they face competition from well renowned South African private companies and other organisations worldwide. The junior employees the organisation attracts do not stay for long in the organisation as competitors then recruit them once they have the necessary skills and experience.

According to Mokone (2016), there is a lack of adequate financial investments in port terminals, which is hampering their adoption of new technology. Top management support is required at port terminals in terms of financial support and encouragement to adopt new ways of doing things in the organisation. A high performance culture is required, which enables adoption of new effective ways of doing business (Ndlovu, 2007).

In a study conducted by Wang, Mileski & Zeng (2017), it was reported that close ties need to be maintained with maritime supply–chain partners to increase throughput volume and reduce throughput uncertainty.

The study conducted by Keceli, Choi, Cha and Aydogdu (2008), reported that top management support, adopters' technical and non-technical readiness, competition and perceived benefits were the factors influencing Port Community System adoption.

Environmental Issues

Port terminals in Durban are facing huge competition from direct and indirect players in the port industry. Direct competition is coming from local organisation who are lobbying for the government to open up the seaport industry to everyone and not let it just be monopolised by a parastatal. Regional players are also posing a threat to port terminals in Durban as ports of Namibia, Mozambique and Tanzania are getting huge funding from the Chinese and Russian government to revamp their port terminals (Vhumbunu, 2016). This poses an indirect threat to port terminals in Durban as it could lead to a loss of its regional customers. Worldwide port terminals are identifying new routes, which are faster and reliable for their delivery of goods, so port terminals in Durban will have to be prepared to meet the new conditions expected by these international port terminals (Trujillo, González & Jiménez, 2013).

Government and municipality laws and regulations are also posing a challenge to ports of Durban operations. The government and the municipality of Durban are reviewing laws and regulations to reduce energy usage, radiation pollution and carbon dioxide emissions to protect the health and improve the safety of people working at port terminals and living near the seaport. Labour relations laws are undergoing review to ensure that individuals from previously disadvantaged backgrounds also have an opportunity of employment.

Another challenge encountered is to satisfy the port terminals customers, who have expectations of a quick and affordable service. They want to have their transactions processed online and in real-time so that they can be able to track and monitor their transactions throughout the process flow (Ndlovu, 2007). Processing customer transactions online will enable them to cut the huge printing costs associated with manually processing the transactions. The other issue is that customers expect the safe and secure processing of confidential information, which manual processes cannot guarantee.

The challenges discussed show that technology is critical from an operational point of view. There is a need for data analytics to provide clarity in governance and enable risk management. Business networks are required to establish connections with suppliers. Automated finance, procurement, and supply chain management are already increasing efficiency and generating significant increases in revenue.

These increases are credited to automation and the new performance-driven culture (Kowalczyk & Buxmann, 2015).

Port Automation

Dynamics such as spatial restraints, pressure to increase efficiency, economic restrictions and the necessity to be ecological add to the present trials of harbours (De Martino, 2014). Expertise and inventions, such as the internet of things, can help to mitigate these challenges and be the driving force pushing the automation of seaports (Zhou, 2013). The final automated port could be the completely computerised seaport where every gadget is linked through the internet of things, where the main drivers in automated seaports are efficiency and productivity improvements. Automating ports involves a combination of equipment and systems setups (Gubbi, Buyya, Marusic & Palaniswami, 2013), which include diverse network tools like radio, LAN, WAN and WLAN, RFID, WIFI and positioning technologies.

The efficiency of the automated seaport depends on the equipment, skills, knowledge and the capability of working collectively to successfully share data, for the advantage of the seaport and its clients (Albino, Berardi & Dangelico, 2015). Data exchange is essential where stakeholders and the business need to strengthen their relationship and improve operations, as was the situation at the Cartagena port terminal. The fostering of close ties with maritime supply–chain partners help increase throughput volume and reduce throughput uncertainty (Wang, Mileski & Zeng, 2017).

Port automation offers the benefit of improved safety and security of people and port facilities by reducing human errors in operation (Martín-Soberón, Monfort, Sapiña, Monterde & Calduch, 2014).

According to Chu, Gailus, Liu, and Ni (2018), port automation involves the integration and co-ordination of five components, namely automated equipment, equipment-control systems, terminal control tower, human–machine interactions and interactions with the port community. Equipment-control systems such as integrated gate-operating software with advanced optical-character-recognition and camera technology allows for automating gate operations and the identification and routing of containers and trucks automatically. A terminal control tower comprises the terminal operating system, decision-making tools, advanced analytics, the digital platform, and interfaces to the port community and customers. Human–machine interactions use technologies like augmented reality and virtual reality, namely direct robots and automated guided vehicles. Interactions with the port community enables a smooth exchange of data and connectivity among liners, logistics service providers, consignees, and customs officials. While the first automated container port was already in existence in Europe in the early 1990s, since then many ports have installed equipment to automate some of the processes in their terminals. Almost 40 partly or fully automated ports now do business in various parts of the world (Chu, Gailus, Liu, and Ni, 2018).

Smart Port Terminals

The vision of a smart port terminal is a port that uses digital technologies to enhance performance, reduce cost and resource consumption by taking care of people and being environmentally responsible. The principle of the smart/intelligent port concept is making the best use of limited resources (streets, waterways and railways) by introducing a control unit that optimises present day handling processes of carriers on land and sea (Angelidou, 2014).

The increasing freight transport volumes, cost pressures, regulatory requirements and the growing demands for sustainability all call for ongoing process optimisation in ports (Ndlovu, 2007). Ports cannot geographically expand forever, and they will have to come up with mechanisms to increase productivity whilst operating in their confined space. The existing infrastructure facilities must be used intelligently and efficiently, as space is limited. The establishment of an intelligent infrastructure is imperative to ensure smooth and efficient traffic flows and, ultimately, trade flows. Information technology platforms such as Bluetooth, hotspots or Wi-Fi, cloud computing, mobile end devices, the internet of things and big data play a key role in implementing this (Dadashi, Wilson, Golightly & Sharples, 2014).

Ports need to brace themselves for a rising volume of transport in maritime traffic. Large ports are the major hubs of this incredibly huge flow of goods. This is where maritime shipping, rail and road all come together and this confluence is confronting logistics with growing challenges. It is important to link together real-time data between companies, people, machines and plants across different, organically grown systems and its landscapes. A smart port is the vision (Ndlovu, 2007). According to Yang, Zhong, Yao, Yu, Fu, & Postolache (2018), a smart port may be defined as a fully automated port where all devices are connected via a network of smart sensors and actuators, wireless devices, and data centers, which constitutes the key infrastructure of the smart port. The major enablers in smart ports are productivity and efficiency gains.

A smart port terminal can enable an organisation to integrate all its operating components and systems, so that it can be able to analyse the data and information available using business intelligence (BI). An automated intelligent port should provide a set of intelligent services, which combines the following characteristics (Ferretti & Schiavone, 2016):

- **Intelligent and Efficient Use of Current Resources and Infrastructures:** The intelligent services should optimize the use of current resources, seeking mechanisms that facilitate the re-use of the infrastructure.
- **Cost Reduction:** The gate automation would have a direct impact on the reduction of the staff assigned to gate control. In addition, this would reduce the gate process time and alleviate queues and pollution.
- **Economic Value:** The intelligent services should create a clear return of the investment and produce economic value through a cost reduction or a new source of income.
- **Time Reduction**: The gate in/out operation at gate terminals is currently under the supervision of terminal staff and police officers. The personnel assigned to these tasks have to check the hard copy documentation or the information prompted in their IT systems against physical items like the container number, truck plate, and trucker identification. The control process takes time and slows down the gate in/out operation. Moreover, it creates truck queues at lanes with its negative impact on cost, time and pollution.
- **Secure Operations:** The supervision and manual tasks are not free of errors and are harder to follow up and trace. The setup of automatic control at gates should guarantee the reliability and security of the port operations. The new systems would check that the operations are fully authorized.
- **Improved Working Conditions:** The people in charge of the supervision have to work outside or in small cabins. The gate automation process will allow people to move into well-equipped control offices.
- **Environmental Sustainability:** The services will take into consideration environmental issues. It will contribute in reducing usage of limited resource and seek for the reduction of the CO_2 footprint.
- **Health Care Responsibility:** Millions of people work at port areas suffering tough conditions during their daily tasks. The intelligent services would bring about an improvement in working conditions. For instance, by providing mobility services and technologies, people can work in better premises.
- **Governance:** The intelligent services will enhance the good management of the ports improving security, safety and other key items such as ensuring the availability, traceability and smooth execution of the port operations. The intelligent services should strive for better control of the tasks. In this way, it is key to have an efficient use of the human resources assigned to supervision tasks.

A smart/intelligent port terminal has to have at least seven mechanisms for it to be fully effective when functioning. These following mechanisms are integral components of a smart/ intelligent port terminal:

- **Internet of Things** for interconnecting all devices and gadgets around the terminal for quicker and easier exchange of data and information.
- **Big Data Analytics** tools for analysing data collected during port terminal operations (Shi, Tao & Voß, 2011).
- **Data Visualization** for deducing meaning from the data analysed and presenting them in a form that business understands.
- **Cloud Computing** A key element to all this is some sort of repository (cloud computing) gathering information about all events related to the port. When analysed and presented in an intelligent way, that data can help achieve the goal of doing things smarter (Kumar & Prakash, 2016).
- **Pervasive Computing** giving intelligence to machinery in terminal operations so human intervention can be minimum.
- **Information Security** to ensure that confidential information for port terminal operations is secure (Ao, 2014).
- **Sensors** such as inertial sensors, ultrasonic sensors, eddy current sensors, radar, lidar, imaging sensors, and RFID readers and tags for the collection of the required data in order to change the "port" into a "smart port." (Yang, Zhong, Yao, Yu, Fu, & Postolache, 2018)

The following are examples of ports that are forerunners of smart digital transformation, and have implemented port automation:

- **Port Amsterdam:** a port that presents a model of "Smart Green Port" based on 3 axes: Environment, Intermodal and ICT (Hollen, van den Bosch & Volberda, 2014).
- **Port Hamburg:** has a model of smart port based on logistics services offered to both foreland and hinterland. The Hamburg smart port 2025 project relies heavily on an intelligent ICT infrastructure and logistic services based on them (Ferretti & Schiavone, 2016).
- **Port Singapore:** has a business driven IT investment and is involved in the development of Maritime Intelligence & Shipping (Hollen, van den Bosch & Volberda, 2014).
- **Port Barcelona:** has made a re-interpretation of the services and ICT applications of the last 15 years, and now presents them as a new IT solution that the port authority offers to its port community, to automate its process and add any technology enhanced services (Hein, 2016).

- **Port Rotterdam:** Erasmus University and the port of Rotterdam launched the smart port Rotterdam Project in 2010, to connect knowledge management with new logistical services of the port of Rotterdam. (Hollen, van den Bosch & Volberda, 2014).
- **Port Kansas:** KC SmartPort promotes and enhances the status of the Kansas City region as a leading logistics centre in USA.

Table 1 illustrates the evolution of port operations from the 1940s to predictions of them by the year 2020.

Conceptual Model

There are limited studies on factors influencing port automation in the literature. This study adapted the Technology–Organization–Environment (TOE) framework to fit the empirical study on factors influencing automation in the port of Durban. The TOE framework emphasis three aspects (Kim, Park, Choi & Min, 2014):

- Technological aspect, which looks at the technology the organisation is currently using in carrying out its operations, as well as technology available

Table 1. Evolution of port terminals

1st Generation	2nd Generation	3rd Generation	4th Generation	5th Generation
1940s	1960s	1980s	2000s	2020s
Mechanic Port	Container Port	EDI Port	Internet Port	Intelligent Port
Mechanical Operation	Free Zone	International network	Global network	ITS port
Handcraft Works	Industrial Area	Integrated centre	Port Community	Logistic community
		Commercial area	Logistic area	Smart city
		EDI Services	Intermodal services	Smart Hinterland
			Internet services	Multi modal services
				Sustainable port

(https://www.slideshare.net/vijayhiranandani/port-operations-management-slideshow)

for the organisation to utilize in accomplishing its tasks although it has not yet been implemented by the firm.

- Organisational aspect, which looks at organisational structure as it influences decision-making and communication flow in the organisation. The scope of the organisation covering size, goals and aims merits consideration, as these affect the rate at which change can be effected in the firm.
- Environmental aspect, which considers issues such as the industry in which the organisation operates, as it determines if it is a technology driven industry or if new technology does not effect change into the sector. Competitors in the environment aspect are important as no organisation wants to be lagging role in determining the environment in which the organisation operates as it sets rules to regulate operations in industries of its country.

The TOE framework was adapted for this study as this framework provides a comprehensive perspective on the factors that contribute to the influence of innovation adoption in organizations. Table 3 provides a summary of the adapted TOE framework categories, constructs, and previous research using these constructs for technological innovation adoption in various domains.

DATA FINDINGS AND ANALYSIS

A quantitative approach was adopted for the empirical study and a survey research instrument was designed, comprising six sections, namely demographics, technological factors, organisational factors, environmental factors, automation of port terminals, as well as challenges and limitations in port operations. The questionnaire consisted of a Likert-scale for all the sections, except the demographics section, and participants were requested to rate the statements on a 5-point Likert rating scale ranging from 'Strongly Agree'(5) to 'Strongly Disagree'(1). Expert reviews and a pilot study were used as mechanisms to test for the validity of the research instrument.

The research setting for the study was the port of Durban. The target population was drawn from the ranks of senior management, middle level employees and IT technicians employed within the Enterprise Information Management Services department as they have the necessary knowledge, IT expertise and experience in using systems to optimise operations. The purposive sampling technique was used to select a sample of 80 employees from the Enterprise Information Management Services (EIMS) department out of a total of 100 employees in the department. An electronic survey (e-survey) developed on Google forms, which is a free online survey offered to Gmail account clients and the link to the e-survey was sent to all employees. The majority responded via the e-survey method while some employees

Table 2. Conceptual model and previous research on technological innovation adoption

Categories	Constructs	Previous research on factors influencing technological innovation adoption
Port Automation	Organisational readiness	Readiness of a company to adopt the new system influenced by technical and non-technical readiness (Keceli, Choi, Cha & Aydogdu, 2008).
	Organisational capability	
	Organisation self-efficacy	
Technological factors	Technological availability	Chalfin (2010) study on the neo-developmental state and the Port of Tema in Ghana.; Lee, Kim & Ahn, (2011) on e-Government service adoption by business users and Rahayu & Day (2015) on E-commerce Adoption by in a Developing Country.
	Technology competence	Rahayu & Day (2015); Oliveira, Thomas & Espadanal (2014) on assessing the determinants of cloud computing on adoption: An analysis of the manufacturing and services sectors; Zhu & Kraemer (2005) on post-Adoption Variations in Usage and Value of E-Business by Organizations: Cross-Country Evidence from the Retail Industry.
	Technology complexity	Brown and Bakhru (2007) on Information Systems Innovation Research and the case RFID.
	Data and information security	Benlian & Hess (2011) on SAAS.
	Perceived benefits	Kuan and Chau (2001) on EDI adoption in small businesses; Brown & Russel (2007) on Radio frequency identification technology.
Organisational Factors	Organisational structure	Rahayu & Day (2015).
	Communication process	Rahayu & Day (2015); Zhu & Kraemer (2005), Post-Adoption Variations in Usage and Value of E-Business by Organizations.
	IT skills	Rahayu & Day (2015).
	Top management support	Brown and Russel (2007) on Radio frequency identification technology.
	Organisational goals	Zhu & Kraemer (2005) on Post-Adoption Variations in Usage and Value of E-Business.
Environmental Factors	Competitive pressure	Rahayu & Day (2015), Zhu & Kraemer, (2005).
	Laws and regulations	Zhu & Kraemer, (2005).
	Customer readiness	Rahayu & Day (2015); Son & Han (2011) on technology readiness effects on post-adoption behaviour; Yousafzai & Yani-de-Soriano (2012) on understanding customer-specific factors underpinning internet banking adoption.

requested to complete the questionnaire on a physical paper. Fifty-five completed questionnaires were received, thereby achieving a 69% successful response rate.

The statistical tests applied to the quantitative data using the Statistical Package for the Social Sciences (SPSS) 22 package were as follows: descriptive statistics in the form of frequency distributions, means and standard deviations; Wilcoxon Signed Ranks test; Regression analysis and the one sample *t*-test.

Demographic Findings

This section presents findings for some of the demographic data collected namely position, ICT experience and port operations experience.

Position

Most of the employees who responded were in the junior manager level comprising 39% of the respondents, followed by the junior level employees and the middle managers with a 29% representation each, and followed by senior managers who had a 4% representation. Figure 2 shows the graphical representation of the position of employees who responded.

ICT_Experience

The majority of respondents with ICT_experience was 27%, represented by two groups, namely 5-9 years and 10-14 years of experience. This was followed by 13% who had 1-4 years' experience, 7% who had more than 20+ years' experience

Figure 2. Employment position

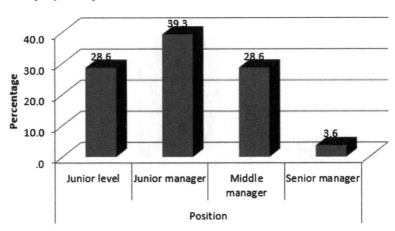

in ICT, and 5% who had less than a year (<1) ICT_Experience. Figure 3 shows a graphical representation of the respondents' experience in ICT.

Port Experience

The majority of respondents had between 1-4 years' experience constituting a 43% representation, followed by 27% who had 5-9 years port working experience, 11% who worked less than a year, 7% with 10-14 years and 15-19 years, and 5% who had more than twenty years' experience. Figure 4 shows a graphical representation of the respondents working experience in the port environment.

Findings on Technological, Organisational and Environmental Factors

This section presents significant results pertaining to the various constructs comprising technological, organisational and environmental factors, and their influence on port automation. The Cronbach's coefficient alpha was used to test the reliability of the constructs in the questionnaire, which fell between .786 and .951, representing acceptable internal reliability. A one-sample t-test and the Wilcoxon Signed Ranks test was used to test if the average agreement measure showed significant agreement or disagreement for the various constructs comprising the factors/categories in the conceptual model. Regression analysis was used to test whether technological factors, organisational factors and environmental factors were predictors of port automation.

Figure 3. ICT_experience

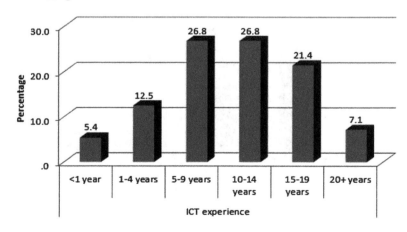

Figure 4. Port_experience

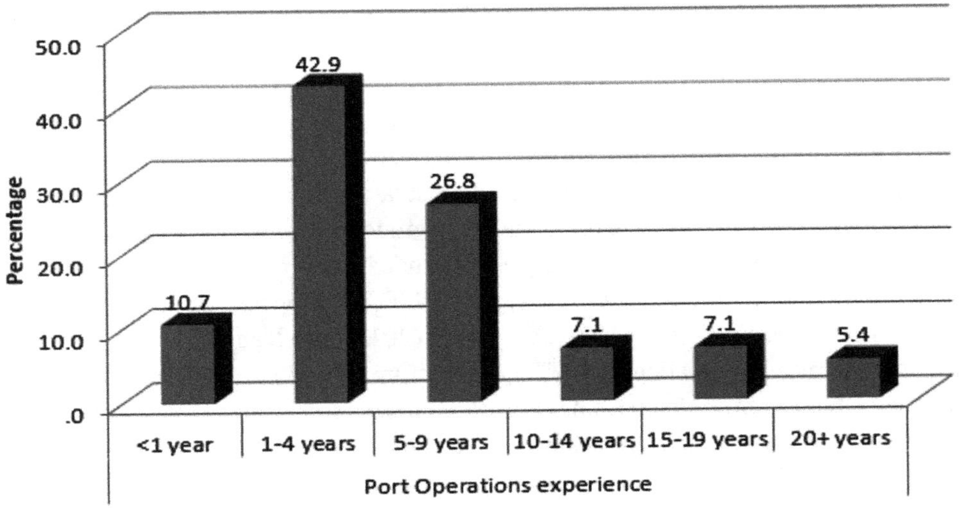

Technological Factors

The one sample *t*-test showed that there is significant disagreement with one aspect and significant agreement with four aspects of the technological factor statements. There was significant disagreement on the following statement measuring technological factors influence:

- The necessary technology to fully automate port terminal operations is already available (M = 2.6042, SD = .76973), t (55) = -3.848, p= .000;

There was significant agreement on the following statements measuring technological factors influence:

- The current technology is compatible to use for entirely automating the port operations (M=3.2634, SD = .90002), t (55) = 2.190, p=.033);
- The current technology is easy and simple to use (M=3.4598, SD = .79598), t (55) = 4.323, p=.000).
- The company's data and information security mechanisms are capable of securing the company's records (M=3.7083, SD = .76558), t (55) = 6.924, p=.000);

- The technology being utilised by the organisation is able to achieve the required perceived benefits (M=3.5821, SD = .82970), t (55) = 5.251, p=.000).

Figure 5 shows a graphical representation of the average measure of the constructs comprising technological factors.

Based on the statistical tests conducted on data relating to technological factors, the findings confirmed that the majority of respondents disagreed that the necessary technology was available, and equally agreed that aspects relating to compatibility, complexity, security and benefits were supported. The finding on available technology concurs with the findings of Ruto & Everlyn (2015) and Kahyarara, (2018), who report on the need for an adequate ICT infrastructure for port automation. The finding on adequate data and information security of current technology is consistent with the view that automation provides improved safety and security of people and port facilities (Martín-Soberón, Monfort, Sapiña, Monterde & Calduch, 2014).

Organisational Factors

The one sample *t*-test showed that there is significant agreement with two aspects of the organisational factor statements. There was significant agreement on the following statements measuring organisational factors influence:

- There is significant agreement that organisation's employees have the IT skills required to implement and maintain IT solutions (M=3.3155, SD = .98251), t (55) = 2.403, p=.020).

Figure 5. Technological factors

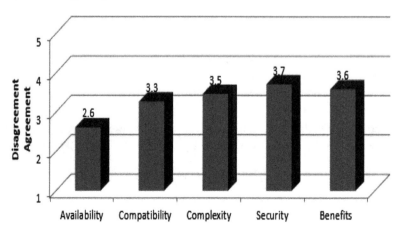

- There is significant agreement that the communication methods/tools (email & meetings, etc.) are effective for running IT operations in the organisation (M=3.48, SD = 1.079), t (55) = 3.345, p=.001).

Figure 6 shows a graphical representation of the average measure of the constructs comprising organisational factors.

Based on the statistical tests conducted on data relating to organisational factors, the findings confirmed that the majority of the respondents disagreed that necessary organisational goals were available, and equally agreed that the other aspects, namely structure, communication, IT skills, and top management support were adequately supported. The finding on IT skills refutes the finding of the study conducted by Trujillo, González & Jiménez (2013), who reported that there is a big issue concerning lack of critical IT skills and their retention and by Chu, Gailus, Liu & Ni (2018), who stated that ports are experiencing challenges of acquiring the specialist capabilities. The finding on communication methods refutes a study conducted by Ndlovu (2007), who stated that there is no clear communication between top-level management and operational employees working at the bottom of the hierarchy.

Environmental Factors

The one sample *t*-test showed that there is significant agreement with three aspects of with the environmental factors statements. There was significant agreement on the following statements measuring environmental factors influence:

Figure 6. Organisational factors

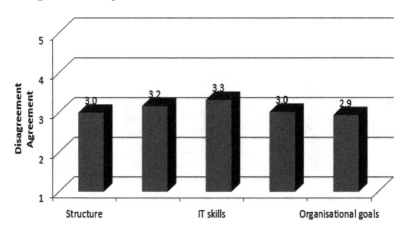

- There is significant agreement that the pressure from competitors ensures the company strives to perform better than its competitors (M=3.3482, SD = 1.00981), t (55) = 2.580, p=.013);
- The organisation's operations adhere to the relevant laws and regulations related to its operations (M=3.5268, SD = .64883), t (55) = 6.076, p=.000);
- The organisation's stakeholders have an influence over the decision to fully automate operations at port terminals. (M=3.4420, SD = .89060), t (55) = 3.714, p=.000).

Figure 7 shows a graphical representation of the average measure of the constructs comprising environmental factors.

Based on the statistical tests conducted on data relating to environmental factors, the findings confirmed that the majority of respondents agreed that pressure from competitors ensures the company strives to perform better than its competitors do, operations adhere to the relevant laws and regulations and stakeholders have an influence over the decision to automate operations at port terminals. The finding on adherence to relevant laws and regulations concurs with the view of Muntean, Nechita, Nistor, Sarpe, (2010) that regulations are necessary to ports. The finding on competitive pressure is consistent with the studies conducted by Keceli, Choi, Cha and Aydogdu (2008) and Rahayu & Day (2015). The finding on trading partners supports the view of Wang, Mileski & Zeng (2017) that there needs to be close relationships with maritime supply–chain partners.

Figure 7. Environmental factors

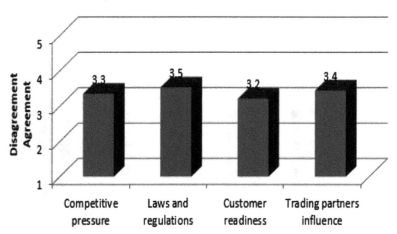

Findings on Port Terminal Automation

The Wilcoxon Signed Ranks test showed that there was significant agreement with the following two statements relating to port automation:

- I think the organisation has the capability to fully automate its port terminal operations (M=3.41, SD = 1.092), t (55) = 2.815, p=.007);
- I think the organisation will successfully automate its entire port terminal operations (M=3.30, SD = 1.043), t (55) = 2.178, p=.034).

Figure 8 shows a graphical representation of the average measure of the constructs pertaining to port automation.

The findings relating to port terminal operation revealed that the majority of respondents agreed that the organisation has the capability to fully automate its port terminal operations and that the organisation will successfully automate its entire port terminal operations. The majority of the respondents disagreed that the organisation is ready to fully automate its port terminal operations. Keceli, Choi, Cha, & Aydogdu (2008) supports the finding on organisational readiness, by arguing that readiness has many facets, namely technical aspects of readiness such as hardware and software capabilities, as well as non-technical aspects such as expertise, expertise and financial readiness.

Figure 8. Port terminal automation

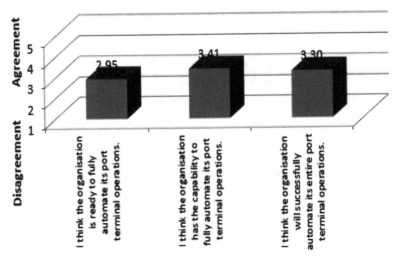

Findings and Analysis of Challenges and Limitations

The Wilcoxon Signed Ranks test showed that there is significant agreement with two and significant disagreement with one of the challenges and limitations statements. There was significant agreement on the following statements measuring challenges and limitations:

- There is significant agreement that computer systems (SAP, GCOS & Navis) for port terminal operations are adequate (M=3.79, SD = .868), t (55) = 6.775, p=.000);
- There is significant agreement that IT employees are skilled enough to run port terminal operations efficiently (M=3.41, SD = .910), t (55) = 3.377, p=.001);

There was significant disagreement on the following statement measuring challenges and limitations:

- Labour (Labour unions and employee committees) are in support of fully automating port operations. (M=2.46, SD = .914), t (55) = -4.387, p=.000).

Figure 9 shows a graphical representation of the challenges and limitations relating to port terminal operations.

While the majority of respondents agreed that computer system were adequate for port terminal operations, the results of the Wilcoxon Signed Ranks test indicated that many respondents perceive the organisation as not having the latest technology (i.e. IoT, Big Data analytics, Visualisation, Cloud Computing capabilities, Pervasive Computing and latest advances in information security) to fully automate its terminal operations. The latest technology, which the ports in Durban currently does not have, is crucial for automating port terminal operations. The result on adequacy of computer systems supports the study conducted by Narsoo, Muslun & Sunhaloo, (2009), who state that efficient ICT is necessary to enable smooth information and knowledge transfer and improve organizational performance and competitiveness.

The finding that IT employees are skilled enough refutes earlier studies by Trujillo, González & Jiménez (2013) and Chu, Gailus, Liu & Ni (2018).

The results of the Wilcoxon Signed Ranks test showed that there is a majority agreement that customers' operating processes are not yet ready for the full automation of port terminal processes. The result needs to be considered in conjunction with the study conducted by Ndlovu (2007), who reported that customers want to have their transactions processed online and in real-time so that they can be able to track and monitor their transactions throughout the process flow.

The majority of the employees also agreed that there is a lack of top management support in the form of financial support to adequately maintain and upgrade terminal operations infrastructure and systems. The result also correlates with the study conducted by Mokone, (2016) which states that the lack of enough financial investments in port terminals is hampering their adoption of new technology.

The majority of the employees also agreed that labour unions and employee committees are not in favour of fully automating port operations. This result also correlates with a prior study conducted by Jones, (2005), who states that labour unions are the biggest resistor to changes in the way employees work in terminal port operations as they presume it will lead to job losses.

Analysis of Relationships Between Factors and Port Automation

This section presents the results of linear regression, which shows the predictors of port automation. Linear regression estimates the coefficients of the linear equation,

Figure 9. Challenges and limitations

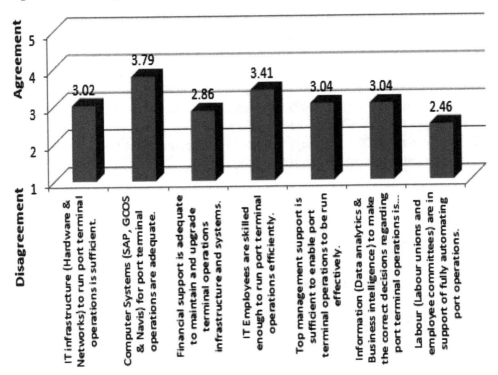

involving one or more independent variables, which best predict the value of the dependent variable (Mielniczuk & Teisseyre, 2014).

Influence of Technological Factors on Port Automation

Regression analysis was used to test whether independent variable technological factors (i.e. availability, compatibility, complexity, security and benefits) were predictors of port automation. Table 3 shows the results obtained from the test.

The regression analysis results also indicated that these technological factor predictors accounted 62.9% ($R^2 = .629$) of the variance of automation, $F (5, 50) = 16.924$, $p<.0005$). Compatibility ($\beta = .321$, $p=.019$) and complexity ($\beta = .662$, $p<.0005$) are both significant predictors of perceptions on port automation.

The result of technology availability as a predictor correlates with prior studies conducted by Chalfin, (2010); Lee, Kim & Ahn, (2011) and Rahayu & Day, (2015), who report that technology availability positively influences the adoption of a new technology. The result of technology competence as a significant predictor correlates with prior studies conducted by Rahayu & Day (2015); Oliveira, Thomas & Espadanal, (2014) and Zhu & Kraemer, (2005), who report that technology competence positively influences the adoption of a new technology. The result of technology complexity as a significant predictor correlates with a prior study conducted by Brown and Bakhru, (2007), who report that complexity is a key factor for successful application of technologies. Data and information security was not found to be a predictor of perceptions on port automation with the results ($\beta = -.223$, $p=.153$). This result refutes a prior study conducted by Benlian & Hess, (2011) who report that security is a major risk factor influencing software as a service adoption. Perceived benefits was found to be a predictor of perceptions on port automation ($\beta = .124$, $p=.380$), which correlates with a prior study conducted by Keceli, Choi, Cha and Aydogdu (2008), who reported that the perceived benefits factor influenced Port Community System adoption.

Table 3. Influence of technological factors on port automation

	Influencing factors	β	p	Result
B1	Availability	.233	.074	Predictor
B2	Compatibility	.321	.019	Significant predictor
B3	Complexity	.662	.000	Significant predictor
B4	Security	-.223	.153	Not a predictor
B5	Benefits	.124	.380	Predictor

Influence of Organisational Factors on Port Automation

Regression analysis was used as a technique to test whether independent variable organisational factors (i.e. structure, communication, IT skills, top management support, organisational goals) predicted the automation of ports. Table 4 shows the results obtained from the test.

The regression analysis results also indicated that these organisational factors predictors account for 55.5% (R2 = .555) of the variance of automation, F (5, 50) = 12.490, p<.0005). Communication (β = .505, p=.008) and IT Skills (β = .384, p=.002) are both significant predictors of perceptions on port automation.

The findings revealed that organisational structure was not a predictor on perceptions of port automation. This result refutes findings of a study conducted by Rahayu & Day, (2015), who report that organisational structure positively influences the adoption of a new technology. The result of communication process as a significant predictor of perceptions on port automation correlates with prior studies conducted by Rahayu & Day, (2015) and Zhu & Kraemer, (2005), who report that communication between stakeholders is crucial for the success of adopting a new technology. The result of IT skills as a significant predictor of perceptions on port automation correlates with a prior study conducted by Rahayu & Day, (2015), who report that IT skills positively influences the adoption of a new technology. The results of top management support as a non-predictor of perceptions on port automation refutes the findings of the study conducted by Keceli, Choi, Cha & Aydogdu (2008) who reported that top management support is a factor that influences user acceptance of port community systems. This result also does not support a prior study conducted by Brown and Russel, (2007), who state that top-management support is crucial in guiding and encouraging the transformation of an organisation from operating manually to automating its process. The result of organisational goals as a non-predictor of perceptions on port automation refutes the findings of a study conducted by Zhu & Kraemer, (2005), who state that organisational goals tend to drive the adoption of the latest technology on the market, if it can help an organisation achieve its goals.

Table 4. Influence of organisational factors on port automation

	Influencing factors	β	p	Result
C1	Structure	-.133	.470	Not a predictor
C2	Communication	.505	.008	Significant Predictor
C3	IT skills	.384	.002	Significant Predictor
C4	Top management support	.215	.228	Predictor
C5	Organisational goals	-.171	.243	Not a predictor

Influence of Environmental Factors on Port Automation

Regression analysis was used to test whether independent variable environmental factors (i.e. competitive pressure, laws and regulations, customer readiness, trading partners influence) predicted port automation. Table 5 shows the results obtained from the test.

The regression analysis results also indicated that these environmental organisational factors predictors account for 49.2% ($R^2 = .492$) of the variance of automation, $F(4, 51) = 12.357$, $p<.0005$. Customer readiness ($\beta = .676$, $p<.0005$) is a significant predictor of perceptions of port automation concerning operating processes and systems integration. This finding correlates with the expectation of customers to have their transactions processed online and in real-time, so that they can be able to track and monitor their transactions throughout the process flow (Ndlovu, 2007). This result refutes findings of prior studies conducted by Rahayu & Day, (2015); Son & Han, (2011) and Yousafzai & Yani-de-Soriano, (2012), who report that customer readiness has no positive and significant correlation with the adoption of a new technology. The results shows that competitive pressure is not a predictor of perceptions on port automation. This does not support the findings of the study conducted by Keceli, Choi, Cha and Aydogdu (2008) who reported that competition is a factor that influences user acceptance of port community systems. This result also refutes the findings of a study conducted by Rahayu & Day (2015), who report that competitive pressure positively influences the adoption of a new technology, but correlates with findings from a study conducted by Zhu & Kraemer (2005), who state that competitor's influence has no direct effect on the adoption of a new technology. The result of laws and regulations as a predictor of perceptions on port automation supports the viewpoint of Muntean, Nechita, Nistor & Sarpe (2010) that community rules and regulations are necessary to ports. This result concurs with the findings of a study conducted by Zhu & Kraemer, (2005), who report that firms facing higher regulatory support are more likely to adopt a new technology. The influence of trading partners on port automation was significant, which correlates with the view of Wang, Mileski & Zeng (2017) that close ties

Table 5. Influence of environmental factors on port automation

	Influencing factors	β	p	Result
D1	Competitive pressure	-.010	.944	Not a predictor
D2	Laws and regulations	.089	.629	Predictor
D3	Customer readiness	.676	.000	Significant Predictor
D4	Trading partners influence	.191	.245	Predictor

need to be maintained with maritime supply–chain partners to increase throughput volume and reduce throughput uncertainty. This result refutes the findings of studies conducted by Rahayu & Day (2015) and Shi & Yan (2016) who report that trading partner's pressure has no positive and significant correlation with the adoption of a new technology.

DISCUSSION AND RECOMMENDATIONS

One of the limitations of conducting the study was that it was restricted to the vicinity of Durban only and included three port terminals instead of covering all ten-port terminals in South Africa. Another limitation was that the study focused only on the constructs of the conceptual model adopted for the study. The target population comprised employees from the EIMS department, instead of all employees from the port terminals in Durban. The study also adopted a quantitative approach, which while consistent with similar studies based on the TOE model, did not provide deeper insights as is possible with a mixed methods research design.

Findings from this study showed that the challenges and limitations faced by port terminals in Durban are that it does not have the latest technology, there is a lack of top management financial support to adequately maintain and upgrade terminal operations infrastructure and systems, and customers' operating processes are not yet ready for the full automation of port terminals. The technological factor predictors accounted for 62.9% ($R2 = .629$) of the variance of port terminal automation, meaning that technological factors have the biggest influence and the latest technology such as IOT, big data analytics, visualization, cloud computing capabilities, pervasive computing and latest advances in information security have to be acquired. The organisational factor predictors accounted for 55.5% of the variance, with factors such as communication and critical IT skills positively influencing perceptions of port automation. The environmental factor predictors accounted for 49.2% of the variance, meaning that environmental factors have the least influence on the port terminal automation, with only customer readiness significantly influencing perceptions of port automation. To promote customer readiness before implementation, there is a need to introduce awareness and training campaigns and ensure customer systems are inter-operable with the intelligent port terminal systems. Current challenges and limitations can be addressed by investing in advanced digitalisation and automation, and by emulating the technologies and characteristics of smart port terminals. The majority of the respondents disagreed that the organisation is ready to fully automate its port terminal operations, but agree that it is capable and will successfully automate its entire port terminal operations.

FUTURE RESEARCH DIRECTIONS

Future research can be conducted test the viability of the conceptual model for similar results in a different context, for example, in other South African provinces, African countries, the Southern African region or the African continent. In addition, other factors, which could affect port terminal automation could be explored, that are not limited to the conceptual model. More studies need to be conducted using different research methodologies to obtain deeper insights into challenges and limitations of port terminal operations. Future studies should focus on implementation issues pertaining to the automation of ports with intelligent services.

CONCLUSION

This study was necessitated by the need to reduce costs and improve performance and productivity at the Durban port terminals using smart technologies and optimizing business processes. Another factor that motivated the study was that competition among port terminals around the world are increasing and ports are beginning to tap into each other's market share. As the competition increases ports are looking for better mechanisms to carry out their operations in a less costly and most effective way.

The TOE framework was utilised in this study as a baseline to assess the extent to which technological, organisational and environmental factors influence automation in the port of Durban. The findings of this study also highlights the current challenges and limitations faced by port terminals in Durban. This study makes a practical contribution by helping companies operating port terminals in South Africa, especially those operating in Durban, to be able to understand and overcome the current challenges and limitations, in an effort to evolve towards the use of smart technologies and transformation in policies and business practices. The study has contributed to the body of knowledge by the successful adaptation of the TOE framework to study automation issues in the transport and logistics industry.

Organisations must seize the opportunity to increase its market share by striving towards fully automating its port terminal operations. As many ports in Africa have not yet fully automated its port terminals, the port of Durban, together with other African countries with automated seaports, is set to lead the way in adopting the disruptive technologies of the fourth industrial revolution. The fourth industrial revolution or 4IR, synonymous with terms such as smart cities, smart factories, smart industries, speaks to a revolution in the production processes, operations as well as products and services. The vision of the smart port includes the use of new and innovative technologies, such as artificial intelligence (AI), autonomous systems, track and trace technology, sensors, the internet of things (IoT), big data analytics, cloud computing and pervasive computing. These developments are set to revolutionize the transport logistics industry yielding positive and far-reaching benefits.

REFERENCES

Africabusinesscommunities. (n.d.). *The future of African ports is also the future of Africa's economic success*. Retrieved November 16, 2018, from https://africabusinesscommunities.com/news/the-future-of-african-ports-is-also-the-future-of-africas-economic-success/

Albino, V., Berardi, U., & Dangelico, R. (2015). Smart Cities: Definitions, Dimensions, Performance, and Initiatives. *Journal of Urban Technology*, *22*(1), 3–21. doi:10.1080/10630732.2014.942092

Angelidou, M. (2014). Smart city policies: A spatial approach. *Cities (London, England)*, *41*, S3–S11. doi:10.1016/j.cities.2014.06.007

Ao, Q. (2014). Analysis the Transformation and Upgrading Path of the Ports in Pearl River Delta. *Applied Mechanics and Materials*, *587-589*, 1771–1775. doi:10.4028/www.scientific.net/AMM.587-589.1771

Benlian, A., & Hess, T. (2011). Opportunities and risks of software-as-a-service: Findings from a survey of IT executives. *Decision Support Systems*, *52*(1), 232–246. doi:10.1016/j.dss.2011.07.007

Brown, A., & Bakhru, A. (2007). Information Systems Innovation Research and the case of RFID. *IFIP International Federation for Information Processing*, *235*, 363–376. doi:10.1007/978-0-387-72804-9_24

Brown, I., & Russell, J. (2007). Radio frequency identification technology: An exploratory study on adoption in the South African retail sector. *International Journal of Information Management*, *27*(4), 250–265. doi:10.1016/j.ijinfomgt.2007.02.007

Chalfin, B. (2010). Recasting maritime governance in Ghana: The neo-developmental state and the Port of Tema. *The Journal of Modern African Studies*, *48*(04), 573–598. doi:10.1017/S0022278X10000546

Chu, F., Gailus, G., Liu, L., & Ni, L. (2018). *The future of automated ports*. Retrieved January 16, 2019, from https://www.mckinsey.com/industries/travel-transport-and-logistics/our-insights/the-future-of-automated-ports.#0

Dadashi, N., Wilson, J., Golightly, D., & Sharples, S. (2014). A framework to support human factors of automation in railway intelligent infrastructure. *Ergonomics*, *57*(3), 387–402. doi:10.1080/00140139.2014.893026 PMID:24670143

De Martino, M. (2014). Sustainable Development Strategies of the Port Authority: The Network Approach. *Advanced Engineering Forum, 11*, 87-95.

Eaton, J., Kortum, S., Neiman, B., & Romalis, J. (2010). *Trade and the Global Recession*. SSRN Electronic Journal. doi:10.2139srn.1692582

Felício, J., & Caldeirinha, V. (2013). The influence of the characterisation factors of the European ports on operational performance: Conceptual model testing. *International Journal of Shipping and Transport Logistics*, *5*(3), 282. doi:10.1504/IJSTL.2013.054191

Ferretti, M., & Schiavone, F. (2016). Internet of Things and business processes redesign in seaports: *The case of Hamburg. Business Process Management Journal*, *22*(2), 271–284. doi:10.1108/BPMJ-05-2015-0079

Gubbi, J., Buyya, R., Marusic, S., & Palaniswami, M. (2013). Internet of Things (IOT): A vision, architectural elements, and future directions. *Future Generation Computer Systems*, *29*(7), 1645–1660. doi:10.1016/j.future.2013.01.010

Hall, P., & Jacobs, W. (2010). Shifting Proximities: The Maritime Ports Sector in an Era of Global Supply Chains. *Regional Studies*, *44*(9), 1103–1115. doi:10.1080/00343400903365110

Hein, C. (2016). Port cityscapes: Conference and research contributions on port cities. *Planning Perspectives*, *31*(2), 313–326. doi:10.1080/02665433.2015.1119714

Hollen, R., van den Bosch, F., & Volberda, H. (2014). Strategic levers of port authorities for industrial ecosystem development. *Maritime Economics & Logistics*, *17*(1), 79–96. doi:10.1057/mel.2014.28

Homayouni, S., & Tang, S. (2015). Optimization of integrated scheduling of handling and storage operations at automated container terminals. *WMU Journal of Maritime Affairs*, *15*(1), 17–39. doi:10.100713437-015-0089-x

Horwitz, F. (2013). An analysis of skills development in a transitional economy: The case of the South African labour market. *International Journal of Human Resource Management*, *24*(12), 2435–2451. doi:10.1080/09585192.2013.781438

Jones, P. (2005). *Maritime Transport Costs and Port Efficiency: A Historical Perspective*. SSRN Electronic Journal. doi:10.2139srn.898468

Kahyarara, G. (2018). Opportunity and Growth Diagnostic of Maritime Transportation in the Eastern and Southern Africa. In *Maritime Transport In Africa: Challenges, Opportunities, and an Agenda for Future Research*. IAME Conference. Retrieved November 10, 2019 from https://unctad.org/meetings/en/Contribution/dtltlbts-AhEM2018d1_Kahyarara_en.pdf

Keceli, Y., Choi, H. R., Cha, Y. S., & Aydogdu, Y. V. (2008). A Study of User Acceptance of Port Community Systems. *ICOVACS 2008 – International Conference on Value Chain Sustainability*. Retrieved January 19, 2019 from https://pdfs.semanticscholar.org/4e35/b8a2c5c519572f18b6edcce60c3e398ccb6f.pdf

Kim, D., Park, K., Choi, G., & Min, K. (2014). A study on the factors that affect the adoption of Smart Water Grid. *Journal of Computer Virology and Hacking Techniques*, *10*(2), 119–128. doi:10.100711416-014-0206-y

Kumar, S., & Prakash, A. (2016). Role of Big Data and Analytics in Smart Cities. *International Journal of Science And Research*, *5*(2), 12–23. doi:10.21275/v5i2.nov161007

Lee, J., Kim, H., & Ahn, M. (2011). The willingness of e-Government service adoption by business users: The role of offline service quality and trust in technology. *Government Information Quarterly*, *28*(2), 222–230. doi:10.1016/j.giq.2010.07.007

Lokuge, P., & Alahakoon, D. (2007). Improving the adaptability in automated vessel scheduling in container ports using intelligent software agents. *European Journal of Operational Research*, *177*(3), 1985–2015. doi:10.1016/j.ejor.2005.12.016

Martín-Soberón, A. M., Monfort, A., Sapiña, R., Monterde, N., & Calduch, D. (2014). Automation in port container terminals. *Procedia: Social and Behavioral Sciences*, *160*, 195–204. doi:10.1016/j.sbspro.2014.12.131

Maspero, E., Van Dyk, E., & Ittmann, H. (2008). Maritime supply chain security: Navigating through a sea of compliance requirements. *Journal of Transport And Supply Chain Management*, *2*(1). doi:10.4102/jtscm.v2i1.44

Maturana, F. (2004). Distributed multi-agent architecture for automation systems. *Expert Systems with Applications*, *26*(1), 49–56. doi:10.1016/S0957-4174(03)00068-X

Mielniczuk, J., & Teisseyre, P. (2014). Using random subspace method for prediction and variable importance assessment in linear regression. *Computational Statistics & Data Analysis*, *71*, 725–742. doi:10.1016/j.csda.2012.09.018

Mokone, T. (2016). *The impact of governance structure on the port performance: a case of Durban Port* (Unpublished Masters dissertation). World Maritime University.

Muntean, M. C., Nechita, D., Nistor, C., & Şarpe, D. (2010). Port management importance in port activities development. In *The 3rd WSEAS International Conference On Urban Planning and Transportation (UPT '10), Latest Trends on Urban Planning and Transportation, Mathematics and Computers in Science and Engineering, A Series of Reference Books and Textbooks*. Corfu Island, Greece: WSEAS Press. Retrieved from www.wseas.org

Naicker, R., & Allopi, D. (2015). Improving performance at the Durban Container Terminal through automation. *Civil Engineering, 23*(9), 74-76. Retrieved 15 January 2019 from https://ir.dut.ac.za/bitstream/10321/2370/1/Naicker_CE_v23_ n9_a17_2015.pdf

Narsoo, J., & Muslun, A., W., & Sameer Sunhaloo, M. (2009). A Radio Frequency Identification (RFID) Container Tracking System for Port Louis Harbor: The Case of Mauritius. *Issues in Informing Science and Information Technology, 6*, 127–142. doi:10.28945/1047

Ndlovu, Z. (2007). Port Infrastructure and Operational Efficiency, and Port Productivity Management. In *PMAESA Maritime Conference* (pp. 1-10). Mahe, Seychelles: PMAESA. Retrieved October 13, 2016, from http://www.pmaesa.org/media/docs/Zeph_Ndlovu_TPT.pdf

Oliveira, T., Thomas, M., & Espadanal, M. (2014). Assessing the determinants of cloud computing adoption: An analysis of the manufacturing and services sectors. *Information & Management, 51*(5), 497–510. doi:10.1016/j.im.2014.03.006

Overendstudio. (n.d.). *Transnet Port Terminals*. Retrieved from: http://www.overendstudio.co.za/online_reports/transnet_ar2014/integrated/pao_tpt.php

Pettit, S., & Beresford, A. (2009). Port development: From gateways to logistics hubs. *Maritime Policy & Management, 36*(3), 253–267. doi:10.1080/03088830902861144

Rahayu, R., & Day, J. (2015). Determinant Factors of E-commerce Adoption by SMEs in Developing Country: Evidence from Indonesia. *Procedia: Social and Behavioral Sciences, 195*, 142–150. doi:10.1016/j.sbspro.2015.06.423

Roso, V., Woxenius, J., & Lumsden, K. (2009). The dry port concept: Connecting container seaports with the hinterland. *Journal of Transport Geography, 17*(5), 338–345. doi:10.1016/j.jtrangeo.2008.10.008

Ruto, W. K., & Datche, E. (2015). Logistical Factors Influencing Port Performance A Case of Kenya Ports Authority (Kpa). *International Journal of Current Research and Review*, *7*(12), 52–58.

Shi, P., & Yan, B. (2016). Factors affecting RFID adoption in the agricultural product distribution industry: Empirical evidence from China. *SpringerPlus*, *5*(1), 2029. doi:10.118640064-016-3708-x PMID:27995006

Shi, X., Tao, D., & Voß, S. (2011). RFID Technology and its Application to Port-Based Container Logistics. *Journal of Organizational Computing and Electronic Commerce*, *21*(4), 332–347. doi:10.1080/10919392.2011.614202

Son, M., & Han, K. (2011). Beyond the technology adoption: Technology readiness effects on post-adoption behavior. *Journal of Business Research*, *64*(11), 1178–1182. doi:10.1016/j.jbusres.2011.06.019

Tongzon, J. (2001). Efficiency measurement of selected Australian and other international ports using data envelopment analysis. *Transportation Research Part A, Policy and Practice*, *35*(2), 107–122. doi:10.1016/S0965-8564(99)00049-X

TransnetNationalPortsAuthority-Port of Durban. (2019). Retrieved January 15, 2019, from https://www.transnetnationalportsauthority.net/ourports/durban/Pages/Overview.aspx

Trujillo, L., González, M., & Jiménez, J. (2013). An overview on the reform process of African ports. *Utilities Policy*, *25*, 12–22. doi:10.1016/j.jup.2013.01.002

Verhoeven, P. (2010). A review of port authority functions: Towards a renaissance? *Maritime Policy & Management*, *37*(3), 247–270. doi:10.1080/03088831003700645

Vhumbunu, C. (2016). Enabling African Regional Infrastructure Renaissance through the China-Africa Partnership: A Trans-Continental Appraisal. *International Journal of China Studies Africa*, *7*(3), 271–300.

Wang, P., Mileski, J. P., & Zeng, Q. (2017). Alignments between strategic content and process structure: The case of container terminal service process automation. *Maritime Economics & Logistics*, 1.

Yang, Y., Zhong, M., Yao, H., Yu, F., Fu, X., & Postolache, O. (2018). Internet of Things for Smart Ports: Technologies and Challenges. *IEEE Instrumentation & Measurement Magazine*, *21*(1), 34–43. doi:10.1109/MIM.2018.8278808

Yousafzai, S., & Yani-de-Soriano, M. (2012). Understanding customer-specific factors underpinning internet banking adoption. *International Journal of Bank Marketing*, *30*(1), 60–81. doi:10.1108/02652321211195703

Yu, M., & Qi, X. (2013). Storage space allocation models for inbound containers in an automatic container terminal. *European Journal of Operational Research, 226*(1), 32–45. doi:10.1016/j.ejor.2012.10.045

Zehendner, E., & Feillet, D. (2014). Benefits of a truck appointment system on the service quality of inland transport modes at a multimodal container terminal. *European Journal of Operational Research, 235*(2), 461–469. doi:10.1016/j.ejor.2013.07.005

Zhou, J. (2013). Digitalization and intelligentization of manufacturing industry. *Advances in Manufacturing, 1*(1), 1–7. doi:10.100740436-013-0006-5

Zhu, K., & Kraemer, K. (2005). Post-Adoption Variations in Usage and Value of E-Business by Organizations: Cross-Country Evidence from the Retail Industry. *Information Systems Research, 16*(1), 61–84. doi:10.1287/isre.1050.0045

ADDITIONAL READING

Barros, C., & Peypoch, N. (2012). Productivity assessment of African seaports with biased technological change. *Transportation Planning and Technology, 35*(6), 663–675. doi:10.1080/03081060.2012.710033

Carlo, H., Vis, I., & Roodbergen, K. (2014). Transport operations in container terminals: Literature overview, trends, research directions and classification scheme. *European Journal of Operational Research, 236*(1), 1–13. doi:10.1016/j.ejor.2013.11.023

Chen, L., Zhang, D., Ma, X., Wang, L., Li, S., Wu, Z., & Pan, G. (2016). Container Port Performance Measurement and Comparison Leveraging Ship GPS Traces and Maritime Open Data. *IEEE Transactions on Intelligent Transportation Systems, 17*(5), 1227–1242. doi:10.1109/TITS.2015.2498409

Dwarakish, G., & Salim, A. (2015). Review on the Role of Ports in the Development of a Nation. *Aquatic Procedia, 4*, 295–301. doi:10.1016/j.aqpro.2015.02.040

Fernández, P., Santana, J., Ortega, S., Trujillo, A., Suárez, J., Domínguez, C., ... Sánchez, A. (2016). Smartport: A Platform for Sensor Data Monitoring in a Seaport Based on firmware. *Sensors (Basel), 16*(3), 417. doi:10.339016030417 PMID:27011192

Notteboom, T. (2016). The adaptive capacity of container ports in an era of mega vessels: The case of upstream seaports Antwerp and Hamburg. *Journal of Transport Geography, 54*, 295–309. doi:10.1016/j.jtrangeo.2016.06.002

KEY TERMS AND DEFINITIONS

Digitization of Ports: Seaports that invest in digitization and innovation to revolutionize shipping and transport logistics.

Efficiency in Seaports: Efficiency in seaports considers measures such as the duration of a ship's stopover in a port, as well as quality processes relating to cargo handling and service to inland transport providers.

Internet of Things (IoT): It is a network of items including sensors and embedded systems, which are connected to the internet and enable physical objects to gather and exchange data.

Market Share: The percentage of total sales of an industry in the market owned by a specific organisation compared to its competitors.

Port Terminal: It is an assembly point were freight (goods, container, and cars) are stored for processing that are to be moved to other destinations, usually from one mode of transportation to another.

Port Terminal Technology: Includes partially automated cranes, automated guided vehicles, and automated yard planning.

Smart Port Terminal: Uses the latest advances in information and communication technology to facilitate the movement of freight faster, using low cost mechanisms, and assures the safety of employees and citizens living around port terminals.

Chapter 11
Environmental Performance in the Waste Management Industry of Africa:
A Measure of Responsible Management

Bibi Zaheenah Chummun
University of KwaZulu-Natal, South Africa

ABSTRACT

In the midst of the Fourth Industrial Revolution, the proliferation of the technology revolution is changing the mindset of people relating to waste management. The mobility of people to the different places of African continent, a hike in industrial advancements, and the increase in the rise of goods consumption among others are fueling the generation of waste across Africa. Although the waste management industry plays a crucial role, reports have shown in the last decade that environmental degradation, pollution, and non-compliances by the activities of waste management companies prevail and impinge on environmental performance. Waste has now become one of the most significant environmental issues that requires attention. This chapter emphasizes on the landscape of the sector of waste management and the challenges facing the waste industry in Africa. The chapter ends with propositions to address those issues in a view to promote environmental performance and ensure responsible management of emerging African markets in the era of the Fourth Industrial Revolution.

DOI: 10.4018/978-1-5225-7638-9.ch011

Copyright © 2019, IGI Global. Copying or distributing in print or electronic forms without written permission of IGI Global is prohibited.

INTRODUCTION

Due to rapid innovation in technology, the global economy, and urbanization, man has established the Fourth Industrial Revolution, which has increased the standard of living. This has led to an increase in industrial processing, which has accelerated the generation of waste. Waste management has rapidly become one of the global environmental issues (Song, Li & Zeng, 2015:1). Due to a rapid increase in population and industrial advancements, there has been an increased generation of waste in Africa. For instance, the waste management sector in South Africa plays a vital role in the South African economy, the sector has been valued at 15.3 billion rand, and contributes to 0.51% of the country's GDP and contributing to economic growth (Department of Environmental Affairs, 2017).

In the last decade, there have been numerous reports of environmental degradation, pollution and non-compliances by the activities of waste management companies that has shown to have strong bearing on responsible management. Responsible management can be described as "seeking to balance the interests of the entire world (people, companies and environment) to prosper for the benefit of both current and future generations". Waste has now become one of the most significant environmental issues that requires attention to enhance responsible management. In this context, the waste management sector plays a vital role in the African economy as waste is generated from all industries, which needs to be disposed of in a legal and accountable manner (Singh, Brueckner, & Padhy, 2015:16). For instance, much emphasis has been placed on the waste sector lately with the National Department of Environmental Affairs (DEA) in South Africa, declaring a "War on Waste". The DEA have been striving to implement measures to ensure that waste is recycled, re-used, reduced and beneficiated. Targets and deadlines have been placed on waste generators and waste management companies to comply with national legislation in order to ensure the protection of the environment, health and safety of the public and to promote responsible management (Young, Davis, Mcneil, Malhotra, Russell, Unsworth, & Clegg, 2015:670).

However, research suggests that sound waste management practices in Africa are not under control by those who are actively involved in waste management (DEA, 2017). Although the intention is there to act responsibly, there are various barriers to good waste behaviour. Also, whilst there is intent to perform proper waste management practices, to enhance environmental performance, there has been weak translation into good behaviour (Godfrey, Scott, & Trois, 2013:295).

Therefore, the study is predicated on the thrust that the main factors affecting environmental performance in the waste industry of African developing countries such as organizational culture, environmental management system and the pro-environmental behaviour of employees can improve environmental performance in the waste industry of African developing countries and ensure responsible management practices.

The chapter focuses mainly on Municipal solid wastes (MSW) that are waste generated everyday although it makes mention of other types of waste in the content of the chapter.

Table 1 highlights the amount of MSW recorded in various cities of Africa.

Over the last five years, MSW has been seen as an environmental management component that can affect the attractiveness of a city, its socio-economic and political development (Nhamo, 2011). This is in line with the "SDGs Transforming our world: the 2030 Agenda for Sustainable Development" which includes Sustainable Development Goal 11: "Make cities and human settlements inclusive, safe, resilient and sustainable". First world-war countries or developed countries have prioritized MSW management by adhering to strict compliance, stringent regulatory framework and creative measures for MSW use, for instance energy generation. Further, they have ensured that MSW figures at the top of development agenda for their cities. This initiative can unlock opportunities of income generation for African cities by adopting waste re-use for the purpose of energy generation. However, the availability and quality of data on MSW are rather compromised and this affects the development agenda of MSW programmes in Africa (Fahmi & Sutton, 2010; UNEP, 2018).

Seven sections form part of the chapter: Section one provides a landscape of the waste management sector as a measure to promote environmental performance and ensure responsible management in the African context. Section two discusses the challenges facing the waste management sector in Africa to enhance environmental performance. The third section addresses the main drivers of environmental performance in the waste industry of Africa. The fourth part of this chapter gives an overview of the current scale of increased waste and E-waste in the African countries. Ways relating to how environmental performance can be enhanced in the waste management industry of African developing countries is provided in section five. Section six provides some recommendations focusing on how environmental

Table 1. Amount of MSW recorded in various cities of Africa during year 2016

African City/Countries	MSW generation rate (kg/capita/day)
Nigeria- Lagos	0,95
Kenya - Nairobi	0,72
Tanzania - Dar es Salaam	0,50
Zambia- Lusaka	0,37
Ethiopia - Addis Ababa	0,32

Source: Kawai and Tasaki (2016)

performance can be promoted in the sector of waste management while the FIR has emerged already. Future research directions are provided in section seven. This chapter provides a conclusion at the end.

BACKGROUND

A Snapshot of the Waste Management Sector With Reference to African Developing Countries

"Waste management" has gained momentum over the last decade and has been embedded within the Sustainable Development Goals. Although there has been an increase the waste generation in Africa, it has been noted that concerted efforts have contributed towards achieving the SDGs goals in the era of a hike in population and industrialization. Recently, there has been an increase of people in the move towards urban places in Sub-Saharan African countries and this trend is expected to continue in the near future. A population of 697 million is expected compared to 298 million in 2035 and by the middle century more than a billion of people is expected to live in urban places (African Development Bank, 2016). As much as urbanization can lead to economic growth engine, it can also generate alongside some challenges. As population count and African urban places grow rapidly, so grows the amount of the waste generated. The change in the patterns of consumption and economic activities can lead to different kinds of waste that should be managed in a decent and appropriate manner to ensure healthy living standards for each and every citizen so as to ensure responsible management. The hike in the population and industrialization in the emerging countries are pressurizing the resources in urban areas to provide for appropriates services of waste management. This is due to the lack of policies that can regulate the emerging informal settlements where the generating of services for waste management are not inadequate or appropriate in most parts of Africa. For instance, there is largely a lack of sanitation, water and waste management services for sixty-two percent of the people who live in the informal settlements of Sub-Saharan African countries (International Labour Organisation, 2013).

Moreover, lately, the waste management sector has been plagued with a significant number of transgressions to national legislation, natural resources, and the health and safety of the public by various industries. The mismanagement of waste has led to the compromise of natural resources such as air, water and land, which has transpired through the mobilization of chemicals and airborne particulates from the incorrect handling and disposal of hazardous waste. Waste management efficacy is not at the desired levels in Africa as compared to international standards, most of the waste generated in Africa is disposed of to landfill sites. Godfrey, Scott, & Trois (2013) stated that only 10% of landfills in South Africa are operated within accordance to national legislation. Policy makers have still a long way ahead to go in order to respond to the sanitary needs of the low-income people. Consequently, role players in the waste management sector have a duty to ensure the protection of the environment and the health and safety of the African public. Therefore, it is imperative to enlighten top management in the waste management sector of the factors that influence environmental performance which will be discussed at a later stage in the chapter. Various practices and procedures can be put in place to ensure that the business activities are conducted in accordance with best environmental methodologies to enhance environmental performance and to ensure the sustained protection of the environment (Hamdoun & Zouaoui, 2017). The communities in the vicinity of waste management activities will benefit from the increased environmental performance as they will not be exposed to the toxic fumes emanating from the waste and landfills. Clients and legislative bodies will be at ease with the fact that their waste is being handled and disposed in an industry which specifically focuses on environmental sustainability and responsible management

CHALLENGES FACING WASTE MANAGEMENT INDUSTRY IN AFRICA

There are different kinds of waste (wastewater, human excreta sludge and municipal solid waste) generated which can have an effect on health and performance of the environment (Song & Zeng, 2015). Most of the waste generation is related to illegal handling, disposal and transboundary movement of waste and has been seen as an ongoing phenomenon which has negative impacts on the health and safety of communities and the environment

One of the main challenges is to meet the Sustained Development Goals on informal settlements relating to the handling of these types of waste in Africa. Although much efforts have been made to enhance waste management at some point the progress has been slowed down by rise in the number of people and industrialisation. Although the government is finally responsible to ensure that the management of waste services is properly handled, the private sector is also an important component for contribution in the process of waste management treatment. The private niche as much as it has contributed in the management of waste services has also proven to be neglectful in complying with legislation wherever applicable and sustainability as well environment protection (Comoglio & Botta, 2012). The issue is the continued manifestation of events, which has led to environmental, and health degradation caused by waste management organisations. Furthermore, the proliferation of 90% of small and micro and medium enterprises in creating employment (50-60% of jobs in developing African countries) in the waste management segment has played an important part in neglecting the compliance with waste management legislation (Singh, Brueckner, & Padhy, 2015). Moreover, another challenge faced by the government recently in many African countries is to come up with a fully-fledged environment which can enable small enterprises to start the waste management services and to create more employment. The lack of Government support in the waste management industry consequently lead to harmful wastes in dump sites that are left unrecycled while could have been managed by small scale entrepreneurs. Nowadays this process is currently taking place by private smallholder scavengers and could have been better managed by the small entrepreneurs with better recycling equipment if they were fully supported by the Government. Further, there is a lack of trained personnel. For instance, the status of MSW in India is poor because the most appropriate methods from waste collection to disposal are not being used. There is a lack of training in MSW and the availability of qualified waste management professionals is limited. There is also a lack of accountability in current MSW systems throughout India (Khajuria, Matsui, Machimura, & Morioka, 2010)

Further, the Fourth Industrial Revolution (FIR) seems to be inevitable and its effect on waste has already been shown to some extent while some of its impact is still forthcoming (Schwab, 2015) The FIR has already started using digital systems and technologies along with waste management in each area such as robotics and sensors. These gadgets inevitably affect the waste market and could review the ways waste management is handled. Waste processors and organisations such as collectors might require some time to familiarise themselves with technologies and be fully informed of how they probably can improve measures of sustainable waste processes and responsible management practices. The shift of the FIR can change the whole paradigm of resources handling and could be a daunting challenge to many waste organisations and stakeholders. For instance, the innovative application of information technology is currently assisting to enhance the MSW management processes through sensors. While this application reduces the turnaround time in unnecessary truck trips and is viewed as a benefit to society as less emission is recorded, the private waste organizations are more likely to be unhappy with this technology as their income model generates revenue even when their trucks collect garbage from bins on a limited basis (Schwab, 2015).

Moreover, there have been instances where organizations have been found guilty of polluting the environment and have regularly received non-compliance notices from the DEA for not meeting the requirements of legislation. Some instances are as follows:

- **Illegal dumping of medical waste:** In 2010, a waste management firm was charged with the illegally dumping of medical waste on virgin soil and the company was issued with a compliance notice for the rehabilitation of the polluted ground (Cox, 2010).
- **Imported waste from Japan, illegally disposed in South Africa:** Imported waste from Japan has been illegally dumped in South Africa. An investigation was underway to the alleged reports of toxic waste such as acids, bitumen and organic material being disposed in non-designated sites which has caused serious damage to the environment and the health of the public and wildlife (Mungadze, 2014).
- **Illegal dump a hazard:** An illegal asbestos dumpsite has caused serious health impacts on the communities in the vicinity of the site. Numerous research studies have shown a link between lung cancer and various other diseases associated with occupational exposure to asbestos fibres. Companies offload the asbestos in this area as they do not wish to pay the fees associated with disposal in a licensed facility (Pieterse, 2015).
- **Toxic cocktail suspected in stink pollutions:** Noxious odours have been emanating from a landfill site in Kwa-Zulu Natal (KZN). Allegations have been made that the fumes from the site are causing detrimental health impacts to the communities. Members of the communities have complained of headaches, respiratory problems and continuous coughing because of the odours (Ntuli, 2016).
- **Landfill bosses criminally charged over smelly dump in many provinces of SA:** Senior members of a waste management firm have been criminally charged due to the environmental and health impact of odour emanating from a landfill site in KZN, the personnel of the company have been charged with contravening the environmental air quality legislation (Wicks, 2017).
- **Open burning:** Open dumping whether it is controlled or uncontrolled is mainly related to waste burning and most popular in Africa (Hoornweg and Bhada-Tata 2012). Nineteen out the fifty largest dumpsites are based in the African continent (United Nations Environment Programme, 2015). Open waste dumping in the African cities are more likely to affect negatively societies at large in a healthy way and environments that are exposed (Jerie, 2016) which is evidence of irresponsible management practices due to missing awareness, lack of enforcement measures and environment regulation.
- **Waste Landslide:** One hundred people were killed in waste landslides in Ethiopia more specifically Addis Ababa in March 2017. Another landslide in 2017 was in Mozambique where sixteen people died as a result of waste slide in Maputo. Two-third of those who died were women (Moshenberg 2018).

- **Waste burning:** Children and women in Ghana most specifically Accra who were asked to discard their waste in burning them in 2017 and were seen to be more prone to respiratory issues due to burning of waste (Moshenberg 2018). Further the agricultural waste open burning for instance rice straw a popular practice in Egypt leads to lung infections and allergic reactions of the exposed victims (Safar and Labib 2010) due to the grey and black smoke loaded by greenhouse gases.

- **Informal land Reclamation-Coastline:** Along the coastal places in Africa, debris and modes of commutation tyres were used as spaces to reclaim land for housing which is scarce and costly for low-income households. According to Frazer-Williams, (2014), this practice has been popular in mangrove land of Sierra Leone coastal area for the poor to build their "habitat". The houses are adjacent to the rivers which are prone to regular floods. Along the coastline the residents discard their waste hence affecting the ocean life which is an obvious example of irresponsible management practices.

Further, as much as data has been scarce and unreliable in the African Waste industry, the lack of waste data is not a new issue although it prevents to provide a holistic waste state in Africa since a decade (Sthiannopkao & Wong, 2013). A more important concern is that research on the drivers of environmental performance in the waste industry of Africa is still at a preliminary stage. Therefore, the research focus of the study relate to these ice-breaking questions: do these companies have environmental management programs in place, does a culture prone to the protection of the environment exist in waste management companies in Africa, and do the staff possess the attitude and behaviour associated with environmental values? Therefore, it is important to identify the main drivers of environmental performance in the waste management industry in the African context.

MAIN DRIVERS OF ENVIRONMENTAL PERFORMANCE IN THE WASTE INDUSTRY OF AFRICA

Dealing with waste management used to be perceived as a cost component in the early days. However, during the last decade, there has been much emphasis on environmental management, organizational culture and pro-environmental behaviour towards environmental performance as organizations are now beginning to allocate significant resources towards environmental compliance and are more committed to environmental performance hence responsible management (Chummun & Gaffar, 2018). What was once seen as a cost sector, is now viewed as a beneficial opportunity and a competitive advantage (Hamdoun & Zouaoui, 2017).

Environment Management

Environmental performance demonstrates a methodology to ascertain the effectiveness of the environmental initiatives an organization or the government put in place to mitigate and protect the environment. Environmental performance can be measured by a variety of indicators dependent on the organization and the type of business such as, waste reduction, waste beneficiation, diversion of waste from landfill, recycling initiatives, energy conservation, green procurement, implementation of an environmental management system and compliance with legislation (Paillé, Boiral, & Jin, 2014). Environmental Management plays a significant role in creating an important rate of environmental performance, profitability and a competitive advantage. Hamdoun and Zouaoui (2017:78) define environmental management as "technical and organizational activities aimed at reducing environmental impact caused by an organizations business operations". Environmental management consists of programs, policies and procedures to enhance and improve environmental performance in the form of recycling, waste management, eco-design, prevention of pollution and promoting sound environmental attitude and behaviour (Hamdoun & Zouaoui, 2017).

One of the most important measures of enhancing environmental performance is through the sound implementation of the Environmental Management System (EMS). An EMS is a global tool utilized for the mitigation of environmental impacts of the activities of a business and continuous improvement concerning environmental performance of an organization and the mitigation of environmental degradation in the waste management industry (Nguyen & Hens, 2015). There are two leading standards which set requirements for an EMS, namely the ISO 14001 and Eco-management & Audit Scheme (EMAS) (Testa, Rizzi, Daddi, Gusmerotti, Frey, & Iraldo, 2014). The African developing countries of which South Africa is mainly one adopts the requirements of the ISO 14001, in the form of South African National Standard (SANS) 14001.

ISO 14001 forms part of a set of standards aimed at environmental management systems called the ISO 14000 family. An organization can achieve an ISO 14001 certification for each site that it operates on, by accredited independent bodies (Gavronski, Paiva, Teixeira, & De Andrade, 2013). The EMS consists of a framework to ensure the protection of the environment, responding to client demands and to changing and challenging environmental conditions. An EMS provides top management with an approach to continuously improve sustainable development by policies, procedures and work instructions in order to assist the organization in ensuring compliance with relevant legislation, efficiency improvement and by protecting the environment and enhancing environmental performance (Nguyen & Hens, 2015).

There has been a significant amount of research which suggests that there is a definite correlation between an EMS and environmental performance. Melnyk, Bititci, Platts, Tobias, & Andersen (2014) provide case studies on the positive relationship of an ISO 14001 EMS and environmental performance. However, there has also been research where there has been no impact on environmental performance, and in some cases the organizations have performed worse once the ISO 14001 was established. Also, a number of research findings have been non-conclusive (Nguyen & Hens, 2015; Testa, Rizzi, Daddi, Gusmerotti, Frey, & Iraldo, 2014).

Comoglio and Botta (2012) argued that an ISO 14001 system does not supply a methodology for continuous improvement or a minimum level of environmental performance indicators. However, Gavronski, Paiva, Teixeira, & De Andrade (2013) suggests that the ISO 14001 does provide a methodology for continuous improvement in the form of a "plan to do check model", which allows managers to improve on the organizations environmental impacts continuously. Many studies of certified businesses both large and small have shown that the standard does indeed contribute to improving environmental performance significantly (Gonzalez-Benito and Gonzalez-Benito, 2005; Potoski & Prakash, 2005). More specifically, several case studies of ISO 14001 certified companies have shown that implementation of the standard has helped reduce environmental impacts, including the volume of waste generated, water and energy consumption, and atmospheric emissions (Chattopadhyay, 2001).

Nguyen and Hens (2015) suggested that there are various published studies which have commonly determined strategies in order to determine the effectiveness of an ISO 14001 system on environmental performance such as:

1. Comparison between environmental performance between pre-and post-certification;
2. Comparison of environmental performance of organisations who have a certified ISO 14001 system and those organisations who do not; and
3. Combination of changes in environmental performance between pre-and post ISO 14001 certifications in certified organizations and between certified and non-certified organisations.

Link Between Environmental Management System and Environmental Performance

Wiengarten and Pagell (2012) have supported the research by Testa et al. (2014) and Valmohammadi and Roshanzamir (2015), whereby the authors confirmed a positive relationship between EMS and environmental performance. The researchers acknowledged that a formal EMS, such as the ISO 14001, significantly improves overall organizational performance, and through an EMS a firm reduces or mitigates the generation of waste and the risk associated with the activities of the business which ultimately has an impact on a firm's financial bottom line. Wiengarten and Pagell (2012) analysed the impact of environmental performance on the market value of organizations, the authors identified that declarations of company environmental initiatives, and especially environmental awards, recognitions and certifications, to the staff of the business have had a positive impact on environmental performance. Massoud, Tabcharani, Nakkash and Jamali (2012) suggests that ISO 14001 certified firms experience a significant reduction in pollution when compared to non-certified companies. Melnyk et al. (2014) undertook a study on small medium enterprises and examined the extent to which ISO certified firms considered various environmental options. The study revealed that the EMS certification had a significant and positive impact on waste management practices among certified firms. Certified firms were found to consider a broader range of environmental practices when compared with their non-certified counterparts. Wiengarten and Pagell (2012) identified that organizations who have an externally certified EMS such as the ISO 14001, experience higher performance rates from environmental campaigns such as waste management services as compared to companies who did not possess or partake in such a system.

Organisational Culture

Moreover, literature suggests that organizational culture plays a vital role in influencing behaviours and attitudes amongst employees, financial performance, organizational effectiveness, and structure (Sanyal & Pal, 2017). Organizational performance relies significantly on a healthy organizational culture (Awadh & Alyahya, 2013:171). The purpose of an organizational culture is to ensure collaboration amongst teams, ensure coherency amongst staff, engage and stimulate employee creativity and innovation, instill values and beliefs, create excitement and enhance and improve organizations' efficiency, which in turn enhances employee attitude and behaviour. These traits will provide the norms of behaviour that employees will follow, which will in turn, translate to pro-environmental behavior amongst employees (Sanyal & Pal, 2017). A cohesive organizational culture is substantially dependent on the number of people collaborating with each other with the aim of accomplishing goals in their environment (Valmohammadi & Roshanzamir, 2015).

There have been numerous studies in literature which depict a positive relationship between organizational culture and pro-environmental behaviour (Awadh & Alyahya, 2013; Hamdoun & Zouaoui, 2017; Hogan & Coote, 2014). One such study was undertaken by Sanyal and Pal (2017), which was conducted in West Bengal amongst 100 employees, spanning different sectors in an organization. The samples were taken from both the private and public sector between managers and non-managerial employees. The study concludes that there is a definite association amongst an organizational culture, environmental awareness and pro-environmental behaviour. The authors put forth suggestions from the questionnaires submitted as to what should be done by the organization in order to facilitate a robust organizational culture which is conducive to environmental awareness and pro-environmental behaviour. Attention was focused on mainly the incorporation of shared values and beliefs through workshops and training programs designed for employees, environmental training that forms an integral part of developing environmental awareness and pro-environmental behavior that includes the importance of organizations sharing a pool of environmental values to employees on a regular basis to enhance environmental performance.

Hamdoun and Zouaoui (2017) stated that in order to facilitate and sustain an environmental culture and commitment there needs to be collaboration between departments of an organization. All employees need to work together and participate in environmental practices to achieve a shared goal which is part of the organizational culture as working in teams encourages friendly competition and the sharing of tacit knowledge (Valmohammadi & Roshanzamir, 2015). In a study by Zsóka (2007), the author stated that the function of environmental values in sustaining a business environmental behaviour with specific focus on environmental values is of paramount importance as it enhances environmental performance .

Pro-Environmental Behavior

Zsóka (2007) made mention of a model, which is called the ABC model and refers to attitude, behaviour and structural settings of behavioural conditions. The theory suggests that the attitude-behaviour relationship will be at its highest when the external and internal factors around it are supportive, which will encourage personnel with negative attitudes towards the environment to act in a more responsible manner. A highly restrictive setting will discourage individuals from performing activities in an environmentally responsible manner. This model is entirely relative to organizational culture, whereas the theory of the model could be used to explain the theory of the impact of organizational culture, which assimilates the C in the model in terms of the conditional setting pertaining to the environmental management in the company. Pro-environmental behaviour in an organization has become crucial as a tool in reducing environmental impacts in the waste industry. Moreover, an employee's willingness to participate and support environmental practices has been identified as a vital step in supporting environmental management goals and enhancing environmental performance (Paille, Chen, Boiral, & Jin, 2014:452). To sustain pro-environmental behaviour in the workplace, environmental values need to be inculcated in the organizational culture.

Several industries (manufacturing, petroleum, textile and mining), amongst others have environmental policies and programs in place. However, these are not adequate in order for organizations to completely react to environmental challenges. Merely changing environmental infrastructure and system changes can only reduce environmental impacts to a limited extent. There has to be a significant cultural and environmental change transformation and behavioural change research can assist organizations in reducing critical environmental issues such as waste management issues and improving environmental performance (Sanyal & Pal, 2017).

THE SCALE OF INCREASED WASTE AND E-WASTE IN DEVELOPING AFRICAN COUNTRIES

One of the most challenging events in any African urban locality nowadays is the collection, treatment, transportation, storage, and eventual disposal of waste (Mgimba & Sanga, 2016). A comparative poor waste management practices which includes dumping of water refuse and abandoned units have compromised the sanitation standards of many African countries. The prevailing increase in the level of urbanization in Africa is expected to continue in the future. However, a major concern is that there are no adequate infrastructural facilities and appropriate land use planning to match up with the demands posed by the urban growth rate especially the slums and ghettos in Africa (Mgimba & Sanga, 2016). Practices such as waste collection, storage, treatment and final disposal have recently been reported to be major problems in cities.

In Africa the total count per year of municipal solid waste in 2012 was approximately one hundred and twenty-five tonnes of which sixty-five percent was generated from SSA countries (Chengula, Lucas & Mzula, 2015). In Africa, the generation of waste is expected to increase to approximately two hundred and forty four million tonnes on an annual basis by year 2025. On average the MSW generation in 2012 was rated at 0.78 kg per capita on a daily basis and is expected that by 2025 to grow to approximately 0.99 kg per capita on a daily basis (Chengula, Lucas & Mzula, 2015). In Africa, the biggest part of a budget for the MSW is allocated to the collection of waste although the total of waste collected in the year 2012 was only 55 per cent of total waste generated compared to 49 percent collected in 2016 (Sanyal & Pal, 2017). This situation is worse in rural spaces.

In Africa, controlled and uncontrolled dumping are the most common waste disposal practices in Africa. Research has shown that recently waste in some dumping areas that are open has been left untreated, and unsegregated with little access to water protection and the trend keeps on increasing (Sanyal & Pal, 2017). The presence of lack of education about waste disposal, recycling and collection have been seen to be increasing as the main cause to manage waste in African countries. According to Organization for Economic Cooperation and Development, on a general font, waste recycling seemingly has not been viewed as a main priority as the average recycling rate for the municipal solid waste in Africa has been estimated at 4 per cent only compared to 30 per cent in 2013 (OECD 2015a, 2015b). There are only a few formal recycling systems in sub-Saharan Africa. Although several municipalities in Africa have implemented some onsite recovery of material facilities (CSIR, 2011), waste recycling has not improved a lot. Hoornweg and Bhada-Tata (2012) put forward that the main causes are related to municipalities that are not fully equipped with the necessary logistics for waste collection and recycling. The waste management services systems in the African countries are facing many obstacles as economies and mobility of population grow and move to urban areas from rural places. Furthermore, the substandard products being imported from other low cost-producing countries and places into Africa giving rise to hazardous waste leads to emerging new waste streams. An urgent need is required for better comprehensive quality data relating to composition, sources and types of wastes which are generated and this information should be revealed to other African countries. By the same token electronic waste (e-waste) which is related to discarded electronic equipment is increasing in the African countries. With the proliferation of the Internet of Technology (IoT) revolutionizing the African countries, the discarded electronic equipment such as cellphones refrigerators, laptops or any electronic device is generating 2.2 millions of e-waste tonnes per year (Baldé, Forti, Gray, Kuehr, & Stegmann, 2017). For example, the number of personal computers and cellphones has increased drastically over the last five years in Africa and this phenomenon is generating millions of tonnes of e-waste per year which are left untreated in many areas (Schluep & Wasswa, 2012). The largest amount of e-waste generated come from three countries mainly South Africa, Senegal and Uganda and the e-waste is estimated to grow by eight times more in the next ten years (Schluep & Wasswa, 2012; Bello, Ismail, & Kabbashi, 2016). This is mainly due to a rapid increase in Electric Electronic Equipment demand and supply in Africa. Furthermore, the lifetime of EEE is very short mainly because of emerging changes and new trends in technology or low-priced charged products (United Nations Environment Programme, 2016).

SUGGESTIONS AS TO HOW ENVIRONMENTAL PERFORMANCE IN LOCALITIES/ORGANISATIONS CAN BE ENHANCED IN THE WASTE MANAGEMENT SECTOR OF AFRICAN COUNTRIES

Partnerships and Collaborations

In order to facilitate and sustain an environmental culture and improve environmental performance and commitment, there is an urgent need to have a collaboration between departments of an organization, where all employees need to work together and participate in environmental practices to enhance environmental performance (Hamdoun & Zouaoui, 2017).

Partnerships and collaborations between private sector organizations and governments could be a good initiative to construct strong infrastructure, waste services and also to tackle waste issues in order to enhance environmental performance. Therefore, the public authority needs to research how collaboration between private sector and public sector can be incentivized for instance to initiate economic incentives and create a more policy- enabling environment. Furthermore, it is also important to consult and collaborate with developed countries to explore how knowledge transfer and right technology can be adapted to the needs of Africa.

Training and Development

In a view to sustain a pro-environmental behaviour in the workplace, environmental values should be embedded in the organizational culture to promote environmental performance through consistent training and development (Zsóka, 2007).

It is important that training and development are made at both levels; bottom-to-top level and top-to-bottom level. The bottom-to-top level comprises tailor-made training for different staff of waste management such as private companies and municipalities. This should involve educating them on the importance of sustainable waste management services and the benefits of complying with legislation; The top-to-bottom level is more customized to equip the senior executives at the governmental level about the benefits of having rational waste management services.

Further, since environmental performance relies on a large extent on the motivation, commitment and leadership of top management who are in a role to implement policies and procedures, motivating employees is needed through rewards and incentives to conduct activities in an environmentally responsible manner which increases environmental performance (Boiral, Baron, & Gunnlaugson, 2014).

It is also important to encourage a pro-environmental behavior amongst employees such as performance management, incentive rewards, recruitment process, and training programs. Therefore, the environmental culture of the company should be incorporated into the recruitment process, and the personnel to be selected should match the attribute and character required for environmental competencies. Human resource management plays a pivotal role in achieving environmental objectives, and if the human resources practices are efficient, they are in a position to understand the company's environmental objectives and can assist in achieving them (Jabbour & Santos,2008).

Further, there is a need to undertake green performance appraisals which provide a platform to continually point out the employee's wrongdoing or downfall with regard to environmental practices, thus more likely to enhance continuous improvement and promote environmental performance (Renwick, Redman, & Maguire, 2013).

There is a need to develop training and capacity building at every level. All African school children should understand the importance of waste management, the effects of poor waste management on the environment and public health, and the role and responsibilities of each individual in the waste management system. This will develop responsible citizens who regard waste as a resource opportunity (Khajuria, Matsui, Machimura, & Morioka, 2010)

Legislation and Enforcement of Appropriate Quality Systems

A good quality managed system has the potential to be a building block for successful environmental management practices. Therefore, the adoption of a formal ISO14001 by many African entities who are not yet compliant with a good quality system should ensure that the management of their business operations towards the environment enhance the company's environmental performance as well as its long-run financial performance (Raj & Seetharaman, 2013). Watson, Klingenberg, Poluto and Grurts (2004) also suggested that total quality management (TQM) techniques assist in improving the overall environmental performance. Raj and Seetharaman (2013) stated that TQM and EMS assist in reducing the cost of the business in respect to environmental clean-up costs, penalties and fines from government and the cost associated with the loss of market share as clients would not want to associate themselves with a company that has caused pollution. Hence the waste management African companies and sector should pay particular attention to a QMS system to enhance the EMS which improves environmental performance.

Further, the waste industry in Africa must ensure compliance with national legislation not only to ensure that the business is performing activities ethically, but also to ensure a competitive advantage as clients want to do business with company's who are actively compliant especially in light of the recent spate of environmental transgressions by waste management companies (Uecker-Mercado & Walker, 2012). This could be a feature for the organizations to work on to promote environmental performance and enhance responsibility management. The African countries must explore the benefits of an enabling policy environment that can attract foreign investors into waste management sector. This is more likely to boost the confidence of investors in Africa's countries waste management sector. Wherever possible a regulatory framework overseeing the waste management sector in African countries should be implemented and governance consolidated to enhance environmental performance and promote responsible management.

RECOMMENDATIONS: SOME SOLUTIONS TO ENHANCE ENVIRONMENTAL PERFORMANCE IN THE WASTE MANAGEMENT SECTOR IN THE FOURTH INDUSTRIAL REVOLUTION

The FIR characterized by technologies will significantly impact on the waste management sector in African countries. The technology revolution is changing our mindset on waste management activities to enhance environmental performance. The number of people migrating to urban areas, change in pattern of consumption and rapid industrialization in African countries are generating more waste nowadays than a decade earlier. Therefore, a new approach on waste management initiatives is needed as follows:

To Develop a Circular Economy Through the Use of Technology

The proliferation and shaping of technology is changing the way that waste management systems and practices can be handled and treated by government, service providers and consumers. In a view of protecting the environment degradation the stakeholders should collaborate in enhancing this initiative. The revolution is to ensure that developing African countries also form part of the emerging trends in technology relating to the waste management sector as the growth in population for the developing African countries is one of the biggest worldwide. The internet of things is proliferating the waste management industry therefore it is important to move towards exploring the benefits related to a circular economy through the use of technology in the waste management industry. This could be done by modelling human industry on nature's processes and researching other ways of re-using and recycling items to mitigate natural resources usage. Circular economy is different to a linear one which involves only "take, make and dispose production model. The main pillar of a circular economy is not only to conserve resources but also per se enhance the conservation. A good approach to efficiently operate in the waste management industry during the Fourth Industrial Revolution and maximize output is through the philosophy of green building. These green buildings, among other benefits to man and environment, will reduce waste generation. Also, the materials used are environment friendly and are recycled efficiently. The products we consume are changing fast, but technology has to ensure these products contain a very high percentage of recyclable materials.

For instance, nowadays approximately 10% only of our waste is reused and recycled while over 90% of waste is landfilled. It will be wise that the African countries bring along technology communication and connectivity for sharing data in assisting in many waste management processes. For instance, using technology in optimising ways that disposal of garbage is being transported for waste removal and collection with enabling automation operations through the use of sensors that can be used dustbins of garbage indicating that there is a need for collection when bins are completely full.

The aforesaid automated process will enable the data to convey real time information to a main control server to help the driver of waste on the different routes to embark on for collection, dustbins to offload and load, projected time to collect and also to supply information on the per kilometer collection cost of waste. After collecting the bins, information on the types of waste can be used to decide which dustbins requires recycling points and /or disposal centres. This information is useful to customers as it provides an invoice and informs them accordingly through the cloud.

Another example is that the Indian-based Tata Motors dealer is using the re-incarnated sales method as a measure of circular economy. The next sales of second-hand products and life materials seem to be effective when Tata Motors refurbishes its products and then offers the same cars and products to earn another income again through a certification process (Den Holder, 2017).

Starbucks, the American Seattle coffee company, has started to convert its food and coffee grounds waste into regular used products by making use of bacteria to produce succinic acid which is ultimately used in detergents, bio-plastics and even medicines, all these are evidence of innovation in the recycling technology (Den Holder, 2017).

Zero Waste Scotland in the United Kingdom is currently supporting individuals and organisations in the development of a circular economy. The Deposit Return scheme of Zero Waste Scotland enables customers to pay a relative lower price than usual when they purchase drinks and get their deposit back at return of the container which is used for recycling (Zero Waste Scotland, 2018).

A study by the World Bank in 2017 put forward that a solid waste of approximately seven millions tons will be recorded every day until 2025, and an increase to two billions of low to middle income consumers until 2030 (World Bank, 2017). It is high time that the circular economy process needs to be adopted in other parts of the world when the FIR is flowing full swing. This situation currently is happening in some countries on a small basis and African countries need to adopt this initiative wherever possible and applicable. Obviously, it will be wise for the suppliers of waste management and other stakeholders to work together as a team and explore solutions to the issues faced by governments and municipalities when adopting technology in waste management processes with a view to enhance environmental performance.

The Need for Developing Finance

Amongst others, government faces important financial restrictions that are not easy to overcome overnight when considering enhancing environmental performance in waste management services in the midst of Industry 4.0. The amount of waste generated is huge and can affect public health, quality of life and the environment. It is not impossible that appropriate solid waste management can be achieved when tools and equipment currently exist. However, the need for funding of these means is important. Although municipalities in African countries allocate 20% to 50% of their budgets on solid waste management, there is a lack of financing solid waste management activities. Therefore there is definitely a need for municipalities to explore opportunities for development finance in Africa and ensure that these funds are transparently and efficiently used such as results-based-financing (RBF) approach to the municipal solid waste sector. This is an innovative development finance tool that helps ensure that public funds are used efficiently and transparently. Many developing countries have started using the RBF such as India (Banna, Bhada-Tata, Ho, & Lee, 2014). Results-based-financing relates where "payments are tied to results and can play an important role in improving municipal solid waste services and outcomes" (Banna et al., 2014).

Reducing Waste Management Costs

Reducing the costs of providing goods and services in the waste management sector is more likely to lower cost to the country and increase a country's GDP (Raj & Seetharam, 2013). It is likely that investors will be more attractive to the competitive costs of waste management and is more probable to enhance environmental performance in the midst of Industry 4.0.

While moving from the linear economy towards a circular one, waste management costs can be reduced through the reduction in collection costs and treatment /disposal costs as follows: Reducing collection costs can be achieved through adjusting to an approach which is decentralised to waste management thereby, will minimize the cost of transportation. This is more likely that community will sort out the waste on a re-used or a recycled basis through technologies that is cheaper and faster in the respective locality (Dainty & Brooke, 2004). This process is a more user-friendly one as it reduces the waste at decentralized community level enabling the waste management services that is more easily managed in Africa to enhance environmental performance in the midst of FIR.

FUTURE RESEARCH DIRECTIONS

The study's results have implications on the management of waste management sector who are seeking on ways to improve their environmental performance and ensure responsible management in the waste industry of African developing countries. The management of waste has been viewed as a critical environmental hurdle in African countries and this affects environmental performance and responsible management. The composition, recycling and composition that can convert waste into useful resources in a view of generating income is more likely to promote responsible management. Such initiatives can be achieved if Africa is to meet up to the international trends and standards of managing waste. In order to achieve the desired results, the African countries need to address the hurdles of managing waste urgently and to get ready forecasted increase in waste of approximately seven billion tons daily and even more waste is expected in the forthcoming century (World Bank, 2017).

These will comprise of exploring new ways of recycling and disposing waste through technologies that needs to be researched in the era of the FIR. For instance, it will be wise to research on how to adopt the e-waste model or regenerative circular economy approach in Africa instead of a linear model of "make, take and dispose waste" in a view to enhance environmental performance and ensure responsible management.in the near future (EACO, 2013; UNEP, 2018). There is also a need to establish a culture which focuses on the protection of the environment and legal compliance, and this should form part of the vision and mission of the company so that all employees, are motivated by the company culture to engage in their work activities in an environmental safe and responsible manner (Hogan & Coote, 2014)

Further, several socio-economic opportunities such as women's empowerment, enterprise development and job creation are more likely to happen if the companies move the waste towards reuse, recovery and recycling (UN-Habitat 2014; EEA, 2011:7). The African companies should review these social innovation opportunities of waste management and explore ways of using them effectively through intensive research initiatives.

Therefore, the above-mentioned elements still have room for research at a near future stage and provide a sound technical base for further enhancement of environmental performance as a measure of responsible management practices in the waste management services sector of African developing countries.

CONCLUSION

This chapter kick-starts with a landscape of the waste management industry in an attempt to enhance environmental performance as a measure of responsible management in emerging markets in the African economies. During the FIR midst, where a change in mindset in treating waste is proliferating the industry, many challenges and disruptions are emerging and hampering the environmental performance which have been taken into account in section two of this chapter. The daunting challenges occurring in the waste industry are countless and will keep on carrying on as the population is expected to grow and so is the amount of waste as previously mentioned in this chapter. The main drivers of environmental performance in the waste management industry has been discussed in section three of the study. The study has also provided enough evidence of the existing status of increased waste over the last decade facing developing nations in Africa. Based on the findings of the chapter, some insightful recommendations namely circular economy approach, socio-economic opportunities amongst others on how to improve environmental performance and promote responsible management in the waste management industry of Africa in this era of Fourth Industrial Revolution which is currently swinging full flow.

REFERENCES

African Development Bank. (2016). *African Economic Outlook 2016: Sustainable Cities and Structural Transformation.* Retrieved May 11, 2018, from http://www.africaneconomicoutlook.org/sites/default/files/content-pdf/eBook_AEO2016.pdf

Awadh, A. M., & Alyahya, M. S. (2013). Impact of organizational culture on employee performance. *International Review of Management and Business Research, 2,* 168.

Baldé, C. P., Forti, V., Gray, V., Kuehr, R., & Stegmann, P. (2017). *The Global E-waste Monitor.* Retrieved May 13, 2018, from https://www.itu.int/en/ITU-D/limate-Change/Documents/GEM%202017/Global-Ewaste%20Monitor%202017%20.pdf

Banna, F., Bhada-Tata, P., Ho, R., & Lee, M. (2014). *Results-based financing for municipal solid waste. Urban development series knowledge papers, 20(2).* Washington, DC: World Bank Group.

Bello, I. A., Ismail, M. N., & Kabbashi, N. A. (2016). Solid Waste Management in Africa: A review. *International Journal of Waste Resources*, *6*(2), 1–4.

Boiral, O., & Paillé, P. (2012). Organizational citizenship behaviour for the environment: Measurement and validation. *Journal of Business Ethics*, *109*(4), 431–445. doi:10.100710551-011-1138-9

Chattopadhyay, S. P. (2001). Improving the speed of ISO 14000 implementation: A framework for increasing productivity. *Managerial Auditing Journal*, *16*(1), 36–40. doi:10.1108/02686900110363636

Chengula, A., Lucas, B. K., & Mzula, A. (2015). Assessing the Awareness, Knowledge, Attitude and Practice of the Community towards Solid Waste Disposal and Identifying the Threats and Extent of Bacteria in the Solid Waste Disposal Sites in Morogoro Municipality in Tanzania. *Journal of Biology, Agriculture and Healthcare*, *5*(3), 54–65.

Chummun, B. Z., & Gaffar, K. (2018). Factors that Influence Environmental Performance in the Waste Management Industry in KwaZulu-Natal. In *12*th *International Business Conference Proceedings* (pp. 1-17). Le Meridian, Mauritius: Academic Press.

Comoglio, C., & Botta, S. (2012). The use of indicators and the role of environmental management systems for environmental performances improvement: A survey on ISO 14001 certified companies in the automotive sector. *Journal of Cleaner Production*, *20*(1), 92–102. doi:10.1016/j.jclepro.2011.08.022

Cox, A. (2010). *Waste Company Head Arrested*. Retrieved May 18, 2018, from http://www.iol.co.za/news/south-africa/waste-company-head-arrested-480897

CSIR. (2011). *Municipal waste management - good practices*. Retrieved May 13, 2018, fromhttps://www.csir.co.za/sites/default/files/Documents/Waste_Management_Toolkit_0.pdf

Dainty, A. R. J., & Brooke, R. J. (2004). Towards improved construction waste minimisation: A need for improved supply chain integration? *Structural Survey*, *22*(1), 20–29. doi:10.1108/02630800410533285

Den Holder, G. (2017). *Circular Economy*. Retrieved May 15, 2018, from, https://www.business2community.com/strategy/need-inspiring-examples-circular-economy-5-01872776

Department of Environmental Affairs. (2017). Waste minimization with relation to producers - fact pack. Pretoria: Department of Environmental Affairs.

East African Communication Organisation (EACO). (2013). *Model Framework for e-waste management.* Retrieved May 21, 2018, from, http://www.eaco.int/admin/docs/reports/Policy_Model_ Framework_June_2013.pdf

European Economic Area (EEA). (2011). *Earnings, jobs and innovation: The role of recycling in a green economy.* European Environment Agency: Report no. 8/2011. Luxembourg: Office for Official Publications of the European Union. Retrieved May 17, 2018, from, https:// www.eea.europa.eu/publications/earnings-jobs-andinnovation-the/download

Fahmi, W., & Sutton, K. (2010). Cairo's contested garbage: Sustainable waste management and the Zabaleen's right to the city. *Sustainability*, *2*(6), 1765–1783. doi:10.3390u2061765

Gavronski, I., Paiva, E. L., Teixeira, R., & De Andrade, M. C. F. (2013). ISO 14001 certified plants in Brazil–taxonomy and practices. *Journal of Cleaner Production*, *39*, 32–41. doi:10.1016/j.jclepro.2012.08.025

Godfrey, L., Scott, D., & Trois, C. (2013). Caught between the global economy and local bureaucracy: The barriers to good waste management practice in South Africa. *Waste Management & Research*, *31*(3), 295–305. doi:10.1177/0734242X12470204 PMID:23377284

González-Benito, J., & González-Benito, Ó. (2005). Environmental proactivity and business performance: An empirical analysis. *Omega*, *33*(1), 1–15. doi:10.1016/j.omega.2004.03.002

Hamdoun, M., & Zouaoui, M. (2017). Impact of Environmental Management on Competitive Advantage of Tunisian Companies: The Mediator Role of Organizational Culture. *International Review of Management and Marketing*, *7*, 76–82.

Hogan, S. J., & Coote, L. V. (2014). Organizational culture, innovation, and performance: A test of Schein's model. *Journal of Business Research*, *67*(8), 1609–1621. doi:10.1016/j.jbusres.2013.09.007

Hoornweg, D., & Bhada-Tata, P. (2012). *What a waste: A Global Review of Solid Waste Management. Urban Development Series Knowledge Papers No. 15.* Washington, DC: World Bank.

International Labour Organisation. (2013). *Decent work in waste management: A baseline study on the ward contractor system in the City of Windhoek.* Geneva: ILO. Retrieved May 17, 2018, from http://www.ilo.org/wcmsp5/ groups/public/---africa/---ro-addis_ababa/---ilo-pretoria/ documents/publication/wcms_243093.pdf

Jabbour, C. J. C., & Santos, F. C. A. (2008). The central role of human resource management in the search for sustainable organizations. *International Journal of Human Resource Management, 19*(12), 2133–2154. doi:10.1080/09585190802479389

Kawai, K., & Tasaki, T. (2016). Revisiting estimates of municipal solid waste generation per capita and their reliability. *Journal of Material Cycles and Waste Management, 18*(1), 1–13. doi:10.100710163-015-0355-1

Khajuria, A., Matsui, T., Machimura, T., & Morioka, T. (2010). Assessment of the challenge of sustainable recycling of municipal solid waste management. *India International Journal of Environmental Technology Management, 13*, 171–187.

Massoud, M., Tabcharani, R., Nakkash, R., & Jamali, D. (2012). *Environmental performance improvement and ISO 14001: case of Lebanon. Environmental Impact.* WIT Press.

Melnyk, S. A., Bititci, U., Platts, K., Tobias, J., & Andersen, B. (2014). Is performance measurement and management fit for the future? *Management Accounting Research, 25*(2), 173–186. doi:10.1016/j.mar.2013.07.007

Mgimba, C., & Sanga, A. (2016). Municipal Solid Waste Composition Characterization for Sustainable Management Systems in Mbeya City, Tanzania. *International Journal of Science Environmental Technology, 5*, 47–58.

Mungazde, S. (2014). *Imported waste from Japan and has been illegally dumped in South Africa.* Retrieved May 13, 2018, from http://www.bdlive.co.za/business/industrials/2014/05/26/interwaste-probe-reaches-across-borders

Nguyen, Q. A., & Hens, L. (2015). Environmental performance of the cement industry in Vietnam: The influence of ISO 14001 certification. *Journal of Cleaner Production, 96*, 362–378. doi:10.1016/j.jclepro.2013.09.032

Nhamo, G. (2011). *Green economy and climate mitigation: Topics of relevance to Africa.* Pretoria: Africa Institute of South Africa.

Ntuli, N. (2016). *Toxic cocktail suspected in stink pollutions busters roped in Campbell's book gets global face.* Retrieved May 12, 2018, from http://sundaytribune.newspaperdirect.com/epaper/viewer.aspx

OECD (2015a). *OECD Environment Statistics, Municipal Waste database.* OECD. doi:10.1787/data-00601-en

OECD. (2015b). *Environment at a Glance 2015: OECD Indicators.* Paris: OECD Publishing. doi:10.1787/9789264235199-

Paillé, P., Chen, Y., Boiral, O., & Jin, J. (2014). The impact of human resource management on environmental performance: An employee-level study. *Journal of Business Ethics, 121*(3), 451–466. doi:10.100710551-013-1732-0

Pieterse, C. (2015). *Illegal Dump a Hazard.* Retrieved May 15, 2018, from http://www.news24.com/SouthAfrica/News/Illegal-dump-a-health-hazard-20150629

Raj, J. R., & Seetharaman, A. (2013). Role of waste and performance management in the construction industry. *Journal of Environmental Science and Technology, 6*(3), 119–129. doi:10.3923/jest.2013.119.129

Renwick, D. W., Redman, T., & Maguire, S. (2013). Green human resource management: A review and research agenda. *International Journal of Management Reviews, 15*(1), 1–14. doi:10.1111/j.1468-2370.2011.00328.x

Sanyal, U., & Pal, D. (2017). Effect of organizational culture in environmental awareness on pro-environmental behaviour at workplace: A new perspective on organizational sustainability. *International Journal of Commerce and Management Research*, 60-65.

Schluep, M., & Wasswa, J. (2012). *e-Waste assessment in Uganda: A situational analysis of e-waste management and generation with special emphasis on personal computers.* Kampala Uganda Clean Prod Cent.

Schwab, K. (2015). The Fourth Industrial Revolution. What it means and how to respond. *Foreign Affairs.* Retrieved May 15, 2018, from, https://www.foreignaffairs.com/articles/2015-12-12/fourth-industrial-revolution

Singh, M., Brueckner, M., & Padhy, P. K. (2015). Environmental management system ISO 14001: Effective waste minimisation in small and medium enterprises in India. *Journal of Cleaner Production, 102*, 285–301. doi:10.1016/j.jclepro.2015.04.028

Song, Q., Li, J., & Zeng, X. (2015). Minimizing the increasing solid waste through zero waste strategy. *Journal of Cleaner Production, 104*, 199–210. doi:10.1016/j.jclepro.2014.08.027

Sthiannopkao, S., & Wong, M. H. (2013). Handling of e-waste in developed and developing countries: Initiatives, practices and consequences. *The Science of the Total Environment, 463-464*, 1147–1153. doi:10.1016/j.scitotenv.2012.06.088 PMID:22858354

Testa, F., Rizzi, F., Daddi, T., Gusmerotti, N. M., Frey, M., & Iraldo, F. (2014). EMAS and ISO 14001: The differences in effectively improving environmental performance. *Journal of Cleaner Production, 68*, 165–173. doi:10.1016/j.jclepro.2013.12.061

Uecker-Mercado, H., & Walker, M. (2012). The value of environmental social responsibility to facility managers: Revealing the perceptions and motives for adopting ESR. *Journal of Business Ethics, 110*(3), 269–284. doi:10.100710551-011-1153-x

UN-Habitat. (2014). *Urbanisation Challenges, Waste Management and Development.* Note prepared for the regional meeting of the ACP-EC Joint Parliamentary Assembly, Mauritius. Retrieved May 15, 2018 from, http://www. europarl.europa.eu/intcoop/ acp/2014_mauritius/pdf/ un_habitat_presentation_en.pdf

United Nations Environment Programme. (2016). *Guidelines for framework legislation for integrated waste management.* United Nations Environment Programme. Retrieved from http://wedocs. unep.org/handle/20.500.11822/22098

United Nations Environmental Programme (UNEP). (2018). *Africa Waste Management Outlook.* United Nations Environment Programme.

Valmohammadi, C., & Roshanzamir, S. (2015). The guidelines of improvement: Relations among organizational culture, TQM and performance. *International Journal of Production Economics, 164*, 167–178. doi:10.1016/j.ijpe.2014.12.028

Watson, K., Klingenberg, B., Polito, T., & Geurts, T. G. (2004). Impact of environmental management system implementation on financial performance: A comparison of two corporate strategies. *Management of Environmental Quality, 15*(6), 622–628. doi:10.1108/14777830410560700

Wicks, J. (2017). *Landfill bosses criminally charged over smelly KZN dump.* Retrieved May 11, 2018, from https://www.timeslive.co.za/news/south-africa/2017-08-17-landfill-bosses-criminally-charged-over-smelly-kzn-dump/

Wiengarten, F., & Pagell, M. (2012). The importance of quality management for the success of environmental management initiatives. *International Journal of Production Economics, 140*(1), 407–415. doi:10.1016/j.ijpe.2012.06.024

World Bank. (2017). *What a Waste: A Global Review of Solid Waste Management.* Retrieved May 15, 2018, from, http://web.worldbank.org/WBSITE/EXTERNAL/ TOPICS/EXTURBANDEVELOPMENT/0%2C%2CcontentMDK%3A23172887~ pagePK%3A210058~piPK%3A210062~theSitePK%3A337178%2C00.html

Young, W., Davis, M., Mcneill, I. M., Malhotra, B., Russell, S., Unsworth, K., & Clegg, C. W. (2015). Changing behaviour: Successful environmental programmes in the workplace. *Business Strategy and the Environment, 24*(8), 689–703. doi:10.1002/ bse.1836

Zero Waste Scotland. (2018). *Our Role in the Circular Economy.* Retrieved May 15, 2018, from, https://www.zerowastescotland.org.uk/circular-economy/our-role

Zsóka, Á. N. (2007). The role of organisational culture in the environmental awareness of companies. *Journal for East European Management Studies*, *12*(2), 109–131. doi:10.5771/0949-6181-2007-2-109

ADDITIONAL READING

Couth, R., & Trois, C. (2012). Cost effective waste management through composting in Africa. *Waste Management (New York, N.Y.)*, *32*(12), 2518–2525. doi:10.1016/j.wasman.2012.05.042 PMID:22857939

FAO. (2017). *Prevention and Disposal of Obsolete Pesticides.* Retrieved May 18, 2018, from http://www.fao.org/agriculture/crops/obsolete-pesticides/why-problem/en/

Kadafa, A., Manaf, L., & Sulaiman, W. (2014). Applications of system analysis techniques in Solid Waste Management assessment. *Polish Journal of Environmental Studies*, 1061–1070.

Mott, R. M. (2016). Improving industrial waste management in Africa. *Journal of Sustainable Development in Africa*, *18*(4), 1520–5509.

Mpofu, T. P. Z. (2013). Urbanization and urban environmental challenges in Sub-Saharan Africa. *Research Journal of Agricultural and Environmental Management*, *2*(6), 127–134.

Udofia, E. A., & Nriagu, J. (2013). Health Care Waste in Africa: A Silent Crises? *Global Health Perspect*, *1*(1), 3–10. doi:10.5645/ghp2013.01.01.02

Xinhua. (2017). *Sub-Saharan Africa's first waste to energy facility to be commissioned in July.* Retrieved May 18, 2018, from http://newsxinhuanet.com/english/2017-05/13/c_136278070.htm

KEY TERMS AND DEFINITIONS

E-Waste: Electronic devices meant for reuse, resale, salvage, recycling, or disposal.

Environmental Management: Technical and organizational activities aimed at reducing environmental impact caused by an organizations business operation.

Environmental Performance: Demonstrates a methodology to ascertain the effectiveness of the environmental initiatives an organization puts in place to mitigate and protect the environment.

Responsibility Management: Finding the right equilibrium to suit the interests of the entire world to enhance welfare.

Waste Management: Activities required to manage waste or garbage from its start to its final disposal.

Chapter 12
Factors Inhibiting Green Supply Chain Management Initiatives in a South African Pharmaceutical Supply Chain

Aveshin Reddy
University of KwaZulu-Natal, South Africa

Micheline Juliana Naude
University of KwaZulu-Natal, South Africa

ABSTRACT

The Fourth Industrial Revolution and increased environmental awareness is forcing business leaders to adapt to the changing environment in functional areas such as the supply chain. This chapter focuses on the role of green supply chain management in achieving a sustainable competitive advantage, exploring the factors that affect green supply chain management initiatives at a leading pharmaceutical manufacturer in Durban. The study used a descriptive and exploratory case study approach in which in-depth interviews were conducted with 10 participants. Content analysis was used to analyze the collected data. The findings of the study reveal that the main factors affecting green supply chain management initiatives include high costs, lack of government support, and pressure to reduce selling prices. Since a limited number of studies have been conducted on this topic, the findings and recommendations of this work contribute to the existing body of research knowledge.

DOI: 10.4018/978-1-5225-7638-9.ch012

Copyright © 2019, IGI Global. Copying or distributing in print or electronic forms without written permission of IGI Global is prohibited.

INTRODUCTION AND BACKGROUND

The Fourth Industrial Revolution has the potential to increase global income levels and improve the quality of life for people. The technologies that underpin the Fourth Industrial Revolution, also known as Industry 4.0, are the internet of things, artificial intelligence, robotics, and the smart factory (Fields & Atiku, 2018). These technologies have created opportunities for businesses to improve efficiencies in the production environment and the supply chain in general by contributing to an improved usage of time, materials, and other resources. These are fundamental to supply chain sustainability and the greening of the supply chain (Duarte & Cruz-Machado, 2017).

The mushrooming of the Fourth Industrial Revolution and of technical innovation will have a significant impact on the supply-side, sustainability, and environmental issues, with long-term gains in efficiency and productivity (Szegedi, Gabriel, & Papp, 2017). Shifts will also occur on the demand-side as growing transparency, consumer engagement, better-informed consumers, and new patterns of consumer behavior will force businesses to change the way they design, market, and deliver products and services (Schwab, 2015). Consequently, business leaders need to understand the changing environment and continuously to innovate. Areas of change include environmental issues, which are amplified by the public's environmental awareness and knowledge of resource depletion. This has already resulted in regulators at various levels implementing stricter regulations (Zhu, Geng, Fujita, & Hashimoto, 2010).

Sustainability and environmental issues are prevalent in supply chains, particularly those which function in highly competitive industries. Supply chain management (SCM) is an important component of a business (Monczka, Handfield, Giunipero, & Patterson, 2016). It affects competitiveness, the way the business operates, how it procures its materials, and how it disposes of its waste (Fawcett, Ellram, & Ogden, 2014). SCM consists of core business processes such as procurement, operations management, logistics, and reverse logistics (Monczka et al., 2016). These processes may negatively impact on the environment, leading to the diminishing of natural resources, problems with air emissions and waste disposal, and increases in natural disasters. This has led to increasing pressure from various stakeholders to improve businesses environmental sustainability (Zhu, Sarkis, & Lai, 2007). In turn, businesses recognise that environmental management is a key strategic issue with the potential to achieve sustainable organisational performance (Diabat & Govindan, 2011). Consequently, the deterioration of the environment and pressure from stakeholders has led businesses to look to their supply chain department to assist in creating a sustainable method of operating (Griskevicius, Tybur, & Van den Bergh, 2010). This has given rise to a supply chain initiative known as green supply chain management (GSCM). It is an approach which seeks to improve the performance of processes and products in line with the requirements of environmental regulations (Luthra, Kumar, Kumar, & Haleen, 2011).

GSCM is adopted by many businesses as a means to improve their environmental performance (Testa & Iraldo, 2010) and to mitigate risks that could arise from toxic materials in a supplier's end product, poor working conditions in a low-cost country, or similar challenges (Hallikas & Lintukangas, 2016). However, many businesses adopt GSCM not only for creating sustainability but also to improve their economic standing (Zhu et al., 2010). Regardless of the reason for implementing GSCM, it is becoming an area of focus for many businesses (Dashore & Sohani, 2013). Therefore, it is important to identify the factors affecting GSCM initiatives in order to improve adoption. South Africa has strong logistics capabilities and currently produces 1% of the world's annual carbon emission output (Pillay & Mbhele, 2015). As far back as 1993, the transport sector was identified as being a large contributor to carbon emissions pollution (Underwood, 1993). Consequently, the South African government has shown an increasing interest in GSCM initiatives in order to keep in line with global trends. It has promoted the efficient and effective use of resources within industries such as the construction sector (Ojo, Mbohwa, & Akinlabi, 2013).

In response to international frameworks on environmental sustainability, the South African government has adopted the National Framework for Sustainable Development (Department of Environmental Affairs, 2008). The purpose is to express the national vision for sustainable development and indicate strategic interventions to re-orientate South Africa's development path in a more sustainable manner. Woolworths, Volkswagen, Standard Bank, Pikitup and Imperial Logistics are some of the businesses within the South African private sector that have taken the initiative to implement GSCM in order to improve sustainability (Van Rensburg, 2015).

Pharmaceutical supply chains are amongst some of the costliest and most complex as the industry is continuously evolving (Faisal, 2015). The industry is known to produce high levels of pollution, particularly on the production side with the production of waste by-products (Narayana, Elias, & Pati, 2014). This production waste is difficult to recycle and dispose of because of the nature of pharmaceutical products (Narayana et al., 2014). This means that GSCM initiatives are difficult to implement and maintain in this industry.

Against this background, the aim of this study was to:

1. Identify external and internal factors affecting GSCM initiatives in a pharmaceutical supply chain at a leading pharmaceutical manufacturer in Durban, South Africa.
2. Provide insight into the measures this manufacturer has in place to improve the adoption of GSCM initiatives in their planning, procurement and logistics departments.

Studies that identify the external and internal factors affecting GSCM initiatives within the South African pharmaceutical manufacturing industry are limited. Therefore, the findings and recommendations of this study contribute to the existing body of knowledge by providing new insights in the field of GSCM. Moreover, the implementation of the proposed recommendations could assist other pharmaceutical manufacturers to improve the adoption of GSCM initiatives. This would enable them to contribute positively towards the sustainability of the natural environment.

The chapter consists of five parts. The first part provides the introduction and background to this study. Next is a review of theory relevant to the research, followed by an explanation of the research methodology. The fourth part presents the results and the findings and explanation thereof, and the chapter concludes with recommendations and concluding remarks.

THEORETICAL REVIEW

The theoretical review provides a brief insight into the South African pharmaceutical industry, GSCM initiatives and the factors affecting GSCM initiatives.

The South African Pharmaceutical Industry

The pharmaceutical industry is a high-risk but high-profit generating industry (Angell, 2004). In South Africa, it plays a key role in society as it supplies high-demand medication to combat epidemics such as tuberculosis, the Human Immunodeficiency Virus, and the Acquired Immune Deficiency Syndrome. With a total revenue in the 2008/2009 financial year of 36.1 billion rand, the industry contributed 1.58% of South Africa's total GDP (Health24, 2013). The South African health care industry is split into the private and public sector. It is estimated that 16% of South Africa's population receives health care from the private sector, with the remaining 84% using public sector services (Minnie, 2015). South Africans spend approximately 1.9% of their household expenditure on pharmaceutical and medical products Health24, 2013). Pharmaceutical companies cater for the needs of both the public and private sector.

Green Supply Chain Management

GSCM has emerged as an important practice for global businesses that are aiming to achieve sustainable profitability and increased market share by improving their environmental performance (Kumar & Chandrakar, 2012; Testa & Iraldo, 2010; Zhu, Sarkis, & Lai, 2008). Diminishing resources, increases in natural disasters, and carbon emissions that arise from supply chain activities give rise to environmental problems. Acid rain and global warming are just two of the factors that have forced businesses to examine the need to improve their environmental sustainability (Kumar & Chandrakar, 2012; Zhu et al., 2007). The motivation for such businesses to adopt GSCM may be ethical and/or commercial. Despite the growing implementation of GSCM and its benefits, many factors still hinder the adoption of GSCM initiatives by businesses (Testa & Iraldo, 2010).

The term "going green" means to incorporate environmentally friendly practices into a business function. The aim is to improve the sustainability of the environment through practices that have a reduced negative effect on climate and the environment as a whole (Kumar & Chandrakar, 2012). Going green can be viewed as a strategic shift for an organisation to improve pollution control and/or avoid pollution (Griskevicius et al., 2010). Going green can also be defined as the development of environmentally friendly products, services, and business processes that reduce a business's overall negative impact on the environment (Green, Zelbst, Meacham, & Bhadauria, 2012).

The concept of GSCM appeared in the late 1990s. It involves the monitoring of environmental management programmes and the incorporation of green practices such as the recycling, remanufacturing and reverse logistics, as well as other green innovations within a business's supply chain (Dhull & Narwal, 2016; Mugabe, 2013). GSCM involves a set of environmental initiatives that enforce the improvement of environmental practices between businesses operating within the same supply chain. In order to reduce challenges facing the environment such as pollution reduction and energy conservation, successful greening of the supply chain depends on the balancing of marketing performance with environmental issues (Kumar & Chandrakar, 2012). Darnall, Jolley and Handfield (2008) posit that GSCM extends throughout the value chain from the supplier to the buyer. It begins at the product design phase, extending to the end of the useful life of the product and finally to the product disposal or recycling phase. Thus, it takes into consideration the environmental impact at each step of the supply chain (Dhull & Narwal, 2016; Kumar & Chandrakar, 2012).

Green Supply Chain Management Initiatives

Some of the most common GSCM initiatives are (1) green purchasing, (2) green production, (3) reverse logistics, (4) green transportation and distribution and (5) green packaging (Attar, Gilaninia, & Homayounfar, 2016). These initiatives are explained below:

Green Procurement

Appolloni, Sun, Jia and Li (2014, p. 3) define green procurement as "the set of purchasing policies, relationships and actions taken in response to environmental concerns". In short, green procurement can be described as a procurement practice that includes environmental considerations (Green et al., 2012). One of the most common types of green procurement is the buying of eco-labelled and environmentally friendly products and materials, as the negative impact of these products on the environment is lower than that of standard products. According to Welter (2012), green procurement affects two key aspects in a pharmaceutical company, namely, (1) corporate social responsibility, and (2) the carbon footprint of pharmaceutical products.

- **Corporate Social Responsibility (CSR):** Is a business's social responsibility to give back to the community and environment, to maintain human rights, and to treat its employees fairly and equitably (Servaes & Tamayo, 2013). A CSR programme entails a business giving some of its resources to reduce some social or environmental impact (Isaksson, Kiessling, & Harvey, 2014). Even though CSR does not generate a profit, it has benefits such as improving public image of a business (Isaksson et al., 2014).
- **The Carbon Footprint**: Is the quantity of carbon emissions that is produced throughout the lifecycle of the product (Trappey, Trappey, Hsiao, Ou, & Chang, 2012). The carbon footprint concept was developed to measure the impact that a product, service or business has on climate change (Scipioni, Manzardo, Mazzi & Mastrobuono, 2012).

Green Production

Green production is production that incorporates environmental sustainability and reduces the impact that the manufacture of the product has on the environment (Sheldon, 2014). Within the pharmaceutical industry, there are two commonly used methods that are used to ensure green production, namely, (1) the use of green technology, and (2) green chemistry (Boltic et al., 2013; Sheldon, 2014).

- Green technology is the use of technology to reduce the pollution that is generally created through production (Boltic et al., 2013). The aim of this technology is to improve the efficiency of production whilst using fewer resources, reducing greenhouse gas emissions, and minimising the degradation of the environment (Ng, Yew, Basiron, & Sundram, 2011).

- Green chemistry is the efficient use of raw materials, preferably renewable materials, the elimination of waste, and the avoidance of hazardous solvents and reagents in the manufacturing of chemical products (Sheldon, 2014).

Reverse Logistics

Reverse logistics is the reverse flow of waste and products back into a business for reuse or disposal (Ivona, Novačko, & Ogrizović, 2014). Reverse logistics is the aspect of logistics that deals with product returns, recycling, waste disposal, re-use of materials, remanufacturing, and repair (Wright, Richey, Tokman, & Palmer, 2011). Pharmaceutical manufacturers generally produce high value chemicals that require effective reverse logistics management, particularly when expired and recalled stock is involved (Narayana et al., 2014). This is because the chemicals used in medication are destructive to the environment if they are exposed to water systems, such as rivers (Jones, Voulvoulis, & Lester, 2001). Since the pharmaceutical industry has a high waste to product ratio, it requires efficient reverse logistics systems that can be used to minimise or mitigate the damage done to the environment by the disposal of waste and expired medicines (Narayana et al., 2014).

Green Transport and Distribution

Green transport and distribution is the use of environmentally friendly transportation or transportation that has a reduced impact on the environment rather than standard transport methods (Ubeda, Arcelus, & Faulin, 2011). An example is the movement towards environmentally friendly fuels and other more efficient methods of transport (Demir, Bektaş, & Laporte, 2014). Green transportation and distribution reduces the overall carbon footprint of a business and a product and improves its environmental performance (Zhang, Methipara, & Lu, 2011).

Green Packaging

Green packaging is important in any green strategy as packaging is one of the main causes of land pollution (Zsidisin & Siferd, 2001). Kümmerer (2010) identifies the following methods that can be used to implement green packaging initiatives:

- Resource reduction strategies entail the use of less packaging per product and thereby reduces the amount of resources used and the pollution caused by their disposal (Zsidisin & Siferd, 2001).

- Recycling of packaging that has been used and is to be disposed of together with the packaging waste generated during production reduces pollution (Zsidisin & Siferd, 2001).

Green packaging in the pharmaceutical industry is critical as pharmaceutical products are highly sensitive and can be compromised by environmental factors such as heat and micro-organisms (Kümmerer, 2010).

Key Factors That Affect Green Supply Chain Management Initiatives

In order to implement and maintain GSCM within a business, it is key that the factors that affect GSCM initiatives are identified (Dhull & Narwal, 2016). These factors can be categorised into external and internal factors. External factors can be defined as those that operate in the macro environment and internal factors as those that operate within the micro environment.

External Factors

Government and Policy Regulation

Globally, policy regulations and laws have been implemented by governments to address factors that have contributed to pollution (Kumar & Chandrakar, 2012) and ultimately the degradation of the environment (Lee & Klassen, 2008, p. 575). These problems have led to climate change, irregular weather patterns, and water scarcity. The aim of policy regulations and laws is to minimise these negative impacts (Kumar & Chandrakar, 2012)

Government and policy regulations impact on GSCM initiatives as they force businesses to meet government targets and, if they do not, in many cases they are penalised (Lee & Klassen, 2008). Diabat and Govindan (2011) stress that in the area of environmental sustainability, most businesses will not spend more than is required to maximise their economic goals Therefore, a lack of government and policy regulations negatively affects GSCM initiatives (Khiewnavawongsa & Schmidt, 2013). Government and policy regulations also impact significantly on the reverse logistics component of a business's supply chain as the disposal and reuse of products after its life cycle is monitored (Sheu, Chou, & Hu, 2005). In other words, because of policy regulations, sustainability becomes a matter of law rather than of choice (Diabat & Govindan, 2011; Lee & Klassen, 2008).

Inbound Logistics

Wu and Dunn (1995) define inbound logistics as the upstream activities linked to the receiving and storage of goods within a business. Inbound logistics include activities such as supplier management, inventory management, and green purchasing (Sellitto, Bittencourt, & Reckziegel, 2015). These activities are dependent on external factors that fall outside of the authority of the business and are focussed on the inwards movement of goods and services into the business (Kumar & Chandrakar, 2012). However, a business can adopt methods to influence upstream factors. Some of these methods include:

- Making it a requirement that all suppliers are ISO14001 accredited (Kumar & Chandrakar, 2012).
- Conducting audits of suppliers' environmental processes (Kumar & Chandrakar, 2012).
- Coordinating and incorporating suppliers into the environmental initiatives of a business, such as GSCM (Kamal & Fernando, 2015).
- Ensuring that the design specifications for products purchased include environmental requirements and standards (Dhull & Narwal, 2016).

Outbound Logistics

Huynh (2013) defines outbound logistics as the downstream movement of the finished goods from the business to the point of its consumption. Outbound logistics includes activities such as the physical distribution of finished goods and some components of marketing (Kumar & Chandrakar, 2012). Outbound logistics is an important downstream factor, which impacts on GSCM initiatives as the activities of logistics produce significant amounts of carbon dioxide (Huynh, 2013).

Competitors

While consumers are becoming more and more sensitive to environmental issues, price sensitivity is also a key factor (Kumar & Chandrakar, 2012). Consequently, globally many businesses focus on improving their environmental performance in order to gain a competitive advantage over their competitors (Diabat & Govindan, 2011). However, other competitors focus only on cost reduction and the production of cheaper products, which makes it difficult for those businesses that focus on environmental initiatives to compete (Dhull & Narwal, 2016). This means that cost pressures from competitors' pricing can deter some businesses from adopting GSCM initiatives.

Suppliers

Suppliers may impact on the GSCM initiatives of a business. For this reason, suppliers should be environmentally compliant by owning and administering a certified environmental management system (Diabat & Govindan, 2011). For example, if suppliers are environmentally compliant, a business can implement green procurement (Zhu, Sarkis & Lai, 2005). Green procurement is a term used to identify the purchasing of goods from environmentally responsible sources (Walker & Brammer, 2009, p. 128). Such policies and practices would mean that businesses could provide design specifications to suppliers in order for these suppliers to build sustainability into their products (Zhu et al., 2005). However, suppliers could oppose environmental collaboration, and this misalignment of goals would be detrimental to GSCM initiatives (Diabat & Govindan, 2011).

Social Responsibility

Various businesses such as Hewlett-Packard posit that it is necessary to give back to the community and society through creating social responsibility programmes (Darnall et al., 2008). A social responsibility focus may drive GSCM initiatives, as businesses tend to focus on what is most important in their community. Conversely, GSCM initiatives may not be a focus area in some communities (Van Rensburg, 2015).

Internal Factors

Management Support and Commitment

The commitment and support of management is a crucial factor in the adoption of any new GSCM initiatives (Lee & Klassen, 2008). Such support and commitment, or the lack thereof, can have a positive or negative effect on the GSCM initiatives (Kumar & Chandrakar, 2012). Support and commitment from management will motivate employees and thus align business goals with sustainable initiatives (Dhull & Narwal, 2016). A lack of management support, on the other hand, is likely to cause employees to be disinterested or apathetic and result in GSCM initiatives failing at the initial stage of introduction (Kumar & Chandrakar, 2012). Figure 1 illustrates the importance of the support and commitment of management when implementing new initiatives.

The commitment and support of top management (Figure 1) is vital for the successful implementation of all new initiatives, and particularly for GSCM initiatives (Diabat & Govindan, 2011). Further, as GSCM initiatives affect the business as a whole, the support of middle management is also vital.

Figure 1. The impact of management commitment on new initiatives
Source: Kumar and Chandrakar (2012, p. 4)

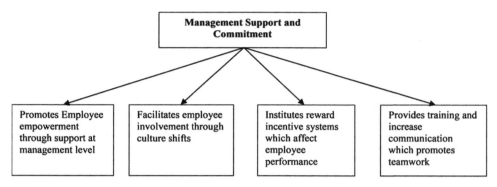

Organisational Structure and Strategy

Organisational structure and strategy can be a positive or negative factor impacting on GSCM initiatives. The ability of a business' strategy to achieve its goals and objectives is dependent on a business's capability (Lee & Klassen, 2008). If strategies are put in place to take a proactive stand to sustainability, they will have a positive impact on GSCM initiatives (Lee & Klassen, 2008). The overall organisational structure of businesses can also impact on GSCM initiatives as it will determine whether GSCM initiatives are viable or not (Zhu et al., 2005). However, as the carbon footprint of some businesses is very small they cannot use GSCM initiatives (Lee & Klassen, 2009).

Organisational Learning

Organisational learning can be defined as the developed capabilities and intelligence that a business and its employees develop over time (Wood & Reynolds, 2013). While the successful implementation of a business's strategies, including sustainable initiatives, are dependent on effective deployment, development and maintenance of capabilities and resources take time (Wood & Reynolds, 2013). Organisational learning is important for continuous improvement of initiatives and better use of business resources (Dalkir, 2005). As a result, organisational learning can be used as a tool to facilitate initiatives such as Environmental Systems Management, ISO 14001, and GSCM initiatives. Organisational learning assists businesses to develop new routines and processes and helps them to identify inefficiencies in current processes and to eliminate these inefficiencies through improved processes (Kumar & Chandrakar, 2012).

Eco-Design

The initial focus of eco-design was on improving a business's products and processes so as to reduce environmental costs. Today, eco-design involves factors outside of the direct control of a business such as relationships with suppliers, recyclers, and consumers (Green et al., 2012). Kumar and Chandrakar (2012) observe that, for eco-design to be successful, there must be good internal cross-functional cooperation between business units and the external partners that form the supply chain. As proof of this, we know that the Environmental Protection Agency in the U.S and Chinese businesses use eco-design as a core aspect of their environmental sustainability initiatives (Kumar & Chandrakar, 2012; Zhu et al., 2005).

Investment Recovery

Investment recovery from a sustainability viewpoint can be defined as a business's strategic use of recycling, reverse logistics, and redeployment to gain greater value from its inputs (Kumar & Chandrakar, 2012). The aim of investment recovery is to convert assets, such as obsolete assets, excess materials, waste, and by-products, into income for the business (Zhu et al., 2005; Zsidisin & Siferd, 2001). Investment recovery can be achieved through the sale of obsolete assets, redeploying unused assets to other corporate locations, and making better use of storage space (Kumar & Chandrakar, 2012). Investment recovery is also an essential component of reverse logistics – recycling, re-use, reduced use, and remanufacturing – a key aspect of GSCM (Green et al., 2012; Narayana et al., 2014).

Cost

Cost is one of the factors that affects GSCM initiatives (Lee & Klassen, 2008). GSCM initiatives can increase or decrease the cost structure of a business (Diabat & Govindan, 2011). For example, some businesses are concerned about the financial implications of GSCM initiatives as these may reduce their bottom line. Thus, cost implications can be a deterrent to the implementation of GSCM initiatives (Khiewnavawongsa & Schmidt, 2013). Such implications would include aspects such as product cost price, raw material cost price, and investment cost. It must be noted that environmentally friendly goods and packaging are often costlier. In addition, other determinants that impact on the costs of operations and the cost of investment come about through changes in the operation, training costs, and the redesigning of processes. On the other hand, businesses can reduce costs through reducing waste fees, reducing government regulatory costs, and reducing energy consumption (Zhu et al., 2005).

Reverse Logistics

Reverse logistics is a key factor in GSCM as it closes the "loop" at the end of a product's lifecycle (Zhu et al, 2008). Reverse logistics can be defined as the disposal and recovery of raw materials, work-in-process, final products, and information (Jumadi & Zailani, 2010). Reverse logistics is essential for processes such as recycling, refurbishing, reducing, re-using, and remanufacturing (Choudhary & Seth, 2011). However, as logistics is a costly function, many businesses chose to outsource this function (Jumadi & Zailani, 2010). In the pharmaceutical industry, one of the main environmental hazards is the waste from production and consumption, and thus reverse logistics plays a crucial role by eliminating waste (Narayana et al., 2014).

Figure 2 summarises the factors that affect GSCM initiatives. These factors form the foundation that guided this study and were used to identify the key factors that affect GSCM initiatives at Pharma X.

The list of factors presented in figure 2 is not exhaustive. For example, factors affecting GSCM initiatives at pharmaceutical companies can change, depending on many variables such as geographic location and the current and future state of the economy (Rossetti, Handfield, & Dooley, 2011).

RESEARCH METHODOLOGY

A single case study approach for this study was adopted in order to identify the factors that inhibit GSCM initiatives in a pharmaceutical supply chain at a leading pharmaceutical manufacturer (hereinafter referred to as Pharma X). Pharma X is located in Durban, South Africa. Furthermore, the study provides insight into the measures this manufacturer has in place to improve the adoption of these initiatives in their planning, procurement and logistics department. Case-study research is descriptive and exploratory and represents the perspective views of participants about

Figure 2. Factors affecting GSCM initiatives
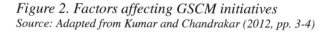
Source: Adapted from Kumar and Chandrakar (2012, pp. 3-4)

a specific object, individuals, or particular situations (Saunders, Lewis & Thornhill, 2016; Yin, 2014). This approach is appropriate in order to provide a deeper insight into the business as well as to identify the factors that Pharma X experiences in expediting their GSCM initiatives. However, as stated by Yin (2014), causal links in case-study research are often difficult to test, and generalisations cannot always be made from single case studies.

The target population for this study was the SCM staff at the Pharma X Durban branch. The Durban branch was selected as the study site as it is one of the key manufacturing pharmaceutical plants in South Africa. A non-probability purposive judgement sampling technique was used to select the participants, who are supply chain staff members from three departments, namely planning, procurement, and logistics. Nine staff members across the three operational areas participated in the study. Table 1 presents the breakdown of the participants.

During the course of the study, Guba's model of trustworthiness, namely credibility, dependability, transferability, and conformability were maintained. Credibility was achieved as the purposive sample included only individuals with expert knowledge, who could contribute meaningful information to the study. Dependability ensures that the study is reliable, and credibility cannot be achieved without dependability (Polit & Beck, 2008:539). To ensure dependability, the mixed approach was followed in that data was collected from various secondary data sources and through conducting interviews with participants. Transferability was achieved with detailed descriptions of the research design, implementation, and data-collection process.

The interviews were conducted by one of the authors of this chapter, using a semi-structured interview guide. The interview guide consisted of open-ended questions and was pre-tested to ensure that the questions were clear and unambiguous. The participants were given the opportunity to ask questions and seek clarity before responding. Therefore, consistency and accuracy were maintained during the interviews, which contributed to the trustworthiness of the results of the study.

In order to ensure reliability, the interviews were recorded by means of handwritten notes and by audio recording. Permission to use a voice recorder was granted by the participants. The recordings were transcribed with the assistance of a Windows

Table 1. List of participants included in this study

Department	Number of Participants
Planning	1
Procurement	5
Logistics	3
Total	**9**

programme known as "Listen N Write" and then checked against the voice recordings for accuracy, with any transcription errors being corrected.

The qualitative data was analysed using content analysis. Content analysis consists of identifying themes and key words in the recording of the interview (Saunders et al, 2016). It is used to "see the meaning" in data obtained from verbal dialogue, visual depictions, and written documents (Krippendorf, 2012). The transcribed data was categorised according to the relevant departments, that is planning, procurement, and logistics, and were then reviewed to identify key words, concepts, sentences, and related themes.

RESULTS AND EXPLANATION OF THE FINDINGS

The results and explanation of the findings are presented according to the purpose and objectives of this study, which are to identify the factors that inhibit GSCM initiatives in a pharmaceutical supply chain at Pharma X and to provide insight into the measures PharmaX has in place to improve the adoption of the GSCM initiatives in their planning, procurement, and logistics department.

Profile of Respondents

Table 2 presents the profile of the participants who took part in this study.

Table 2. Profile of the participants

Participant (N=9)	Position	Department	Years in company	Highest level of education	Number of employees in department
Participant 1	Buyer	Procurement	11	Matric	5
Participant 2	Team Leader	Warehouse	1	Diploma	23
Participant 3	Team Leader	Warehouse and planning	1	Undergraduate Degree	23
Participant 4	Senior Buyer	Procurement	4	Diploma	5
Participant 5	Buyer	Procurement	7	Matric	5
Participant 6	Junior Buyer	Procurement	2	Undergraduate Degree	5
Participant 7	Warehouse Manager	Warehouse	5	Diploma	22
Participant 8	Buyer	Procurement	10	Diploma	7
Participant 9	Team Leader	Warehouse	12	Matric	23

Factors Affecting GSCM Initiatives at Pharma X

This section presents the factors that affect GSCM initiatives at Pharma X. The results are tabulated in Table 3. Only the factors that inhibit GSCM initiatives at Pharma X are dealt with.

External Factors

Government Legislation

From Table 3, it is clear that all participants indicated that government legislation has impacted on GSCM initiatives at Pharma X. Seven of the participants noted that government legislation has a positive effect on GSCM, whereas three participants believed that it had a negative effect. One participant stated that it has both a positive and negative effect on GSCM, noting that a lack of government legislation relative

Table 3. Factors affecting GSCM initiatives at Pharma X

	Factors	Yes N=9	How factors affect Pharma X*	
			Positive	Negative
	External Factors			
1.	Government legislation	9	7	3
2.	Logistics	3	2	-
3.	Competition	1	1	-
4.	Social	1	1	-
	Internal Factors			
1.	Cost	9	7	5
2..	Organisational structure and strategy	8	7	1
3.	Management support and commitment	7	7	-
4.	Investment recovery	5	5	2
5.	Organisational learning	2	2	-
6.	Reverse logistics	1	-	1
	Other Factors			
1.	Lack of manpower	1	-	1
2.	Lack of awareness	1	-	1

* The frequencies do not equal the number of participants (n) due to multiple responses being possible from each participant.

to green initiatives would negatively impact on GSCM initiatives. The participants stated:

It has a positive impact because it forces all companies to implement green into their company. Pharma X does a lot of green things, but other companies aren't like that. So, it's essential, I think. (Participant 2)

It has a positive effect on us because it gives us guidelines to GSCM. Without it we would have to define our own ways to go green things like that. (Participant 1)

Negative effect because of the lack of government encouragement and policy on green initiatives. Also, the actual policing of those things, so whether we have the policy and the legislation in place, how do we police it effectively and ensure that people are actually following it. We should have professionals that are in those positions not just anybody, understand the policy and legislation and they must know each company's impact on it. They must be able to enforce those rules and regulations, not just having that on paper. (Participant 7)

These statements are in line with the comments made by Dhull and Narwal (2016), Diabat and Govindan (2011), and Khiewnavawongsa and Schmidt (2013), namely, that government regulations have a considerable impact on GSCM initiatives. These authors are of the opinion that a lack of government regulation would negatively impact on GSCM initiatives, as it is a key driver of GSCM initiatives.

Internal Factors

Cost

All participants identified cost as factor that affects GSCM initiatives at Pharma X. The findings revealed that cost can have either a positive or negative affect on GSCM initiatives. The participants stated:

It will affect prices, but I mean if it's expensive it will be negative. If it saves money it will be positive. So, it can be either. (Participant 3)

Yes, the company might implement it, if its cost is low. But if the cost is high, then they won't do it. So, cost is very important. (Participant 9)

It is definitely a big positive factor, we save money, so it drives us more towards green practices like GSCM. Without it, the only benefit would be saving the environment and it wouldn't be driven as much overall. (Participant 1)

These statements are in line with those by Diabat and Govindan (2011), Khiewnavawongsa and Schmidt (2013), Lee and Klassen (2008), and Zhu et al. (2005), who posit that GSCM initiatives can increase or decrease cost structure of a business. Businesses can also reduce costs through reducing waste fees, government regulation costs, and reduced energy consumption.

Organisation Structure and Strategy

Eight participants identified organisational structure and strategy as a factor affecting GSCM. Seven participants indicated that organisational structure and strategy have a positive impact, and one indicated that they have a negative impact on GSCM initiatives. The participants stated:

It does because we are always trying to improve green in the company like with Sean's idea, it comes from management support, so we focus on green where we can. So, it is positive overall. (Participant 1)

The structure will help us because you can communicate ideas to them. (Participant 9)

They do support it and it does have a positive effect overall. Pharma X will implement GSCM initiatives. (Participant 5)

Right now, if we look at Pharma X's organisational structure we have a Safety Health Environment Risk & Quality Manager in place, so there is a focus on that perspective and Pharma X, looks at basically Environment health and safety, from a very serious light and we don't joke about it. We are very serious about it and it's not just seen as just we meet every month and we have stats being presented, we look at it from the point of view as, so what can we always do better and that is always recorded, as what are we going to look at next. So, it has a positive effect on us. (Participant 7)

These responses are in line with observations by Lee and Klassen (2008) and Zhu et al. (2005) that organisational structure and strategy can be either a driver or an inhibitor of GSCM initiatives. In addition, the overall organisational structure of businesses can affect GSCM initiatives, as it will determine whether GSCM initiatives are viable or not.

Investment Recovery

Five participants indicated that investment recovery is a factor that affects GSCM. Whilst all participants identified it as a positive factor, one participant identified it as both a positive and negative factor. The participants stated:

I guess it affects green positively especially here because it helps us save money like with reduced waste so we get more recovery of investment, so it is positive. (Participant 2)

In our case I would say it has a positive effect because we get more for what we put in, like with using the bio-degradable board, we save money and we help the environment. (Participant 1)

For example, to increase our bay size will be beneficial because we can offload closer to the building and the hyster will require less movement and it uses a lot of diesel. But it will cost a lot and you can't see returns so it hasn't been implemented. (Participant 7)

These findings are in line with those by Green et al. (2012), Kumar and Chandrakar (2012), Narayana et al. (2014), and Zhu et al. (2005), who note that the strategic use of sustainability techniques (such as recycling, reverse logistics, and redeployment) allows for a business to recover its investment in these techniques by obtaining increased value from inputs such as materials and assets.

Reverse Logistics

One participant identified reverse logistics as a negative factor affecting GSCM at Pharma X. This participant remarked:

Overall it will save the company money because I mean you are recycling material and getting refunded in a way because it will help the bottom line and the environment. But in this business, it's negative, because the material can't be reused most of the time.

This aligns with comments made by Choudhary and Seth (2011), Jumadi and Zailani (2010), and Narayana et al. (2014:381), who note that while reverse logistics is essential for processes such as recycling, refurbishing, re-use, and remanufacturing, it can have a negative effect in the pharmaceutical industry. In the pharmaceutical industry, one of the main environmental hazards is the waste from production and consumption, which is difficult to recycle and reuse.

Other Factors Affecting GSCM at Pharma X

Two other factors were identified by the participants (Table 3) that were not listed as factors affecting GSCM initiatives in the interview guide. These two factors, identified by two participants (one each), are lack of manpower and lack of awareness.

Lack of Manpower

The participant who identified lack of manpower as a negative factor impacting on Pharma X's GSCM initiatives stated:

The other factor is time and the short hours we work – we run a 24-hour factory. We need more people. When the business expands it becomes more strenuous because we need more people, but none are given to us. So, we can't do too many initiatives.

Lack of Awareness

The participant who identified lack of awareness as a factor negatively impacting on Pharma X's GSCM initiatives stated:

I think awareness would be the most critical thing. Within the organisation I think they are, but remember we are not all working in an environment where we can sort of drive this thing, but getting people to come and drive it and sort of communicate it to everyone at the facility, I think that would give others that are not working in that particular environment more understanding and more sort of initiative to go with this concept.

Processes That Pharma X Has in Place to Improve the Adoption of the GSCM Initiatives

The findings in Table 3 reveal that there are more positive than negative factors affecting GSCM. The aim of this section was to present the processes Pharma X has in place to improve the adoption of GSCM initiatives. These are presented in Table 4.

From the results gathered from the participants (Table 4), it was found that only four participants stated that Pharma X has processes to improve the adoption of GSCM initiatives.

One participant remarked that Pharma X does not have processes in improve the adoption of the initiatives, whilst three were unsure whether they had such process.

I'm not sure though, I must be honest. (Participant 5)

Table 4. Process to improve the GSCM initiatives

Participant	Processes Pharma X has in place to overcome the factors that inhibit their GSCM initiatives
Participant 1	Not sure
Participant 2	Improving consolidation Reverse logistics
Participant 3	Not sure
Participant 4	Reduction of cost
Participant 5	Not sure
Participant 6	Reduction of cost
Participant 7	Policies and procedures as drivers of GSCM
Participant 8	Not sure
Participant 9	No

Not that I can see. (Participant 9)

No, I don't think we have any in place, as far as I know. (Participant 3)

However, other participants said:

Definitely, our policies and procedures are great drivers of consciousness when it comes to those things and doing it right always, and it is self-policed. Not right now I think whatever we've talked about, we've rolled out, but it doesn't stop us from thinking more, just that currently our focus is a bit different. (Participant 7)

Yes, definitely because as a buyer in the procurement department my objective is always to look for alternate suppliers who are cheaper and who are of the same quality of the materials so we can also mitigate that cost factor by looking for suppliers that can mitigate that cost factor and provide that same grade of materials, also by buying in bulk quantities we can reduce cost, so cost is not a problem in that area. And also, by negotiating with suppliers on a monthly basis to get best price out of them, without reducing the quality of the product. (Participant 6)

From the results, it can be concluded that the participants of this study are not sure whether Pharma X has procedures to improve the adoption of GSCM initiatives. That does not mean that the company does not have any in place but that the participants may not be aware of them.

RECOMMENDATIONS

It is recommended that Pharma X focus on improving their adoption of GSCM initiatives. Successful implementation of GSCM calls for collaboration between all stakeholders in the supply chain and the government.

- **Government Legislation:** This presents the regulations and rules set forth by the government sector to reduce environment degradation through the reduction of greenhouse gases and carbon emissions (Kumar & Chandrakar, 2012). Government should engage with industry to find ways of expediting GSCM projects, such as offering more incentives. The benefits of expediting GSCM for both government and industry would be reduced greenhouse gases, carbon emissions, reduced waste, reduced reliance on energy sources, lower production costs, and a sustainable South African industry sector.
- **Cost:** One way to reduce cost implications is through improving the initial design of the product, waste recycling, green manufacturing, and green logistics. For example, products should be designed to ensure reliability and durability and to be easy to assemble, distribute, and dispose of. Harmful processes in the manufacturing process should be eliminated, and the product must always meet customer requirements.
- **Environmental Technologies:** It is also recommended that environmental technologies are used. These green technologies consist of machinery that operates in the same way as normal machinery and is commonly used in the package printing industry, but which reduces carbon emissions (Vachon & Klassen, 2006).
- **Organisational Structure and Strategy:** These are key for the successful implementation of GSCM. Consequently, top management has to offer support and resources for efficient implementation. Kumar and Chandrakar (2012) posit that the use of dedicated champions is important in improving support and commitment in a business, since a lack of support and commitment at the initial stages is recognised as one of causes of failure of a business's GSCM initiatives. These champions can play a key role in an organisational cultural shift and can educate staff on the purpose and benefits of GSCM initiatives. This would deal with the lack of awareness factor.
- **Customers:** A study conducted by Griskevicius et al. (2010) found that the current generation of consumers prefer green products to normal products. Consequently, making consumers aware of green initiatives could improve the return on investment of a business, as it would impact on their buying preferences and loyalty.

LIMITATIONS AND RECOMMENDATIONS FOR FUTURE RESEARCH

This study is not without its limitations. These are as follows:

- The study is limited to three departments within Pharma X, and therefore results do not provide a holistic view of the entire organisation.
- The results cannot be generalised to other companies in the pharmaceutical industry as they are unique to Pharma X.

The true impact of the Fourth Industrial Revolution on sustainability and environmental issues will only be seen in the future (Szegedi et al., 2017). In the meantime, further and ongoing research will be required in GSCM. Possible areas for future research include the following:

- While this study was specific to Pharma X, future research could focus on identifying whether the factors identified in the study are prevalent throughout the pharmaceutical industry.
- It may be that the factors affecting GSCM initiatives vary between businesses. Hence future research could focus on improving the adoption of GSCM initiatives.
- Research could focus on the relationship between GSCM factors and the practices of the pharmaceutical industry.

CONCLUSION

The study identified factors that affect GSCM initiatives at Pharma X and the measures it has in place to improve the adoption of these initiatives in their planning, procurement, and logistics department. In addressing the objectives of this study, semi-structured interviews were carried out with nine participants at Pharma X. The interview guide consisted of open-ended questions that were formulated from the literature review. The literature review focused on two key areas that pertain to the study, firstly, GSCM and the pharmaceutical industry, and secondly, other essential information that laid the foundation for the study.

The study is qualitative and face-to-face semi-structured in-depth interviews were conducted to gather empirical data. This data was analysed, and the results were tabulated and presented. The findings identified various factors affecting GSCM initiatives such as high costs, lack of government support, and pressure to reduce selling prices at the company that was studied; processes used by the company to overcome these factors were also identified.

The value of this study is that, since a limited number of studies have been conducted on the factors affecting green supply chain management initiatives within the South African pharmaceutical sector, the findings and recommendations here contribute to the existing body of research knowledge by providing new insights in the field of GSCM. Through this study, the factors affecting GSCM initiatives at Pharma X have been identified as well as the procedures that have been put in place to overcome the negative factors. Managers should be aware of the pressure that drives companies to implement GSCM initiatives and what the factors are that affect such initiatives. Being better informed about these factors and making good decisions in determining GSCM initiatives will lead to better results and improve shareholder returns.

REFERENCES

Angell, M. (2004). Excess in the pharmaceutical industry. *Canadian Medical Association Journal*, *171*(12), 1451–1453. doi:10.1503/cmaj.1041594 PMID:15583183

Appolloni, A., Sun, H., Jia, F., & Li, X. (2014). Green procurement in the private sector: A state of the art review between 1996 and 2013. *Journal of Cleaner Production*, *85*, 122–133. doi:10.1016/j.jclepro.2014.08.106

Attar, M., Gilaninia, S., & Homayounfar, M. (2016). A study of the effect of green supply chain management's components on the performance of the pharmaceutical distribution companies system in Iran. *Arabian Journal of Business and Management Review*, *5*(8), 48–54.

Boltic, Z., Ruzic, N., Jovanovic, M., Savic, M., Jovanovic, J., & Petrovic, S. (2013). Cleaner production aspects of tablet coating process in pharmaceutical industry: Problem of VOCs emission. *Journal of Cleaner Production*, *44*(1), 123–132. doi:10.1016/j.jclepro.2013.01.004

Choudhary, M., & Seth, N. (2011). Integration of green practices in supply chain environment-The practices of inbound, operational, outbound and reverse logistics. *International Journal of Engineering Science and Technology*, *3*(6), 4993–4995.

Dalkir, K. (2005). *Knowledge management in theory and practice*. Amsterdam: Elsevier, Butterworth-Heinemann.

Darnall, N., Jolley, G. J., & Handfield, R. (2008). Environmental management systems and green supply chain management: Complements for sustainability? *Business Strategy and the Environment, 17*(1), 30–45. doi:10.1002/bse.557

Dashore, K., & Sohani, N. (2013). Green supply chain management – barriers & drivers: A review. *International Journal of Engineering Research & Technology, 2*(4), 2021–2030.

Demir, E., Bektaş, T., & Laporte, G. (2014). A review of recent research on green road freight transportation. *European Journal of Operational Research, 237*(3), 775–793. doi:10.1016/j.ejor.2013.12.033

Department of Environmental Affairs. (2008). *National framework for sustainable development*. Pretoria, South Africa: Department of Environmental Affairs.

Dhull, S., & Narwal, M. (2016). Drivers and barriers in green supply chain management adaptation: A state-of-art review. *Uncertain Supply Chain Management, 4*(1), 61–76. doi:10.5267/j.uscm.2015.7.003

Diabat, A., & Govindan, K. (2011). An analysis of the drivers affecting the implementation of green supply chain management. *Resources, Conservation and Recycling, 55*(6), 659–667. doi:10.1016/j.resconrec.2010.12.002

Duarte, S., & Cruz-Machado, V. (2017). An investigation of lean and green supply chain in the Industry 4.0. *Proceedings of the 2017 International Conference on Industrial Engineering and Operations Management*.

Faisal, M. (2015). Research analysis on barriers to green supply chain management in pharmaceutical industries. *Review of Public Administration and Management, 3*(1), 1–5. doi:10.4172/2315-7844.1000176

Fawcett, S. E., Ellram, L. M., & Ogden, J. A. (2014). *Supply chain management: From vision to implementation*. London: Pearson.

Fields, Z., & Atiku, S. O. (2018). Collaborative approaches for communities of practice activities enrichment. In N. Baporikar (Ed.), *Knowledge integration strategies for entrepreneurship and sustainability* (pp. 304–333). Hershey, PA: IGI Global. doi:10.4018/978-1-5225-5115-7.ch015

Green, K. W. Jr, Zelbst, P. J., Meacham, J., & Bhadauria, V. S. (2012). Green supply chain management practices: Impact on performance. *Supply Chain Management*, *17*(3), 290–305. doi:10.1108/13598541211227126

Griskevicius, V., Tybur, J. M., & Van den Bergh, B. (2010). Going green to be seen: Status, reputation, and conspicuous conservation. *Journal of Personality and Social Psychology*, *98*(3), 392–404. doi:10.1037/a0017346 PMID:20175620

Hallikas, J., & Lintukangas, K. (2016). Purchasing and supply: An investigation of risk management performance. *International Journal of Production Economics*, *171*, 487–494. doi:10.1016/j.ijpe.2015.09.013

Health24. (2013). *The pharmaceutical industry at a glance.* Retrieved from http://www.health24.com/Medical/Meds-and-you/Inside-the-lab/The-pharmaceutical-industry-at-a-glance-20130521

Huynh, P. (2013). *Outbound transportation and its environmental impact: case company: Drilling Mud Corporation (Vietnam)* (Unpublished Bachelor thesis). Haaga-Helia University of Applied Sciences, Helsinki, Finland.

Isaksson, L., Kiessling, T., & Harvey, M. (2014). Corporate social responsibility: Why bother. *Organizational Dynamics*, *43*(1), 64–72. doi:10.1016/j.orgdyn.2013.10.008

Ivona, B., Novačko, L., & Ogrizović, D. (2014). Processing reverse logistics inventories. *Scientific Journal of Maritime Research*, *28*(1), 10–16.

Jones, O. A. H., Voulvoulis, N., & Lester, J. N. (2001). Human pharmaceuticals in the aquatic environment a review. *Environmental Technology*, *22*(12), 1383–1394. doi:10.1080/09593330.2001.11090873 PMID:11873874

Jumadi, H., & Zailani, S. (2010). Integrating green innovations in logistics services towards logistics service sustainability: A conceptual paper. *Environmental Research Journal*, *4*(4), 261–271. doi:10.3923/erj.2010.261.271

Kamal, A. N. A., & Fernando, Y. (2015). Review of supply chain integration on green supply chain management (GSCM). In V. González-Prida & A. Raman (Eds.), *Promoting sustainable practices through energy engineering and asset management* (pp. 348–368). Hershey, PA: IGI Global. doi:10.4018/978-1-4666-8222-1.ch015

Khiewnavawongsa, S., & Schmidt, E. K. (2013). Barriers to green supply chain implementation in the electronics industry. In *Proceedings of 2013* (pp. 226–230). Industrial Engineering and Engineering Management. doi:10.1109/IEEM.2013.6962408

Krippendorff, K. (2012). *Content analysis: An introduction to its methodology* (3rd ed.). London: Sage.

Kumar, R., & Chandrakar, R. (2012). Overview of green supply chain management: Operation and environmental impact at different stages of the supply chain. *International Journal of Engineering and Advanced Technology*, *1*(3), 1–6.

Kümmerer, K. (2010). Why green and sustainable pharmacy? In K. Kümmerer & M. Hempel (Eds.), *Green and sustainable pharmacy* (pp. 3–10). Berlin, Germany: Springer. doi:10.1007/978-3-642-05199-9_1

Lee, S. Y., & Klassen, R. D. (2008). Drivers and enablers that foster environmental management capabilities in small- and medium-sized suppliers in supply chains. *Production and Operations Management*, *17*(6), 573–586. doi:10.3401/poms.1080.0063

Luthra, S., Kumar, V., Kumar, S., & Haleen, A. (2011). Barriers to implement green supply chain management in automobile industry using interpretive structural modeling technique: An Indian perspective. *Journal of Industrial Engineering and Management*, *4*(2), 231–257. doi:10.3926/jiem.2011.v4n2.p231-257

Minnie, T. (2015). *A review of the South African pharmaceutical landscape.* Retrieved from http://www.utipharma.co.za/documents/198965/199128/UTi+November+2015+-+South+Africa+V1.pdf/c9c979e4-41ce-4d2c-94dc-e24f5d8c1b43

Monczka, M. R., Handfield, B. R., Giunipero, C. L., Patterson, J. L., & Waters, D. (2016). *Purchasing and supply chain management* (6th ed.). Boston, MA: Cengage Learning.

Mugabe, A. Y. (2013). *Green management practices and supply chain performance of pharmaceutical companies in Nairobi* (Unpublished Masters dissertation). University of Nairobi, Kenya.

Narayana, A. S., Elias, A., & Pati, K. R. (2014). Reverse logistics in the pharmaceuticals industry: A systemic analysis. *International Journal of Logistics Management*, *25*(2), 379–398. doi:10.1108/IJLM-08-2012-0073

Ng, F. Y., Yew, F. K., Basiron, Y., & Sundram, K. (2011). A renewable future driven with Malaysian palm oil-based green technology. *Journal of Oil Palm. Environmental Health*, *2*, 1–7.

Ojo, E., Mbohwa, C., & Akinlabi, E. (2013). *An analysis of green supply chain management in South Africa and Nigeria: A comparative study*. In *Proceedings of the International Conference on Integrated Waste Management and Green Energy Engineering* (pp. 315-319). University of Johannesburg.

Pillay, K., & Mbhele, T. P. (2015). The challenges of green logistics in the Durban road freight industry. *Environment and Ecology*, *6*(1), 64–73.

Polit, D. F., & Beck, C. T. (2008). *Nursing research: Generating and assessing evidence for nursing practice* (8th ed.). Philadelphia, PA: Wolters Kluwer Health/ Lippincott Williams & Wilkins.

Rossetti, C. L., Handfield, R., & Dooley, K. J. (2011). Forces, trends, and decisions in pharmaceutical supply chain management. *International Journal of Physical Distribution & Logistics Management*, *41*(6), 601–622. doi:10.1108/09600031111147835

Saunders, M., Lewis, P., & Thornhill, A. (2016). *Research methods for business students* (7th ed.). Harlow, UK: Pearson.

Schwab, K. (2015). The Fourth Industrial Revolution: What it means and how to respond. *Snapshot*. Retrieved from https://www.foreignaffairs.com/articles/2015-12-12/fourth-industrial-revolution

Scipioni, A., Manzardo, A., Mazzi, A., & Mastrobuono, M. (2012). Monitoring the carbon footprint of products: A methodological proposal. *Journal of Cleaner Production*, *36*, 94–101. doi:10.1016/j.jclepro.2012.04.021

Sellitto, M. A., Bittencourt, S. A., & Reckziegel, B. I. (2015). Evaluating the implementation of GSCM in industrial supply chains: Two cases in the automotive Industry. *Chemical Engineering Transactions*, *43*, 1315–1320.

Servaes, H., & Tamayo, A. (2013). The impact of corporate social responsibility on firm value: The role of customer awareness. *Management Science*, *59*(5), 1045–1061. doi:10.1287/mnsc.1120.1630

Sheldon, R. A. (2014). Green and sustainable manufacture of chemicals from biomass: State of the art. *Green Chemistry*, *16*(3), 950–963. doi:10.1039/C3GC41935E

Sheu, J. B., Chou, Y. H., & Hu, C. C. (2005). An integrated logistics operational model for green-supply chain management. *Transportation Research Part E, Logistics and Transportation Review*, *41*(4), 287–313. doi:10.1016/j.tre.2004.07.001

Szegedi, Z., Gabriel, M., & Papp, I. (2017). Green supply chain awareness in the Hungarian automotive industry. *Polish Journal of Management Studies*, *16*(1), 259–268. doi:10.17512/pjms.2017.16.1.22

Testa, F., & Iraldo, F. (2010). Shadows and lights of GSCM (green supply chain management): Determinants and effects of these practices based on a multi-national study. *Journal of Cleaner Production*, *18*(10), 953–962. doi:10.1016/j.jclepro.2010.03.005

Trappey, A. J., Trappey, C. V., Hsiao, C. T., Ou, J. J., & Chang, C. T. (2012). System dynamics modelling of product carbon footprint life cycles for collaborative green supply chains. *International Journal of Computer Integrated Manufacturing*, *25*(10), 934–945. doi:10.1080/0951192X.2011.593304

Ubeda, S., Arcelus, F. J., & Fau Linton, J. (2011). Green logistics at Eroski: A case study. *International Journal of Production Economics*, *131*(1), 44–51. doi:10.1016/j.ijpe.2010.04.041

Underwood, J. D. (1993). Going green for profit. *EPA Journal*, *19*(3), 9–15.

Vachon, S., & Klassen, R. D. (2006). Extending green practices across the supply chain: The impact of upstream and downstream integration. *International Journal of Operations & Production Management*, *26*(7), 795–821. doi:10.1108/01443570610672248

Van Rensburg, S. L. J. (2015). *A framework in green logistics for companies in South Africa* (Unpublished Masters' dissertation). University of South Africa.

Walker, H., & Brammer, S. (2009). Sustainable procurement in the United Kingdom public sector. *Supply Chain Management*, *14*(2), 128–137. doi:10.1108/13598540910941993

Welter, V. (2012). *Sustainable procurement of pharmaceuticals: Time to act.* Retrieved from http://www.who.int/medicines/areas/policy/IPC_dec2012_Volker_procurement.pdf

Wood, S., & Reynolds, J. (2013). Knowledge management, organisational learning and memory in UK retail network planning. *Service Industries Journal*, *33*(2), 150–170. doi:10.1080/02642069.2011.614340

Wright, R. E., Richey, R. G., Tokman, M., & Palmer, J. C. (2011). Recycling and reverse logistics. *The Journal of Applied Business and Economics*, *12*(5), 9.

Wu, H. J., & Dunn, S. C. (1995). Environmentally responsible logistics systems. *International Journal of Physical Distribution & Logistics Management*, *25*(2), 20–38. doi:10.1108/09600039510083925

Yin, R. K. (2014). *Case study research: Design and methods* (5th ed.). Thousand Oaks, CA: Sage.

Zhang, L., Methipara, J., & Lu, Y. (2011, January). *Internalizing congestion and environmental externalities with green transportation financing policies.* Paper presented at the 90th Annual Meeting of the Transportation Research Board, Washington, DC.

Zhu, Q., Geng, Y., Fujita, T., & Hashimoto, S. (2010). Green supply chain management in leading manufacturers. Case studies in Japanese large companies. *Management Research Review*, *33*(4), 380–392. doi:10.1108/01409171011030471

Zhu, Q., Sarkis, J., & Lai, K. H. (2005). Green supply chain management: Pressures, practices and performance within the Chinese automobile industry. *International Journal of Operations & Production Management*, *25*(5), 449–468. doi:10.1108/01443570510593148

Zhu, Q., Sarkis, J., & Lai, K. H. (2007). Green supply chain management: Pressures, practices and performance within the Chinese automobile industry. *Journal of Cleaner Production*, *15*(11-12), 1041–1052. doi:10.1016/j.jclepro.2006.05.021

Zhu, Q., Sarkis, J., & Lai, K. H. (2008). Confirmation of a measurement model for green supply chain management practices implementation. *International Journal of Production Economics, 111*(2), 261–273. doi:10.1016/j.ijpe.2006.11.029

Zsidisin, G. A., & Siferd, S. P. (2001). Environmental purchasing: A framework for theory development. *European Journal of Purchasing & Supply Management, 7*(1), 61–73. doi:10.1016/S0969-7012(00)00007-1

KEY TERMS AND DEFINITIONS

Green Supply Chain Management (GSCM): The incorporation of environmental practices into supply chain activities so as to improve environmental performance and reduce a business's negative impact on the environment.

Logistics: The movement and management of goods and services. It includes transportation, warehousing, and inventory management.

Operations Management: The transformation of inputs into outputs.

Procurement: The buying of goods and services for a business to meet its needs.

Reverse Logistics: The aspect of logistics that deals with product returns, recycling, waste disposal, reuse of materials, remanufacturing, and repair of defected goods.

Supply Chain: The value adding chain of the movement of resources from the procurement phase up until its consumption and disposal by the end user.

Supply Chain Management (SCM): The management of the flow of products through procurement, manufacturing, distribution, sales, and disposal.

Sustainability: The reduction of waste so as to maintain natural resources and the environment for future generations.

Compilation of References

Abadi, M. (2018, January). 15 books Bill Gates, Jezz Bezos, and Elon Musk think everyone should read. *Business Insider*. Retrieved from https://www.businessinsider.de/bill-gates-jeff-bezos-elon-musk-favorite-books-2017-11

Abernathy, W. J., & Utterback, J. M. (1978). Patterns of industrial innovation. *Technology Review*, *52*(5), 109–119.

Adams, D. (1979). *The Hitchhiker's Guide to the Galaxy*. London, UK: Pan Books.

Adams, R., Jeanrenaud, S., Bessant, J., Denyer, D., & Overy, P. (2016). Sustainability-oriented innovation: A systematic review. *International Journal of Management Reviews*, *18*(2), 180–205. doi:10.1111/ijmr.12068

Africabusinesscommunities. (n.d.). *The future of African ports is also the future of Africa's economic success*. Retrieved November 16, 2018, from https://africabusinesscommunities.com/news/the-future-of-african-ports-is-also-the-future-of-africas-economic-success/

African Development Bank. (2016). *African Economic Outlook 2016: Sustainable Cities and Structural Transformation*. Retrieved May 11, 2018, from http://www. africaneconomicoutlook. org/sites/default/files/content-pdf/eBook_AEO2016.pdf

Agarwal, N., & Brem, A. (2012). Frugal and reverse innovation—literature overview and case study insights from a German MNC in India and China. *Proceedings of the 18th International Conference on Engineering, Technology and Innovation*.

Agarwal, S. R., & Kalmár, T. (2015). *Sustainability in project management: Eight principles in practice* (Master's thesis). Umeå School of Business and Economics, Sweden. Retrieved from http://umu.diva-portal.org/smash/get/diva2:899231/FULLTEXT01.pdf

Agor, W. H. (1986). The logic of intuition: How top executives make important decisions. *Organizational Dynamics*, *14*(3), 5–18. doi:10.1016/0090-2616(86)90028-8

Aguilar-Fernandez, M. E., Otegi-Olaso, J. R., & Cruz-Villazón, C. (2015). Analysing sustainability in project life cycle and business models from the perspective of the sustainable innovation drivers. *Proceedings of the 8th International Conference on Intelligent Data Acquisition and Advanced Computing Systems*. 10.1109/IDAACS.2015.7341354

Ahlstrom, D. (2010). *Innovation and Growth: How Business Contributes to Society, 2010.* Retrieved October 19, 2018, from SSRN: https://ssrn.com/abstract=2643390

Ajike & Neoma. (2015). Green marketing: A tool for achieving sustainable development of Nigeria. *International Journal of Advanced Research in Statistics, Management and Finance.*

Aksin-Sivrikaya, S., & Bhattacharya, C. B. (2017). Where Digitalization Meets Sustainability: Opportunities and Challenges. In T. Osburg & C. Lohrmann (Eds.), *Sustainability in a Digital World. CSR, Sustainability, Ethics & Governance.* Cham: Springer. doi:10.1007/978-3-319-54603-2_3

Albarosa, F., & Musura, R. E. V. (2016). *Social Sustainability Aspects of Agile Project Management* (Master's thesis). Umeå School of Business and Economics, Sweden. Retrieved from https://umu.diva-portal.org/smash/get/diva2:1070296/FULLTEXT01.pdf

Albert, M., Breßler, J., & Hüsig, S. (2017). Expansive Learning through contradictions of sustainability. In J. A. Arevalo (Ed.), *Handbook of Sustainability in Management Education - In Search of a Multidisciplinary, Innovative and Integrated Approach.* Edward Elgar Publishing. doi:10.4337/9781785361241.00021

Albino, V., Berardi, U., & Dangelico, R. (2015). Smart Cities: Definitions, Dimensions, Performance, and Initiatives. *Journal of Urban Technology, 22*(1), 3–21. doi:10.1080/10630732.2014.942092

Alexander, B. (2017). Disruption of the Retail Ecosystem: The South African e-Retail Imperative. *Proceedings Of The European Conference On Management, Leadership & Governance*, 32-39.

Allievi, F., Vinnari, M., & Luukkanen, J. (2015). Meat consumption and production: Analysis of efficiency, sufficiency and consistency of global trends. *Journal of Cleaner Production, 92*(1), 142–151. doi:10.1016/j.jclepro.2014.12.075

Anderson, J., & Markides, C. (2007). Strategic Innovation at the base of the pyramid. *MIT Sloan Management Review, 49*(49116), 83–88.

Andoni, E., Hannot, R., & Andoni, E. (2017). Politicising Responsible Innovation: Responsibility as Inclusive Governance. *IJIS, 1*(1), 20–36. doi:10.3724/SP.J.1440.101003

Andres, A. (2012). *Measuring Academic Research: How to Undertake a Bibliometric Study.* Cambridge, UK: Chandos Publishing.

Angelidou, M. (2014). Smart city policies: A spatial approach. *Cities (London, England), 41*, S3–S11. doi:10.1016/j.cities.2014.06.007

Angell, M. (2004). Excess in the pharmaceutical industry. *Canadian Medical Association Journal, 171*(12), 1451–1453. doi:10.1503/cmaj.1041594 PMID:15583183

Ansari, Z. N., & Kant, R. (2017). A state-of-art literature review reflecting 15 years of focus on sustainable supply chain management. *Journal of Cleaner Production, 142*, 2524–2543. doi:10.1016/j.jclepro.2016.11.023

Ansoff, H. I. (1965). *Corporate strategy*. New York: McGraw-Hill.

Ao, Q. (2014). Analysis the Transformation and Upgrading Path of the Ports in Pearl River Delta. *Applied Mechanics and Materials*, *587-589*, 1771–1775. doi:10.4028/www.scientific. net/AMM.587-589.1771

Appadurai, A. (2010). *Modernity at Large. Cultural Dimensions of Globalization* (9th ed.). Minneapolis, MN: University of Minnesota Press. (Original work published 1996)

Appolloni, A., Sun, H., Jia, F., & Li, X. (2014). Green procurement in the private sector: A state of the art review between 1996 and 2013. *Journal of Cleaner Production*, *85*, 122–133. doi:10.1016/j.jclepro.2014.08.106

Archibugi, D. (2017a). Blade Runner economics: Will innovation lead the economic recovery? *Research Policy*, *46*(3), 535–543. doi:10.1016/j.respol.2016.01.021

Archibugi, D. (2017b). The social imagination needed for an innovation-led recovery. *Research Policy*, *46*(3), 554–556. doi:10.1016/j.respol.2016.09.018

Arevalo, J. A., & Mitchell, S. F. (2017). Handbook of Sustainability in Management Education. In *Search of a Multidisciplinary, Innovative and Integrated Approach*. Edward Elgar Publishing. doi:10.4337/9781785361241

Armstrong, N. (1969). *Recorded live broadcast transcript*. Retrieved from http://apollo11.spacelog. org/07:09:32:24/#log-line-639144

Armstrong, C. M., Niinimäki, K., Kujala, S., Karell, E., & Lang, C. (2015). Sustainable product-service systems for clothing: Exploring consumer perceptions of consumption alternatives in Finland. *Journal of Cleaner Production*, *97*, 30–39. doi:10.1016/j.jclepro.2014.01.046

Arnold, M. (2010). Stakeholder dialogues for sustaining cultural change. *International Studies of Management & Organization*, *40*(3), 61–77. doi:10.2753/IMO0020-8825400304

Arnold, M. (2016). *Systemic Structural Constellations and Sustainability in Academia: A New Method for Sustainable Higher Education*. Taylor & Francis. doi:10.4324/9781315403465

Arnold, M. (2017a). Fostering sustainability by linking co-creation and relationship management concepts. *Journal of Cleaner Production*, *140*(Part 1), 179–188. doi:10.1016/j.jclepro.2015.03.059

Arnold, M. G. (2017b). Corporate social responsibility representation of the German water-supply and distribution companies: From colourful to barren landscapes. *International Journal of Innovation and Sustainable Development*, *11*(1), 1–22. doi:10.1504/IJISD.2017.080655

Arnold, M. G. (2018). Combining conscious and unconscious knowledge within human-machine-interfaces to foster sustainability with decision-making concerning production processes. *Journal of Cleaner Production*, *179*, 581–592. doi:10.1016/j.jclepro.2018.01.070

Association for Project Management. (n.d.). *APM supports sustainability outlooks.* Retrieved July 13, 2006, from: http://www.blackpool.ac.uk/sites/default/files/documents /apm_supports_sustainability_oultooks.pdf

Attar, M., Gilaninia, S., & Homayounfar, M. (2016). A study of the effect of green supply chain management's components on the performance of the pharmaceutical distribution companies system in Iran. *Arabian Journal of Business and Management Review, 5*(8), 48–54.

Australian Institute of Project Management. (n.d.). *AIPM website.* Retrieved December 11, 2017, from http:// www.aipm.com.au/

Awadh, A. M., & Alyahya, M. S. (2013). Impact of organizational culture on employee performance. *International Review of Management and Business Research, 2,* 168.

Axelos. (2017). *Projects in Controlled Environments* (PRINCE2). Norwich: The Stationery Office.

Baker, L., Eggers, W., Gonzalez, R., & Vaughn, A. (2012). *Public sector, disrupted. How disruptive innovation can help government achieve more for less.* Deloite Govlab Study. Deloitte Development LLC.

Baker, T., Miner, A., & Easley, D. (2003). Improvising firms: Bricolage, retrospective interpretation and improvisational competencies in the founding process. *Research Policy, 32,* 255–276. doi:10.1016/S0048-7333(02)00099-9

Baker, T., & Nelson, R. E. (2005). Creating something from nothing: Resource construction through entrepreneurial bricolage. *Administrative Science Quarterly, 50*(3), 329–366. doi:10.2189/asqu.2005.50.3.329

Baldassarre, B., Calabretta, G., Bocken, N. M. P., & Jaskiewicz, T. (2017). Bridging sustainable business model innovation and user-driven innovation: A process for sustainable value proposition design. *Journal of Cleaner Production, 147,* 175–186. doi:10.1016/j.jclepro.2017.01.081

Baldé, C. P., Forti, V., Gray, V., Kuehr, R., & Stegmann, P. (2017). *The Global E-waste Monitor.* Retrieved May 13, 2018, from https://www.itu.int/en/ITU-D/limate-Change/Documents/GEM%20 2017/Global-Ewaste%20Monitor%202017%20.pdf

Ball, R., & Tunger, D. (2005). Bibliometrische Analysen - Daten, Fakten und Methoden. Jülich, Germany: Forschungszentrum Jülich.

Bankers Association for Finance and Trade (BAFT), Euro Banking Association (EBA), Factors Chain International (FCI), International Chamber of Commerce (ICC), & International Trade and Forfaiting Association (ITFA). (2016). Standard Definitons for Techniques of Supply Chain Finance. *Global Supply Chain Finance Forum.* Retrieved from https https://www.tradefinance.training/library/files/Standard%20Definitions%20for%20Techniques%20of%20Supply%20Chain%20Finance.pdf

Banna, F., Bhada-Tata, P., Ho, R., & Lee, M. (2014). *Results-based financing for municipal solid waste. Urban development series knowledge papers, 20(2).* Washington, DC: World Bank Group.

Barnes, L., & Lea-Greenwood, G. (2006). Fast fashioning the supply chain: Shaping the research agenda. *Journal of Fashion Marketing and Management: An International Journal*, *10*(3), 259–271. doi:10.1108/13612020610679259

Bassett, C., Steinmueller, E., & Voss, G. (2013). *Better made up. The mutual influence of science fiction and innovation.* Nesta Working Paper, No. 13/07. Retrieved from http://www.nesta.org.uk/wp13-07

Beattie, V., & Smith, S. J. (2013). Value creation and business models: Refocusing the intellectual capital debate. *The British Accounting Review*, *45*(4), 243–254. doi:10.1016/j.bar.2013.06.001

Beckert, J. (2013). Imagined futures: Fictional expectations in the economy. *Theory and Society*, *42*(3), 219–240. doi:10.100711186-013-9191-2

Bedenlier, S., Kondakci, Y., & Zawacki-Richter, O. (2018). Two decades of research into the internationalization of higher education: Major themes in the *Journal of Studies in International Education* (1997-2016). *Journal of Studies in International Education*, *22*(2), 108–135. doi:10.1177/1028315317710093

Behringer, C. (2017). Digitalisierung und CSR in der Finanzberatung. In A. Hildebrandt & W. Landhäußer (Eds.), *CSR und Digitalisierung. Management-Reihe Corporate Social Responsibility*. Berlin: Springer Gabler. doi:10.1007/978-3-662-53202-7_54

Bello, I. A., Ismail, M. N., & Kabbashi, N. A. (2016). Solid Waste Management in Africa: A review. *International Journal of Waste Resources*, *6*(2), 1–4.

Benlian, A., & Hess, T. (2011). Opportunities and risks of software-as-a-service: Findings from a survey of IT executives. *Decision Support Systems*, *52*(1), 232–246. doi:10.1016/j.dss.2011.07.007

Bentham, J. (2009). *An Introduction to the Principles of Morals and Legislation*. Dover, UK: Dover Publications. (Original work published 1781)

Bergere, F. (2016). Ten years of PPP: An initial assessment. *OECD Journal on Budgeting*, *15*(1), 31–123. doi:10.1787/budget-15-5jm3rx2qbxbq

Bharadwaj, A., Sawy, O., Pavlou, P., & Venkatraman, N. (2013). Digital Business Strategy: Towards a Next Generation of Insights. *Management Information Systems Quarterly*, *37*(2), 471–482. doi:10.25300/MISQ/2013/37:2.3

Bhatti, Y. (2012). *What is frugal, what is innovation? Towards a theory of frugal innovation* (SSRN Working Paper). Retrieved from Social Science Research Network website: https://papers.ssrn.com/sol3/papers.cfm?abstract_id=2005910

Bhatti, Y., & Ventresca, M. (2012). *The emerging market for frugal innovation - fad, fashion, or fit?* (SSRN Working Paper). Retrieved from Social Science Research Network website: https://papers.ssrn.com/sol3/papers.cfm?abstract_id=2005983

Bhatti, Y., & Ventresca, M. (2013). *How can 'frugal innovation' be conceptualized?* Said Business School Working Paper.

Birtchnell, T. (2013). *Indovation: Innovation and a Global Knowledge Economy in India.* Basingstoke, UK: Palgrave MacMillan. doi:10.1057/9781137027412

Blackford, R. (2017). *Science Fiction and the Moral Imagination.* Springer. doi:10.1007/978-3-319-61685-8

Blal, I., Singal, M., & Templin, J. (2018). Airbnb's effect on hotel sales growth. *International Journal of Hospitality Management, 73*, 85–92. doi:10.1016/j.ijhm.2018.02.006

Blok, V., Tempels, T.,Pietersma, E. & Jansen, L. (2017). *Exploring Ethical Decision Making in Responsible Innovation: The Case of Innovations for Healthy Food.* doi:10.1007/978-3-319-64834-7_12

Blok, V., Hoffmans, L., & Wubben, E. F. M. (2015). Stakeholder engagement for responsible innovation in the private sector: Critical issues and management practices. *Journal on Chain and Network Science, 15*(2), 147–164. doi:10.3920/JCNS2015.x003

Bocken, N. M. P., Short, S. W., Rana, P., & Evans, S. (2014). A literature and practice review to develop sustainable business model archetypes. *Journal of Cleaner Production, 65*, 42–56. doi:10.1016/j.jclepro.2013.11.039

Boiral, O., & Paillé, P. (2012). Organizational citizenship behaviour for the environment: Measurement and validation. *Journal of Business Ethics, 109*(4), 431–445. doi:10.100710551-011-1138-9

Boltic, Z., Ruzic, N., Jovanovic, M., Savic, M., Jovanovic, J., & Petrovic, S. (2013). Cleaner production aspects of tablet coating process in pharmaceutical industry: Problem of VOCs emission. *Journal of Cleaner Production, 44*(1), 123–132. doi:10.1016/j.jclepro.2013.01.004

Bondarouk, T., & Brewster, C. (2016). Conceptualising the future of HRM and technology research. *International Journal of Human Resource Management, 27*(21), 2652–2671. doi:10.1080/09585192.2016.1232296

Bonekamp, L., & Sure, M. (2015). Consequences of Industry 4.0 on human labour and work organisation. *Journal of Business and Media Psychology, 6*(1), 33–40.

Bonte, D. (2018). *The Role of Smart Cities for Economic Development.* New York: ABI Research.

Boons, F., & Lüdeke-Freund, F. (2013). Business models for sustainable innovation: State-of-the-art and steps towards a research agenda. *Journal of Cleaner Production, 45*, 9–19. doi:10.1016/j.jclepro.2012.07.007

Börjeson, N., & Boström, M. (2018). Towards reflexive responsibility in a textile supply chain. *Business Strategy and the Environment, 27*(2), 230–239. doi:10.1002/bse.2012

Botta, A., De Donato, W., Persico, V., & Pescapé, A. (2016). Integration of Cloud computing and Internet of Things: A survey. *Future Generation Computer Systems, 56*, 684–700. doi:10.1016/j.future.2015.09.021

Bound, K., & Thornton, I. (2012). *Our frugal future: Lesson from India's innovation System.* London, UK: NESTA.

Bowersox, D. J., Closs, D. J., & Stank, T. P. (2003). How to master cross-enterprise collaboration. *Supply Chain Management Review, 7*(4), 18–27.

Brem, A., & Wolfram, P. (2014). Research and development from the bottom up - Introduction of terminologies for new product development in emerging markets. *Journal of Innovation and Entrepreneurship, 3*(9).

Brettel, M., Friederichsen, N., Keller, M., & Rosenberg, M. (2014). How Virtualization Decentralization and Network Building Change the Manufacturing Landscape An Industry 4.0. *Perspective, 8*(1), 37–44.

Brockhoff, K. (1999): Forschung und Entwicklung: Planung und Kontrolle (5th ed.). München, Germany: Oldenburg.

Brookes, B. C. (1990). Biblio-, sciento-, infor-metrics?? what are we talking about? In L. Egghe & R. Rousseau (Eds.), *Informetrics, 89/90* (pp. 31–43). London, Ontario, Canada: Elsevier.

Brown, A., & Bakhru, A. (2007). Information Systems Innovation Research and the case of RFID. *IFIP International Federation for Information Processing, 235*, 363–376. doi:10.1007/978-0-387-72804-9_24

Brown, I., & Russell, J. (2007). Radio frequency identification technology: An exploratory study on adoption in the South African retail sector. *International Journal of Information Management, 27*(4), 250–265. doi:10.1016/j.ijinfomgt.2007.02.007

Brown, J. S., & Hagel, J. (2005). Innovation blowback: Disruptive management practices from Asia. *The McKinsey Quarterly, 1*(1), 35–45.

Brown, T., & Wyatt, J. (2010). Design thinking for social innovation. *Stanford Social Innovation Review, 8*(1), 30–35.

Brundtland, G. H. (1987). *Our common future: World commission on environment and development.* Oxford, UK: Oxford University Press.

Bruno, G. (1999). *De Immenso et Innumerabilibus Liber I-VI. Das Unermeßliche und Unzählbare.* 6 Bücher. Peißenberg: Skorpion-Verlag. (Original work published 1591)

Bryman, A. (2015). *Social research methods* (5th ed.). Oxford, UK: Oxford University Press.

Brynjolfsson, E., & McAfee, A. (2014). *The second machine age: Work, progress, and prosperity in a time of brilliant technologies.* WW Norton & Company.

Bubel, D., Ostraszewska, Z., Turek, T., & Tylec, A. (Eds.). (2015). Innovation in developing countries - a new approach. In *Proceedings of the, 10th International Conference on European Integration - Realities and Perspectives (EIRP Vol.10).* Galati, Romania: Danubius University Press.

Bucher, J. (2016). *Die Proliferation der Möglichkeiten und Anforderungen. Über Infrastrukturinnovationen und ihre wirtschaftliche und soziale Adaption.* Paper presented at the 1. interdisziplinäre Konferenz zur Zukunft der Wertschöpfung. Retrieved from http://www.openproduction.info/wp-content/uploads/2016/12/161205_Konferenzband_Zukunft-der-Wertschöpfung_2016_digital.pdf

Bundeskartellamt (BKA). (2015). *Digitale Ökonomie – Internetplattformen zwischen Wettbewerbsrecht, Privatsphäre und Verbraucherschutz.* Tagung des Arbeitskreises Kartellrecht. Retrieved July 13, 2018, from https://www.bundeskartellamt.de/SharedDocs/Publikation/DE/Diskussions_Hintergrundpapier/AK_Kartellrecht_2015_Digitale_Oekonomie.pdf?__blob=publicationFile&v=2

Burget, M., Bardone, E., & Pedaste, M. (2017). Definitions and conceptual dimensions of responsible research and innovation: A literature review. *Science and Engineering Ethics*, *23*(1), 1–19. doi:10.100711948-016-9782-1 PMID:27090147

Burri, M. (2017). *Current and Emerging Trends in Disruptive Technologies: Implications for the Present and Future of EU's Trade Policy.* doi:10.2861/96860

Callon, M., Lascoumes, P., & Barthe, Y. (2009). *Acting in an Uncertain World: An Essay on Technical Democracy.* Cambridge, MA: MIT Press.

Cao, M., & Zhang, Q. (2011). Supply chain collaboration impact on collaborative advantage and firm performance. *Journal of Operations Management*, *29*(3), 163–180. doi:10.1016/j.jom.2010.12.008

Cappelli, P., Singh, H., Singh, J., & Useem, M. (2010). The India way: Lessons for the US. *The Academy of Management Perspectives*, *24*(2), 6–24. doi:10.5465/amp.24.2.6

Caputo, A., Marzi, G., & Pellegrini, M. M. (2016). The Internet of Things in manufacturing innovation processes: Development and application of a conceptual framework. *Business Process Management Journal*, *22*(2), 383–402. doi:10.1108/BPMJ-05-2015-0072

Cartwright, C., & Yinger, M. (2007). *Project management competency development framework.* Paper presented at PMI Global Congress (EMEA 2017), Budapest, Hungary.

Carvalho, M. M., & Rabechini, R. Jr. (2017). Can project sustainability management impact project success? An empirical study applying a contingent approach. International Journal of Project Management. *International Journal of Project Management*, *35*(6), 1120–1132. doi:10.1016/j.ijproman.2017.02.018

Castoriadis, C. (1997). *The Castoriadis Reader* (D. A. Curtis, Trans. & Ed.). Cambridge, UK: Blackwell Publishers.

Castoriadis, C. (1998). *The Imaginary Institution of Society* (K. Blarney, Trans.). Cambridge, UK: MIT Press.

Cavalho, Edson, & Mataers. (2018). Manufacturing in the fourth industrial revolution: A positive perspective in sustainable manufacturing. *Procedia Manufacturing, 21*, 671-678.

Chalfin, B. (2010). Recasting maritime governance in Ghana: The neo-developmental state and the Port of Tema. *The Journal of Modern African Studies*, *48*(04), 573–598. doi:10.1017/S0022278X10000546

Chataway, J., Hanlin, R., & Kaplinsky, R. (2014). Inclusive innovation - an architecture for policy development. *Innovation and Development*, *4*(1), 33–54. doi:10.1080/2157930X.2013.876800

Chattopadhyay, S. P. (2001). Improving the speed of ISO 14000 implementation: A framework for increasing productivity. *Managerial Auditing Journal*, *16*(1), 36–40. doi:10.1108/02686900110363636

Chengula, A., Lucas, B. K., & Mzula, A. (2015). Assessing the Awareness, Knowledge, Attitude and Practice of the Community towards Solid Waste Disposal and Identifying the Threats and Extent of Bacteria in the Solid Waste Disposal Sites in Morogoro Municipality in Tanzania. *Journal of Biology, Agriculture and Healthcare*, *5*(3), 54–65.

Choudhary, M., & Seth, N. (2011). Integration of green practices in supply chain environment- The practices of inbound, operational, outbound and reverse logistics. *International Journal of Engineering Science and Technology*, *3*(6), 4993–4995.

Chowdhury, G. G. (2016). How to improve the sustainability of digital libraries and information Services? *Journal of the Association for Information Science and Technology*, *67*(10), 2379–2391. doi:10.1002/asi.23599

Christen, M., & Schmidt, S. (2012). A Formal Framework for Conceptions of Sustainability - a Theoretical Contribution to the Discourse in Sustainable Development. *Sustainable Development*, *20*(6), 400–410. doi:10.1002d.518

Christensen, C. M., Baumann, H., Ruggles, R., & Sadler, T. M. (2006). Disruptive Innovation for Social Change. *Harvard Business Review*. Retrieved from http://hbr.org/2006/12/disruptive-innovation-for-social-change/ar/1

Christensen, C. M. (1997). *The innovator's dilemma: when new technologies cause great firms to fail*. Boston, MA: Harvard Business School Press.

Christensen, C. M. (2000). *The innovator's dilemma*. New York: Harper Collins Publishers.

Christensen, C. M. (2006). The ongoing process of building a theory of disruption. *Journal of Product Innovation Management*, *23*(1), 39–55. doi:10.1111/j.1540-5885.2005.00180.x

Christensen, C. M., Baumann, H., Ruggles, R., & Sadtler, T. M. (2006). Disruptive innovation for social change. *Harvard Business Review*, *84*(12), 94–101. PMID:17183796

Christensen, C. M., & Bower, J. L. (1995, January). Disruptive technologies: Catching the wave. *Harvard Business Review*, 43–53.

Christensen, C. M., & Overdorf, M. (2000, March). Meeting the challenge of disruptive change. *Harvard Business Review*, 66–76.

Christensen, C. M., & Raynor, M. (2003). *The Innovators Solution: Creating and Sustaining Successful Growth*. Cambridge, MA: Harvard Business School Press.

Chu, F., Gailus, G., Liu, L., & Ni, L. (2018). *The future of automated ports*. Retrieved January 16, 2019, from https://www.mckinsey.com/industries/travel-transport-and-logistics/our-insights/the-future-of-automated-ports.#0

Chummun, B. Z., & Gaffar, K. (2018). Factors that Influence Environmental Performance in the Waste Management Industry in KwaZulu-Natal. In *12th International Business Conference Proceedings* (pp. 1-17). Le Meridian, Mauritius: Academic Press.

Clarke, A. C. (1961). *A Fall of Moondust*. London, UK: Galloncz.

Clark, P. (2003). *Organizational innovations*. London: SAGE Publications.

Cloete, F., De Coning, C., Wissink, H. F., & Rabie, B. (2018). *Improving Public Policy for Good Governance* (4th ed.). Pretoria: Van Schaik.

Committee on Payments and Market Infrastructures (CPMI). (2015). Digital currencies. *Bank for International Settlements*. Retrieved from https://www.bis.org/cpmi/publ/d137.pdf

Comoglio, C., & Botta, S. (2012). The use of indicators and the role of environmental management systems for environmental performances improvement: A survey on ISO 14001 certified companies in the automotive sector. *Journal of Cleaner Production*, *20*(1), 92–102. doi:10.1016/j.jclepro.2011.08.022

Conschafter, S. J. (2017). Charting a path for cities in the Second Machine Age with or without the car: A focus on the human experience. *Journal of Urban Regeneration and Renewal*, *10*(2), 116–127.

Cooper, H. (1989). *Integrating research* (2nd ed.). London: Sage.

Cooper, H., Hedges, L. V., & Valentine, J. C. (2009). *The handbook of research synthesis and meta-analysis* (2nd ed.). New York, NY: Russell Sage Foundation.

Cooper, R. G. (1983). A process model for industrial new product development. *IEEE Transactions on Engineering Management*, *30*(1), 2–11. doi:10.1109/TEM.1983.6448637

Cooper, R. G. (1996). Overhauling the new product process. *Industrial Marketing Management*, *25*(6), 465–482. doi:10.1016/S0019-8501(96)00062-4

Cooper, R. G., & Kleinschmidt, E. J. (1990). *New Products: The Key Factors in Success*. Chicago, IL: American Marketing Association.

Costa, G., Mavrommatis, A., Vila, M., & Valdes, S. (2017). Collaborative Relationships Between Manufacturers and Retailers: A Supply Chain Collaboration Framework. In F. Martínez-López, J. Gázquez-Abad, K. Ailawadi, & M. Yagüe-Guillén (Eds.), *Advances in National Brand and Private Label Marketing. Springer Proceedings in Business and Economics*. Cham: Springer. doi:10.1007/978-3-319-59701-0_21

Courtial, J. P. (1998). Comments on Leydesdorff's article. *Journal of the American Society for Information Science*, 49(1), 98–98. doi:10.1002/(SICI)1097-4571(199801)49:1<98::AID-ASI14>3.0.CO;2-1

Cowen, T. (2011). *The Great Stagnation: How America Ate All the Low-Hanging Fruit of Modern History, Got Sick, and Will (Eventually) Feel Better.* New York: Dutton.

Cox, A. (2010). *Waste Company Head Arrested.* Retrieved May 18, 2018, from http://www.iol.co.za/news/south-africa/waste-company-head-arrested-480897

Cox, M. W., & Alm, R. (2017). *The Imagination Age. America's fourth wave of economic progress.* Retrieved from https://www.smu.edu/-/media/Site/Cox/CentersAndInstitutes/ONeilCenter/Research/AnnualReports/2017AnnualReport.ashx?la=en

Cretchley, J., Rooney, D., & Gallois, C. (2010). Mapping a 40-year history with Leximancer: Themes and concepts in the Journal of Cross-Cultural Psychology. *Journal of Cross-Cultural Psychology*, 41(3), 318–328. doi:10.1177/0022022110366105

CSIR. (2011). *Municipal waste management - good practices.* Retrieved May 13, 2018, from https://www.csir.co.za/sites/default/files/Documents/Waste_Management_Toolkit_0.pdf

D'Souza, A., Wortmann, H., Huitema, G., & Velthuijsen, H. (2015). A business model design framework for viability; a business ecosystem approach. *Journal of Business Models*, 3(2), 1–29.

Da Silva, F. M., Bártolo, H. M., Bártolo, P., Almendra, R., Roseta, F., Almeida, H. A., & Lemos, A. C. (2017). Challenges for Technology Innovation: An Agenda for the Future. In *Proceedings of the International Conference on Sustainable Smart Manufacturing.* Lisbon, Portugal: CRC Press.

Dadashi, N., Wilson, J., Golightly, D., & Sharples, S. (2014). A framework to support human factors of automation in railway intelligent infrastructure. *Ergonomics*, 57(3), 387–402. doi:10.1080/00140139.2014.893026 PMID:24670143

Dainty, A. R. J., & Brooke, R. J. (2004). Towards improved construction waste minimisation: A need for improved supply chain integration? *Structural Survey*, 22(1), 20–29. doi:10.1108/02630800410533285

Dalkir, K. (2005). *Knowledge management in theory and practice.* Amsterdam: Elsevier, Butterworth-Heinemann.

Daneshpour, H. (2015). Integrating Sustainability into Management of Project. *International Journal of Environmental Sciences and Development*, 6(4), 321–325. doi:10.7763/IJESD.2015.V6.611

Dapp, M., Balta, D., & Krcmar, H. (2017). Blockchain - Disruption der öffentlichen Verwaltung? Eine Technologie zur Neugestaltung der Verwaltungsprozesse. *Konrad Adenauer Stiftung.* Retrieved from http://www.kas.de/wf/doc/kas_49305-544-1-30.pdf?170622171027

Darnall, N., Jolley, G. J., & Handfield, R. (2008). Environmental management systems and green supply chain management: Complements for sustainability? *Business Strategy and the Environment, 17*(1), 30–45. doi:10.1002/bse.557

Dashore, K., & Sohani, N. (2013). Green supply chain management – barriers & drivers: A review. *International Journal of Engineering Research & Technology, 2*(4), 2021–2030.

DaSilva, C. M., & Trkman, P. (2014). Business model: What it is and what it is not. *Long Range Planning, 47*(6), 379–389. doi:10.1016/j.lrp.2013.08.004

De Man, J. C., & Strandhagen, J. O. (2017). An Industry 4.0 Research Agenda for Sustainable Business Models. *Procedia CIRP, 63*, 721–726. doi:10.1016/j.procir.2017.03.315

De Martino, M. (2014). Sustainable Development Strategies of the Port Authority: The Network Approach. *Advanced Engineering Forum, 11*, 87-95.

Deland, D. (2009). Sustainability through project management and net impact. In *Proceedings of the PMI Global Congress 2009*. Philadelphia, PA: Project Management Institute.

Demir, E., Bektaş, T., & Laporte, G. (2014). A review of recent research on green road freight transportation. *European Journal of Operational Research, 237*(3), 775–793. doi:10.1016/j.ejor.2013.12.033

Den Holder, G. (2017). *Circular Economy.* Retrieved May 15, 2018, from, https://www.business2community.com/strategy/need-inspiring-examples-circular-economy-5-01872776

Department of Environmental Affairs. (2008). *National framework for sustainable development.* Pretoria, South Africa: Department of Environmental Affairs.

Department of Environmental Affairs. (2017). Waste minimization with relation to producers - fact pack. Pretoria: Department of Environmental Affairs.

Dhull, S., & Narwal, M. (2016). Drivers and barriers in green supply chain management adaptation: A state-of-art review. *Uncertain Supply Chain Management, 4*(1), 61–76. doi:10.5267/j.uscm.2015.7.003

Diabat, A., & Govindan, K. (2011). An analysis of the drivers affecting the implementation of green supply chain management. *Resources, Conservation and Recycling, 55*(6), 659–667. doi:10.1016/j.resconrec.2010.12.002

Dias, A. C., Almendra, R., & Silva, F. (2017). Design education facing Europe 2020—a reflection on demands: FAULisbon as the case study. In Challenges for Technology Innovation (Vol. 287, No. 292, pp. 287-292). Routledge in association with GSE Research.

Dickson, M. A., & Chang, R. K. (2015). Apparel manufacturers and the business case for social sustainability: 'World class' CSR and business model innovation. *Journal of Corporate Citizenship, 57*(57), 55–72. doi:10.9774/GLEAF.4700.2015.ma.00006

Die Geschichte der Plattform Industrie 4.0. (n.d.). Retrieved from https://www.plattform-i40.de/I40/Navigation/DE/Plattform/Plattform-Industrie-40/plattform-industrie-40.html

Ding, K., Jiang, P., & Zheng, M. (2017). Environmental and economic sustainability-aware resource service scheduling for industrial product service systems. *Journal of Intelligent Manufacturing*, *28*(6), 1303–1316. doi:10.100710845-015-1051-7

Dini, P. (2007). A Scientific Foundation for Digital Ecosystems. In F. Nachira, A. Nicloai, & ... (Eds.), *Digital Business Ecosystems, Information Society and Media* (pp. 24–47). Luxembourg: Office for Official Publications of the European Communities.

Dobrovnik, M., Herold, D., Fürst, E., & Kummer, S. (2018). Blockchain for and in Logistics: What to Adopt and Where to Start. *Logistics 2018, 2*(3), 18. Retrieved from https://www.mdpi.com/2305-6290/2/3/18

Dominish, E., Retamal, M., Sharpe, S., Lane, R., Rhamdhani, M., Corder, G., ... Florin, N. (2018). "Slowing" and "Narrowing" the Flow of Metals for Consumer Goods: Evaluating Opportunities and Barriers. *Sustainability*, *10*(4), 1096. doi:10.3390u10041096

Drescher, D. (2017). *Blockchain-Basics*. Springer Berlin APress.

Dreyer, M., Chefneux, L., Goldberg, A., Von Heimburg, J., Patrignani, N., Schofield, M., & Shilling, C. (2017). Responsible innovation: A complementary view from industry with proposals for bridging different perspectives. *Sustainability*, *9*(10), 1719. doi:10.3390u9101719

Duarte, S., & Cruz-Machado, V. (2018). Exploring Linkages Between Lean and Green Supply Chain and the Industry 4.0. In *Proceedings of the Eleventh International Conference on Management Science and Engineering Management. ICMSEM 2017. Lecture Notes on Multidisciplinary Industrial Engineering*. Springer.

Duarte, S., & Cruz-Machado, V. (2017). An investigation of lean and green supply chain in the Industry 4.0. *Proceedings of the 2017 International Conference on Industrial Engineering and Operations Management*.

Duncu. (2013). The contribution of sustainable marketing for sustainable development. *Management and Marketing Challenges for the Knowledge Society, 8*(2), 385-400.

East African Communication Organisation (EACO). (2013). *Model Framework for e-waste management*. Retrieved May 21, 2018, from, http://www.eaco.int/admin/docs/reports/Policy_Model_ Framework_June_2013.pdf

Eaton, J., Kortum, S., Neiman, B., & Romalis, J. (2010). *Trade and the Global Recession*. SSRN Electronic Journal. doi:10.2139srn.1692582

Ebbesen, J. B., & Hope, A. (2013). Re-imagining the Iron Triangle: Embedding Sustainability into Project Constraints. *PM World Journal*, *2*(3), 1–13.

Elkington, J. (1994). Towards the sustainable corporation: Win-win-win business strategies for sustainable development. *California Management Review*, *36*(2), 90–100. doi:10.2307/41165746

Elkington, J. (1997). *Cannibals with Forks: The Triple Bottom Line of 21st Century Business.* Oxford, UK: Capstone Publishing.

Ellram, L. M. (1991). Supply-chain management: The industrial organization perspective. *International Journal of Physical Distribution & Logistics Management, 21*(1), 13–22. doi:10.1108/09600039110137082

Elo, S., & Kyngäs, H. (2007). The qualitative content analysis process. *Journal of Advanced Nursing, 62*(1), 107–115. doi:10.1111/j.1365-2648.2007.04569.x PMID:18352969

Erdmann, L., & Hilty, L. M. (2010). Scenario analysis. *Journal of Industrial Ecology, 14*(5), 826–843. doi:10.1111/j.1530-9290.2010.00277.x

Eriksson, D., & Svensson, G. (2015). Elements affecting social responsibility in supply chains. *Supply Chain Management, 20*(5), 561–566. doi:10.1108/SCM-06-2015-0203

Ernest and Young. (2017). *Public Sector Innovation: From Ideas to Actions.* Retrieved from http://www.ey.com/ca/en/industries/government---public-sector/ey-public-sector-innovation-ideas-actions

Ethikrat, D. (2017). Big Data und Gesundheit–Datensouveränität als informationelle Freiheitsgestaltung. *Vorabfassung vom, 30.*

European Economic Area (EEA). (2011). *Earnings, jobs and innovation: The role of recycling in a green economy.* European Environment Agency: Report no. 8/2011. Luxembourg: Office for Official Publications of the European Union. Retrieved May 17, 2018, from, https:// www. eea.europa.eu/publications/earnings-jobs-andinnovation-the/download

European Space Agency ESA. (2004): Tales of Innovation and Imagination: Selected Stories from the 2003 Clarke-Bradbury International Science Fiction Competition. D. Raitt & B. Warmbein (Eds.). Retrieved from www.esa.int/esapub/sp/sp546/sp546web.pdf

Evans, S., Vladimirova, D., Holgado, M., Van Fossen, K., Yang, M., Silva, E. A., & Barlow, C. Y. (2017). Business model innovation for sustainability: Towards a unified perspective for creation of sustainable business models. *Business Strategy and the Environment, 26*(5), 597–608. doi:10.1002/bse.1939

Fahmi, W., & Sutton, K. (2010). Cairo's contested garbage: Sustainable waste management and the Zabaleen's right to the city. *Sustainability, 2*(6), 1765–1783. doi:10.3390u2061765

Faisal, M. (2015). Research analysis on barriers to green supply chain management in pharmaceutical industries. *Review of Public Administration and Management, 3*(1), 1–5. doi:10.4172/2315-7844.1000176

Farley, H. M., & Smith, Z. A. (2014). *Sustainability: If It's Everything, Is It Nothing?* New York: Routledge.

Fawcett, S. E., Ellram, L. M., & Ogden, J. A. (2014). *Supply chain management: From vision to implementation.* London: Pearson.

Feldman, M. S., & Pentland, B. T. (2003). Reconceptualizing organizational routines as a source of flexibility and change. *Administrative Science Quarterly*, *48*(1), 94–118. doi:10.2307/3556620

Felício, J., & Caldeirinha, V. (2013). The influence of the characterisation factors of the European ports on operational performance: Conceptual model testing. *International Journal of Shipping and Transport Logistics*, *5*(3), 282. doi:10.1504/IJSTL.2013.054191

Ferretti, M., & Schiavone, F. (2016). Internet of Things and business processes redesign in seaports: The case of Hamburg. *Business Process Management Journal*, *22*(2), 271–284. doi:10.1108/BPMJ-05-2015-0079

Fields, Z., & Atiku, S. O. (2018). Collaborative approaches for communities of practice activities enrichment. In N. Baporikar (Ed.), *Knowledge integration strategies for entrepreneurship and sustainability* (pp. 304–333). Hershey, PA: IGI Global. doi:10.4018/978-1-5225-5115-7.ch015

Fischer, A., & Pascucci, S. (2017). Institutional incentives in circular economy transition: The case of material use in the Dutch textile industry. *Journal of Cleaner Production*, *155*, 17–32. doi:10.1016/j.jclepro.2016.12.038

Fischer, C. (2017). Environmental protection for sale: Strategic green industrial policy and climate finance. *Environmental and Resource Economics*, *66*(3), 553–575. doi:10.100710640-016-0092-5

Fjeldstad, Ø. D., & Snow, C. C. (2018). Business models and organization design. *Long Range Planning*, *51*(1), 32–39. doi:10.1016/j.lrp.2017.07.008

Flechtheim, O. K. & Joos, E. (1991). *Ausschau halten nach einer besseren Welt*. Berlin: Dietz.

Fletcher, K. (2010). Slow fashion: An invitation for systems change. *Fashion Practice*, *2*(2), 259–266. doi:10.2752/175693810X12774625387594

Flyverbom, M., Deibert, R., & Matten, D. (2017). The Governance of Digital Technology, Big Data, and the Internet: New Roles and Responsibilities for Business. *Business & Society*, 1–17.

Ford, S., & Despeisse, M. (2016). Additive manufacturing and sustainability: An exploratory study of the advantages and challenges. *Journal of Cleaner Production*, *137*, 1573–1587. doi:10.1016/j.jclepro.2016.04.150

Franco, M. A. (2017). Circular economy at the micro level: A dynamic view of incumbents' struggles and challenges in the textile industry. *Journal of Cleaner Production*, *168*, 833–845. doi:10.1016/j.jclepro.2017.09.056

Frappier, M., Meynell, L., & Brown, J. R. (2012). *Thought Experiments in Science, Philosophy, and the Arts*. London, UK: Routledge. doi:10.4324/9780203113271

Frischmann, B. M. (2005). An Economic Theory of Infrastructure and Commons Management. *Minnesota Law Review*, *89*, 917–1030.

Frischmann, B. M. (2012). *Infrastructure. The Social Value of Shared Resources*. New York: Oxford University Press. doi:10.1093/acprof:oso/9780199895656.001.0001

Fuentes, C., & Sörum, N. (2018). Agencing ethical consumers: Smartphone apps and the socio-material reconfiguration of everyday life. *Consumption Markets & Culture*, 1–26.

Fysikopoulos, A., Pastras, G., Alexopoulos, T., & Chryssolouris, G. (2014). On a generalized approach to manufacturing energy efficiency. *International Journal of Advanced Manufacturing Technology*, *73*(9-12), 1437–1452. doi:10.100700170-014-5818-3

Gabriel, M., & Pessl, E. (2016). Industry 4.0 and sustainability impacts: Critical discussion of sustainability aspects with a special focus on future of work and ecological consequences. *Annals of the Faculty of Engineering Hunedoara*, *14*(2), 131.

Gadiesh, O., Leung, P., & Vestring, T. (2007). The battle for China's good-enough market. *Harvard Business Review*, *85*(9), 81–89.

Gardetti, M. A., & Torres, A. L. (2012). Introduction. *Journal of Corporate Citizenship*, *45*(45), 5–15. doi:10.9774/GLEAF.4700.2012.sp.00003

Gareis, R. (2013). Re-Thinking Project Initiation and Project Management by Considering Principles of Sustainable Development. In A. G. Silvius & J. Tharp (Eds.), *Sustainability Integration for Effective Project Management* (pp. 129–143). Hershey, PA: IGI Global. doi:10.4018/978-1-4666-4177-8.ch008

Gareis, R., Heumann, M., & Martinuzzi, A. (2010). Relating sustainable development and project management: a conceptual model. In *Proceedings of the PMI Research Conference 2010*. Newtown Square, PA: Project Management Institute.

Gareis, R., Heumann, M., & Martinuzzi, A. (2011). What can project management learn from considering sustainability principles? *Project Perspectives*, *33*, 60–65.

Gates, B. (2018). *5 books worth reading this summer*. Retrieved from https://www.gatesnotes.com/About-Bill-Gates/Summer-Books-2018

Gavronski, I., Paiva, E. L., Teixeira, R., & De Andrade, M. C. F. (2013). ISO 14001 certified plants in Brazil–taxonomy and practices. *Journal of Cleaner Production*, *39*, 32–41. doi:10.1016/j.jclepro.2012.08.025

Gawer, A., & Cusumano, M. A. (2014). Industry platforms and ecosystem innovation. *Journal of Product Innovation Management*, *31*(3), 417–433. doi:10.1111/jpim.12105

Gebhardt, C. (2017). Humans in the Loop: The Clash of Concepts in Digital Sustainability in Smart Cities. In T. Osburg & C. Lohrmann (Eds.), *Sustainability in a Digital World. CSR, Sustainability, Ethics & Governance* (pp. 85–93). Cham: Springer. doi:10.1007/978-3-319-54603-2_7

Geisler, S., Zelazny, M., Christmann, S., & Hagenhoff, S. (2011, June). Empirical analysis of usage and acceptance of software distribution methods on mobile devices. In *Mobile Business (ICMB), 2011 Tenth International Conference on* (pp. 210-218). IEEE.

Geissbauer, R., Vedso, J., & Schrauf, S. (2016). Industry 4.0: building the digital enterprise: 2016 global industry 4.0 survey. PwC.

George, G., Macgahan, A., & Prabhu, J. (2012). Innovation for inclusive growth: Towards a theoretical framework and a research agenda. *Journal of Management Studies*, *49*(4), 662–683. doi:10.1111/j.1467-6486.2012.01048.x

GeSI Report. (2015). *System Transformation: how digital solutions will drive progress towards the sustainable development goals.* Accenture Strategy. Retrieved March 14, 2018, from www.systemtransformation-sdg.gesi.org

Gilbert, R., Stevenson, D., Girardet, H., & Stren, R. (1996). *Making cities work: The role of local authorities in the urban environment.* London: Earthscan.

Godfrey, L., Scott, D., & Trois, C. (2013). Caught between the global economy and local bureaucracy: The barriers to good waste management practice in South Africa. *Waste Management & Research*, *31*(3), 295–305. doi:10.1177/0734242X12470204 PMID:23377284

Godin, B., & Lane, J. P. (2013). *"Pushes and Pulls": The Hi(story) of the Demand Pull Model of Innovation, Project on the Intellectual History of Innovation* (Working Paper No. 13). Retrieved from http://www.csiic.ca/PDF/Demand-pull.pdf

Goedknegt, D., & Silvius, A. J. G. (2012). *The implementation of sustainability principles in project management.* Paper presented on the 26th IPMA World Congress, Creta, Greece.

Goedknegt, D. (2012). Sustainability in project management: A case study at University of Applied Sciences Utrecht. *PM World Journal*, *1*(4), 1–18.

Gogate, A. S., & Pande, S. S. (2008). Intelligent layout planning for rapid prototyping. *International Journal of Production Research*, *46*(20), 5607–5631. doi:10.1080/00207540701277002

Golicic, S. L., Foggin, J. H., & Mentzer, J. T. (2003). Relationship magnitude and its role in interorganizational relationship structure. *Journal of Business Logistics*, *24*(1), 57–75. doi:10.1002/j.2158-1592.2003.tb00032.x

González-Benito, J., & González-Benito, Ó. (2005). Environmental proactivity and business performance: An empirical analysis. *Omega*, *33*(1), 1–15. doi:10.1016/j.omega.2004.03.002

Gonzalez-Chiñas, D. (2010). *La cadena de suministro inteligente.* Retrieved from https://cadenadesuministro.wordpress.com/2010/08/09/la-cadena-de-suministro-inteligente/

Goodland, R. (1995). The concept of environmental sustainability. *Annual Review of Ecology and Systematics*, *26*(1), 1–24. doi:10.1146/annurev.es.26.110195.000245

Gordon, R. J. (2015). *The Rise and Fall of American Growth: The U.S. Standard of Living since the Civil War.* Princeton, NJ: Princeton University Press.

Govindarajan, V. (2012). A reverse innovation playbook. *Harvard Business Review*, *90*(4), 120–124.

Govindarajan, V., & Ramamurti, R. (2011). Reverse Innovation, Emerging Markets, and Global Strategy. *Global Strategy Journal*, *1*(3-4), 191–205. doi:10.1002/gsj.23

Govindarajan, V., & Trimble, C. (2012). *Reverse innovation: create far from home, win everywhere.* Boston, MA: Harvard Business School Press. doi:10.5437/08956308X5506003

Graf, R., & Herzog, B. (2016). Von der Geschichte der Zukunftsvorstellungen zur Geschichte ihrer Generierung. Probleme und Herausforderungen des Zukunftsbezugs im 20. Jahrhundert. *Geschichte und Gesellschaft (Vandenhoeck & Ruprecht), 42*(3), 497–515. doi:10.13109/gege.2016.42.3.497

Gräfrath, B. (1993). *Ketzer, Dilettanten und Genies. Grenzgänger der Philosophie.* Hamburg, Germany: Junius.

Greening, L. A., Greene, D. L., & Difiglio, C. (2000). Energy efficiency and consumption—the rebound effect—a survey. *Energy Policy, 28*(6-7), 389–401. doi:10.1016/S0301-4215(00)00021-5

Green, K. W. Jr, Zelbst, P. J., Meacham, J., & Bhadauria, V. S. (2012). Green supply chain management practices: Impact on performance. *Supply Chain Management, 17*(3), 290–305. doi:10.1108/13598541211227126

Griskevicius, V., Tybur, J. M., & Van den Bergh, B. (2010). Going green to be seen: Status, reputation, and conspicuous conservation. *Journal of Personality and Social Psychology, 98*(3), 392–404. doi:10.1037/a0017346 PMID:20175620

Groover, H. (2016). As Seattle Uber Drivers Try to Unionize, the Company Doubles Down on a Scare Campaign. *The Stranger.* Retrieved from https://www.thestranger.com/news/2016/12/07/24731875/can-uber-convince-its-drivers-they-dont-need-a-union

Gubbi, J., Buyya, R., Marusic, S., & Palaniswami, M. (2013). Internet of Things (IOT): A vision, architectural elements, and future directions. *Future Generation Computer Systems, 29*(7), 1645–1660. doi:10.1016/j.future.2013.01.010

Gundry, L. K., Kickul, J. R., Griffiths, M. D., & Bacq, S. C. (2007). Creating social change out of nothing: the role of entrepreneurial bricolage in social entrepreneurs' catalytic innovations. In G. T. Lumpkin & J. A. Katz (Eds.), *Social and sustainable entrepreneurship: Advances in entrepreneurship, firm emergence, and growth* (pp. 1–24). Bingley, UK: Emereld Group Publishing.

Gupta, A. (2010). Empathetic innovations: Connections across boundaries. In R. Mashelkar (Ed.), *Timeless Inspirator - Reliving Gandhi* (pp. 43–57). Pune, India: Sakal Papers.

Gupta, A. (2012). Innovations for the poor by the poor. *International Journal of Technological Learning, Innovation and Development, 5*(1-2), 28–39.

Gupta, A., & Wang, H. (2009). *Getting China and India right: strategies for leveraging the world's fastest-growing economies for global advantage.* San Francisco, CA: Wiley.

Haddud, A., DeSouza, A., Khare, A., & Lee, H. (2017). Examining potential benefits and challenges associated with the Internet of Things integration in supply chains. *Journal of Manufacturing Technology Management, 28*(8), 1055–1085. doi:10.1108/JMTM-05-2017-0094

Hallikas, J., & Lintukangas, K. (2016). Purchasing and supply: An investigation of risk management performance. *International Journal of Production Economics*, *171*, 487–494. doi:10.1016/j.ijpe.2015.09.013

Hall, J., Matos, S., Sheehan, L., & Silvestre, B. (2012). Entrepreneurship and innovation at the base of the pyramid: A recipe for inclusive growth or social exclusion? *Journal of Management Studies*, *49*(4), 785–812. doi:10.1111/j.1467-6486.2012.01044.x

Hall, P., & Jacobs, W. (2010). Shifting Proximities: The Maritime Ports Sector in an Era of Global Supply Chains. *Regional Studies*, *44*(9), 1103–1115. doi:10.1080/00343400903365110

Hamacher, S. (2014). *Exploring the frugal innovation process: an empirical study of a new emerging market phenomenon* (Master's thesis). Copenhagen Business School. Retrieved from http://studenttheses.cbs.dk/handle/10417/4943

Hamdoun, M., & Zouaoui, M. (2017). Impact of Environmental Management on Competitive Advantage of Tunisian Companies: The Mediator Role of Organizational Culture. *International Review of Management and Marketing*, *7*, 76–82.

Hang, C., Chen, J., & Subramian, A. M. (2010). Developing disruptive products for emerging economies: Lessons from Asian cases. *Research Technology Management*, *53*(4), 21–26. doi:10.1080/08956308.2010.11657637

Hart, S. (2011). Taking the green leap to the base of the pyramid. In T. London & S. L. Hart (Eds.), *Next Generation Business Strategies for the Base of the Pyramid. New Approaches for Building Mutual Value* (pp. 79–101). Upper Saddle River, NJ: Pearson Education.

Hart, S. L., & Christensen, C. M. (2002). The great leap: Driving innovation from the base of the pyramid. *MIT Sloan Management Review*, *44*(1), 51–56.

Harwood, I., Gapp, R. P., & Stewart, H. J. (2015). Cross-check for completeness: Exploring a novel use of Leximancer in a grounded theory study. *Qualitative Report*, *20*(7), 1029–1045.

Haubro, A. P., Lomholt, H. A., Lueg, R., Nielsen, S. V., & Knudsen, U. (2015). Tactical and strategic choices in business models: Evidence from a Danish fashion outlet. *Journal of Fashion Marketing and Management*, *19*(3), 274–289. doi:10.1108/JFMM-07-2014-0056

Health24. (2013). *The pharmaceutical industry at a glance*. Retrieved from http://www.health24.com/Medical/Meds-and-you/Inside-the-lab/The-pharmaceutical-industry-at-a-glance-20130521

Hein, C. (2016). Port cityscapes: Conference and research contributions on port cities. *Planning Perspectives*, *31*(2), 313–326. doi:10.1080/02665433.2015.1119714

Herrmann, C., Schmidt, C., Kurle, D., Blume, S., & Thiede, S. (2014). Sustainability in manufacturing and factories of the future. *International Journal of Precision Engineering and Manufacturing-green Technology*, *1*(4), 283–292. doi:10.100740684-014-0034-z

Herrmann-Fankhänel, A. (2019). How to take Advantage of Online Platforms like the Sharing Economy does. In Co-Creation: Reshaping Business and Society in the Era of Bottom-up Economics. Springer. doi:10.1007/978-3-319-97788-1_7

Herrmann-Fankhänel, A., Dreßler, A., & Hüsig, S. (2017). JointExpertise – ein internationales Projekt mit Schwerpunkt auf Nachhaltigkeit sowie verantwortungsbewussten und global orientiertem Handeln. *CWG-Dialog*, *2*(22), 5–6.

Heuser, M.-L. (2015). Raumontologie und Raumfahrt um 1600 und 1900. *Reflex*, *6*, 1–15.

Hoejmose, S., Brammer, S., & Millington, A. (2012). "Green" supply chain management: The role of trust and top management in B2B and B2C markets. *Industrial Marketing Management*, *41*(4), 609–620. doi:10.1016/j.indmarman.2012.04.008

Hofmann, E., & Rüsch, M. (2017). Industry 4.0 and the current status as well as future prospects on logistics. *Computers in Industry*, *89*, 23–34. doi:10.1016/j.compind.2017.04.002

Hogan, S. J., & Coote, L. V. (2014). Organizational culture, innovation, and performance: A test of Schein's model. *Journal of Business Research*, *67*(8), 1609–1621. doi:10.1016/j.jbusres.2013.09.007

Ho, J. C., & Chen, H. (2018). Managing the Disruptive and Sustaining the Disrupted: The Case of Kodak and Fujifilm in the Face of Digital Disruption. *The Review of Policy Research*, *35*(3), 352–371. doi:10.1111/ropr.12278

Hollen, R., van den Bosch, F., & Volberda, H. (2014). Strategic levers of port authorities for industrial ecosystem development. *Maritime Economics & Logistics*, *17*(1), 79–96. doi:10.1057/mel.2014.28

Hölsgens, R., Schultze, J., Anttila, V., Kozarev, V., Linford, S., Martin, L., ... Popper, R. (2017). Lessons from a multi-level/stakeholder approach to sustainable innovation actions analysis. In R. Popper & G. Velasco (Eds.), *Sustainable Innovation Policy Advice* (pp. 76–86). Brussels, Belgium: European Commission.

Homayouni, S., & Tang, S. (2015). Optimization of integrated scheduling of handling and storage operations at automated container terminals. *WMU Journal of Maritime Affairs*, *15*(1), 17–39. doi:10.100713437-015-0089-x

Hoornweg, D., & Bhada-Tata, P. (2012). *What a waste: A Global Review of Solid Waste Management. Urban Development Series Knowledge Papers No. 15*. Washington, DC: World Bank.

Hope, A. J., & Moehler, R. (2014). Balancing Projects with Society and the Environment: A Project, Programme and Portfolio Approach. *Procedia: Social and Behavioral Sciences*, *119*, 358–367. doi:10.1016/j.sbspro.2014.03.041

Hopp, C., Antons, D., Kaminski, J., & Salge, T. O. (2018). What 40 Years of Research Reveals About the Difference Between Disruptive and Radical Innovation. *Harvard Business Review*. Retrieved from https://hbr.org/2018/04/what-40-years-of-research-reveals-about-the-difference-between-disruptive-and-radical-innovation

Horowitz, T., & Massey, G. (1991). *Thought experiments in science and philosophy.* Retrieved from http://philsci-archive.pitt.edu/3190/

Horwitz, F. (2013). An analysis of skills development in a transitional economy: The case of the South African labour market. *International Journal of Human Resource Management, 24*(12), 2435–2451. doi:10.1080/09585192.2013.781438

Hossain, M. S., & Muhammad, G. (2016). Cloud-assisted industrial internet of things – enabled framework for health monitoring. *Computer Networks, 101,* 192–202. doi:10.1016/j.comnet.2016.01.009

Houben, R., & Snyers, A. (2018). *Cryptocurrencies and blockchain: Legal context and implications for financial crime, money laundering and tax evasion.* European Parliament. Policy Department of Economic, Scientific and Quality of Life Policies. Retrieved from http://www.europarl.europa.eu/cmsdata/150761/TAX3%20Study%20on%20cryptocurrencies%20and%20blockchain.pdf

Howarth, R. B. (1997). Defining Sustainability: An Overview. *Land Economics, 73*(4), 445–457.

Howell, R., van Beers, C., & Doorn, N. (2018). Value capture and value creation: The role of information technology in business models for frugal innovations in Africa. *Technological Forecasting and Social Change, 131,* 227–239. doi:10.1016/j.techfore.2017.09.030

Hughes, G. D., & Chafin, D. C. (1996). Turning New Product Development into a Continuous Learning Process. *Journal of Product Innovation Management, 13*(2), 89–104. doi:10.1016/0737-6782(95)00112-3

Hüsig, S. (2014). A Typology for Radical Innovation Projects based on an Innovativeness Framework. *International Journal of Innovation and Technology Management, 11*(4).

Hüsig, S., & Kohn, S. (2003). Factors Influencing the Front End of the Innovation Process: A Comprehensive Review of Selected Empirical NPD and Explorative FFE Studies. *10th International Product Development Management Conference,* Brussels, Belgium.

Hüsig, S., Timar, K., & Doblinger, C. (2014). The influence of regulation and disruptive potential on incumbents' sub-market entry decision and success in the context of a network industry. *Journal of Product Innovation Management, 31*(5), 1039–1056. doi:10.1111/jpim.12143

Huynh, P. (2013). *Outbound transportation and its environmental impact: case company: Drilling Mud Corporation (Vietnam)* (Unpublished Bachelor thesis). Haaga-Helia University of Applied Sciences, Helsinki, Finland.

Immelt, J., Govindarajan, V., & Trimble, C. (2009). How GE is disrupting itself. *Harvard Business Review, 87*(10), 56–65.

International Association of Project Managers. (2010). *PM Guide 2.0: Guideline for the Certification of Project Managers.* Liechtenstein: Author.

International Labour Organisation. (2013). *Decent work in waste management: A baseline study on the ward contractor system in the City of Windhoek*. Geneva: ILO. Retrieved May 17, 2018, from http://www.ilo.org/wcmsp5/ groups/public/---africa/---ro-addis_ababa/---ilo-pretoria/ documents/publication/wcms_243093.pdf

International Project Management Association. (2006). *IPMA Competence Baseline, Version 3.0*. Author.

International Union for Conservation of Natural Resources. (1991). *Caring for the Earth: A strategy for sustainable living*. Sterling, VA: Earthscan.

Isaksson, L., Kiessling, T., & Harvey, M. (2014). Corporate social responsibility: Why bother. *Organizational Dynamics*, *43*(1), 64–72. doi:10.1016/j.orgdyn.2013.10.008

Ittmann, H. W. (2015). The impact of big data and business analytics on supply chain management. *Journal of Transport and Supply Chain Management*, *9*(1), 1–9. doi:10.4102/jtscm.v9i1.165

Ivona, B., Novačko, L., & Ogrizović, D. (2014). Processing reverse logistics inventories. *Scientific Journal of Maritime Research*, *28*(1), 10–16.

Jabbour, C. J. C., & Santos, F. C. A. (2008). The central role of human resource management in the search for sustainable organizations. *International Journal of Human Resource Management*, *19*(12), 2133–2154. doi:10.1080/09585190802479389

Jayachandran, P. (2017). The difference between public and private blockchain. *IBM-Research*. Retrieved from https://www.ibm.com/ blogs/blockchain/2017/05/the-difference-between-public-and-private-blockchain/

Jessen, H. (2011). Die Auslieferung von Gütern ohne Vorlage eines Konnossements: Neuere Empfehlungen für die Praxis bei der Verwendung des "Letter of indemnity." TranspR.

Johnson, B. D. (2009). *Science Fiction Prototypes Or: How I Learned to Stop Worrying about the Future and Love Science Fiction*. Paper presented at the 5th International Conference on Intelligent Environments. Retrieved from https://www.researchgate.net/publication/220992681_ Science_Fiction_Prototypes_Or_How_I_Learned_to_Stop_Worrying_about_the_Future_and_ Love_Science_Fiction

Johnson, B. D. (2010). *Science Fiction for Scientists!! An Introduction to SF Prototypes and Brain Machines*. Paper presented at Creative-Science 2010. Retrieved from http://dces.essex. ac.uk/Research/iieg/papers/SF_Prototyping(Paper).pdf

Johnson, B. D. (2011a). *Science Fiction Prototyping: Designing the Future with Science Fiction*. San Rafael, CA: Morgan & Claypool.

Johnson, B. D. (2011b). *Love and God and Robots. The Science Behind the Science Fiction Prototype "Machinery of Love and Grace."* Paper presented at Creative-Science 2011. Retrieved from http://dces.essex.ac.uk/Research/iieg/abstracts_CS11/CS11_ Johnson(abstract).pdf

Jonas, H. (1985). *Technik, Medizin und Ethik: Zur Praxis des Prinzips Verantwortung*. Leipzig, Germany: Insel Verlag.

Jonas, H. (1984). The Imperative of Responsibility. In *Search of Ethics for the Technological Age* (H. Jonas & D. Herr, Trans.). Chicago, IL: University of Chicago Press. (Original work published 1979)

Jones, Clarke-Hill, Comfort, & Hillier. (2008). Marketing and sustainability. Marketing Intelligence and Planning, 26(2), 123-130.

Jones, O. A. H., Voulvoulis, N., & Lester, J. N. (2001). Human pharmaceuticals in the aquatic environment a review. *Environmental Technology*, 22(12), 1383–1394. doi:10.1080/09593330. 2001.11090873 PMID:11873874

Jones, P. (2005). *Maritime Transport Costs and Port Efficiency: A Historical Perspective*. SSRN Electronic Journal. doi:10.2139srn.898468

Joseph, N., & Marnewick, C. (2016). Incorporating the dimensions of sustainability into information systems projects. *Southern African Business Review*, 20(1), 530–556. doi:10.25159/1998-8125/6062

Joyce, A., & Paquin, R. L. (2016). The triple layered business model canvas: A tool to design more sustainable business models. *Journal of Cleaner Production*, 135, 1474–1486. doi:10.1016/j.jclepro.2016.06.067

Jumadi, H., & Zailani, S. (2010). Integrating green innovations in logistics services towards logistics service sustainability: A conceptual paper. *Environmental Research Journal*, 4(4), 261–271. doi:10.3923/erj.2010.261.271

Kaal, W. A., & Vermeulen, E. P. M. (2017). How to Regulate Disruptive Innovation—From Facts to Data. *Journal of Jurimetrics*, 57, 169–209.

Kagermann, H. (2015). *Change Through Digitization—Value Creation in the Age of Industry 4.0*. In H. Albach, H. Meffert, A. Pinkwart, & R. Reichwald (Eds.), *Management of permanent change* (pp. 23–45). New York: Springer Gabler.

Kahn, P. H. (2011). *Technological nature: Adaptation and the future of human life*. MIT Press.

Kahyarara, G. (2018). Opportunity and Growth Diagnostic of Maritime Transportation in the Eastern and Southern Africa. In *Maritime Transport In Africa: Challenges, Opportunities, and an Agenda for Future Research*. IAME Conference. Retrieved November 10, 2019 from https://unctad.org/meetings/en/Contribution/dtltlbts-AhEM2018d1_Kahyarara_en.pdf

Kaltofen, T. (2016, Oktober 18). Blockchain im Einsatz. *Computerwoche*. Retrieved from https://www.computerwoche.de/a/blockchain-im-einsatz,3316539

Kamal, A. N. A., & Fernando, Y. (2015). Review of supply chain integration on green supply chain management (GSCM). In V. González-Prida & A. Raman (Eds.), *Promoting sustainable practices through energy engineering and asset management* (pp. 348–368). Hershey, PA: IGI Global. doi:10.4018/978-1-4666-8222-1.ch015

Kamble, S. S., Gunasekaran, A., & Gawankar, S. A. (2018). Sustainable Industry 4.0 framework: A systematic literature review identifying the current trends and future perspectives. *Process Safety and Environmental Protection*, *117*, 408–425. doi:10.1016/j.psep.2018.05.009

Kant, I. (1788). *Critic der practischen Vernunft*. Retrieved from http://www.deutschestextarchiv. de/book/show/kant_pvernunft_1788

Kant, I. (2004). Grundlegung der Metaphysik der Sitten. Immanuel Kant: Grundlegung zur Metaphysik der Sitten. Göttingen, Germany: Vandenhoeck & Ruprecht. (Original work published 1785)

Kanter, R. M. (2008). Transforming giants. *Harvard Business Review*, *86*(1), 43–52, 136. PMID:18271317

Kaplan, S. M. (1999). Discontinuous Innovation and the growth paradox. *Strategy and Leadership*, *27*(2), 16–21. doi:10.1108/eb054631

Kaplinsky, R. (1990). *The Economies of Small: Appropriate Technology in a Changing World*. London, UK: Intermediate Technology Press. doi:10.3362/9781780440729

Kaplinsky, R. (2011). Schumacher meets Schumpeter: Appropriate technology below the radar. *Research Policy*, *40*(2), 193–203. doi:10.1016/j.respol.2010.10.003

Kassicieh, S. K., Kirchhoff, B. A., Walsh, S. T., & McWhorter, P. J. (2002). The role of small firms in the transfer of disruptive technologies. *Technovation*, *22*(2), 667–674. doi:10.1016/S0166-4972(01)00064-5

Kaulartz, M. (2016). Die Blockchain-Technologie. *Computer und Recht, 7*.

Kawai, K., & Tasaki, T. (2016). Revisiting estimates of municipal solid waste generation per capita and their reliability. *Journal of Material Cycles and Waste Management*, *18*(1), 1–13. doi:10.100710163-015-0355-1

Keceli, Y., Choi, H. R., Cha, Y. S., & Aydogdu, Y. V. (2008). A Study of User Acceptance of Port Community Systems. *ICOVACS 2008 – International Conference on Value Chain Sustainability*. Retrieved January 19, 2019 from https://pdfs.semanticscholar.org/4e35/b8a2c5c519572f18b6edcce60c3e398ccb6f.pdf

Keeys, L. A. (2012). Emerging sustainable development strategy in projects: A theoretical framework. *PM World Journal*, *1*(2), 1–15.

Kepler, J. (2010). Der Traum, oder: Mond-Astronomie. Somnium sive astronomia lunaris. In Mit einem Leitfaden für Mondreisende von Beatrix Langner. Berlin: Matthes & Seitz. (Original work published 1593)

Khajuria, A., Matsui, T., Machimura, T., & Morioka, T. (2010). Assessment of the challenge of sustainable recycling of municipal solid waste management. *India International Journal of Environmental Technology Management, 13,* 171–187.

Khiewnavawongsa, S., & Schmidt, E. K. (2013). Barriers to green supply chain implementation in the electronics industry. In *Proceedings of 2013* (pp. 226–230). Industrial Engineering and Engineering Management. doi:10.1109/IEEM.2013.6962408

Khilji, N., Duan, Y., Lewis, R., Bukoye, T., & Luton, U. K. (2017, July). Incorporating Knowledge Management Tools in the UK Local Government towards Improved Planning Support Services. In *ICICKM 2017 14th International Conference on Intellectual Capital Knowledge Management & Organisational Learning: ICICKM 2017* (p. 122). Academic Conferences and Publishing Limited.

Khurana, K., & Ricchetti, M. (2016). Two decades of sustainable supply chain management in the fashion business: An appraisal. *Journal of Fashion Marketing and Management, 20*(1), 89–104. doi:10.1108/JFMM-05-2015-0040

Kim, D., Park, K., Choi, G., & Min, K. (2014). A study on the factors that affect the adoption of Smart Water Grid. *Journal of Computer Virology and Hacking Techniques, 10*(2), 119–128. doi:10.100711416-014-0206-y

Kim, W. C., & Mauborgne, R. (2005). *Blue ocean strategy: How to create uncontested market space and make competition irrelevant.* Boston, MA: Harvard Business School Press.

King, R. J. (2007). *The Emergence of a New Global Culture in the Imagination Age.* British Council Essays.

Kirchhof, S., & Brandtweiner, R. (2011). Sustainability in projects: An analysis of relevant sustainability aspects in the project management process based on the three pillars model. In C. A. Brebbia & E. Beriatos (Eds.), *Sustainable Development And Planning* (pp. 527–535). Southampton, UK: WIT Press. doi:10.2495/SDP110441

Kivilä, J., Martinsuo, M., & Vuorinen, L. (2017). Sustainable project management through project control in infrastructure projects. *International Journal of Project Management, 35*(5), 1167–1183. doi:10.1016/j.ijproman.2017.02.009

Klassen, R. D., & Vereecke, A. (2012). Social issues in supply chains: Capabilities link responsibility, risk (opportunity), and performance. *International Journal of Production Economics, 140*(1), 103–115. doi:10.1016/j.ijpe.2012.01.021

Köksal, D., Strähle, J., Müller, M., & Freise, M. (2017). Social sustainable supply chain management in the textile and apparel industry: A literature review. *Sustainability, 9*(100), 1–32.

Kontis, V., Bennett, J. E., Mathers, C. D., Li, G., Foreman, K., & Ezzati, M. (2017). Future life expectancy in 35 industrialised countries: Projections with a Bayesian model ensemble. *Lancet, 389*(10076), 1323–1335. doi:10.1016/S0140-6736(16)32381-9 PMID:28236464

Kopp, U. (2013). Systemische Nachhaltigkeitskompetenzen für Führungskräfte–Erfahrungen mit Aufstellungsarbeit in der Managementaus- und weiterbildung. *Die Unternehmung*, *67*(2), 126–151. doi:10.5771/0042-059X-2013-2-126

Kortan, W., & Gad, G. (2014). Knowledge: for social innovation. *Journal of American Science, 10*(2), 143-147.

Krippendorff, K. (2012). *Content analysis: An introduction to its methodology* (3rd ed.). London: Sage.

Krishnan, R. (2010). *From jugaad to systematic innovation: The challenge for India*. Bangalore, India: Utpreraka Foundation.

Krys, C. (2017). Megatrends–Rahmenbedingungen für unternehmerische Nachhaltigkeit. In CSR und Strategisches Management (pp. 45-65). Springer Gabler. doi:10.1007/978-3-662-49457-8_2

Kubicek, B., & Korunka, C. (2017). The Present and Future of Work: Some Concluding Remarks and Reflections on Upcoming Trends. In *Job Demands in a Changing World of Work* (pp. 153–162). Cham: Springer. doi:10.1007/978-3-319-54678-0_9

Kudłak, R., Martinuzzi, A., Schönherr, N., & Krumay, B. (2015). Quo vadis responsible fashion? Contingencies and trends influencing sustainable business models in the wearing apparel sector. *Journal of Corporate Citizenship*, *57*(57), 33–54. doi:10.9774/GLEAF.4700.2015.ma.00005

Kuhlman, T., & Farrington, J. (2010). What is sustainability? *Sustainability*, *2*(11), 3436–3448. doi:10.3390u2113436

Kuka. (2017). *Into the cloud with KUKA SmartConnect.frictionwelding*. Retrieved from https://www.kuka.com/en-ch/press/news/2017/09/industrie-40-innovation-award

Kumar, N., & Puranam, P. (2012). *India inside: The emerging innovation challenge to the west*. Boston, MA: Harvard Business Press.

Kumar, R., & Chandrakar, R. (2012). Overview of green supply chain management: Operation and environmental impact at different stages of the supply chain. *International Journal of Engineering and Advanced Technology*, *1*(3), 1–6.

Kumar, S., & Prakash, A. (2016). Role of Big Data and Analytics in Smart Cities. *International Journal of Science And Research*, *5*(2), 12–23. doi:10.21275/v5i2.nov161007

Kümmerer, K. (2010). Why green and sustainable pharmacy? In K. Kümmerer & M. Hempel (Eds.), *Green and sustainable pharmacy* (pp. 3–10). Berlin, Germany: Springer. doi:10.1007/978-3-642-05199-9_1

Kupper, F., Klaassen, P., Rijnen, M., Vermeulen, S., & Broerse, J. (2015). *Report on the Quality Criteria of Good Practice Standards in RRI, Deliverable 3.1 RRI Tools*. Amsterdam: Athena Institute, VU University Amsterdam.

Kvochko, H. (2013). Five ways technology can help the economy. *World Economic Forum.* Retrieved October 19, 2018, from https://www.weforum.org/agenda/2013/04/five-ways-technology-can-help-the-economy

Labuschagne, C., & Brent, A. C. (2004). *Sustainable project life cycle management: Aligning project management methodologies with the principles of sustainable development.* Paper presented at the Project Management South Africa International Conference, Johannesburg, South Africa.

Lambert, D., & Cooper, M. (2000). Issues in supply chain management. *Industrial Marketing Management, 29*(1), 65–83. doi:10.1016/S0019-8501(99)00113-3

Lambert, S. C. (2015). The importance of classification to business model research. *Journal of Business Models, 3*(1), 49–61.

Lamnek, S. (1988). Qualitative Social Science. In Methodology. Beltz PVU.

Laschewski, C. (2017*). Der Blockchain-Algorithmus: Eine GoB-konforme digitale Buchführung?* Retrieved from https://www.maersk.com/news/2018/06/29/maersk-and-ibm-introduce-tradelens-blockchain-shipping-solution

Lasi, H., Fettke, P., Kemper, H. G., Feld, T., & Hoffmann, M. (2014). Industry 4.0. *Business & Information Systems Engineering, 6*(4), 239–242. doi:10.100712599-014-0334-4

Lazonick, W. (2004). Indigenous innovation and economic development: Lessons from china's leap into the information age. *Industry and Innovation, 11*(4), 273–297. doi:10.1080/1366271042000289360

Lee, J., Kim, H., & Ahn, M. (2011). The willingness of e-Government service adoption by business users: The role of offline service quality and trust in technology. *Government Information Quarterly, 28*(2), 222–230. doi:10.1016/j.giq.2010.07.007

Lee, S. Y., & Klassen, R. D. (2008). Drivers and enablers that foster environmental management capabilities in small- and medium-sized suppliers in supply chains. *Production and Operations Management, 17*(6), 573–586. doi:10.3401/poms.1080.0063

Leonhard, G., & von Kospoth, C. A. G. (2017). Exponential technology versus linear humanity: Designing a sustainable future. In T. Osburg & C. Lohrmann (Eds.), *Sustainability in a Digital World. CSR, Sustainability, Ethics & Governance* (pp. 77–83). Cham: Springer. doi:10.1007/978-3-319-54603-2_6

Leonhardt, F., & Wiedemann, A. (2015). *Realigning Risk Management in the Light of Industry 4.0.* Amsterdam: Academic Press. 10.2139srn.2678947

Leuschner, R., Rogers, D. S., & Charvet, F. F. (2013). A Meta-Analysis of Supply Chain Integration and Firm Performance. *The Journal of Supply Chain Management, 49*(2), 34–57. doi:10.1111/jscm.12013

Lévi-Strauss, C. (1967). *The savage mind.* Chicago, IL: University of Chicago Press.

Leximancer Pty Ltd. (2018). *Leximancer*™ (Version 4.50). Author.

Leydesdorff, L. (1997). Why words and co-words cannot map the development of the sciences. *Journal of the American Society for Information Science*, *48*(5), 418–427. doi:10.1002/(SICI)1097-4571(199705)48:5<418::AID-ASI4>3.0.CO;2-Y

Liesch, P. W., Håkanson, L., McGaughey, S. L., Middleton, S., & Cretchley, J. (2011). The evolution of the international business field: A scientometric investigation of articles published in its premier journal. *Scientometrics*, *88*(1), 17–42. doi:10.100711192-011-0372-3

Lin, J., & Lee, S. T. (2012, November). Mapping 12 years of communication scholarship: themes and concepts in the Journal of Communication. In *International Conference on Asian Digital Libraries* (pp. 359-360). Springer. 10.1007/978-3-642-34752-8_53

Linkov, I., Trump, B. D., Poinsatte-Jones, K., & Florin, M. V. (2018). Governance strategies for a sustainable digital world. *Sustainability*, *10*(2), 440. doi:10.3390u10020440

Lokuge, P., & Alahakoon, D. (2007). Improving the adaptability in automated vessel scheduling in container ports using intelligent software agents. *European Journal of Operational Research*, *177*(3), 1985–2015. doi:10.1016/j.ejor.2005.12.016

London, T. (2009). Making better investments at the base of the pyramid. *Harvard Business Review*, *87*(5), 106–113.

London, T., & Hart, S. L. (2004). Reinventing strategies for emerging markets: Beyond the transnational model. *Journal of International Business Studies*, *35*(5), 350–370. doi:10.1057/palgrave.jibs.8400099

Long, T. B., Looijen, A., & Blok, V. (2018). Critical success factors for the transition to business models for sustainability in the food and beverage industry in the Netherlands. *Journal of Cleaner Production*, *175*, 82–95. doi:10.1016/j.jclepro.2017.11.067

Lubberink, R., Blok, V., Van Ophem, J., & Omta, O. (2017). Lessons for Responsible Innovation in the Business Context: A Systematic Literature Review of Responsible, Social and Sustainable Innovation Practices. *Sustainability*, *9*(5), 721. doi:10.3390u9050721

Lubberink, R., Blok, V., Van Ophem, J., Velde, G., & Omta, O. (2017). Innovation For Society: Towards a Typology of Developing Innovations by Social Entrepreneurs. *Journal of Social Entrepreneurship*, 1–27. doi:10.1080/19420676.2017.1410212

Lueg, R., Medelby Pedersen, M., & Clemmensen, S. N. (2015). The role of corporate sustainability in a low-cost business model: A case study in the Scandinavian fashion industry. *Business Strategy and the Environment*, *24*(5), 344–359. doi:10.1002/bse.1825

Lund-Thomsen, P., & Lindgreen, A. (2014). Corporate social responsibility in global value chains: Where are we now and where are we going? *Journal of Business Ethics*, *123*(1), 11–22. doi:10.100710551-013-1796-x

Lundvall, B.-Å. (1985). *Product innovation and user-producer interaction*. Aalborg, Denmark: Aalborg University Press.

Lundvall, B.-Å. (2017). Is there a technological fix for the current global stagnation?: A response to Daniele Archibugi, Blade Runner economics: Will innovation lead the economic recovery? *Research Policy*, *46*(3), 544–549. doi:10.1016/j.respol.2016.06.011

Lu, Q. (2000). *China's leap into the information age: Innovation and organization in the computer industry*. New York, NY: Oxford University Press. doi:10.1093/acprof:o so/9780198295372.001.0001

Luthra, S., Kumar, V., Kumar, S., & Haleen, A. (2011). Barriers to implement green supply chain management in automobile industry using interpretive structural modeling technique: An Indian perspective. *Journal of Industrial Engineering and Management*, *4*(2), 231–257. doi:10.3926/jiem.2011.v4n2.p231-257

Lynch, K. (2017). How disruptive technologies are eroding our trust in government. *The Globe and Mail*. Retrieved from https://www.theglobeandmail.com/opinion/how-disruptive-technologies-are-eroding-our-trust-in-government/article34857043/

Lynley, M. (2012). *Elon Musk Wants To Invent A Fifth Mode Of Transportation Called 'Hyperloop'*. Retrieved from https://www.businessinsider.com/elon-musk-is-kicking-around-an-idea-that-would-send-you-from-san-francisco-to-los-angeles-in-30-minutes-2012-7?IR=T

Lyons, G., Mokhtarian, P., Dijst, M., & Böcker, L. (2018). The dynamics of urban metabolism in the face of digitalization and changing lifestyles: Understanding and influencing our cities. *Resources, Conservation and Recycling*, *132*, 246–257. doi:10.1016/j.resconrec.2017.07.032

Machi, L., & McEvoy, B. (2017). *The Literature Review: Six Steps to success* (3rd ed.). London: Corwin.

Magee, C. (1993). The Age of Imagination. Coming Soon to a Civilization Near You. *Second International Symposium: National Security & National Competitiveness: Open Source Solutions Proceedings*, *1*, 95–98.

Magretta, J. (2002). Why business models matter. *Harvard Business Review*. Available at: https://hbr.org/2002/05/why-business-models-matter

Marcelino-Sádaba, S., González-Jaen, L. F., & Pérez-Ezcurdia, A. (2015). Using project management as a way to sustainability: From a comprehensive review to a framework definition. *Journal of Cleaner Production*, *99*, 1–16. doi:10.1016/j.jclepro.2015.03.020

Marnewick, C. (2017). Information system project's sustainability capability levels. *International Journal of Project Management*, *35*(6), 1151–1166. doi:10.1016/j.ijproman.2017.02.014

Martens, M. L., & Carvalho, M. M. (2013). An exploratory study of sustainability evaluation in project management. *Product: Management & Development*, *11*(2), 111–117. doi:10.4322/pmd.2013.019

Martens, M. L., & Carvalho, M. M. (2015). The challenge of introducing sustainability into project management function: Multiple-case studies. *Journal of Cleaner Production*, *117*, 29–40. doi:10.1016/j.jclepro.2015.12.039

Martín-Soberón, A. M., Monfort, A., Sapiña, R., Monterde, N., & Calduch, D. (2014). Automation in port container terminals. *Procedia: Social and Behavioral Sciences*, *160*, 195–204. doi:10.1016/j.sbspro.2014.12.131

Maspero, E., Van Dyk, E., & Ittmann, H. (2008). Maritime supply chain security: Navigating through a sea of compliance requirements. *Journal of Transport And Supply Chain Management*, *2*(1). doi:10.4102/jtscm.v2i1.44

Massoud, M., Tabcharani, R., Nakkash, R., & Jamali, D. (2012). *Environmental performance improvement and ISO 14001: case of Lebanon. Environmental Impact*. WIT Press.

Matser, I. (2017). Leading Change in Ongoing Technological Developments: An Essay. In Sustainability in a Digital World. Springer International.

Maturana, F. (2004). Distributed multi-agent architecture for automation systems. *Expert Systems with Applications*, *26*(1), 49–56. doi:10.1016/S0957-4174(03)00068-X

Mayner, L., & Arbon, P. (2015). Defining disaster: The need for harmonisation of terminology. *Australasian Journal of Disaster and Trauma Studies*, *19*, 21–26.

Mayring, P. (2015). *Qualitative Inhaltsanalyse: Grundlagen und Techniken* (12th ed.). Weinheim, Germany: Beltz.

McKinsey Global Institute (MGI). (2013). *Disruptive technologies: Advances that will transform life, business, and the global economy*. Retrieved February 19, 2019, from https://www.mckinsey.com/~/media/mckinsey/business%20functions/mckinsey%20digital/our%20insights/disruptive%20technologies/mgi_disruptive_technologies_full_report_may2013.ashx

McKinsey Global Institute (MGI). (2018). *Notes from the AI Frontier. Insights from Hundreds of Use Cases*. McKinsey and Company. Retrieved October 19, 2018, from https://www.mckinsey.com/~/media/McKinsey/Global%20Themes/Artificial%20Intelligence/Notes%20from%20the%20AI%20frontier%20Applications%20and%20value%20of%20deep%20learning/MGI_Notes-from-AI-Frontier_Discussion-chapter.ashx

Melnyk, S. A., Bititci, U., Platts, K., Tobias, J., & Andersen, B. (2014). Is performance measurement and management fit for the future? *Management Accounting Research*, *25*(2), 173–186. doi:10.1016/j.mar.2013.07.007

Mfeka, B. (2018). Rationalisation of state-owned enterprises has become inevitable. *BusinessDay*. Retrieved from https://www.businesslive.co.za/bd/opinion/2018-12-05-rationalisation-of-state-owned-enterprises-has-become-inevitable/

Mgimba, C., & Sanga, A. (2016). Municipal Solid Waste Composition Characterization for Sustainable Management Systems in Mbeya City, Tanzania. *International Journal of Science Environmental Technology*, *5*, 47–58.

Michaelides, R., Bryde, D., & Ohaeri, U. S. (2014). Sustainability from a project management perspective: are oil and gas supply chains ready to embed sustainability in their projects? In *Proceedings of the Project Management Institute Research and Education Conference*. Newtown Square, PA: Project Management Institute.

Michaud, T. (2017). *Innovation, Between Science and Science Fiction*. London, UK: ISTE Ltd. doi:10.1002/9781119427568

Mielniczuk, J., & Teisseyre, P. (2014). Using random subspace method for prediction and variable importance assessment in linear regression. *Computational Statistics & Data Analysis*, *71*, 725–742. doi:10.1016/j.csda.2012.09.018

Mill, J. S. (1861). *Utilitarianism*. Retrieved from https://en.wikisource.org/wiki/Utilitarianism

Millard, J. (2014). Development Theory. In J. Howaldt, A. Butzin, D. Domanski, & C. Kaletka (Eds.), Theoretical approaches to social innovation – a critical literature review (pp. 34-59). Collaborative project: Social Innovation - Driving Force of Social Change.

Miner, A., Bassof, P., & Moorman, C. (2001). Organizational improvisation and learning: A field study. *Administrative Science Quarterly*, *46*(2), 304–337. doi:10.2307/2667089

Minges, M. (2016). Exploring the Relationship between Broadband and Economic Growth. Background Chapter – Digital Dividends. *World Development Report*. Retrieved October 19, 2018, from http://pubdocs.worldbank.org/en/391452529895999/WDR16-BP-Exploring-the-Relationship-between-Broadband-and-Economic-Growth-Minges.pdf

Ministerium für Umwelt, Klima und Energiewirtschaft Baden-Württemberg (MUKEBW). (2018). *Digitalisierung als Motor für mehr Nachhaltigkeit. Runder Tisch "Nachhaltige Digitalisierung" des Umweltministeriums*. Retrieved from https://www.nachhaltigkeitsstrategie.de/erleben/rueckblick/nachhaltige-digitalisierung.html

Minnie, T. (2015). *A review of the South African pharmaceutical landscape*. Retrieved from http://www.utipharma.co.za/documents/198965/199128/UTi+November+2015+-+South+Africa+V1.pdf/c9c979e4-41ce-4d2c-94dc-e24f5d8c1b43

Missimer, M., Robèrt, K.-H., & Broman, G. (2017). A strategic approach to social sustainability – Part 1: Exploring the social system. *Journal of Cleaner Production*, *140*, 32–41. doi:10.1016/j.jclepro.2016.03.170

Mokone, T. (2016). *The impact of governance structure on the port performance: a case of Durban Port* (Unpublished Masters dissertation). World Maritime University.

Moldavska, A., & Welo, T. (2017). The concept of sustainable manufacturing and its definitions: A content-analysis based literature review. *Journal of Cleaner Production*, *166*, 744–755. doi:10.1016/j.jclepro.2017.08.006

Moller, J. (2008). A Critical Note on 'The Rise of Illiberal Democracy'. *Australian Journal of Political Science*, *43*(3), 555–561. doi:10.1080/10361140802267316

Monczka, M. R., Handfield, B. R., Giunipero, C. L., Patterson, J. L., & Waters, D. (2016). *Purchasing and supply chain management* (6th ed.). Boston, MA: Cengage Learning.

Monto, M., Ganesh, L. S., & Varghese, K. (2005). *Sustainability and Human Settlements: Fundamental Issues, Modeling and Simulations*. New Delhi, India: Sage Publications.

Morris, P. W. G., Pinto, J. K., & Söderlund, J. (2012). *The Oxford Handbook of Project Management*. New York: Oxford University Press.

Moudud-Ul-Huq S. (2014). The Role of Artificial Intelligence in the Development of Accounting Systems: A Review. *IUP Journal of Accounting Research & Audit Practices, 13*(2), 7-19.

Mougayar, W. (2011). *The business blockchain: promise, practice, and application of the next internet technology*. Hoboken, NJ: John Wiley & Sons.

Mugabe, A. Y. (2013). *Green management practices and supply chain performance of pharmaceutical companies in Nairobi* (Unpublished Masters dissertation). University of Nairobi, Kenya.

Mukherjee, S. (2017). *Welspun initiates digitization drive towards cashless economy*. Retrieved from https://techseen.com/2017/01/11/welspun-digitization-cashless/

Müller, J. M., Kiel, D., & Voigt, K. I. (2018). What drives the implementation of Industry 4.0? The role of opportunities and challenges in the context of sustainability. *Sustainability, 10*(1), 247. doi:10.3390u10010247

Müller-Mielitz, S., & Lux, T. (Eds.). (2016). *E-Health-Ökonomie*. Springer-Verlag.

Mungazde, S. (2014). *Imported waste from Japan and has been illegally dumped in South Africa*. Retrieved May 13, 2018, from http://www.bdlive.co.za/business/industrials/2014/05/26/interwaste-probe-reaches-across-borders

Muntean, M. C., Nechita, D., Nistor, C., & Şarpe, D. (2010). Port management importance in port activities development. In *The 3rd WSEAS International Conference On Urban Planning and Transportation (UPT '10), Latest Trends on Urban Planning and Transportation, Mathematics and Computers in Science and Engineering, A Series of Reference Books and Textbooks*. Corfu Island, Greece: WSEAS Press. Retrieved from www.wseas.org

Musk, E. (2013). *Hyperloop Alpha*. Retrieved from http://www.spacex.com/sites/spacex/files/hyperloop_alpha-20130812

Naicker, R., & Allopi, D. (2015). Improving performance at the Durban Container Terminal through automation. *Civil Engineering, 23*(9), 74-76. Retrieved 15 January 2019 from https://ir.dut.ac.za/bitstream/10321/2370/1/Naicker_CE_v23_n9_a17_2015.pdf

Nakamoto, S. (2018). *Bitcoin: A Peer-to-Peer Electronic Cash System*. Retrieved from https://bitcoin.org/bitcoin.pdf

Narasimhan, R., & Kim, S. (2002). Effect of supply chain integration on the relationship between diversification and performance: Evidence from Japanese and Korean firms. *Journal of Operations Management*, 20(3), 303–323. doi:10.1016/S0272-6963(02)00008-6

Narayana, A. S., Elias, A., & Pati, K. R. (2014). Reverse logistics in the pharmaceuticals industry: A systemic analysis. *International Journal of Logistics Management*, 25(2), 379–398. doi:10.1108/IJLM-08-2012-0073

Narsoo, J., & Muslun, A., W., & Sameer Sunhaloo, M. (2009). A Radio Frequency Identification (RFID) Container Tracking System for Port Louis Harbor: The Case of Mauritius. *Issues in Informing Science and Information Technology*, 6, 127–142. doi:10.28945/1047

Ndlovu, Z. (2007). Port Infrastructure and Operational Efficiency, and Port Productivity Management. In *PMAESA Maritime Conference* (pp. 1-10). Mahe, Seychelles: PMAESA. Retrieved October 13, 2016, from http://www.pmaesa.org/media/docs/Zeph_Ndlovu_TPT.pdf

Ngai, E. W., Chau, D. C., & Chan, T. L. A. (2011). Information technology, operational, and management competencies for supply chain agility: Findings from case studies. *The Journal of Strategic Information Systems*, 20(3), 232–249. doi:10.1016/j.jsis.2010.11.002

Ng, F. Y., Yew, F. K., Basiron, Y., & Sundram, K. (2011). A renewable future driven with Malaysian palm oil-based green technology. *Journal of Oil Palm. Environmental Health*, 2, 1–7.

Nguyen, Q. A., & Hens, L. (2015). Environmental performance of the cement industry in Vietnam: The influence of ISO 14001 certification. *Journal of Cleaner Production*, 96, 362–378. doi:10.1016/j.jclepro.2013.09.032

Nhamo, G. (2011). *Green economy and climate mitigation: Topics of relevance to Africa*. Pretoria: Africa Institute of South Africa.

Niinimäki, K., & Hassi, L. (2011). Emerging design strategies in sustainable production and consumption of textiles and clothing. *Journal of Cleaner Production*, 19, 1876–1883.

Nishida, A., Koshijima, I., & Umeda, T. (2014). The deployment of sustainable P2M. In *Proceedings of International Conference on Engineering*. Bergamo, Italy: Institute of Electrical and Electronics Engineers.

Nordhaus, W. D. (2015). *Are We Approaching an Economic Singularity? Information Technology and the Future of Economic Growth (No. w21547)*. National Bureau of Economic Research. doi:10.3386/w21547

Ntuli, N. (2016). *Toxic cocktail suspected in stink pollutions busters roped in Campbell's book gets global face*. Retrieved May 12, 2018, from http://sundaytribune.newspaperdirect.com/epaper/viewer.aspx

OECD & ITU. (2011). *M-Government: Mobile Technologies for Responsive Governments and Connected Societies*. Paris: OECD Publishing. doi:10.1787/9789264118706-en

OECD (2015a). *OECD Environment Statistics, Municipal Waste database.* OECD. doi:10.1787/data-00601-en

OECD. (2003). *ICT and Economic Growth.* Paris: OECD Publishing. Retrieved October 28, 2013, from http://www.cla.org.pt/docs/OCDE_TIC.PDF

OECD. (2014). *Recommendation of the Council on Digital Government Strategies.* OECD Publishing. Retrieved October 28, 2013, from http://www.oecd.org/gov/digital-government/Recommendation-digital-government-strategies.pdf

OECD. (2015b). *Environment at a Glance 2015: OECD Indicators.* Paris: OECD Publishing. doi:10.1787/9789264235199-

Oehlmann, I. (2011). *The sustainable footprint methodology.* Cologne, Germany: Lambert Academic Publishing.

Oesterreich, T. D., & Teuteberg, F. (2016). Understanding the implications of digitisation and automation in the context of Industry 4.0: A triangulation approach and elements of a research agenda for the construction industry. *Computers in Industry, 83,* 121–139. doi:10.1016/j.compind.2016.09.006

Ogburn, W. F. (1966). *Social change: With respect to cultural and original nature.* Oxford, UK: Delta Books.

Oh, D.-S., Phillips, F., Park, S., & Lee, E. (2016). Innovation ecosystems: A critical examination. *Technovation, 54,* 1–6. doi:10.1016/j.technovation.2016.02.004

Ojo, E., Mbohwa, C., & Akinlabi, E. (2013). *An analysis of green supply chain management in South Africa and Nigeria: A comparative study.* In *Proceedings of the International Conference on Integrated Waste Management and Green Energy Engineering* (pp. 315-319). University of Johannesburg.

Okland, A. (2015). Gap Analysis for Incorporating Sustainability in Project Management. *Procedia Computer Science, 64*(1877), 103-109.

Oliveira, T., Thomas, M., & Espadanal, M. (2014). Assessing the determinants of cloud computing adoption: An analysis of the manufacturing and services sectors. *Information & Management, 51*(5), 497–510. doi:10.1016/j.im.2014.03.006

Opazo-Basáez, M., Vendrell-Herrero, F., & Bustinza, O. F. (2018). Uncovering Productivity Gains of Digital and Green Servitization: Implications from the Automotive Industry. *Sustainability, 10*(5).

Ortmann, G. (2013). Brave New World und wie neu sie wirklich ist. *ZFO - Zeitschrift Führung + Organisation, 82*(5), 338-339.

Osburg, T., & Lohrmann, C. (Eds.). (2017). *Sustainability in a Digital World. CSR, Sustainability, Ethics & Governance.* Cham: Springer. doi:10.1007/978-3-319-54603-2

Osterwalder, A., Pigneur, Y., & Tucci, C. L. (2005). Clarifying business models: Origins, present, and future of the concept. *Communications of the Association for Information Systems, 16*, 1–25. doi:10.17705/1CAIS.01601

Ostraszewska, Z., & Tylec, A. (2015). Reverse innovation – how it works. *International Journal of Business and Management, 3*(1), 57–74. doi:10.20472/BM.2015.3.1.004

Otegi-Olaso, J. R., Aguilar-Fernández, M. E., & Cruz-Villazón, C. (2015). Towards sustainable project management: A literature review. In *Proceedings of the 19th International Congress on Project Management and Engineering*. Granada, Spain: International Project Management Association.

Overendstudio. (n.d.). *Transnet Port Terminals*. Retrieved from: http://www.overendstudio.co.za/online_reports/transnet_ar2014/integrated/pao_tpt.php

Owen, R., Stilgoe, J., Macnaghten, P., Gorman, M., Fisher, E., & Gustion, D. (2013). A Framework for responsible innovation. In R. Owen, J. Bessant, & M. Heintz (Eds.), *Responsible innovation* (pp. 27–50). London: Wiley. doi:10.1002/9781118551424.ch2

Paillé, P., Chen, Y., Boiral, O., & Jin, J. (2014). The impact of human resource management on environmental performance: An employee-level study. *Journal of Business Ethics, 121*(3), 451–466. doi:10.100710551-013-1732-0

Pansera, M. (2014). *Discourses of innovation and development - Insights from ethnographic case studies in Bangladesh and India* (Unpublished doctoral dissertation). University of Exeter, UK.

Pansera, M. (2013). Frugality, grassroots and inclusiveness - new challenges for mainstream innovation theories. *African Journal of Science, Technology, Innovation and Development, 5*(6), 469–478.

Pansera, M., & Sarkar, S. (2016). Crafting sustainable development solutions – Frugal innovations of grassroots entrepreneurs. *Sustainability, 8*(1), 1–25. doi:10.3390u8010051

Parry, M. E., & Kawakami, T. (2016). The Encroachment Speed of Potentially Disruptive Innovations with Indirect Network Externalities: The Case of E-Readers. *Product Development & Management Association, 34*(2), 141–158. doi:10.1111/jpim.12333

Pavie, X. (2014). The Importance of Responsible Innovation and the Necessity of 'Innovation-Care'. *Philosophy of Management, 13*(1), 21–42. doi:10.5840/pom20141313

Peattie, K. (2001). Towards sustainability: The third age of green marketing. *The Marketing Review, 2*(2), 129–146. doi:10.1362/1469347012569869

Pedersen, E. R. G., Gwozdz, W., & Hvass, K. K. (2018). Exploring the relationship between business model innovation, corporate sustainability, and organisational values within the fashion industry. *Journal of Business Ethics, 149*(2), 267–284. doi:10.100710551-016-3044-7

Petrick, I. J., & Juntiwasarakij, S. (2011). The rise of the rest: Hotbeds of innovation in emerging markets. *Research Technology Management, 54*(4), 24–29. doi:10.5437/08956308X5404009

Pettit, S., & Beresford, A. (2009). Port development: From gateways to logistics hubs. *Maritime Policy & Management, 36*(3), 253–267. doi:10.1080/03088830902861144

Peukert, B., Benecke, S., Clavell, J., Neugebauer, S., Nissen, N. F., Uhlmann, E., ... Finkbeiner, M. (2015). Addressing sustainability and flexibility in manufacturing via smart modular machine tool frames to support sustainable value creation. *Procedia CIRP, 29,* 514–519. doi:10.1016/j.procir.2015.02.181

Pieterse, C. (2015). *Illegal Dump a Hazard.* Retrieved May 15, 2018, from http://www.news24.com/SouthAfrica/News/Illegal-dump-a-health-hazard-20150629

Pillay, K., & Mbhele, T. P. (2015). The challenges of green logistics in the Durban road freight industry. *Environment and Ecology, 6*(1), 64–73.

Plessner, H. (1975). Die Stufen des Organischen und der Mensch. Einleitung in die philosophische Anthropologie (3rd ed.). Berlin: Walter de Gruyter. (Original work published 1928) doi:10.1515/9783110845341

Polit, D. F., & Beck, C. T. (2008). *Nursing research: Generating and assessing evidence for nursing practice* (8th ed.). Philadelphia, PA: Wolters Kluwer Health/ Lippincott Williams & Wilkins.

Popper, R., Velasco, G., & Popper, M. (2017b). *CASI-F: Common Framework for the Assessment and Management of Sustainable Innovation, CASI project report.* Deliverable 6.2. Retrieved from http://www.futuresdiamond.com/casi2020/casi-f/

Popper, R., Popper, M., & Velasco, G. (2017a). Towards a more responsible sustainable innovation assessment and management culture in Europe. *Engineering Management in Production and Services, 9*(4), 7–20. doi:10.1515/emj-2017-0027

Popper, R., Velasco, G., & Ravetz, J. (2016). *State-of-the-art of Sustainable Innovation: Climate action, environment, resource efficiency and raw materials.* Brussels, Belgium: European Commission.

Porter, M. E., & Heppelmann, J. E. (2015). How smart, connected products are transforming companies. *Harvard Business Review, 93*(10), 96–114.

Porter, M., & Heppelmann, J. (2014). How Smart Connected Products are Transforming Competition. *Harvard Business Review, 92*(11), 64–88.

Prabhu, J., & Jain, S. (2015). Innovation and entrepreneurship in India - Understanding jugaad. *Asia Pacific Journal of Management, 32*(4), 843–868. doi:10.100710490-015-9445-9

Prahalad, C. K., & Hart, S. L. (2002). The fortune at the bottom of the pyramid. *Strategy + Business, 22,* 2-14.

Prahalad, C. K. (2004). *The fortune at the bottom of the pyramid: Eradicating poverty through profits.* Upper Saddle River, NJ: Pearson Education.

Prahalad, C. K. (2006). The innovation sandbox. *Strategy and Business, 44,* 1–10.

Prahalad, C. K. (2012). Bottom of the pyramid as a source of breakthrough innovations. *Journal of Product Innovation Management*, *29*(1), 6–12. doi:10.1111/j.1540-5885.2011.00874.x

Prahalad, C. K., & Mashelkar, R. A. (2010). Innovation's Holy Grail. *Harvard Business Review*, *88*(7), 1–11.

Prause, G. (2015). Sustainable business models and structures for Industry 4.0. *Journal of Security and Sustainability Issues*, *5*(2), 159–169. doi:10.9770/jssi.2015.5.2(3)

Prause, G. (2016). E-Residency: A business platform for Industry 4.0? *Entrepreneurship and Sustainability Issues*, *3*(3), 216–227. doi:10.9770/jesi.2016.3.3(1)

Preuveneers, D., & Ilie-Zudor, E. (2017). The intelligent industry of the future: A survey on emerging trends, research challenges and opportunities in Industry 4.0. *Journal of Ambient Intelligence and Smart Environments*, *9*(3), 287–298. doi:10.3233/AIS-170432

Prisecaru, P. (2016). Challenges of the fourth industrial revolution. *Knowledge Horizons. Economics*, *8*(1), 57.

Pritchard, A. (1969). Statistical Bibliography or Bibliometrics. *The Journal of Documentation*, *25*, 348–349.

Project Management Institute. (2008). *A Guide to the Project Management Body of Knowledge (PMBOK guide)* (4th ed.). Newtown Square, PA: Project Management Institute.

Qiu, X., Luo, H., Xu, G., Zhong, R., & Huang, G. Q. (2015). Physical assets and service sharing for IoT-enabled Supply Hub in Industrial Park (SHIP). *International Journal of Production Economics*, *159*, 4–15. doi:10.1016/j.ijpe.2014.09.001

Qi, Y., Zhao, X., & Sheu, C. (2011). The impact of competitive strategy and supply chain strategy on business performance: The role of environmental uncertainty. *Decision Sciences*, *42*(2), 371–389. doi:10.1111/j.1540-5915.2011.00315.x

Quarshie, A. M., Salmi, A., & Leuschner, R. (2016). Sustainability and corporate social responsibility in supply chains: The state of research in supply chain management and business ethics journals. *Journal of Purchasing and Supply Management*, *22*(2), 82–97. doi:10.1016/j.pursup.2015.11.001

Radjou, N., Prabhu, J., & Ahuja, S. (2012). *Jugaad innovation: Think frugal, be flexible, generate breakthrough growth*. San Francisco, CA: Wiley.

Rahayu, R., & Day, J. (2015). Determinant Factors of E-commerce Adoption by SMEs in Developing Country: Evidence from Indonesia. *Procedia: Social and Behavioral Sciences*, *195*, 142–150. doi:10.1016/j.sbspro.2015.06.423

Rajala, R., Hakanen, E., Mattila, J., Seppälä, T., & Westerlund, M. (2018). How Do Intelligent Goods Shape Closed-Loop Systems? *California Management Review*, *60*(3), 20–44. doi:10.1177/0008125618759685

Raj, J. R., & Seetharaman, A. (2013). Role of waste and performance management in the construction industry. *Journal of Environmental Science and Technology, 6*(3), 119–129. doi:10.3923/jest.2013.119.129

Rammler, S. (2017). Digital Fuel for the Mobility Revolution: The Opportunities and Risks of Applying Digital Technologies to the Mobility Sector. In T. Osburg & C. Lohrmann (Eds.), *Sustainability in a Digital World. CSR, Sustainability, Ethics & Governance* (pp. 159–171). Cham: Springer. doi:10.1007/978-3-319-54603-2_13

Rauter, R., Jonker, J., & Baumgartner, R. J. (2017). Going one's own way: Drivers in developing business models for sustainability. *Journal of Cleaner Production, 140*, 144–154. doi:10.1016/j.jclepro.2015.04.104

Rawat, A. (2015). *SI, 2 - Trajectory of change - Remodelling India's national innovation system for sustainable development & inclusive growth.* Paper presented at the, 24th International Association for Management of Technology Conference (IAMOT '15), Cape Town, South Africa.

Ray, P. K., & Ray, S. (2010). Resource-constrained innovation for emerging economies: The case of the indian telecommunications industry. *IEEE Transactions on Engineering Management, 57*(1), 144–156. doi:10.1109/TEM.2009.2033044

Ray, S., & Ray, P. K. (2011). Product innovation for the people's car in an emerging economy. *Technovation, 31*(5–6), 216–227. doi:10.1016/j.technovation.2011.01.004

Renwick, D. W., Redman, T., & Maguire, S. (2013). Green human resource management: A review and research agenda. *International Journal of Management Reviews, 15*(1), 1–14. doi:10.1111/j.1468-2370.2011.00328.x

Ries, E. (2011). *The lean startup: How today's entrepreneurs use continuous innovation to create radically successful businesses.* New York, NY: Random House.

Roehrich, J. K., Grosvold, J., & Hoejmose, S. U. (2014). Reputational risks and sustainable supply chain management: Decision making under bounded rationality. *International Journal of Operations & Production Management, 34*(5), 695–719. doi:10.1108/IJOPM-10-2012-0449

Rogers, E. M. (2003). *Diffusion of innovations* (5th ed.). New York, NY: Free Press.

Rosca, E., Arnold, M., & Bendul, J. C. (2017). Business models for sustainable innovation: An empirical analysis of frugal products and services. *Journal of Cleaner Production, 162*, S133–S145. doi:10.1016/j.jclepro.2016.02.050

Rosca, E., Bendul, J. C., & Arnold, M. (2016). Business models for sustainable innovation - an empirical analysis of frugal products and services. *Journal of Cleaner Production, 20*, 133–145.

Roser, M., & Esteban, O. (2018). *World Population Growth.* Retrieved October 28, 2018, from https://ourworldindata.org/world-population-growth

Roso, V., Woxenius, J., & Lumsden, K. (2009). The dry port concept: Connecting container seaports with the hinterland. *Journal of Transport Geography, 17*(5), 338–345. doi:10.1016/j.jtrangeo.2008.10.008

Rossek, D. (2018). *Implementing Industry 4.0 in packaging*. Retrieved from http://www.connectivity4ir.co.uk/article/149744/Implementing-Industry-4-0-in-packaging.aspx

Rosselet, C. (2013). *Andersherum zur Lösung; Die Organisationsaufstellung als Verfahren der intuitiven Entscheidungsfindung.* Zürich: Versus. doi:10.24096/9783039097371

Rossetti, C. L., Handfield, R., & Dooley, K. J. (2011). Forces, trends, and decisions in pharmaceutical supply chain management. *International Journal of Physical Distribution & Logistics Management, 41*(6), 601–622. doi:10.1108/09600031111147835

Ruto, W. K., & Datche, E. (2015). Logistical Factors Influencing Port Performance A Case of Kenya Ports Authority (Kpa). *International Journal of Current Research and Review, 7*(12), 52–58.

Samuelson, P., & Scotchmer, S. (2002). The law and economics of reverse engineering. *The Yale Law Journal, 111*(7), 1575–1663. doi:10.2307/797533

Sánchez, M. A. (2015). Integrating sustainability issues into project management. *Journal of Cleaner Production, 96*, 319–330. doi:10.1016/j.jclepro.2013.12.087

Sanders, A., Elangeswaran, C., & Wulfsberg, J. (2016). Industry 4.0 implies lean manufacturing: Research activities in industry 4.0 function as enablers for lean manufacturing. *Journal of Industrial Engineering and Management, 9*(3), 811–833. doi:10.3926/jiem.1940

Sanders, N. R. (2007). An empirical study of the impact of e-business technologies on organizational collaboration and performance. *Journal of Operations Management, 25*(6), 1332–1347. doi:10.1016/j.jom.2007.01.008

Santarius, T. (2017). Die dunkle Seite des „smart everything" – Gesellschaft revolutionieren statt Wachstum generieren. Agora, 42(2), 70-74.

Sanyal, U., & Pal, D. (2017). Effect of organizational culture in environmental awareness on pro-environmental behaviour at workplace: A new perspective on organizational sustainability. *International Journal of Commerce and Management Research*, 60-65.

Sarasvathy, S. D. (2001). Causation and effectuation: Toward a theoretical shift from economic inevitability to entrepreneurial contingency. *Academy of Management Review, 26*(2), 243–263. doi:10.5465/amr.2001.4378020

Satoglu, S., Ustundag, A., Cevikcan, E., & Durmusoglu, M. B. (2018). Lean Transformation Integrated with Industry 4.0 Implementation Methodology. In F. Calisir & H. Camgoz Akdag (Eds.), *Industrial Engineering in the Industry 4.0 Era. Lecture Notes in Management and Industrial Engineering.* Cham: Springer. doi:10.1007/978-3-319-71225-3_9

Saunders, M., Lewis, P., & Thornhill, A. (2016). *Research methods for business students* (7th ed.). Harlow, UK: Pearson.

Schaefer, K., Corner, P. D., & Kearins, K. (2015). Social, environmental and sustainable entrepreneurship research: What is needed for sustainability-as-flourishing? *Organization & Environment*, *28*(4), 394–413. doi:10.1177/1086026615621111

Schaltegger, S., Hansen, E. G., & Lüdeke-Freund, F. (2016). Business models for sustainability: Origins, present research, and future avenues. *Organization & Environment*, *29*(1), 3–10. doi:10.1177/1086026615599806

Schlötter, P. (2005). Familiar language and its discovery. System constellations are not random - the empirical evidence [Vertraute Sprache und ihre Entdeckung. Systemaufstellungen sind kein Zufallsprodukt - der empirische Nachweis, in German]. Carl-Auer-Verlag.

Schluep, M., & Wasswa, J. (2012). *e-Waste assessment in Uganda: A situational analysis of e-waste management and generation with special emphasis on personal computers*. Kampala Uganda Clean Prod Cent.

Schmitt, J., & Renken, U. (2012). How to earn money by doing good! Shared value in the apparel industry. *Journal of Corporate Citizenship*, *45*(45), 79–103. doi:10.9774/GLEAF.4700.2012.sp.00007

Schneidewind, U., & Augenstein, K. (2016). Three schools of transformation thinking: The impact of ideas, institutions, and technological innovation on transformation processes. *GAIA – Ecological Perspectives for Science and Society*, *25*(2), 88-93. doi:10.14512/gaia.25.2.7

Scholz, R. W. (2016). Sustainable digital environments: What major challenges is humankind facing? *Sustainability*, *8*(8), 726. doi:10.3390u8080726

Schumacher, E. F. (1973). *Small is beautiful*. New York: Harper & Row.

Schumpeter, J. A. (1912). Theorie der wirtschaftlichen Entwicklung. Berlin: Duncker & Humblot.

Schumpeter, J. A. (1942). *Capitalism, socialism and democracy*. New York, NY: Harper.

Schütz, A. (1971). Wissenschaftliche Interpretation und Alltagsverständnis menschlichen Handelns. In A. Schütz (Ed.), Gesammelte Aufsätze I. Das Problem der sozialen Wirklichkeit (pp. 3-54). Den Haag, The Netherlands: Martinus Njihoff. doi:10.1007/978-94-010-2858-5_1

Schwab, K. (2015). The Fourth Industrial Revolution. What it means and how to respond. *Foreign Affairs*. Retrieved May 15, 2018, from, https://www.foreignaffairs.com/articles/2015-12-12/fourth-industrial-revolution

Schwab, K. (2015). The Fourth Industrial Revolution: What it means and how to respond. *Snapshot*. Retrieved from https://www.foreignaffairs.com/articles/2015-12-12/fourth-industrial-revolution

Schwab, K. (2015, December). The Fourth Industrial Revolution. What It Means and How to Respond. *Foreign Affairs*. Retrieved from https://www.foreignaffairs.com/articles/2015-12-12/fourth-industrial-revolution

Schwab, K. (2017). *The Fourth Industrial Revolution*. London, UK: Portfolio Penguin.

Schwab, K., & Davis, N. (2018). *Shaping the Future of the Fourth Industrial Revolution: A guide to building a better world.* London, UK: Portfolio Penguin.

Scipioni, A., Manzardo, A., Mazzi, A., & Mastrobuono, M. (2012). Monitoring the carbon footprint of products: A methodological proposal. *Journal of Cleaner Production, 36,* 94–101. doi:10.1016/j.jclepro.2012.04.021

Sehgal, V., Dehoff, K., & Panneer, G. (2010). The importance of frugal engineering. *Strategy Business, 59,* 1–5.

Sellitto, M. A., Bittencourt, S. A., & Reckziegel, B. I. (2015). Evaluating the implementation of GSCM in industrial supply chains: Two cases in the automotive Industry. *Chemical Engineering Transactions, 43,* 1315–1320.

Servaes, H., & Tamayo, A. (2013). The impact of corporate social responsibility on firm value: The role of customer awareness. *Management Science, 59*(5), 1045–1061. doi:10.1287/mnsc.1120.1630

Seuring, S., & Müller, M. (2008). From a literature review to a conceptual framework for sustainable supply chain management. *Journal of Cleaner Production, 16*(15), 1699–1710. doi:10.1016/j.jclepro.2008.04.020

Seyfang, G., & Smith, A. (2007). Grassroots innovations for sustainable development: Towards a new research and policy agenda. *Environmental Politics, 16*(4), 584–603. doi:10.1080/09644010701419121

Shafer, S. M., Smith, H. J., & Linder, J. C. (2005). The power of business models. *Business Horizons, 48*(3), 199–207. doi:10.1016/j.bushor.2004.10.014

Shahira, E.-A., & Korlam, W. (2014). Exploring environmental sustainability performance in the Cellular telecommunication industry in Egypt. In *Proceedings on 28th Environmental conference.* University of Oldenburg.

Sharma, A., & Iyer, G. R. (2012). Resource-constrained product development: Implications for green marketing and green supply chains. *Industrial Marketing Management, 41*(4), 599–608. doi:10.1016/j.indmarman.2012.04.007

Sheldon, R. A. (2014). Green and sustainable manufacture of chemicals from biomass: State of the art. *Green Chemistry, 16*(3), 950–963. doi:10.1039/C3GC41935E

Sheu, J. B., Chou, Y. H., & Hu, C. C. (2005). An integrated logistics operational model for green-supply chain management. *Transportation Research Part E, Logistics and Transportation Review, 41*(4), 287–313. doi:10.1016/j.tre.2004.07.001

Shi, P., & Yan, B. (2016). Factors affecting RFID adoption in the agricultural product distribution industry: Empirical evidence from China. *SpringerPlus, 5*(1), 2029. doi:10.118640064-016-3708-x PMID:27995006

Shi, X., Tao, D., & Voß, S. (2011). RFID Technology and its Application to Port-Based Container Logistics. *Journal of Organizational Computing and Electronic Commerce*, *21*(4), 332–347. do i:10.1080/10919392.2011.614202

Shobhit, S. (2018, April). Public, Private, Permissioned Blockchains Compared. *Investopedia*. Reviewed from https://www.investopedia.com/news/public-private-permissioned-blockchains-compared/

Shrouf, F., & Miragliotta, G. (2015). Energy management based on Internet of Things: Practices and framework for adoption in production management. *Journal of Cleaner Production*, *100*, 235–246. doi:10.1016/j.jclepro.2015.03.055

Siew, R. Y. J., Balatbat, M. C. A., & Carmichael, D. G. (2016). Measuring project sustainability maturity level – a fuzzy-based approach. *International Journal of Sustainable Development*, *19*(1), 76–100. doi:10.1504/IJSD.2016.073680

Silva, M. (2015). Future-Proof: Foresight as a Tool towards Project Legacy Sustainability. *Project Management World Journal*, *4*(5), 350–362.

Silvius, A. J. G. (2012a). *The role of Organizational Change in Green IS: Integrating Sustainability in Projects*. Paper presented at International Conference on Information Resources Management (Conf-IRM), Vienna, Austria.

Silvius, A. J. G. (2012c). *Sustainability in project management: Vision, mission, ambition*. Paper presented at the PM Summit 2012, Istanbul, Turkey.

Silvius, A. J. G., & Schipper, R. (2012). *Sustainability in Project Management Competences*. Paper presented on the 26th IPMA World Congress, Creta, Greece.

Silvius, A. J. G. (2012b). Change the game: Sustainability in projects and project management. In S. Seidel, J. Recker, & J. Brocke (Eds.), *Green BPM - Towards the Environmentally Sustainable Enterprise* (pp. 161–177). Berlin, Germany: Springer. doi:10.1007/978-3-642-27488-6_10

Silvius, A. J. G. (2016). Sustainability as a competence of Project Managers. *PM World Journal*, *5*(4), 1–13.

Silvius, A. J. G., & Schipper, R. (2010). A maturity model for integrating sustainability in projects and project management. In *Proceedings of the 24th World Congress of the International Project Management Association*. Istanbul: International Project Management Association.

Silvius, A. J. G., & Schipper, R. (2014a). Sustainability in project management: A literature review and impact analysis. *Social Business*, *4*(1), 63–96. doi:10.1362/204440814X13948909253866

Silvius, A. J. G., & Schipper, R. (2014b). Sustainability in Project Management Competencies: Analyzing the Competence Gap of Project Managers. *Journal of Human Resource and Sustainability Studies*, *2*(2), 40–58. doi:10.4236/jhrss.2014.22005

Silvius, A. J. G., & Schipper, R. (2015). A Conceptual Model for Exploring the Relationship between Sustainability and Project Success. *Procedia Computer Science, 64,* 334–342. doi:10.1016/j.procs.2015.08.497

Silvius, A. J. G., & Schipper, R. (2016). Exploring the relationship between sustainability and project success -conceptual model and expected relationships. *International Journal of Information Systems and Project Management, 4*(3), 5–22.

Silvius, A. J. G., Schipper, R., & Nedeski, S. (2013). Sustainability in Project Management: Reality Bites. *PM World Journal, 2*(2), 1–183.

Silvius, A. J. G., Schipper, R., Planko, J., van den Brink, J., & Köhler, A. (2012). *Sustainability in project management.* London: Gower Publishing.

Silvius, A. J. G., & Tharp, J. (2013). *Sustainability Integration for Effective Project Management.* Hershey, PA: IGI Global. doi:10.4018/978-1-4666-4177-8

Silvius, A. J. G., van den Brink, J., & Köhler, A. (2012). The impact of sustainability on project management. In H. Linger & J. Owen (Eds.), *The Project as a Social System* (pp. 183–200). Victoria, Australia: Monash University Publishing.

Singer, P. (2011). *Practical Ethics* (3rd ed.). Cambridge, UK: Cambridge University Press. (Original work published 1979) doi:10.1017/CBO9780511975950

Singh, M., Brueckner, M., & Padhy, P. K. (2015). Environmental management system ISO 14001: Effective waste minimisation in small and medium enterprises in India. *Journal of Cleaner Production, 102,* 285–301. doi:10.1016/j.jclepro.2015.04.028

Smith, A. (2005). The alternative technology movement: An analysis of its framing and negotiation of technology development. *Human Ecology, 12*(2), 106–119.

Smith, A. E., & Humphreys, M. S. (2006). Evaluation of unsupervised semantic mapping of natural language with Leximancer concept mapping. *Behavior Research Methods, 38*(2), 262–279. doi:10.3758/BF03192778 PMID:16956103

Smith, G. O. (1976). *The Complete Venus Equilateral.* New York, NY: Ballantine.

Soeffner, H.-G. (2004). *Auslegung des Alltags – Der Alltag der Auslegung.* Konstanz, Germany: UVK.

Song, Q., Li, J., & Zeng, X. (2015). Minimizing the increasing solid waste through zero waste strategy. *Journal of Cleaner Production, 104,* 199–210. doi:10.1016/j.jclepro.2014.08.027

Soni, P., & Krishnan, R. T. (2014). Frugal innovation - aligning theory, practice, and public policy. *Journal of Indian Business Research, 6*(1), 29–47. doi:10.1108/JIBR-03-2013-0025

Son, M., & Han, K. (2011). Beyond the technology adoption: Technology readiness effects on post-adoption behavior. *Journal of Business Research, 64*(11), 1178–1182. doi:10.1016/j.jbusres.2011.06.019

Sooknanan, D., Bahadoorsingh, S., Joshi, A., & Sharma, D. P. (2016). Smart Grid Analysis for the Caribbean Region. *West Indian Journal of Engineering, 38*(2).

Sowa, J. F. (2000). *Knowledge representation: logical, philosophical, and computational foundations* (Vol. 13). Pacific Grove, CA: Brooks/Cole.

Stahlbock, R., Heilig, S., Voß, S. (2018, December). Blockchain in der maritimen Logistik. *HMD Praxis der Wirtschaftsinformatik, 55*(6).

Stan, L. (2017). The management of innovation in the context of structural funds. *Manager,* 25.

Sthiannopkao, S., & Wong, M. H. (2013). Handling of e-waste in developed and developing countries: Initiatives, practices and consequences. *The Science of the Total Environment, 463-464,* 1147–1153. doi:10.1016/j.scitotenv.2012.06.088 PMID:22858354

Stilgoe, J., Owen, R., & Macnaghten, P. (2013). Developing a framework for responsible innovation. *Research Policy, 42*(9), 1568–1580. doi:10.1016/j.respol.2013.05.008

Stock, T., Bietz, T., Alva, D., Swat, M., Seliger, G., and Bähre, D. (2015). Design and Control of Manufacturing Systems for Enabling Energy-Efficiency and-Flexibility. *The Journal of Innovation Impact,* 438-49.

Stock, T., & Seliger, G. (2016). Opportunities of sustainable manufacturing in industry 4.0. *Procedia CIRP, 40,* 536–541. doi:10.1016/j.procir.2016.01.129

Stüer, C., Hüsig, S., & Biala, S. (2010). How to Create and Sustain an Open and Radical Innovation Capability in the Fuzzy Front End? The Case of Vodafone R&D Germany and Selected Ongoing Radical Innovation Projects. *International Journal of Product Development, 11*(3/4), 196–219. doi:10.1504/IJPD.2010.033958

Sturgeon, N. (2018, July 10). Henry Kissinger pens ominous warning on dangers of artificial intelligence. *RT Question More.* Retrieved July 13, 2018, from https://www.rt.com/news/432425-henry-kissinger-artificial-intelligence/

Sullivan, K., Thomas, S., & Rosano, M. (2018). Using industrial ecology and strategic management concepts to pursue the Sustainable Development Goals. *Journal of Cleaner Production, 174,* 237–246. doi:10.1016/j.jclepro.2017.10.201

Swirski, P. (2013). *From Literature to Biterature: Lem, Turing, Darwin, and Explorations in Computer Literature, Philosophy of Mind, and Cultural Evolution.* London, UK: McGill-Queen's University Press.

Swirski, P. (2015). *Stanislaw Lem: Philosopher of the Future.* Liverpool, UK: Liverpool University Press. doi:10.5949/liverpool/9781781381861.001.0001

Swirski, P., & Osadnik, W. M. (2014). *Lemography: Stanislaw Lem in the Eyes of the World.* Liverpool, UK: Liverpool University Press. doi:10.5949/liverpool/9781781381205.001.0001

Szegedi, Z., Gabriel, M., & Papp, I. (2017). Green supply chain awareness in the Hungarian automotive industry. *Polish Journal of Management Studies*, *16*(1), 259–268. doi:10.17512/pjms.2017.16.1.22

Talbot, J., & Venkataraman, R. (2011). Integration of sustainability principles into project baselines using a comprehensive indicator set. *International Business & Economics Research Journal*, *10*(9), 29–40.

Tam, G. C. K. (2010). The program management process with sustainability considerations. Journal of Project. *Program & Portfolio Management*, *1*(1), 17–27. doi:10.5130/pppm.v1i1.1574

Teece, D. J. (2010). Business models, business strategy, and innovation. *Long Range Planning*, *43*(2-3), 172–194. doi:10.1016/j.lrp.2009.07.003

Teoh, J. E. M., Chua, C. K., Liu, Y., & An, J. (2017). 4D printing of customised smart sunshade. In Challenges for Technology Innovation (Vol. 105, No. 108, pp. 105-108). Routledge in association with GSE Research.

Terrio, M. (2014). *Examining reverse innovation and collaboration: a case study in the context of Uganda* (Master's thesis). Aalto University. Retrieved from https://aaltodoc.aalto.fi/handle/123456789/15275

Testa, F., & Iraldo, F. (2010). Shadows and lights of GSCM (green supply chain management): Determinants and effects of these practices based on a multi-national study. *Journal of Cleaner Production*, *18*(10), 953–962. doi:10.1016/j.jclepro.2010.03.005

Testa, F., Rizzi, F., Daddi, T., Gusmerotti, N. M., Frey, M., & Iraldo, F. (2014). EMAS and ISO 14001: The differences in effectively improving environmental performance. *Journal of Cleaner Production*, *68*, 165–173. doi:10.1016/j.jclepro.2013.12.061

Thom, N. (1992). Innovationsmanagement. Bern: Schweizerische Volksbank.

Thomas, D. A. (2014). Searching for significance in unstructured data: Text mining with Leximancer. *European Educational Research Journal*, *13*(2), 235–256. doi:10.2304/eerj.2014.13.2.235

Tiwari, R., & Herstatt, C. (2012). Assessing India's lead market potential for cost-effective innovations. *Journal of Indian Business Research*, *4*(2), 97–115. doi:10.1108/17554191211228029

Tobias, J. (2016, August 1). *Blockchain in der Finanzbranche: eine disruptive Technologie?* Bank und Markt.

Todeschini, B. V., Cortimiglia, M. N., Callegaro-de-Menezes, D., & Ghezzi, A. (2017). Innovative and sustainable business models in the fashion industry: Entrepreneurial drivers, opportunities, and challenges. *Business Horizons*, *60*(6), 759–770. doi:10.1016/j.bushor.2017.07.003

Tongzon, J. (2001). Efficiency measurement of selected Australian and other international ports using data envelopment analysis. *Transportation Research Part A, Policy and Practice*, *35*(2), 107–122. doi:10.1016/S0965-8564(99)00049-X

Toonen, H. M., & Bush, S. R. (2018). The digital frontiers of fisheries governance: Fish attraction devices, drones and satellites. *Journal of Environmental Policy and Planning*, 1–13. doi:10.10 80/1523908X.2018.1461084

TransnetNationalPortsAuthority-Port of Durban. (2019). Retrieved January 15, 2019, from https://www.transnetnationalportsauthority.net/ourports/durban/Pages/Overview.aspx

Trappey, A. J., Trappey, C. V., Hsiao, C. T., Ou, J. J., & Chang, C. T. (2012). System dynamics modelling of product carbon footprint life cycles for collaborative green supply chains. *International Journal of Computer Integrated Manufacturing*, *25*(10), 934–945. doi:10.1080/0 951192X.2011.593304

Trimble, C. (2012). Reverse innovation and the emerging-market growth imperative. *Ivey Business Journal*, *76*(2), 19–21.

Trujillo, L., González, M., & Jiménez, J. (2013). An overview on the reform process of African ports. *Utilities Policy*, *25*, 12–22. doi:10.1016/j.jup.2013.01.002

Tufinio, S. P., Mooi, H., Ravestijn, W., Bakker, H., & Boorsma, M. (2013). Sustainability in Project Management. *International Journal of Engineering*, *6*(1), 91–101.

Ubeda, S., Arcelus, F. J., & Fau Linton, J. (2011). Green logistics at Eroski: A case study. *International Journal of Production Economics*, *131*(1), 44–51. doi:10.1016/j.ijpe.2010.04.041

Uecker-Mercado, H., & Walker, M. (2012). The value of environmental social responsibility to facility managers: Revealing the perceptions and motives for adopting ESR. *Journal of Business Ethics*, *110*(3), 269–284. doi:10.100710551-011-1153-x

Ulrich, K. T., & Eppinger, S. D. (1995). *Product design and development*. New York, NY: McGraw-Hill.

Underwood, J. D. (1993). Going green for profit. *EPA Journal*, *19*(3), 9–15.

UN-Habitat. (2014). *Urbanisation Challenges, Waste Management and Development*. Note prepared for the regional meeting of the ACP-EC Joint Parliamentary Assembly, Mauritius. Retrieved May 15, 2018 from, http://www. europarl.europa.eu/intcoop/acp/2014_mauritius/pdf/un_habitat_presentation_en.pdf

United Nations Environment Programme. (2016). *Guidelines for framework legislation for integrated waste management*. United Nations Environment Programme. Retrieved from http://wedocs. unep.org/handle/20.500.11822/22098

United Nations Environmental Programme (UNEP). (2018). *Africa Waste Management Outlook*. United Nations Environment Programme.

United Nations, Department of Economic and Social Affairs, Population Division. (2017). *World Population Prospects: The 2017 Revision, Key Findings and Advance Tables*. Working Paper No. ESA/P/WP/248.

Upton, E. (2016). *The evolving relationship between sustainability and marketing.* Corporate Citizenship Briefing. News and Analysis on Resp.

Vachon, S., & Klassen, R. D. (2006). Extending green practices across the supply chain: The impact of upstream and downstream integration. *International Journal of Operations & Production Management, 26*(7), 795–821. doi:10.1108/01443570610672248

Vallance, S., Perkins, H. C., & Dixon, J. E. (2011). What is social sustainability? A clarification of concepts. *Geoforum, 42*(3), 342–348. doi:10.1016/j.geoforum.2011.01.002

Valmohammadi, C., & Roshanzamir, S. (2015). The guidelines of improvement: Relations among organizational culture, TQM and performance. *International Journal of Production Economics, 164*, 167–178. doi:10.1016/j.ijpe.2014.12.028

Van Rensburg, S. L. J. (2015). *A framework in green logistics for companies in South Africa* (Unpublished Masters' dissertation). University of South Africa.

Vázquez-Casielles, R., Iglesias, V., & Varela-Neira, C. (2017). Manufacturer–distributor relationships: Role of relationship-specific investment and dependence types. *Journal of Business and Industrial Marketing, 32*(8), 1245–1260. doi:10.1108/JBIM-10-2016-0244

Verhoeven, P. (2010). A review of port authority functions: Towards a renaissance? *Maritime Policy & Management, 37*(3), 247–270. doi:10.1080/03088831003700645

Verworn, B., & Herstatt, C. (2000). *Modelle des Innovationsprozesses* (Working Paper No. 6). Retrieved from http://nbn-resolving.de/urn:nbn:de:gbv:830-opus-1607

Vhumbunu, C. (2016). Enabling African Regional Infrastructure Renaissance through the China-Africa Partnership: A Trans-Continental Appraisal. *International Journal of China Studies Africa, 7*(3), 271–300.

Von Hippel, E. (2005). *Democratizing Innovation.* Cambridge, MA: MIT Press. doi:10.7551/mitpress/2333.001.0001

Von Zedtwitz, M., Corsi, S., Søberg, P. V., & Frega, R. (2015). A typology of reverse innovation. *Journal of Product Innovation Management, 32*(1), 12–28. doi:10.1111/jpim.12181

Voshmgir, S. (2016). Blockchains: Smart Contracts und das Dezentrale Web. *Technologiestiftung Berlin.* Retrieved from https://www.technologiestiftung-berlin.de/fileadmin/daten/media/publikationen/170130_BlockchainStudie.pdf

Walker, B., Carpenter, S., Anderies, J., Abel, N., Cumming, G., Janssen, M., ... Pritchard, R. (2002). Resilience management in social-ecological systems: A working hypothesis for a participatory approach. *Conservation Ecology, 6*(1), 14. doi:10.5751/ES-00356-060114

Walker, H., & Brammer, S. (2009). Sustainable procurement in the United Kingdom public sector. *Supply Chain Management, 14*(2), 128–137. doi:10.1108/13598540910941993

Walsh, S., Kirchhoff, B., & Newbert, S. (2000). Differentiating market strategies for disruptive technologies. *IEEE Transactions on Engineering Management*, *49*(4), 341–351. doi:10.1109/TEM.2002.806718

Wang, P., Mileski, J. P., & Zeng, Q. (2017). Alignments between strategic content and process structure: The case of container terminal service process automation. *Maritime Economics & Logistics*, 1.

Wang, S., Wan, J., Li, D., & Zhang, C. (2016). Implementing smart factory of industrie 4.0: An outlook. *International Journal of Distributed Sensor Networks*, *12*(1), 1–10. doi:10.1155/2016/3159805

Wang, W. Y. C., Pauleen, D. J., & Zhang, T. (2017). How social media applications affect B2B communications and improve business performance of SME. *Industrial Marketing Management*, *54*, 4–14. doi:10.1016/j.indmarman.2015.12.004

Watson, K., Klingenberg, B., Polito, T., & Geurts, T. G. (2004). Impact of environmental management system implementation on financial performance: A comparison of two corporate strategies. *Management of Environmental Quality*, *15*(6), 622–628. doi:10.1108/14777830410560700

Webster, F. E. Jr. (1992). The changing role of marketing in the corporation. *Journal of Marketing*, *56*(4), 1–17. doi:10.1177/002224299205600402

Weissbrod, I., & Bocken, N. M. P. (2017). Developing sustainable business experimentation capability: A case study. *Journal of Cleaner Production*, *142*, 2663–2676. doi:10.1016/j.jclepro.2016.11.009

Weller, A., & Bucher, J. (2016). Visualisierte Imaginationen der Lebenswelt und der Einfluss der Medien. In J. Raab & R. Keller (Eds.), Wissensforschung - Forschungswissen. Beiträge zum 1. Sektionskongress der Wissenssoziologie (pp. 595-607). Weinheim, Germany: Belz Juventa.

Welter, V. (2012). *Sustainable procurement of pharmaceuticals: Time to act*. Retrieved from http://www.who.int/medicines/areas/policy/IPC_dec2012_Volker_procurement.pdf

Whittles, G. (2019). Uber drivers fight back with spotters. *Mail and Guardian*. Retrieved from https://mg.co.za/article/2017-09-15-00-uber-drivers-fight-back-with-spotters

Wicks, J. (2017). *Landfill bosses criminally charged over smelly KZN dump*. Retrieved May 11, 2018, from https://www.timeslive.co.za/news/south-africa/2017-08-17-landfill-bosses-criminally-charged-over-smelly-kzn-dump/

Wiengarten, F., & Pagell, M. (2012). The importance of quality management for the success of environmental management initiatives. *International Journal of Production Economics*, *140*(1), 407–415. doi:10.1016/j.ijpe.2012.06.024

Williamson, P. (2010). Cost innovation: Preparing for a "value-for-money" revolution. *Long Range Planning*, *43*(2-3), 343–353. doi:10.1016/j.lrp.2009.07.008

Windell, A. C. (2007). *The impact of disruptive technologies on designated organisations within the IT industry in South Africa* (Unpublished Masters Dissertation). University of Pretoria.

Wisner, J., & Keah, C. (2000). Supply chain management and its impact on purchasing. *The Journal of Supply Chain Management, 36*(4), 33–42. doi:10.1111/j.1745-493X.2000.tb00084.x

Witt, J. (1996). Grundlagen für die Entwicklung und die Vermarktung neuer Produkte. In J. Witt (Ed.), Produktinnovation. Entwicklung und Vermarktung neuer Produkte (pp. 169-183). München, Germany: Vahlen.

Witzig, P., & Salomon, V. (2018). *Cutting out the middleman: a case study of blockchain-induced reconfigurations in the Swiss Financial Services Industry.* Working Paper 1. Université de Neuchâtel. Retrieved from http://www.unine.ch/files/live/sites/ maps/files/shared/documents/wp/WP-1_2018_Witzig%20and%20Salomon.pdf

Womack, J., Jones, D., & Roos, D. (1991). *The machine that changed the world.* New York, NY: Harper-Collins.

Wood, S., & Reynolds, J. (2013). Knowledge management, organisational learning and memory in UK retail network planning. *Service Industries Journal, 33*(2), 150–170. doi:10.1080/0264 2069.2011.614340

Woolridge, A. (2010). The world turned upside down. A special report on innovation in emerging markets. *The Economist.* Retrieved from http://www.economist.com/node/15879369

World Bank Group. (2017). Distributed Ledger Technology (DLT) and blockchain. *FinTech note, 1.* Retrieved from http://documents.worldbank.org/curated/en/ 1779115137140622215/pdf/122140-WP-PUBLIC-Distributed-Ledger-Technology-and-Blockchain-Fintech-Notes.pdf

World Bank. (2017). *What a Waste: A Global Review of Solid Waste Management.* Retrieved May 15, 2018, from, http://web.worldbank.org/WBSITE/EXTERNAL/TOPICS/EXTURBAND EVELOPMENT/0%2C%2CcontentMDK%3A23172887~pagePK%3A210058~piPK%3A21006 2~theSitePK%3A337178%2C00.html

World Bank. (2018). *World Bank Open Data - 2018 update of World Development Indicators available.* Retrieved October 28, 2018, from https://data.worldbank.org/

World Economic Forum (WEF). (2019). *The Fourth Industrial Revolution.* Retrieved February 28, 2019, from https://www.weforum.org/focus/fourth-industrial-revolution

World Economic Forum. (2015, September). Deep Shift - Technology Tipping Points and Societal Impact. *Survey Report.* Reviewed from http://www3.weforum.org/docs/WEF_ GAC15_Technological_Tipping_Points_report_2015.pdf

Wright, R. E., Richey, R. G., Tokman, M., & Palmer, J. C. (2011). Recycling and reverse logistics. *The Journal of Applied Business and Economics, 12*(5), 9.

Wu, H. J., & Dunn, S. C. (1995). Environmentally responsible logistics systems. *International Journal of Physical Distribution & Logistics Management, 25*(2), 20–38. doi:10.1108/09600039510083925

Yang, M., Evans, S., Vladimirova, D., & Rana, P. (2017). Value uncaptured perspective for sustainable business model innovation. *Journal of Cleaner Production, 140*, 1794–1804. doi:10.1016/j.jclepro.2016.07.102

Yang, Y., Zhong, M., Yao, H., Yu, F., Fu, X., & Postolache, O. (2018). Internet of Things for Smart Ports: Technologies and Challenges. *IEEE Instrumentation & Measurement Magazine, 21*(1), 34–43. doi:10.1109/MIM.2018.8278808

Yan, J., Xin, S., Liu, Q., Xu, W., Yang, L., Fan, L., ... Wang, Q. (2014). Chen, Bo., Wang, Q. (2014). Intelligent supply chain integration and management based on cloud of things. *International Journal of Distributed Sensor Networks, 10*(3), 624839. doi:10.1155/2014/624839

Yeo, N. C. Y., Pepin, H., & Yang, S. S. (2017). Revolutionery technology adoption for manufacturing industry. *Proceedings of the 24th CIRP Conference on life Cycle Engineering*, 17-21.

Yin, R. K. (2014). *Case study research: Design and methods* (5th ed.). Thousand Oaks, CA: Sage.

Yoo, Y., Boland, R. J. Jr, Lyytinen, K., & Majchrzak, A. (2012). Organizing for Innovation in the Digitized World. *Organization Science, 23*(5), 1398–1408. doi:10.1287/orsc.1120.0771

Young, W., Davis, M., Mcneill, I. M., Malhotra, B., Russell, S., Unsworth, K., & Clegg, C. W. (2015). Changing behaviour: Successful environmental programmes in the workplace. *Business Strategy and the Environment, 24*(8), 689–703. doi:10.1002/bse.1836

Yousafzai, S., & Yani-de-Soriano, M. (2012). Understanding customer-specific factors underpinning internet banking adoption. *International Journal of Bank Marketing, 30*(1), 60–81. doi:10.1108/02652321211195703

Yu, M., & Qi, X. (2013). Storage space allocation models for inbound containers in an automatic container terminal. *European Journal of Operational Research, 226*(1), 32–45. doi:10.1016/j.ejor.2012.10.045

Yu, X., Nguyen, B., & Chen, Y. (2016). Internet of things capability and alliance: Entrepreneurial orientation, market orientation, and product and process innovation. *Internet Research, 26*(2), 402–434. doi:10.1108/IntR-10-2014-0265

Zakaria, F. (2016). America's democracy has become illiberal. *Washington Post*. Retrieved October 28, 2018, from https://www.washingtonpost.com/opinions/america-is-becoming-a-land-of-less-liberty/2016/12/29/2a91744c-ce09-11e6-a747-d03044780a02_story.html?noredirect=on&utm_term=.0f4e78bc5557

Zawacki-Richter, O., & Latchem, C. (2018). Exploring four decades of research in Computers & Education. *Computers & Education, 122*, 136–152. doi:10.1016/j.compedu.2018.04.001

Zawacki-Richter, O., & Naidu, S. (2016). Mapping research trends from 35 years of publications in Distance Education. *Distance Education, 37*(3), 245–269. doi:10.1080/01587919.2016.1185079

Zehendner, E., & Feillet, D. (2014). Benefits of a truck appointment system on the service quality of inland transport modes at a multimodal container terminal. *European Journal of Operational Research*, *235*(2), 461–469. doi:10.1016/j.ejor.2013.07.005

Zeng, M., & Williamson, P. J. (2007). *Dragons at your door: How Chinese cost innovation is disrupting the rules of global competition.* Boston, MA: Harvard Business School Press.

Zero Waste Scotland. (2018). *Our Role in the Circular Economy.* Retrieved May 15, 2018, from, https://www.zerowastescotland.org.uk/circular-economy/our-role

Zeschky, M. B., Winterhalter, S., & Gassmann, O. (2014a). Resource-constrained innovation - Classification and implications for multinational firms. *Proceedings of the XXV Innovation for Sustainable Economy and Society Conference (ISPIM XXV '14).*

Zeschky, M. B., Widenmayer, B., & Gassmann, O. (2011). Frugal innovation in emerging markets. *Research Technology Management*, *54*(4), 38–45. doi:10.5437/08956308X5404007

Zeschky, M. B., Winterhalter, S., & Gassmann, O. (2014b). From cost to frugal and reverse innovation: Mapping the field and implications for global competitiveness. *Research Technology Management*, *57*(4), 20–27.

Zhang, L., Methipara, J., & Lu, Y. (2011, January). *Internalizing congestion and environmental externalities with green transportation financing policies.* Paper presented at the 90th Annual Meeting of the Transportation Research Board, Washington, DC.

Zhong, R. Y., Huang, G. Q., Lan, S., Dai, Q. Y., Chen, X., & Zhang, T. (2015). A big data approach for logistics trajectory discovery from RFID-enabled production data. *International Journal of Production Economics*, *165*, 260–272. doi:10.1016/j.ijpe.2015.02.014

Zhong, R. Y., Xu, X., Klotz, E., & Newman, S. T. (2017). Intelligent Manufacturing in the Context of Industry 4.0: A Review. *Engineering*, *3*(5), 616–630. doi:10.1016/J.ENG.2017.05.015

Zhou, J. (2013). Digitalization and intelligentization of manufacturing industry. *Advances in Manufacturing*, *1*(1), 1–7. doi:10.100740436-013-0006-5

Zhou, Y., Zhang, X., Zhuang, G., & Zhou, N. (2015). Relational norms and collaborative activities: Roles in reducing opportunism in marketing channels. *Industrial Marketing Management*, *46*, 147–159. doi:10.1016/j.indmarman.2015.01.014

Zhu, K., & Kraemer, K. (2005). Post-Adoption Variations in Usage and Value of E-Business by Organizations: Cross-Country Evidence from the Retail Industry. *Information Systems Research*, *16*(1), 61–84. doi:10.1287/isre.1050.0045

Zhu, Q., Geng, Y., Fujita, T., & Hashimoto, S. (2010). Green supply chain management in leading manufacturers. Case studies in Japanese large companies. *Management Research Review*, *33*(4), 380–392. doi:10.1108/01409171011030471

Zhu, Q., Sarkis, J., & Lai, K. H. (2005). Green supply chain management: Pressures, practices and performance within the Chinese automobile industry. *International Journal of Operations & Production Management, 25*(5), 449–468. doi:10.1108/01443570510593148

Zhu, Q., Sarkis, J., & Lai, K. H. (2007). Green supply chain management: Pressures, practices and performance within the Chinese automobile industry. *Journal of Cleaner Production, 15*(11-12), 1041–1052. doi:10.1016/j.jclepro.2006.05.021

Zhu, Q., Sarkis, J., & Lai, K. H. (2008). Confirmation of a measurement model for green supply chain management practices implementation. *International Journal of Production Economics, 111*(2), 261–273. doi:10.1016/j.ijpe.2006.11.029

Zinnöcker, T. (2017). Nachhaltigkeit, Energiewende und Digitalisierung. In A. Hildebrandt & W. Landhäußer (Eds.), *CSR und Digitalisierung. Management-Reihe Corporate Social Responsibility.* Berlin: Springer Gabler. doi:10.1007/978-3-662-53202-7_15

Zott, C., Amit, R., & Massa, L. (2011). The business model: Recent developments and future research. *Journal of Management, 37*(4), 1019–1042. doi:10.1177/0149206311406265

Zsidisin, G. A., & Siferd, S. P. (2001). Environmental purchasing: A framework for theory development. *European Journal of Purchasing & Supply Management, 7*(1), 61–73. doi:10.1016/S0969-7012(00)00007-1

Zsóka, Á. N. (2007). The role of organisational culture in the environmental awareness of companies. *Journal for East European Management Studies, 12*(2), 109–131. doi:10.5771/0949-6181-2007-2-109

Zuckerberg, M. (2015). *A Year of Books.* Retrieved from https://www.facebook.com/ayearofbooks/

About the Contributors

Ziska Fields was an Associate Professor and Academic Leader at the University of KwaZulu-Natal, South Africa. She recently joined the University of Johannesburg. For this book, her affiliation will still be the University of KwaZulu-Natal. Professor Fields has 13 years' experience in the Financial Industry in South Africa and has 11 years' Higher Education experience. Her qualifications include a BA (Communication Sciences), Diploma in Management Studies, MBA (Cum Laude) and PhD. She teaches various Management and Entrepreneurship courses at undergraduate and postgraduate levels. Her research focus area and passion is theoretical and applied creativity across various disciplines and contexts. She also developed two theoretical models to measure creativity in South Africa, focusing on the youth and tertiary education. She also has various other research areas, which include Entrepreneurship, Management, Innovation, Higher Education, Responsible Management Education, Artificial Intelligence, Future Studies and Information Technology. She edited three books titled "Incorporating Business Models and Strategies into Social Entrepreneurship", "Collective creativity for responsible and sustainable business practice" and "Handbook of Research on Information and Cyber Security in the Fourth Industrial Revolution". She has published various book chapters and papers in internationally recognized journals and presented various conference papers. She is a member of the South African Institute of Management (SAIM), Ethics Institute of SA (EthicsSA) and Institute of People Management (IPM).

Stefan Huesig is holder of the chair for Innovation Research and Technology Management at the Technische Universitat Chemnitz, Germany. Before he had several positions in academia such as Interim Professor at the Chair of Innovation Research and Sustainable Resource Management at the TU Chemnitz, as an Associate Professor at the Department of Innovation and Technology Management at the University of Regensburg, Germany or as Deputy Director and founder of a new Institute for Innovation and Technology Management at the University of Economics in Prague (Czech Republic). Moreover, he had visiting positions at the Leeds School of Business at the University of Colorado (USA), Aston Business

School, Aston University in Birmingham (UK) and the Fudan University in Shanghai (China). In addition to his academic activities Prof. Dr. Hüsig was active in research and consulting projects in collaboration with Mannesmann, Vodafone, Continental or the Fraunhofer Institute. He holds a Habilitation in Business Administration, a PhD in Innovation Management and a Diploma in Business Administration from University of Regensburg.

* * *

Martin Albert is a research associate at the Professorship of Innovation Research and Technology Management at the Technische Universität Chemnitz, Germany. He holds a Diploma in Business Administration & Engineering and a PhD in Engineering from Technische Universität Chemnitz. He is interested in the combination of sustainability, technology, and innovation.

Marlen Gabriele Arnold is professor in the field of Corporate Management and Sustainability at the Chemnitz University of Technology. Since her beginning of her scientific career she has been dealing with strategic questions regarding sustainability and innovation including sustainability tools and assessments. Marlen Arnold worked in several research projects at the University of Oldenburg, the Technical University of Munich and the Institute for Ecological Economy Research (IÖW) in Berlin. She was a research fellow at the Hanken School of Economics and the University of Vaasa, Finland. Her main fields of research are to be found in strategic management, innovation management, open innovation processes, participation, evolutionary approaches and biomimicry.

Julien Bucher studied Political Sciences, Literature Studies and Philosophy and works as a Research Fellow at the Chair of Innovation Research and Management of Technology at the Chemnitz University of Technology.

Bibi Zaheenah Chummun is a Senior Lecturer at the University of KwaZulu-Natal (UKZN) Graduate School of Business and Leadership (GSB&L) based on Westville Campus in Durban - South Africa. Dr. Chummun has published several papers in the field of management, microenterprises, microfinance, microinsurance and financial inclusion. She is supervising Masters and PhD students in the field of management. She is a Chartered Insurer from the Chartered Insurance Institute in UK. She obtained her MBA from Nelson Mandela Metropolitan University (NMMU-South Africa) in 2010 and her PhD is from North West University (NWU-South Africa). Dr. Chummun is originally from the island of Mauritius.

Anne Fischer is a research assistant at Chair of Corporate Environmental Management and Sustainability, Chemnitz University of Technology.

Dagmar Gesmann-Nuissl is the chair of the Professorship for Private Law and Intellectual Property Rights, Chemnitz University of Technology, Germany. She is researching in the interface of innovation, technology and law and is inter alia associate editor of the legal journal "Zeitschrift zum Innovations- und Technikrecht" (InTeR) – "Journal for Innovation and Technology Law".

Friedrich Mickel is currently studying for a Master's degree in Management & Organisation Studies at the Technische Universität Chemnitz, Germany. He holds a Bachelor of Science degree in Management and Economics (2018). He is interested in project management and sustainable development of organisations.

John Mukomana is a holder of a Mcom & BSc Honours Degree in Information Systems and Technology, certified as a CISA, CRISC & SAP GRC. An ICT specialist who has amassed vast experience in IT & Cyber Security, IT Governance, Risk Management, IT Auditing, Internal Control Monitoring and Compliance. Currently interested in the adoption of Innovative, digital & smart technological processes to improve business strategies and operations.

Micheline Naude obtained her DCom in supply chain management in 2010 at the University of South Africa. She currently is an associate professor at the University of KwaZulu-Natal where she has been lecturing supply chain management for the past fifteen years at undergraduate and postgraduate level. She spent the first 20 years of her career in commerce and industry (the last seven years in the purchasing field). She has published several articles and has presented various conference papers locally and internationally. She was the Academic Leader for the discipline of Marketing and Supply Chain Management for three years and is currently the Programme Coordinator for the Self-Funded Teaching Programmes.

Indira Padayachee is a Senior Lecturer in Information Systems & Technology at the University of KwaZulu-Natal, where she has taught a number of subjects including Systems Analysis and Design, Database Design and Management, Software Engineering and Human Computer Interaction. Prior to that she was employed at the Durban University of Technology at the rank of Associate Director in the Department of Computer Studies. Indira has a PhD in Information Systems obtained from the University of South Africa. She has published articles in Alternation, the South African Computer Journal and the Journal of Contemporary Management. In addition, she has presented research papers in various peer-reviewed conferences, namely SACLA, the Annual Conference on World Wide Web Applications and SAICSIT. Her research interests include eLearning, smart education, information security, human-computer interaction and information technology adoption.

Aveshin Reddy completed his Masters study at the University of KwaZulu-Natal in 2016. He is currently writing up his PhD study, also at the University of KwaZulu-Natal.

Katja Schneider is a research associate at the Chair of Corporate Environmental Management and Sustainability at Chemnitz University of Technology. Katja holds a Master's degree in International Energy Economics and Business Administration from Leipzig University and Moscow State Institute of International Relations. Before she has joined Chemnitz University of Technology Katja worked mainly as a researcher in a project funded by the German Federal Ministry of Education and Research investigating innovative technologies for resource efficiency and their contribution to increasing sustainability. In her doctoral thesis Katja focuses on social sustainability in business models in the textile industry. Another central theme of her research relates to sustainability marketing and communication strategies for textile business model innovations.

Jorge Tarifa-Fernandez is a Research Fellow in the Department of Economics and Business at the University of Almería. He received the MBA Degree in 2012 from the University of Almería and the Ph.D. in 2017 also in the University of Almería. His research interests include supply chain management, environmental management, and strategy.

Henry Wissink (PhD) is educated and broadly skilled in the fields of public sector governance, public policy analysis, development studies, organisation- and leadership development. Prior to joining UKZN, his academic and professional career of 28 years, he was employed as an academic at the University of Stellenbosch, the PE Technikon, that later became the Nelson Mandela Metropolitan University in 2005. He primarily served in academic management capacities since 1991, firstly as a Head of Department of Public Administration and Law, and later Dean of the Faculty of Commerce and Governmental Studies. His own teaching background focused on training and educating public servants and prospective entrants to public service in South Africa, as well as broadly schooled professionals who could contribute to more effective governance and public policy-making at all levels of government. He has also made many international study visits to universities and institutions in many parts of the world, and lectured in public policy analysis and development management for Africa at two USA universities in North Carolina and Ohio State.

During this time he played a significant role in promoting his institutions in the areas of education and training, and forming international partnerships with schools and institutes globally. He also spent four years working as a business consultant, and developed an online-learning platform to educate and train public servants in local government according to the demands of their job functions. During his career, he produced more than 100+ academic and scholarly outputs, which include 35 peer reviewed papers at national and international conferences, published 8 academic textbooks as author/co-author; published 45+ articles and chapters in peer reviewed journals and textbooks as well as 19 popular and unpublished research publications. He has served as Dean and Head of the School of Management, IT and Governance, since his appointment in November 2011, and completed his tenure at the end of 2016.

Index

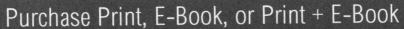

Purchase Print, E-Book, or Print + E-Book

IGI Global books can now be purchased from three unique pricing formats:
Print Only, E-Book Only, or Print + E-Book. Shipping fees apply.

www.igi-global.com

Recommended Reference Books

ISBN: 978-1-5225-2016-0
© 2017; 375 pp.
List Price: $200

ISBN: 978-1-5225-0886-1
© 2017; 251 pp.
List Price: $160

ISBN: 978-1-5225-2075-7
© 2017; 2,266 pp.
List Price: $185

ISBN: 978-1-5225-1865-5
© 2017; 443 pp.
List Price: $200

ISBN: 978-1-5225-19614-4
© 2017; 365 pp.
List Price: $210

ISBN: 978-1-5225-1005-5
© 2015; 370 pp.
List Price: $205

Looking for free content, product updates, news, and special offers?

Join IGI Global's mailing list today and start enjoying exclusive perks sent only to IGI Global members.
Add your name to the list at **www.igi-global.com/newsletters**.

Publisher of Peer-Reviewed, Timely, and Innovative Academic Research

www.igi-global.com   Sign up at www.igi-global.com/newsletters   **f** facebook.com/igiglobal   **t** twitter.com/igiglobal

Ensure Quality Research is Introduced to the Academic Community

Become an IGI Global Reviewer for Authored Book Projects

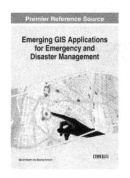

Premier Reference Source

Emerging GIS Applications for Emergency and Disaster Management

Premier Reference Source

Managerial Strategies and Green Solutions for Project Sustainability

Premier Reference Source

Comparative Approaches to Using R and Python for Statistical Data Analysis

Premier Reference Source

Solutions for High-Touch Communications in a High-Tech World

The overall success of an authored book project is dependent on quality and timely reviews.

In this competitive age of scholarly publishing, constructive and timely feedback significantly expedites the turnaround time of manuscripts from submission to acceptance, allowing the publication and discovery of forward-thinking research at a much more expeditious rate. Several IGI Global authored book projects are currently seeking highly qualified experts in the field to fill vacancies on their respective editorial review boards:

Applications may be sent to:
development@igi-global.com

Applicants must have a doctorate (or an equivalent degree) as well as publishing and reviewing experience. Reviewers are asked to write reviews in a timely, collegial, and constructive manner. All reviewers will begin their role on an ad-hoc basis for a period of one year, and upon successful completion of this term can be considered for full editorial review board status, with the potential for a subsequent promotion to Associate Editor.

If you have a colleague that may be interested in this opportunity, we encourage you to share this information with them.

www.igi-global.com

Celebrating 30 Years of Scholarly
Knowledge Creation & Dissemination

InfoSci®-Books

A Collection of 4,000+ Reference Books Containing Over 87,000 Full-Text Chapters Focusing on Emerging Research

This database is a collection of over 4,000+ IGI Global single and multi-volume reference books, handbooks of research, and encyclopedias, encompassing groundbreaking research from prominent experts worldwide. These books are highly cited and currently recognized in prestigious indices such as: Web of Science™ and Scopus®.

Librarian Features:

- No Set-Up or Maintenance Fees
- Guarantee of No More Than A 5% Annual Price Increase
- COUNTER 4 Usage Reports
- Complimentary Archival Access
- Free MARC Records

Researcher Features:

- Unlimited Simultaneous Users
- No Embargo of Content
- Full Book Download
- Full-Text Search Engine
- No DRM

To Find Out More or To Purchase This Database:

www.igi-global.com/infosci-books

eresources@igi-global.com • Toll Free: 1-866-342-6657 ext. 100 • Phone: 717-533-8845 x100

www.igi-global.com

IGI Global Proudly Partners with

Enhance Your Manuscript with
eContent Pro International's Professional
Copy Editing Service

Expert Copy Editing

eContent Pro International copy editors, with over 70 years of combined experience, will provide complete and comprehensive care for your document by resolving all issues with spelling, punctuation, grammar, terminology, jargon, semantics, syntax, consistency, flow, and more. In addition, they will format your document to the style you specify (APA, Chicago, etc.). All edits will be performed using Microsoft Word's Track Changes feature, which allows for fast and simple review and management of edits.

Additional Services

eContent Pro International also offers fast and affordable proofreading to enhance the readability of your document, professional translation in over 100 languages, and market localization services to help businesses and organizations localize their content and grow into new markets around the globe.

IGI Global Authors Save 25% on eContent Pro International's Services!

Scan the QR Code to Receive Your 25% Discount

The 25% discount is applied directly to your eContent Pro International shopping cart when placing an order through IGI Global's referral link. Use the QR code to access this referral link. eContent Pro International has the right to end or modify any promotion at any time.

Email: customerservice@econtentpro.com

econtentpro.com

ARE YOU READY TO
PUBLISH YOUR RESEARCH?

IGI Global
DISSEMINATOR OF KNOWLEDGE

IGI Global offers book authorship and editorship opportunities across 11 subject areas, including business, healthcare, computer science, engineering, and more!

Benefits of Publishing with IGI Global:

- Free one-to-one editorial and promotional support.

- Expedited publishing timelines that can take your book from start to finish in less than one (1) year.

- Choose from a variety of formats including: Edited and Authored References, Handbooks of Research, Encyclopedias, and Research Insights.

- Utilize IGI Global's eEditorial Discovery® submission system in support of conducting the submission and blind-review process.

- IGI Global maintains a strict adherence to ethical practices due in part to our full membership to the Committee on Publication Ethics (COPE).

- Indexing potential in prestigious indices such as Scopus®, Web of Science™, PsycINFO®, and ERIC – Education Resources Information Center.

- Ability to connect your ORCID iD to your IGI Global publications.

- Earn royalties on your publication as well as receive complimentary copies and exclusive discounts.

Get Started Today by Contacting the Acquisitions Department at:
acquisition@igi-global.com

CPSIA information can be obtained
at www.ICGtesting.com
Printed in the USA
BVHW011521260419
546565BV00014B/57/P

9 781522 576389